1. Night jumps also formed part of parachute training. (Photo: Airborne Forces Museum)

2. A Halifax rear gunner's view of a Horsa *en route* for Normandy. (Photo: Museum of Army Flying)

'Go To It!'

3. Queen Elizabeth talks to two members of the Glider Pilot Regiment. (Photo: Imperial War Museum)

The Illustrated History of The
6th Airborne Division
Peter Harclerode

This book is dedicated to all
members of the 6th Airborne
Division, and in particular
to the memory of those of them
who did not come home.

"GO TO IT!"

The Illustrated History of The 6th Airborne Division

Peter Harclerode

CAXTON EDITIONS

This edition published in the United Kingdom in 2000 by Caxton Editions
20 Bloomsbury Street, London WC1B 3QA
a member of the Caxton Publishing Group

Designed by Clive Hardy
Typesetting and Reproduction by Airegraphic Limited
17-18 Enterprise Park, Old Lane, Beeston, Leeds
Cover design by Open Door Limited

Title: "Go To It!"
ISBN: 1-84067-136-X

Printed in Singapore by Star Standard Industries (Pte) Ltd

4. Sniper and patrol commander edge forward cautiously towards the edge of the trees from where they can observe the terrain beyond.
(Photo: Imperial War Musuem)

Contents

Acknowledgements

The writing of this book has been very much a labour of love and I am greatly indebted to a large number of former members of 6th Airborne Division for giving so freely of their time and for providing me with documentary and photographic material in addition to personal accounts of actions in which they were involved. This is their story and this book belongs to them and their former comrades.

I have drawn on both published and unpublished material, the latter based on interviews with several members of the division as well as written personal accounts and material discovered in the archives of The Parachute Regiment. Unfortunately there are periods in the division's history which were not covered photographically at the time, such as the advance to the Seine, and this has inevitably resulted in an absence of illustrations at certain points in the book.

General Sir Nigel Poett very kindly agreed to write the foreword and to check my facts for accuracy. General Sir Kenneth Darling and Brigadier James Hill also devoted much time to checking my facts, as well as supplying me with much material, whilst Lieutenant General Sir Napier Crookenden was kind enough to supply me with photographs and documents from his personal collection. I am most grateful to them and to Major General Dare Wilson who very kindly checked my chapter on the division's operations in Palestine, much of my information being based on his own excellent book *Cordon & Search With 6th Airborne Division In Palestine 1945-48*.

Others who also provided me with much assistance include: Brigadiers Geoffrey Proudman, Ken Timbers and John Lewindon; Colonels Stan Brackenbury, Paddy de Burgh, John Tillett and David Mallam; Lieutenant Colonels Fraser Eadie, Rex Gladwyn, Harry Rice, Bill Corbould and Michael Young; Majors Guy Radmore, John Shave, Owen Brownlow-Wray, John Howard, John Sim, Robin Rigby, John Slater, Bill Chidgey, Morris Fogwell, John Cross and Charles Strafford; Captains John Turner and John Irwin; Messrs Dan Hartigan, M. R. Bailey, Harry Foot, Brian Baxter, Matt Wells, Charles Collins, Harry Long, F. Westell, Ron Dixon, Barry Boswell, J. Enstone, Jim Absalom, Norman Stocker, Bobbie Brown, Reg Barrett-Cross, T. Backshell, L. Mitchell, Brian Owen, Dr Peter Thwaites, David Fletcher, Dick Sweetland, Bob Cross, John Hillyer-Funke, W. Blunt, F. Atcherley, C. Bailey, Howard Hardy, H. Iredale, R. Tucker, Ted Farr, Lou Billingsley, B. Downing, Gilbert White, Ken Walton, R. P. Tucker, Ian Hogg and A. W. Sweetlove.

I would like to express my appreciation and gratitude to all of them, and in particular to those who very kindly loaned photographs for use in the book.

I would also like to extend special thanks to Major Jack Watson who was responsible for putting the idea of the book into my head and who dealt so patiently with the endless stream of questions with which I constantly plied him.

My thanks also go to Jane Carmichael, Keeper of Photographs at the Imperial War Museum in London, and her staff for supplying so many of the photographs, and to Simon Anglim, Diana Andrews and Stan Ward of the Airborne Forces Museum for the hours of patient help that they provided during my research. In addition, I would like to express my appreciation to Colonel Hamish MacGregor, Regimental Colonel The Parachute Regiment, for his kindness in granting me access to the regimental archives. I would also like to acknowledge the kind permission of the Institute of Royal Engineers for me to use the title *Go To It!*, this having previously been the title of Major John Shave's history of 3rd Parachute Squadron RE which was published in 1948.

Finally, I want to thank my long-suffering wife, Gilly, for her great patience and unfailing support during the writing of this book.

Peter Harclerode

Pegasus

6TH AIRBORNE DIVISION

"Wake, Take and Tame."
Athene's words
That roused Bellerophon from out his swoon,
To find a silken bridle at his side;
And grazing near, the wingèd horse,
That fabled Pegasus, till now the wild,
Untamed offspring of the Gorgon's blood;
But now in thrall
And at the virgin Goddess's command.
Then true to plighted oath
Made to Iobatés, the false Lycian king,
To rid his savaged land of the Chimaera —
Half goat, half dragon, belching smoke and flame —
He soared aloft and shot his arrows down;
Then landed to complete the *coup de grâce,*
Till burning, blackened land
Was drenched and drowned beneath the monster's blood.

So runs the myth...
But t'was no myth that summer eve
When wingèd Horsas, stabled rank on rank,
Each with its silken bridle,
Stood waiting consummation of our oath.
The days of training past;
The days and nights when quiet hamlets throbbed
To beat of engine and the snarl of power.
Grey, peaceful villages of rough-hewn stone —
Hinton, Aston, Buckland, Bampton —
Adding in their leisured, gentle way
A vital portion to the sum of war.
The time had come at last:
The promised entry to the Promised Land;
And as new day began
"Heavenly o'er the startled Hell,
Holy, where the Accursed dwell,"
The Great Adventure passed.
Through wind and moon-flecked cloud, airborne,
They sailed for Caen Canal and River Orne.

The myth come true!
Bellerophon again looked down,
    This time to trace
The conquered soil of an unconquered race;
And landed to deliver mortal blow,
The spearhead of the Monster's overthrow.

Athene's words obeyed —
    Now for ever framed,
As those that kept their plighted oath,
And Woke, and Took, and Tamed.

Keith Horan

Foreword

by

General Sir Nigel Poett KCB DSO

This is the story of the 6th Airborne Division; a story packed with action, courage and achievement during the division's five years of service to the nation.

General Richard Gale was a leader of men and a fine trainer of troops. He was only too well aware of the short time available to make his division ready for battle and he told his men, "Go to it!". They did just that.

6th Airborne Division was formed with every man a volunteer and every volunteer a picked man. Those who won the Red Beret were a proud body. Each man knew that he belonged to a *corps d'élite* and that he was a man apart amongst skilled solidiers. All members of the division knew that they would soon be matched against the best soldiers of Hitler's *Wehrmacht* who would be strongly entrenched behind the guns, concrete, and wire of the Atlantic Wall, well protected against assault from the air or sea.

Each airborne soldier, in addition to his skills, needed spirit — the type of indomitable spirit which led the men of 3rd Parachute Brigade, when dropped in the marshes and dykes of the River Dives, to extricate themselves, complete their tasks and, against seemingly impossible odds, rejoin their units. This was the same spirit which inspired Howard's company at Pegasus Bridge, Otway's 9th Parachute Battalion at the Merville Battery, Pine Coffin's 7th Parachute Battalion at Benouville, McLeod's company of Canadians at Varaville, and Johnson's 12th Parachute Battalion and Bampfylde's company of Devons at Breville.

It was such spirit and qualities, under the leadership of General Gale and later under General Bols, which led to the successful accomplishment of every task the division was set and to the successes during the advance to the Seine: the assaults on the heights of Putot and Dozuli, and the liberation of Pont L'Eveque.

The same manifested themselves during the bitterly cold days in the Ardennes and the gallant action at Bures by 13th Parachute Battalion. Later, during the holding by the division of a sector of the Maas and then the great battle of the Rhine Crossing when, alongside the 17th US Airborne Division, a splendid success was achieved. Finally, in the advance across Germany to the Baltic with 6th Airborne Division in the lead on the Allied left flank.

Yes, General Gale ordered "Go to it!" We in the 6th Airborne Division certainly took him at his word.

Great Durnford   **Nigel Poett**
20th May 1990

5. A Vickers medium machine gun detachment awaiting inspection. (Photo: Imperial War Museum)

Prologue

On the night of 5th June 1944, starting at 2256 hours, six Halifax bombers took off at one-minute intervals from an RAF airfield at Tarrant Rushton in Dorset. In tow behind them were six Horsa gliders carrying troops of the 6th Airborne Division's 6th Airlanding Brigade: 'D' Company of the 2nd Battalion The Oxfordshire & Buckinghamshire Light Infantry, under the command of Major John Howard who was travelling in the leading glider with No. 1 Platoon commanded by Lieutenant Den Brotheridge. Howard's company was reinforced by two platoons of his battalion's 'B' Company and a detachment of thirty sappers of No. 2 Platoon of 249th Field Company Royal Engineers under the command of Captain Jock Neilson. As the aircraft climbed to a maximum altitude of between four and five thousand feet, clear moonlight reflected on the Channel below and revealed the dark outline of the French coast ahead of them. The mission of this gliderborne force was to capture intact two bridges in enemy occupied Normandy. It was known that both of them had been prepared for demolition by the enemy.

Just over an hour-and-a-quarter later, the six combinations of tug aircraft and gliders reached their release points over the French coast west of Cabourg at an altitude of five thousand feet. Prior to the gliders being released, the navigator of each Halifax carefully briefed his glider pilot over the intercom on his position and height, the wind speed, course and airspeed.

Having been released from their tugs, the gliders flew silently towards their target landing areas which were about six or seven miles alway. For the pilots it was difficult to see or to recognise any landmarks in the darkness. The leading glider, piloted by Staff Sergeant Jim Wallwork, reached the Bois de Bavent, one of the largest wooded areas in Normandy, which was the checkpoint where the first three gliders were required to make a wide circular turn. However, Wallwork was unable to see the woods where they should have been — straight ahead on his port bow. Putting his glider through a ninety degree turn to starboard, he saw below him the two bridges spanning the Caen Canal at Benouville and the River Orne at Ranville. His own target was the canal bridge.

Wallwork applied half flap until he had descended to a height of one thousand feet and carried out another ninety degree turn to starboard, at which point he told his co-pilot, Staff Sergeant John Ainsworth MM, to deploy the glider's arrester parachute. The braking effect was immediate and the aircraft steadied down to the correct speed for landing. Just before the Horsa crash landed, Wallwork told Ainsworth to jettison the parachute arrester gear as he flew towards the small triangular landing zone south-east of the canal bridge. Touching down at a speed of around 90mph, the glider careered into a barbed wire obstacle.

As the aircraft came to a shattering halt, Wallwork and Ainsworth were both hurled through the perspex of their cockpit into a barbed wire entanglement and were knocked unconscious in the process. Unknown to them they were the first Allied troops to touch French soil on D-Day. The two pilots had landed their passengers on the precise spot indicated during their briefing by Major John Howard prior to the operation.

Incredibly, the German troops guarding the bridge, some of whom were only fifty yards away, had heard the noise of the first

6. The Caen Canal bridge at Benouville which was the objective of Nos. 1, 2 and 3 Platoons of Major John Howard's *coup de main* force.
(Photo: Airborne Forces Museum)

glider landing but had assumed it to be caused by debris falling from a crippled Allied bomber.

Major Howard and the other passengers in Wallwork's glider were very briefly knocked unconscious. Howard himself had been thrown against the interior of the roof of the glider when his seat belt broke with the force of the landing. When he regained consciousness seconds later, he thought he had been blinded until he realised that his helmet had been forced down over his ears and eyes. Scrambling out of the wreckage, he looked up and was astounded to see the bridge only fifty yards away from where he stood, the nose of the glider through the enemy barbed wire defences. There was no firing — complete surprise had been achieved. The others in the glider also came to within a second or two and immediately started to break their way out of the damaged doors at the front and rear of the aircraft.

Forcing their way out, Lieutenant Den Brotheridge and No. 1 Platoon extricated themselves from Wallwork's glider. Taking one section with him, Brotheridge ran straight through the wire and headed for the bridge. As he did so, from the darkness behind came the sound of the second glider, piloted by Staff Sergeants Boland and Hobbs, making its landing. In order to avoid Wallwork's glider, Boland had to swerve and in so doing broke the back of his own Horsa. The force of the impact was such that the platoon commander of No. 2 Platoon, Lieutenant David Wood, was ejected forcibly from the glider. However, his platoon immediately formed up around him exactly as planned and Wood moved forward to link up with his company commander who was waiting for him near the bridge. Howard told Wood to proceed with his platoon's "Number Two task" which Wood knew meant the clearing of the German trenches, machine gun positions and an anti-tank emplacement on the eastern bank. Without any more ado, Wood and his platoon launched themselves into the task.

As they did so the third glider, piloted by Staff Sergeants Barkway and Boyle, hurtled in. Captain John Vaughan of the Royal Army Medical Corps, who was a medical officer with a parachute unit but who had volunteered for this daunting mission, was thrown out of the glider and into the mud by a nearby pond. He was accompanied by Lieutenant Sandy Smith, the platoon commander of No. 3 Platoon, who immediately staggered to his feet and started for the bridge followed by elements of his platoon although half a dozen of his men were still trapped in the wreckage of the glider. The time was now around 0020 hours in the morning of the 6th June.

Meanwhile, Lieutenant Den Brotheridge and his platoon had already run up an embankment on to the bridge. As they did so, a German rifleman opened fire at Howard and his radio operator, Corporal Tappenden, who were now at the top of the embankment. Brotheridge and his platoon went running across the bridge, Brotheridge himself shooting a German sentry who had just fired a warning flare. At the same time, Corporal Jack Bailey and other members of the leading section of No. 1 Platoon knocked out a pillbox with grenades. Meanwhile, the sappers were checking the bridge for demolition charges and were cutting any wires that they found.

By now fully alerted, the Germans were fighting back. As Brotheridge threw a grenade at a machine gun position, knocking it out in the process, he was hit in the neck. As he fell in

7. The canal bridge seen from the eastern end. (Photo: Airborne Forces Museum)

the middle of the road at the western end of the bridge, the rest of his platoon came running over the bridge after him, firing their weapons from the hip and throwing grenades as they systematically neutralised all opposition.

Meanwhile Lieutenant David Wood and No. 2 Platoon proceeded to deal with the German positions, including a 20mm gun emplacement, at the eastern end of the bridge. As they did so, they found that many of the enemy troops had fled. Wood discovered a machine gun which his platoon commandeered as they occupied the enemy positions. As he went back to report to Howard that his tasks were completed, however, he came under fire from a machine gun and was hit in the leg. As his platoon sergeant had also been wounded, one of his section commanders, Corporal Godbold, took over command of the platoon.

As soon as Lieutenant Sandy Smith and his No. 3 Platoon reached the bridge, Major John Howard dispatched them across it to establish defensive positions on the western side and to reinforce No. 1 Platoon. Smith himself was wounded shortly afterwards by a grenade. Although he killed the German who had thrown it, he was hit by fragments as the grenade exploded and one of his wrists was badly injured.

Meanwhile the gliders carrying Howard's other three platoons were landing for an assault on the Orne bridge at Ranville nearby. Unfortunately the crew of the fourth and leading glider, Staff Sergeants Lawrence and Shorter, had been cast off at the wrong location after being ordered to make a blind release by the captain of their tug aircraft. Consequently they had landed Howard's company second in command, Captain Brian Priday, and Lieutenant Tony Hooper's No. 4 Platoon five miles to the east near two

bridges crossing the River Dives and a canal. Their glider landed by one of these bridges which Priday and his men promptly captured. After realising that they were in the wrong place, they started making their way back towards their objective.

However, the crew of the sixth glider, Staff Sergeants Howard and Baacke, had carried out another remarkable feat of flying. They had succeeded in landing their Horsa in the centre of their landing zone, a field surrounded by trees north-west of the river bridge. After initial opposition from a machine gun had been neutralised by a direct hit from a mortar manned by Sergeant Thornton, Lieutenant Dennis Fox's No. 6 Platoon was able to secure the bridge, which was found undefended, within a matter of a few minutes. The fifth glider, piloted by Staff Sergeants Pearson and Guthrie and carrying Lieutenant Tod Sweeney's No. 5 Platoon, had landed seven hundred yards short. By the time Sweeney and his men reached the western end of the bridge, Fox's platoon were already deployed on the other side.

Within fifteen minutes of landing, both bridges had been secured and the success signal "Ham and Jam", indicating that both the bridges had been captured intact, was transmitted by radio. Major John Howard and the men of his *coup de main* force were the first Allied troops to land in Occupied France on D-Day. At 0050 hours in the morning of 6th June 1944, the sound of approaching aircraft heralded the arrival of 3rd and 5th Parachute Brigades.

Thus the 6th Airborne Division went to war for the first time and received its baptism of fire. However, the story of the division begins just over twelve months previously...

8. A magnificent feat of flying: the three gliders of Staff Sergeants Wallwork, Boland and Barkway on the eastern bank of the canal. The nose of Wallwork's glider breached the wire defences. (Photo: Airborne Forces Museum)

9. A close-up of Staff Sergeant Wallwork's glider, showing its wrecked nose through which he and Staff Sergeant Ainsworth were thrown on impact. In the background lies Staff Sergeant Boland's glider, its fuselage snapped in half.
(Photo: Airborne Forces Museum)

10. An assault force-eye view of the approach on the eastern bank to the bridge which is in the background behind the trees. On the left, through the trees, can be seen the Gondree family's cafe on the far side of the canal.
(Photo: Imperial War Museum)

11. A view of the canal bridge, subsequently christened 'Pegasus Bridge'.
(Photo: Imperial War Museum)

12. Three members of D Company 2nd Battalion The Oxfordshire & Buckinghamshire Light Infantry who took part in the operation. *Left to right:* Pte Frank Gardner, Capt Brian Priday and L/Cpl B. H. Lambley. (Photo: Imperial War Museum)

13. The bridge over the River Orne which was the objective of Nos. 4, 5 and 6 Platoons. Staff Sergeant Howard's glider can be seen on the western bank of the river where it landed near the bridge which was taken by No. 6 Platoon. (Photo: Imperial War Museum)

14. Major John Howard who commanded the *coup de main* force. (Photo: Airborne Forces Museum)

Formation

It was a glorious sunny day on 7th May 1943 when Major General Richard Gale drove to Syrencot House, at Figheldean in Wiltshire, to assume command of the newly-established 6th Airborne Division. Gale was in a very happy frame of mind, looking forward eagerly to the task of forming his new command. Having previously commanded the 1st Parachute Brigade and having spent the previous year as Deputy Director of Air in the War Office, he was familiar with the problems connected with assembling a new airborne forces formation.

Such was the fledgling nature of the division that not even its headquarters was fully established although it had begun to form on the 3rd May. The War Office orders of the 23rd April 1943 had laid down a phased programme of formation for the division. This allowed thirty per cent of the divisional headquarters to be formed immediately, thirty per cent to be formed on the 1st June and the remainder to be reviewed in September of the same year. On the day of Gale's arrival, the division's Assistant Adjutant and Quartermaster General, Lieutenant Colonel Shamus Hickie, appeared together with the Assistant Director of Ordnance Services, Lieutenant Colonel John Fielding. Shortly afterwards they were followed by the GSO 1 (Operations), Lieutenant Colonel Bobby Bray. At the same time, there was a steady flow of arrivals in the form of clerks, orderlies, batmen, drivers, military police and other essential personnel. Transport arrived,

together with mounds of packing cases containing stationery, typewriters, furniture and all the necessary paraphernalia required to operate a divisional headquarters. Within a very short space of time order grew out of chaos and on the 14th May, just seven days after assuming command, Gale issued his first Divisional Routine Order.

As far as its formations and units were concerned, 6th Airborne Division was to take over 3rd Parachute Brigade, 3rd Parachute Squadron Royal Engineers, 224th Parachute Field Ambulance Royal Army Medical Corps, 2nd Battalion The Oxfordshire & Buckinghamshire Light Infantry and the 1st Battalion The Royal Ulster Rifles from the 1st Airborne Division. These would provide the nucleus upon which the new division would be formed. The War Office orders also directed that Headquarters 6th Airlanding Brigade was to be formed and that the brigade should consist of the 2nd Battalion The Oxfordshire & Buckinghamshire Light Infantry and the 1st Battalion The Royal Ulster Rifles, both battalions having previously been part of 1st Airlanding Brigade. In addition, 5th Parachute Brigade and the majority of divisional troops were to be formed on the 1st June. A review of any further units would take place in September.

The 3rd Parachute Brigade was commanded by Brigadier James Hill DSO MC who was a very experienced airborne soldier who

15. Major General R. N. Gale OBE MC, General Officer Commanding 6th Airborne Division. (Photo: Imperial War Musuem)

16. Brigadier S. J. L. Hill DSO MC, Commander 3rd Parachute Brigade, seen here talking to Major Don Wilkins of 1st Canadian Parachute Battalion. (Photo: Imperial War Museum)

had served as a regular officer in the Royal Fusiliers before the war and was a member of Lord Gort's command post during the Battle of France in 1940 where he was awarded the MC. He joined Airborne Forces late in 1941 as second in command of 1st Parachute Battalion which he was later to command in the North African landings where he won a DSO and the French Legion of Honour. His brigade comprised the 7th (Light Infantry), 8th (Midlands) and 9th (Eastern Counties) Parachute Battalions. During its operations in North Africa, 1st Parachute Brigade had suffered heavy casualties and had to draw reinforcements from the only source available, 3rd Parachute Brigade, which was consequently very weak in numbers.

Hill recalls that late in May he was summoned by General Gale and told that he would take the one and only Canadian parachute battalion into his brigade. He was delighted and excited at the prospect of adding some of Canada's toughest fighting men to 3rd Parachute Brigade, but he did not like the task of selecting the battalion which the Canadians were to replace and which would then form the spearhead of the newly formed 5th Parachute Brigade. He had no option but to release his senior unit, 7th Parachute Battalion, for this role.

1st Canadian Parachute Battalion, after its arrival in England, went straight to Ringway to undergo training in British parachute techniques and joined the brigade on the 11th August 1943.

The month of May also saw the formation of 6th Airlanding Brigade at Bulford, under the command of Brigadier the Honourable Hugh Kindersley who had previously commanded a tank battalion of the Scots Guards in the Guards Armoured Division. Kindersley was to subsequently distinguish himself by

qualifying as both a parachutist and a glider pilot. Shortly after the 2nd Battalion The Oxfordshire & Buckinghamshire Light Infantry and the 1st Battalion The Royal Ulster Rifles joined the brigade, a third battalion was added. This was the 12th Battalion The Devonshire Regiment which had until then been employed on defence duties on the south-west coast.

On the 1st July, 5th Parachute Brigade was formed at Bulford and was added to the division. Its commander was Brigadier Nigel Poett who was a regular officer late of the Durham Light Infantry. The brigade initially comprised two new battalions: the 12th (Yorkshire) and 13th (Lancashire) Parachute Battalions, 7th (Somerset Light Infantry) Parachute Battalion subsequently being added.

Divisional and brigade troops were also posted into the division during the following month of June. These included the division's artillery, consisting of the 53rd (Worcestershire Yeomanry) Airlanding Light Regiment, the 3rd and 4th Airlanding Anti-Tank Batteries and the 2nd Airlanding Light Anti-Aircraft Battery, all of the Royal Artillery. Other units included those from the Royal Signals, Royal Engineers, Royal Army Service Corps, Royal Army Ordnance Corps, Royal Electrical & Mechanical Engineers, Royal Army Medical Corps, Intelligence Corps and the Corps of Military Police.

On the 22nd September 1943, the War Office ordered the formation of the remainder of divisional troops, less a second composite company of RASC which was to begin forming in cadre in November, for expansion later, and less the Airlanding Reconnaissance Squadron whose requirement was to be reviewed at the end of October. In the event, it was never formed.

17. Brigadier The Hon H. K. M. Kindersley MC, Commander 6th Airlanding Brigade. (Photo: Imperial War Museum)

18. Brigadier J. H. N. Poett, Commander 5th Parachute Brigade. (Photo: Gen Sir Nigel Poett)

Order of Battle

In 1943, a British infantry division numbered 757 officers and 16,764 men organised into two infantry brigades, each of three infantry battalions, and a tank brigade. Principal support was in the form of the artillery which comprised three field regiments, an anti-tank regiment and a light anti-aircraft regiment. Additional support came from the Royal Signals, Royal Engineers, Royal Electrical & Mechanical Engineers, Royal Army Service Corps, Royal Army Ordnance Corps, Royal Army Medical Corps, Corps of Military Police and other arms. The divisional headquarters included intelligence, field security and defence sections.

The establishment of a wartime airborne division differed in that the tank brigade was replaced by the airlanding brigade and in the fact that its support elements were drastically reduced in the interests of air mobility. Artillery support consisted of one airlanding light regiment of three batteries, two batteries of anti-tank artillery, a battery of light anti-aircraft artillery and later on an artillery forward observation unit, whilst armour consisted of an airborne armoured reconnaissance regiment of light tanks, Bren carriers and scout cars. This obviously limited the airborne division's ability to fight a prolonged action against powerful enemy forces possessing a large amount of armour and thus made it imperative that link-ups with ground forces had to be achieved sooner rather than later.

Headquarters 6th Airborne Division

Major General Gale's staff consisted of the following: the GSO 1 (Operations), Lieutenant Colonel Bobby Bray of the Duke of Wellington's Regiment who was the principal staff officer; the GSO 1 (Air), Lieutenant Colonel Bill Bradish of the Royal Irish Fusiliers, who was responsible for all aspects of training with aircraft as well as divisional aircraft loading plans; the GSO 2 (Operations), Major David Baird of the Argyll & Sutherland Highlanders; the GSO 3 (Operations), Captain M. R. Spurling of the Royal Artillery; the GSO 3 (Air), Captain Nick Pratt of the 15th/19th The King's Royal Hussars; the GSO 2 (Intelligence), Major Gerry Lacoste of the Royal Artillery; the GSO 3 (Intelligence), Captain J. H. Max of the Royal Armoured Corps, the GSO 3 (CW), Captain W. D. Burton of the Royal Armoured Corps; two Intelligence Officers who were Captain Freddie Scholes of the Intelligence Corps and Captain V. L. Clarke of the Herefordshire Light Infantry; the Assistant Adjutant & Quartermaster General, Lieutenant Colonel Shamus Hickie of The King's Own Yorkshire Light Infantry, who was the officer ultimately responsible for administrative affairs within the division; the Deputy Assistant Adjutant General, Major H. J. Darlington of the King's Own Border Regiment; the Deputy Assistant Quartermaster General, Major E. J. O'B. Croker of the Leicestershire Regiment; the Staff Captain (Q), Captain C. C. Norbury of The Essex Regiment, the Staff Captain (A), Lieutenant R. G. Ellis of the Royal Welch Fusiliers; Lieutenant Colonel M. McEwan, the Assistant Director Medical Services; and Lieutenant Colonel John Fielding, the Assistant Director Ordnance Services. Captain Tom Haughton, of The Royal Ulster Rifles, was Major General Gale's *aide de camp.*

19. A platoon of one of 6th Airlanding Brigade's battalions deploys from its Horsa glider during an exercise. (Photo: Imperial War Museum)

Responsibility for artillery support lay with the division's Commander Royal Artillery, Lieutenant Colonel Jack Norris, whilst all Sapper operations in the division were co-ordinated by the Commander Royal Engineers, Lieutenant Colonel Frank Lowman. Communications were the responsibility of the Commander Royal Signals, Lieutenant Colonel D. 'Pigmy' Smallman-Tew, whilst all supply matters were the domain of the Commander Royal Army Service Corps, Lieutenant Colonel J. L. Watson. Lieutenant Colonel R. V. Powditch was the division's Commander Royal Electrical & Mechanical Engineers and thus was ultimately responsible for the maintenance of all the division's weapons and vehicles.

The Parachute Brigades

The two parachute brigades each comprised a brigade headquarters and three parachute infantry battalions. Each had attached to it a parachute engineer squadron and a parachute field ambulance.

In 3rd Parachute Brigade, 8th Parachute Battalion, which had been raised from the 13th Battalion The Royal Warwickshire Regiment, was under the command of the redoubtable Lieutenant Colonel Alistair Pearson, who had previously been a Territorial Army officer in the Highland Light Infantry and who had already won three DSOs and an MC in North Africa whilst commanding 1st Parachute Battalion. 9th Parachute Battalion, raised from

the 10th Battalion The Essex Regiment, was initially commanded by Lieutenant Colonel Martin Lindsay, who was a Royal Scots Fusilier and one of the first to undergo parachute training in 1940, but shortly after formation was taken over by Lieutenant Colonel Terence Otway of The Royal Ulster Rifles. 1st Canadian Parachute Battalion was commanded by Lieutenant Colonel George Bradbrooke.

In 5th Parachute Brigade 7th Parachute Battalion, which had been raised from the 10th Battalion The Somerset Light Infantry, was commanded by Lieutenant Colonel Geoffrey Pine-Coffin of The Devonshire Regiment. 12th Parachute Battalion, raised from the 10th Battalion The Green Howards, was initially commanded by Lieutenant Colonel Reggie Parker, himself a Green Howard, and subsequently by Lieutenant Colonel Johnny Johnson. 13th Parachute Battalion, raised from the 2nd/4th Battalion The South Lancashire Regiment, was commanded by Lieutenant Colonel Peter Luard who was a regular officer in The Oxfordshire & Buckinghamshire Light Infantry.

The parachute battalion's jumping strength numbered five hundred and fifty all ranks. Its organisation consisted of a battalion headquarters, a headquarter company, a machine gun platoon with four Vickers medium machine guns, a mortar platoon with six 3-inch mortars and three rifle companies.

The rifle companies, each numbering five officers and a hundred and twenty men, were organised into a company headquarters and three platoons of thirty-six men each.

20. A platoon commander issues orders to his men during his platoon's deployment after landing by glider. (Photo: Imperial War Museum)

The Airlanding Brigade

The airlanding brigade was larger in numbers and carried some heavier weapons and more equipment, its role being to reinforce the two parachute brigades and to fly in the guns, transport, stores and supplies which would be required on the ground. The brigade consisted of a headquarters and three infantry battalions, and had attached to it an engineer field company and an airlanding field ambulance.

Two of the airlanding battalions were pre-war regular units: the 2nd Battalion The Oxfordshire & Buckinghamshire Light Infantry, which was commanded by Lieutenant Colonel Michael Roberts, and the 1st Battalion The Royal Ulster Rifles which was commanded by Lieutenant Colonel Jack Carson. The 12th Battalion The Devonshire Regiment had been raised originally as a coastal defence unit to guard the coasts of its home county. It was commanded by Lieutenant Colonel Dick Stevens who was a regular officer and himself a Devon.

The airlanding battalion was considerably larger than its parachute counterpart, numbering approximately eight hundred all ranks. It comprised a battalion headquarters, a headquarter company which included a reconnaissance platoon and a pioneer platoon, four rifle companies and a support company which itself comprised: a machine gun platoon with four Vickers .303 machine guns, a mortar platoon with four 3-inch mortars and an anti-tank platoon equipped with eight 6-pounder anti-tank guns.

The rifle companies each numbered six officers and approximately a hundred and fifty other ranks, and consisted of a company headquarters and four platoons of thirty-six men. In addition, each rifle company also possessed its own section of two 3-inch mortars.

Divisional Troops

Pathfinders

Each airborne division included a pathfinder company in its order of battle. The role of this unit was to be inserted ahead of a main drop and to reconnoitre and secure the drop zones for the parachute units and the landing zones for the gliders, subsequently marking them out with panels and smoke canisters and positioning directional radio beacons to 'home' in the transport aircraft on to the DZs and LZs.

In the 6th Airborne Division this role was carried out by the 22nd Independent Parachute Company which was raised and commanded by Major Francis Lennox Boyd of the Royal Scots Greys. The company was organised as a company headquarters and three platoons, each of which comprised one officer and thirty-two other ranks. Each platoon consisted of three sections or 'sticks' commanded by a sergeant or corporal. For pathfinding tasks, each stick was equipped with the Eureka ground-to-air radio beacon which transmitted homing signals to Rebecca receivers fitted in transport aircraft. In addition, coloured cloth panels were carried for use as drop zone markers laid out in the

21. The division's pathfinders were the men of 22nd Independent Parachute Company, a group of whom are seen here. *Back row, left to right:* Sergeants Matt Wells, Stan Pearson, Ray Wilkins, 'Smudger' Smith and Jock Lindores. *Kneeling* Sergeant Rob Ramage and Company Sergeant Major 'Mac' McGuinness. (Photo: Mr F. T. Wells)

form of a 'T'. For night drops, 6-volt battery-powered Holophane lamps were used to mark DZs: an orange lamp was placed at the end of each arm of the 'T' whilst a green one was located at the base. Operated by a member of the stick, this was used to flash the drop zone code letter at the approaching transport aircraft.

The 22nd Independent Parachute Company was a particularly interesting unit in that over sixty per cent of its members were German speaking Jews who had fled persecution in Nazi dominated countries. On joining the British Army they adopted British pseudonyms.

6th Airborne Armoured Reconnaissance Regiment

The 6th Airborne Armoured Reconnaissance Regiment (Royal Armoured Corps) was formed at Larkhill in 1942 from 'C' Special Service Light Tank Squadron. Commanded by Major, subsequently Lieutenant Colonel, Godfrey Stewart of the 13th/18th Royal Hussars, it consisted of troops drawn from regiments of the 1st Armoured Division: the Queen's Bays, the 9th Queen's Royal Lancers, the 10th Royal Hussars and the 1st and 2nd Royal Tank Regiments. Subsequently the squadron was redesignated the Airborne Light Tank Squadron and became part of the then newly-formed 1st Airborne Division.

On 1st Airborne Division's departure for the Sicily landings, the squadron was left behind in England and was transferred to 6th Airborne Division on its formation. On joining the division, it was redesignated the 6th Airborne Armoured Reconnaissance Regiment and was reinforced by volunteers from the Royal Armoured Corps Depot and other armoured units.

After expansion, the regiment consisted of a regimental headquarters, a squadron of light tanks, a reconnaissance squadron, a support squadron, a headquarters squadron and a REME light aid detachment. It also included signals and medical elements. The tank squadron comprised five sabre troops, equipped with Tetrarch light tanks armed with two-pounder guns, and a headquarters troop of four tanks of which two were armed with three-inch howitzers. Regimental Headquarters consisted of two Tetrarchs, also armed with three-inch howitzers. The reconnaissance squadron comprised a squadron headquarters and four troops of either two Bren carriers and a Dingo scout car or alternatively two scout cars and a Bren carrier — this depending on the loading of the glider in which they were to be carried — and a number of motorcyclists. The support squadron comprised a troop of 4.2-inch mortars and two troops of medium machine guns. The headquarters squadron was equipped with Rota trailers which carried fuel in the tyres of their wheels and ammunition in their box bodies, and which were towed by jeeps.

The regiment also possessed a Harbour Party which consisted of one officer and fifteen men who were trained parachutists. Their role was to drop in with one of the leading parachute units and to reconnoitre and secure the harbour area to which the regiment would deploy immediately after landing by glider.

Royal Artillery

53rd (Worcestershire Yeomanry) Airlanding Light Regiment RA

The division's main artillery support came from the 53rd (Worcestershire Yeomanry) Airlanding Light Regiment Royal Artillery, commanded by Lieutenant Colonel Tony Teacher. Originally the Queen's Own Worcestershire Hussars, in 1922 the regiment became the 100th (Worcestershire & Oxfordshire Yeomanry) Field Brigade RA, consisting of four batteries. In 1939, it was redesignated the 53rd (Worcestershire Yeomanry) Anti-Tank Regiment RA. In 1943, the regiment's title was changed yet again to 53rd (Worcestershire Yeomanry) Airlanding Light Regiment RA. It comprised a regimental headquarters and three batteries: 210th Airlanding Light Battery RA commanded by Major the Honourable Charles Russell, 211th Airlanding Light Battery RA commanded by Major Jim Craigie and 212th Airlanding Light Battery RA commanded by Major Matt Gubbins. Each battery consisted of a battery headquarters and two troops, each of four 75mm pack howitzers.

Responsibility for forward observation for the guns of the airlanding light regiment was initially that of the regiment's own FOO parties who accompanied the infantry battalions of all three brigades, those accompanying the parachute battalions being trained parachutists. These would be augmented for the Normandy campaign by volunteers from supporting artillery regiments in the corps under whose command the division was operating.

The three battery commanders of 53rd Airlanding Light Regiment were each located at one of the three brigade headquarters, acting as links between their FOOs with the infantry battalions and the batteries.

2nd Forward Observation Unit (Airborne) RA

In August 1944, as a result of the experiences of the Normandy campaign, 2nd Forward Organisation Unit RA (Airborne) was formed at Winterbourne Gunner under the command of Major, later Lieutenant Colonel, Harry Rice. This unit consisted of a headquarters and three sections: No. 3 Section, which comprised Royal Artillery personnel, and Nos. 5 & 6 Sections which consisted of personnel from the Royal Canadian Artillery. Each of these consisted of six teams, each comprising a captain and three gunner signallers. Subsequently each section was augmented by a subaltern who was a counter-mortar officer. One section was attached to each brigade: Nos. 3 & 5 Sections being attached to 3rd & 5th Parachute Brigades respectively and No. 6 Section to 6th Airlanding Brigade. Equipped with jeep-mounted and man-pack radios, their role was to establish observation posts from which they would direct the fire of the division's own guns and that of supporting artillery from other divisions.

22. Private MacGregor of 22nd Independent Parachute Company, seen here fully equipped prior to embarking on exercise.
(Photo: Mr F. T. Wells)

23. Men of 6th Airborne Armoured Reconnaissance Regiment unloading their Tetrarch light tank from a Hamilcar glider at RAF Tarrant Rushton. (Photo: Imperial War Museum)

In November 1944, fire liaison parties of Royal Canadian Artillery personnel were added to the unit. Commanded by Major Roy Harrison, they were located with the guns of the artillery of other divisions supporting 6th Airborne Division. There were four such parties, each consisting of a captain, driver and two signallers.

In March 1945 the unit was augmented further by jeep-mounted sound-ranging and radar sections, consisting of a total of two subalterns and twenty gunners, because of the increasing amount of counter-mortar work being carried out by the unit. However, the FOO teams were by then already very experienced in locating enemy mortars by listening and taking bearings which, when crossed, indicated the baseplate locations.

3rd, 4th & 6th Airlanding Anti-Tank Batteries RA

Anti-tank artillery support for the two parachute brigades in the division was provided by 3rd and 4th Airlanding Anti-Tank Batteries RA, commanded by Majors Nick Cranmer and Peter Dixon respectively. 6th Airlanding Brigade possessed 6-pounder anti-tank guns in each of the support companies of its infantry battalions.

Both batteries were new units raised in July 1943 during the division's period of formation. Each consisted of a battery headquarters and four troops of four guns each, being initally equipped with a total of sixteen 6-pounder anti-tank guns. In 1944, the fourth troop in each battery was re-equipped with the heavier 17-pounder gun which was capable of destroying even the heaviest of German tanks.

In January 1945 6th Airlanding Anti-Tank Battery RA was formed from the 2nd Airlanding Light Anti-Aircraft Battery RA, with the role of providing anti-tank defence for divisional troops. During the following month, all three batteries were regimented

into 2nd Airlanding Anti-Tank Regiment RA which was commanded by Lieutenant Colonel F. E. 'Bill' Allday.

2nd Airlanding Light Anti-Aircraft Battery RA

2nd Airlanding Light Anti-Aircraft Battery RA, raised in May 1943 and commanded by Major W. A. H. Rowat, provided air defence support for the division. It was equipped with a total of eighteen 40mm Bofors anti-aircraft guns and forty-eight 20mm Hispano-Suiza (Oerlikon) anti-aircraft cannon. The number and type of gun deployed by the battery depended on operational requirements. The battery comprised a battery headquarters and three troops, each troop comprising six sections. In January 1945, the battery was converted to the anti-tank role and was redesignated 6th Airlanding Anti-Tank Battery RA.

Royal Signals

6th Airborne Divisional Signals

6th Airborne Divisional Signals, commanded by Lieutenant Colonel D. 'Pigmy' Smallman-Tew, was responsible for maintaining and operating radio and line communications from divisional headquarters forward to all three brigade headquarters and the rear link between the division and the corps under whose command it was operating. It was also responsible for ground-to-air nets for air support, communications with artillery giving support from outside the division, and long range links with the division's base in England from which all air resupply was mounted.

Divisional Signals comprised a headquarter company and three signals companies. No. 1 Company provided the infrastructure and communications for the divisional headquarters. No. 2 Company provided signals sections for each brigade headquarters,

24-25. *Above:* A gun detachment of 53rd (Worcestershire Yeomanry) Airlanding Light Regiment Royal Artillery with its US M8 75mm pack howitzer. *Above right:* A photograph of Captain O. E. Brownlow-Wray MC of 53rd (WY) Airlanding Light Regiment RA, showing the pear blossom cap badge and 'collar dogs' of the Worcestershire Yeomanry which were worn by the officers of the regiment. Warrant officers, NCOs and gunners wore the Royal Artillery's insignia. (Photos: Imperial War Museum & Maj O. E. Brownlow-Wray MC)

the airlanding light artillery regiment, the armoured reconnaissance regiment and the engineers. Those sections allocated to brigades each consisted of two officers and seventy-three other ranks which comprised radio operators, linesmen and cipher operators. They were responsible for operating and maintaining radio and line communications forward to battalions, as well as the rear link communications back to divisional headquarters. No. 3 Company provided the division's base signals organisation in England.

Royal Engineers

3rd & 591st Parachute Squadrons RE

The two parachute squadrons were each attached to one of the two parachute brigades, the 3rd to 3rd Parachute Brigade and the 591st to 5th Parachute Brigade. They were commanded by Majors J. C. A. 'Tim' Roseveare and Andy Wood respectively. Both comprised a squadron headquarters and three troops of thirty men commanded by captains and consisting of three sections, each of which consisted of a subaltern and nine NCOs and sappers.

249th Field Company RE

249th Field Company RE, commanded by Major Sandy Rutherford, was attached to 6th Airlanding Brigade. It consisted of a company headquarters and three platoons. Each platoon was commanded by a captain who had a subaltern as his second in command and a platoon sergeant. The platoons each comprised three sections of eight sappers commanded by a corporal, and were organised in a 'duplication' system. When travelling in Horsa gliders, which in any case accommodated up to thirty men, one half of the platoon would travel in one aircraft with the platoon commander whilst the other half travelled with the second in command. In the event of one aircraft not reaching its objective, there would still be the other half-platoon available to carry out the tasks allotted to the platoon.

286th Field Park Company RE

286th Field Park Company RE, under the command of Major

Jack Waters, was attached to the divisional headquarters and held all engineer stores and plant, providing logistical support to other Sapper units within the division. It was comprised of a company headquarters, a plant troop, a workshop troop and a stones troop.

Royal Army Medical Corps

224th & 225th Parachute Field Ambulances RAMC

The medical support for the two parachute brigades was provided by 224th and 225th Parachute Field Ambulances, commanded respectively by Lieutenant Colonel D. H. Thompson and Lieutenant Colonel Bruce Harvey, which were attached to 3rd and 5th Parachute Brigades respectively. These two units each consisted of nine Royal Army Medical Corps officers and just over one hundred other ranks. They each comprised a headquarters element, two field surgical teams and four clearing sections.

195th Airlanding Field Ambulance RAMC

195th Airlanding Field Ambulance, under the command of Lieutenant Colonel Bill Anderson, was attached to 6th Airlanding Brigade. It was organised on similar lines to its parachute counterparts but was larger in numbers.

Specially designed and purpose-built medical and surgical equipment, including blood plasma, was dropped in containers by parachute and carried in gliders.

In addition to the field ambulances, a medical officer and an RAMC medical platoon were attached to each battalion in the division.

Royal Army Service Corps

Resupply was a vital factor in successful airborne operations and the responsibility for this lay with the division's Royal Army Service Corps units. These consisted of 716th Light Composite Company RASC commanded by Major A. Jones, 398th Composite Company RASC commanded by Major M. E. Phipps, and 63rd Composite Company RASC commanded by Major A. C. Bille-Top.

398th and 63rd Composite Companies consisted of a company headquarters, three transport platoons, a composite platoon and a workshop platoon. Equipped with 3-ton trucks, their role was the packing of all stores into containers and panniers and the movement of them to airfields where they were responsible for loading them on to aircraft. These two companies also provided the air dispatch crews and a large percentage of their personnel were parachute trained.

716th Light Composite Company also consisted of a company headquarters and three platoons of which one was a parachute platoon. It was equipped with jeeps, each of which had two trailers, which were deployed by glider and were pre-loaded with a certain amount of ammunition, supplies and other stores to start the supply dumps on landing. The company's role was to jump or airland with the forward elements of the division and to collect and distribute the stores from the dropping zone which had been dropped by the air dispatch crews of the other two companies.

The roles of both air dispatchers and ground teams were particularly hazardous due to the fact that whilst the enemy might have been taken by surprise by an initial airborne assault, by the time resupply was required they would have been fully alerted and thus both transport aircraft and drop zones would be likely to come under heavy fire.

Royal Army Ordnance Corps

6th Airborne Division Ordnance Field Park RAOC

The RAOC element in the division was 6th Airborne Division Ordnance Field Park commanded by Major W. L. Taylor. It numbered approximately eighty personnel in total, all of whom were trained storemen and drivers. The unit was equipped with 3-ton trucks, jeeps and trailers which were fitted with bins which contained MT and radio spares. Fifty per cent of the members of the unit were trained as parachutists, the other half being trained in the airlanding role. When deployed, the field park was positioned in the divisional maintenance area in proximity to the REME workshops.

Royal Electrical & Mechanical Engineers

6th Airborne Division Workshop REME

Maintenance and repairs of weapons and vehicles within the division was the responsibility of 6th Airborne Division Workshop REME which was commanded by Major E. B. Bonniwell.

During operations the workshop normally deployed an Advance Workshop Detachment, some personnel by parachute and the rest in three gliders; each Horsa containing four men, a jeep and lightweight trailer, plus technical stores. The three trailers contained a generator, radio repair equipment and machinery respectively. The machinery trailer was equipped with precision lathes, portable electric drills, bench grinders and vices. In addition to the Advanced Workshop Detachment, the workshop also deployed light aid detachments with each brigade as well as with the engineer, signals, artillery and armoured elements of the division.

Corps of Military Police

6th Airborne Division Provost Company

6th Airborne Division Provost Company, commanded by Captain Irwin, represented the Corps of Military Police within the division. In addition to the normal provost role, the company had the added tasks of signing routes to airfields and signing within them to dispersal areas. As operations became more imminent, the provost role was the sealing and security of camps and airfields and, immediately prior to an operation, the security of movement of personnel to mounting airfields which then had to be sealed and secured. In the event of an operation being

postponed, the sealing and security of airfields was vital to its success.

On arrival on a drop zone, the airborne military policemen had two tasks. Firstly, the direction of all personnel arriving on the DZ to their correct locations in order that reorganisation was effected swiftly. Secondly, the organisation of the security of the divisional headquarters. In addition, the MPs were responsible for the safe custody of prisoners handed over to them by units who had captured them, and for the safety of civilians caught up in the fighting. It was also the task of the provost company to reconnoitre and provide guidance in respect of routes off the drop zone to objectives, and, where applicable, to sign an axis.

Intelligence Corps

317 Field Security Section (Airborne) Int Corps

Security within the division, and interrogation of captured enemy personnel was the responsibility of 317 Field Security Section (Airborne) which was formed in June 1943. Commanded initially by Captain Donaldson-Loudon, it comprised one officer, a warrant officer, four sergeants and twelve corporals. Prior to D-Day, the section was reinforced by a further eleven NCOs, some of whom came from the 1st Airborne Division, and Captain F. G. Macmillan took over command on Captain Donaldson-Loudon's departure to the Special Operations Executive.

During the six months prior to D-Day, the section's main role was to supervise the strict security in the division's transit camps. For operational matters, the section operated under the GSO 2 (Intelligence) in the divisional headquarters. For technical or personnel matters, and for intelligence policy, it worked under Headquarters Intelligence Corps (Field). During operations, when not carrying out field security tasks, personnel of the section fought as infantry.

Glider Pilot Regiment

Although it was not part of the two airborne divisions which it supported, The Glider Pilot Regiment performed a role which was an integral element of the major wartime airborne operations.

It was comprised of two battalions which were redesignated in 1943 as Nos. 1 & 2 Wings, commanded by Lieutenant Colonel Iain Murray DSO and Lieutenant Colonel John Place respectively. Each wing was intially established as having six squadrons, each comprised of four flights. In addition there was the Independent Squadron which took part in operations in North Africa and the landings in southern France.

All squadrons were equipped with the Airspeed Horsa which could accommodate up to thirty troops or alternatively small vehicles, such as jeeps and trailers, or support weapons such as 6-pounder anti-tank guns. The exception was C Squadron of No. 1 Wing which was equipped with the Hamilcar which was designed to carry heavy weapons and equipment such as 17-pounder anti-tank guns or light tanks.

Glider pilots were drawn from volunteers throughout the British Army and later the RAF. After an initial weeding-out process, they underwent an aircrew selection board before proceeding to an RAF Elementary Flying Training School for basic training on Tiger Moths. From there they proceeded to a Glider Training School for basic glider instruction on Hotspurs. On completion of that stage of their training, pilots were sent to a Heavy Glider Conversion Unit for introduction to the Horsa. Later, after joining their squadrons, some were selected to fly the Hamilcar.

In addition to being trained to fly, members of The Glider Pilot Regiment were instructed in a wide range of military skills, including the use of support weapons. This was the "Total Soldier" concept espoused by the Commander Glider Pilots, Brigadier George Chatteron DSO, which required glider pilots to be able to perform any role required of them after the airborne phase of an operation had been completed.

26. Officers of 6th Airborne Divisional Signals on the occasion of a visit by HRH The Princess Royal, Colonel-in-Chief Royal Signals. *Back row, left to right:* Lt Bradshaw, 2/Lt Gladwyn, Lt Ingham, Lt Curtis, Lt Aitchison, 2/Lt Gilbert, Lt MacMaster. *Centre row:* Lt Hart, Capt Austin, Capt Wilks, Capt Westwood, 2/Lt Royle, Lt Smith, RSM Carr. *Front row:* Capt Fenton, Lady-in Waiting, Brig Prescott, Lt Col Smallman-Tew, HRH The Princess Royal, Lt Gen Wemyss CB DSO MC, Maj Gen Raisson OBE MC, Maj Donald, Capt Holbrook.
(Photo: Col S. W. Brackenbury MBE)

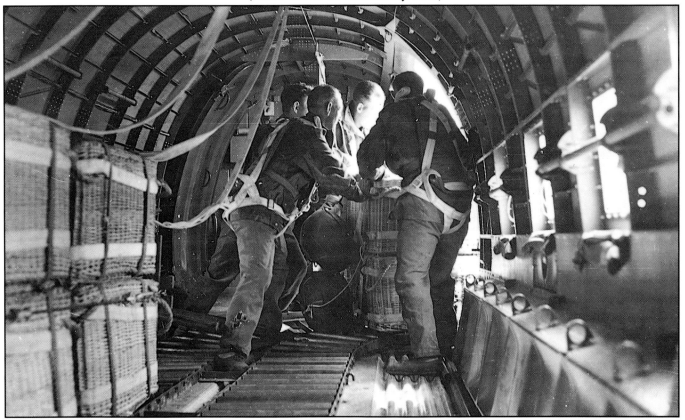

27. Air dispatchers of one of the division's RASC composite companies dispatching panniers from a Dakota.
(Photo: Imperial War Museum)

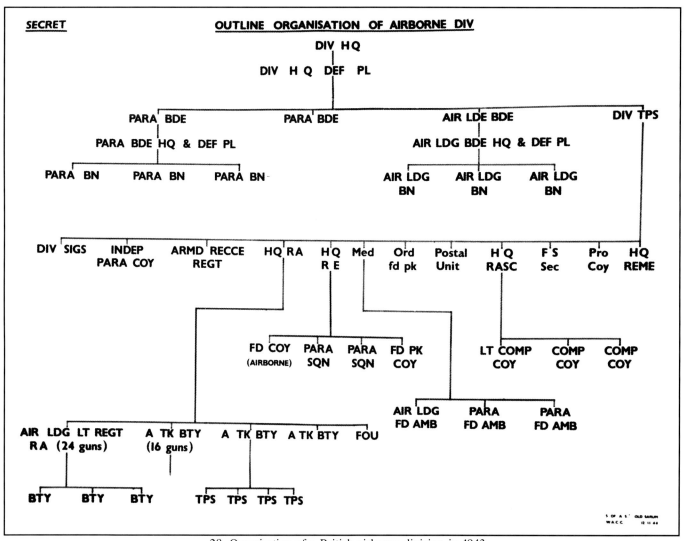

OUTLINE ORGANISATION OF AIRBORNE DIV

DIV HQ

DIV H Q DEF PL

PARA BDE — PARA BDE — AIR LDE BDE — DIV TPS

PARA BDE HQ & DEF PL

PARA BN — PARA BN — PARA BN

AIR LDG BDE HQ & DEF PL

AIR LDG BN — AIR LDG BN — AIR LDG BN

DIV SIGS — INDEP PARA COY — ARMD RECCE REGT — HQ RA — HQ R E — Med — Ord fd pk — Postal Unit — H Q RASC — F S Sec — Pro Coy — HQ REME

FD COY (AIRBORNE) — PARA SQN — PARA SQN — FD PK COY

LT COMP COY — COMP COY — COMP COY

AIR LDG FD AMB — PARA FD AMB — PARA FD AMB

AIR LDG LT REGT R A (24 guns) — A TK BTY (16 guns) — A TK BTY — A TK BTY — FOU

BTY — BTY — BTY

TPS TPS TPS TPS

S OF A S OLD SARUM
WACC   12 11 44

28. Organisation of a British airborne division in 1943.

30. An instructor of the Army Physical Training Corps supervises volunteers during part of the selection course. In the background on the left of the picture can be seen the 'trainasium' on which all volunteers were tested for their ability to overcome any fear of heights. (Photo: Imperial War Museum)

29. *Left:* All volunteers for Airborne Forces were required to undergo a stringent and exhaustive selection course before being accepted. This included a rigorous programme of physical fitness training.
(Photo: Imperial War Museum)

Training

As soon as he had assumed command, Gale wasted no time in starting to prepare his division for war. Despite the fact that some units earmarked for the division had as yet not joined it, training commenced almost immediately. This inevitably placed a considerable strain on all ranks, especially unit commanders and staff officers.

Only just over a month after the first element of divisional headquarters had formed on the 3rd May, 'Exercise Pegasus' took place. Its purpose was to study the role of an airborne division acting in support of an assault on the north-west coast of Europe. The tasks posed in the exercise mirrored those with which the division was to be faced almost exactly a year later, including: the capture of a fortified coastal gun battery, the denial to the enemy of ground from which amphibious assault operations could be observed, and the delaying of enemy reserves reaching the battle until objectives had been taken by assault divisions.

Parachute Training

Meanwhile, those troops in the division's parachute units who were not already parachutists had to qualify as such. This applied particularly to the newly formed 12th and 13th Parachute Battalions whose members had previously been ordinary infantrymen. When these two units were converted to their new role, officers and men were asked if they wished to volunteer for parachute training. About fifty per cent remained and subsequently qualified as parachutists, battalion strengths later being made up with men from other units who volunteered for service with airborne forces and who successfully qualified as parachutists.

Prior to undergoing parachute training, trainees had to successfully complete a selection course at the Airborne Forces Depot at Hardwick Hall. By any standards, the course was a harsh one. Troops underwent a fortnight of intensive physical tests in the gymnasium, on the assault course and on the roads and cross-country. Organised in small squads, each supervised by an Army Physical Training Corps instructor, recruits carried out everything 'at the double' whilst being watched carefully for any signs of weakness. The purpose of the course was to find those men who possessed the high degree of stamina and self-discipline so essential in a paratrooper. The failure rate was high and the fate which all recruits dreaded was to be "RTU'd" — "Returned To Unit". Those who were successful in passing the selection course went on to carry out their parachute training at No.1 Parachute Training School at Ringway, near Manchester.

The course at Ringway lasted two weeks. It consisted firstly of a period of a week devoted to 'synthetic' ground training during which the trainee parachutist learned how to exit correctly from an aircraft, how to control his parachute in the air and how to land correctly. Fuselages of Whitleys, and subsequently Dakotas, Stirlings, Halifaxes and Albemarles, were positioned in the hangers at Ringway. From these trainees jumped whilst learning the correct position for an exit. Other training aids included trapezes, in which trainees swung whilst learning correct flight drills, and wooden chutes down which they slid before falling and rolling. There was also the 'Fan' which consisted of a drum around which was wound a steel cable, the end of which was attached to a parachute harness. When a trainee jumped from a platform twenty feet from the ground, his weight caused the drum to revolve; however, its speed was controlled by two vanes which acted as air brakes and thus allowed the trainee to land with the same impact as he would when using a parachute. Another piece of training apparatus, invented by the 1st Polish Parachute Brigade, was a one hundred foot tower constructed of steel girders from the top of which protruded a long steel arm. Suspended from this by a cable was a parachute canopy stretched

31. Trainees learn the correct method of making an exit from a Whitley bomber, using a full scale mock-up of the aircraft's aperture. (Photo: Imperial War Museum)

32. Correct flight drills, and how to control the parachute during a descent, were taught on the 'trapeze'.
(Photo: Imperial War Museum)

across a large metal hoop. On launching himself from the tower on the command "Go!", the trainee found himself suspended in mid-air beneath the canopy. After he had practised his flight drills and adopted the correct position for landing, the cable was released and he floated to the ground.

Synthetic training was followed at the end of the first week by two descents from a balloon. These were not popular. The slow, swaying and silent ascent of the balloon to the jump height of seven hundred feet frequently added nausea to the tribulations of the trainees who were inevitably suffering from nervousness. Trainees sat in the 'cage' suspended below the balloon, in a 'stick' of four seated around the hole in the centre of the floor. On a command from the RAF instructor, the first man to jump swung his legs into the hole and adopted a position of sitting to attention whilst gripping the rim behind him. On the command "Go!", he thrust himself forward, bringing his hands to his side and keeping his feet together in a position of attention. This was followed by a stomach-churning drop of a hundred and twenty feet before the trainee's parachute opened. Needless to say, the sensation of the parachute opening was a thrilling one but any feeling of bliss was soon interrupted by an instructor on the ground shouting instructions through a megaphone with regard to the correct flight drills and position for landing. Those who were short and stocky had little difficulty in mastering the parachute roll, whilst those who were tall with long legs tended to find it more difficult. However, there were generally few severe casualties.

Balloon descents were followed by five from an aircraft. These were carried out firstly in 'slow pairs' and then in 'quick pairs'. Subsequently trainees jumped in sticks of five and finally in sticks of ten. Whilst not such a nauseating process as jumping from a balloon, parachuting from a Whitley could nonetheless be somewhat disconcerting if the correct position was not maintained when making an exit through the aircraft's floor, the result being one or two rather dramatic somersaults which normally resulted in "the twists" — the front and rear sets of rigging lines becoming twisted together, restricting the proper development of the parachute canopy and thus increasing the rate of descent as well as preventing control of the parachute. The same problems faced parachutists jumping from other converted bombers which were subsequently used, namely Halifaxes, Stirlings and Albemarles, but which had never been designed for such use. It was not until the arrival of the Dakota that exits could be made from a door in the side of the fuselage rather than the floor, thus making life somewhat easier and relatively more enjoyable for the parachutist.

Other problems which faced parachutists included the 'blown periphery' which occurred when part of the periphery of the canopy was blown inwards and subsequently outwards through the rigging lines, thus producing a second inverted canopy. Another type of blown periphery occurred when part of the canopy blew between two rigging lines after which the canopy tended to roll up at the skirt. Other types of malfunctions included the 'streamer', which occurred when a canopy failed to

33. Learning how to roll correctly to absorb the impact of landing. (Photo: Imperial War Museum)

open at all.

Once trainees had completed their total of seven descents at Ringway, they were presented with the coveted parachute wings and returned to join their units within the division.

Glider Training

The men of the 12th Battalion The Devonshire Regiment had a different but equally hazardous type of training to undergo. Their new role as an airlanding battalion required them to become fully familiar with the skills of going to war in gliders. The other two battalions in 6th Airlanding Brigade, the 1st Battalion The Royal Ulster Rifles and the 2nd Battalion The Oxfordshire & Buckinghamshire Light Infantry, having previously formed part of 1st Airlanding Brigade, were already trained and experienced in the use of gliders.

The main workhorse of the airlanding brigade was the Airspeed Horsa glider. Flown by two pilots of the Glider Pilot Regiment, this aircraft could carry a total of thirty infantrymen. Alternatively, it could carry a jeep and trailer, or a 6-pounder anti-tank gun, or an M8 75mm pack howitzer. Heavier equipment, such as light tanks or 17-pounder anti-tank guns and their tractors, were carried in huge Hamilcar gliders.

Passengers in the Horsa sat on wooden benches on either side of the fuselage, each securely strapped in. Unfortunately for them, however, when the glider was airborne behind its tug aircraft it tended to move in a surging motion as the tow-rope tightened or slackened. In addition, it pitched, rolled and yawed. This soon resulted in causing nausea, even amongst those with the strongest of stomachs. This problem was never overcome despite efforts to develop airsickness remedies.

Another somewhat disconcerting experience for Horsa passengers was to fly at the rear of a large formation of bombers towing gliders. The turbulence caused by a large number of four-engined aircraft resulted in gliders sometimes finding themselves at the end of a taut tow-rope one moment, and the next almost level with their tugs whilst their tow-ropes hung in a huge loop behind and below them.

The most nerve-racking time for those travelling in gliders was on landing. As the aircraft made its final approach, the second pilot would call "Brace! Brace!" through the cockpit door. All passengers would then put their arms round the shoulders of the men on either side of them and lift their feet off the floor.

Once the glider had landed and had come to a halt, it was necessary for its passengers to disembark via doors at the front port and rear starboard sides of the fuselage and to deploy rapidly. In the case of equipment and vehicles, these also had to be unloaded as quickly as possible. Initially, this was effected via the large loading door in the front port side. Subsequently, by 1944, the Horsa was modified so as to allow the nose to be swung aside and the tail unit to be detached from the main fuselage so that equipment or vehicles could be unloaded at the front or rear via ramps.

Training for airlanding troops also included the loading and

34. Synthetic training included jumping from fuselage mock-ups suspended in hangars. (Photo: Imperial War Museum)

35. A trainee preparing to jump from the tower. (Photo: Imperial War Museum)

lashing of a wide range of weapons, equipment and vehicles in gliders. The aircraft were fitted with strongpoints to which loads had to be securely fastened by metal lashings. It was essential that the glider's balance had to be maintained in flight and this was done by keeping its centre of gravity steady. For this reason, therefore, each load had to be worked out with maximum care with regard to its exact position and where it was to be loaded and lashed down. The lashings themselves had to be extremely strong and capable of resisting the shock of a crash landing. The effect of a 6-pounder anti-tank gun or jeep breaking loose from its lashings on the sudden cessation of forward movement of the glider would have been catastrophic and would have resulted in the death of both pilots. Unfortunately such events did occasionally occur on operations.

In addition to their parachute or glider training, all units of the 6th Airborne Division worked hard at their respective military skills. Throughout the latter half of 1943, battalions and brigades concentrated on tactical training at all levels, from the individual soldier through section, platoon, company and battalion exercises. Days and nights were spent on exercise, frequently beginning with parachute and glider insertions and more often than not ending with a twenty mile route march back to barracks. Every man in the division, including the divisional commander and those on the staff at divisional and brigade levels, marched, jumped and exercised. The standard of fitness and ability became extremely high as a result of the ceaseless and intensive programme of training and a tremendous *esprit de corps* began to manifest itself.

Staff training was not ignored either. Major General Gale conducted a programme of exercises and study days for his officers, all of which included problems relating to administration and air movement. These were aimed at the types of operations with which the division was likely to be tasked in the future. Gale himself had studied closely the German airborne operations early in the war at Eben Emael in 1940 and the capture of the Corinth Canal bridge in 1941. He insisted that special staff exercises were conducted, these being designed to practise efficient operation under adverse conditions of the type likely to be encountered during airborne operations. A standard layout of divisional headquarters, designed to adapt to differing ground conditions, was drawn up and practised during exercises.

Administrative training was also carried out, covering all aspects including resupply and casualty evacuation. All divisional exercises included full scale resupply by Royal Air Force and US Army Air Corps aircraft by day and night. This was where the division's Royal Army Service Corps units played their part. They were responsible for all aspects of resupply, including the air dispatch of containers from delivering aircraft, their collection and clearance from drop zones and setting up resupply in the field. The division's medical units were exercised fully in the handling of casualties during these exercises, with 'wounded' personnel being processed through the complete medical evacuation process from rendering of first aid to simulated field surgery.

Meanwhile the divisional intelligence staff, under the GSO 2 (Intelligence) Major Gerry Lacoste, studied the German dispositions along the entire northern coast of France, including details of their defensive works, their gun positions, wire obstacles, minefields, anti-airborne troop defences and also the known details of their plans to counter airborne landings.

By the end of 1943, considerable progress had been achieved. However, all the hard work and training enabled the division to achieve the required results only just in time because it was ordered to mobilize on the 23rd December, less than eight months after its formation, and to prepare for operations by the 1st February of the following year. The fact that it was able to do so on time was a tremendous achievement.

36. Descending from the tower. The rate of descent was controlled by a cable attached to the apex of the parachute. (Photo: Imperial War Museum)

37. Two 'sticks' about to make their first descents from a balloon. (Photo: Imperial War Museum)

38. "Red On!" A trainee parachutist watching the RAF dispatcher for the signal to make his exit from a Whitley.
(Photo: Imperial War Museum)

39. A trainee making a descent from a Whitley over the DZ at Tatton Park. Note the kitbag which carries his personal equipment.
(Photo: Airborne Forces Museum)

40. Whitleys dropping trainees over the DZ at Tatton Park.
(Photo: Airborne Forces Museum)

42. A safe landing but the parachutist had to collapse his canopy quickly and release himself from his harness to avoid being dragged. (Photo: Imperial War Museum)

41. *Left:* A trainee parachutist during a descent, assuming the correct position for landing.
(Photo: Imperial War Museum)

43. Paratroops also learned to jump from other types of aircraft, including Albemarles, Stirlings, Halifaxes and Dakotas. Here the hatch has just been opened prior to a 'stick' jumping from an Albemarle. (Photo: Imperial War Museum)

44. *Centre left:* "Red On!"
(Photo: Imperial War Museum)

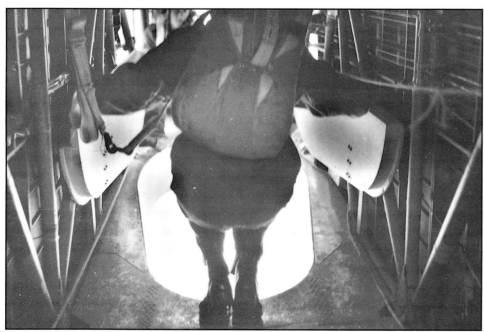

45. *Above:* "Green On! Go!"
(Photo: Imperial War Museum)

46. A view through the hatch showing a canopy deploying. (Photo: Imperial War Museum)

47. The safety and lives of parachutists depended upon the meticulous care taken in the packing of parachutes by specially trained WAAFs.
(Photo: Imperial War Museum)

49. *Opposite page, top:* Parachutists don their parachutes prior to embarking on an exercise.
(Photo: Imperial War Museum)

50. *Opposite page, bottom left:* Boarding a Dakota.
(Photo: Imperial War Museum)

51. *Opposite page, bottom right:* The RAF dispatcher secures himself to his safety strop.
(Photo: Imperial War Museum)

48. Regular parachute descents figured largely in unit training within 6th Airborne Division. Two members of a parachute battalion draw their parachutes. (Photo: Imperial War Museum)

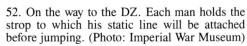

52. On the way to the DZ. Each man holds the strop to which his static line will be attached before jumping. (Photo: Imperial War Museum)

53. *Centre left:* Hooking up. Each man fastens the end of his static line to the strop connecting it to the anchor point in the aircraft.
(Photo: Imperial War Museum)

54. *Centre right:* "Red On!"
(Photo: Imperial War Museum)

55. *Bottom left:* "Green On! Go!" Jumping with equipment. This man is carrying a kitbag, which contains his personal equipment, and an LMG valise. (Photo: Imperial War Museum)

56. *Bottom right:* Dakotas dropping elements of one of the division's parachute brigades during an exercise in south-west England.
(Photo: Imperial War Museum)

No.1 PTS

When first I came to PTS
My CO he advised,
"Take lots and lots of underwear,
You'll need it I surmise."
But I replied. "By Gad Sir!
No matter what befalls,
I'll always keep my trousers clean
When jumping thro' the hole."

Jumping thro' the hole,
Jumping thro' the hole,
I'll always keep my trousers clean
When jumping thro' the hole.

I went into the hangar,
Instructor by my side,
And on Kilkenny's Circus
Had many a glorious ride.
On these ingenious gadgets
You'll soon learn how to fall
And keep your feet together
When jumping thro' the hole.

Jumping thro' the hole,
Jumping thro' the hole,
I'll always keep my trousers clean
When jumping thro' the hole.

They swung me on the swing, boys
They pushed me down the chute,
They showed me the high aperture
I thought it rather cute.
Said they, "This apparatus will teach you,"
I recall, "to centralise your C of G
When jumping thro' the hole."

Jumping thro' the hole,
Jumping thro' the hole,
I'll always keep my trousers clean
When jumping thro' the hole.

One morning very early,
Damp and cold and dark,
They took me in a so-called bus
Out to Tatton Park.
In keeping with the weather,
Said I to one and all,
"I take a dim and misty view
Of jumping thro' the hole."

Jumping thro' the hole
Jumping thro' the hole,
I'll always keep my trousers clean
When jumping thro' the hole.

They fitted me with a parachute
And a helmet for my head,
The sergeant looked with expert eye
"They'll fit you fine," he said,
"I'll introduce you now to Bessie,
That is what we call
That nice balloon from which you'll soon
Be jumping thro' the hole."

Jumping thro' the hole,
Jumping thro' the hole,
I'll always keep my trousers clean
When jumping thro' the hole.

"Okay! Up six hundred!
Four to drop!" Said he.
"Four to drop! Good God!" I cried,
"One of them is me!"
So clinging very grimly
To the handles on the floor,
I cursed the day I volunteered
For jumping thro' the hole.

Jumping thro' the hole,
Jumping thro' the hole,
I'll always keep my trousers clean
When jumping thro' the hole.

I hit the deck, I rang the bell,
I twisted twenty times,
I came down with both feet entangled
In my rigging lines.
But floating gently down to earth,
I didn't care at all
For I had kept my trousers clean
When jumping thro' the hole.

Jumping thro' the hole,
Jumping thro' the hole,
I'll always keep my trousers clean
When jumping thro' the hole.

57. A flight of the Glider Pilot Regiment. The highest standards of discipline and turnout were insisted upon throughout the regiment. Glider pilots were trained in a very wide variety of skills and weapons in order to be able to carry out a number of roles after landings had taken place.
(Photo: Museum of Army Flying)

58. *Right:* Basic flying training for glider pilots was carried out on the Tiger Moth.
(Photo: Museum of Army Flying)

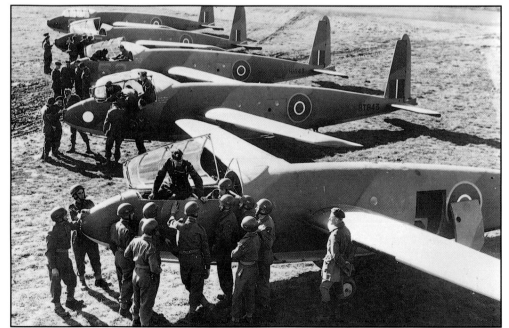

59. Basic glider training was carried out on the Hotspur. Trainee pilots are pictured here with their RAF instructors.
(Photo: Museum of Army Flying)

The board in the photograph reads:

AIRCRAFT TYPE	Nº	PILOT	TIME OUT	E.T.A	TIME IN	DESTINATION OR EXERCISE
HOTSPUR	J	SGT SPOTTO				LOCAL LANDING
"	A	F/O PRANG				ROUTE 2
"	C	SGT DROPIT				ROUTE 5
"	L	F/O FLAPE				ROUTE 5
"	T	P/O TIBSY				PINPOINTING
"	U	LT MATEY				X-COUNTRY

MET REPORT

60. Trainee pilots being briefed prior to a training flight. (Photo: Museum of Army Flying)

61. *Opposite page, top:* A Hotspur takes off in tow behind a Whitley.
(Photo: Airborne Forces Museum)

63. A trainee pilot climbs out of his Hotspur after completing a night flight.
(Photo: Imperial War Museum)

64. A trainee pilot undergoing practical instruction in maintenance on a Hotspur.
(Photo: Imperial War Museum)

62. *Opposite page, bottom:* A close-up view of a Hotspur cockpit. An RAF instructor explains the layout of the instrument panel to a trainee. (Photo: Museum of Army Flying)

65. Aircraft recognition formed an important part of a glider pilot's training.
(Photo: Imperial War Museum)

66. Classroom instruction included such subjects as navigation. Two trainee pilots seen here are studying air photographs.
(Photo: Imperial War Museum)

67. After qualifying for their 'wings', glider pilots progressed to a Heavy Glider Conversion Unit where they converted to Horsas for the final part of their technical flying training. Tactical flying was taught when pilots arrived at their squadrons.
(Photo: Imperial War Museum)

68. RAF aircrew briefing glider pilots prior to a flight.
(Photo: Imperial War Museum)

69. A Horsa being waved forward for take-off.
(Photo: Imperial War Museum)

70. Horsa taking off behind a Halifax bomber.
(Photo: Imperial War Museum)

71. A Horsa descending with full flap applied.
These huge compressed air-operated flaps had a
powerful braking effect and enabled the aircraft
to dive at a steep angle during its approach before
landing. (Photo: Imperial War Museum)

73. 'The Total Soldier'. A glider pilot in full battle order, ready to carry out any role required of him once he had delivered troops or equipment to the battlefield.
(Photo: Museum of Army Flying)

72. A glider pilot in flying gear, standing by the nose of a Horsa.
(Photo: Museum of Army Flying)

74. Aircrew and glider pilots at a briefing. A very close relationship developed between the RAF and the Glider Pilot Regiment. (Photo: Airborne Forces Museum)

75. Air Chief Marshal Sir Trafford Leigh-Mallory addresses glider pilots at the end of a large night flying exercise. (Photo: Imperial War Museum)

76. The interior of a Horsa glider, facing aft and showing a platoon of airlanding infantry. On the right-hand edge of the picture can be seen the loading ramp door in the closed position.
(Photo: Museum of Army Flying)

78. All glider loads had to be securely fastened with steel shackles. Two members of the 12th Battalion The Devonshire Regiment are seen here securing a load to strongpoints inside a Horsa. Behind them is a trailer similarly secured. (Photo: Imperial War Museum)

77. *Left:* A view, facing forward, of the interior of a Horsa. The open door at the far end of the aircraft shows a glimpse of the cockpit.
(Photo: Imperial War Museum)

79. Royal Enfield lightweight motorcycles secured in position inside a Horsa.
(Photo: Imperial War Museum)

80. A 6-pounder anti-tank gun being loaded aboard a Horsa. The gun had to be traversed on its carriage when being loaded via the loading door in the forward port side of the fuselage.
(Photo: Museum of Army Flying)

81. *Bottom left:* A jeep being loaded aboard a Horsa. This aircraft could also accommodate, in addition to the jeep, a trailer or 6-pounder anti-tank gun and its crew.
(Photo: Imperial War Museum)

82. *Below:* The Mk.2 Horsa was fitted with nose and tail units which were hinged and thus could be swung aside to facilitate the loading or unloading of jeeps, trailers, 6-pounder anti-tank guns or Bofors 40mm anti-aircraft guns via ramps at the front or rear of the glider.
(Photo: Imperial War Museum)

83. A Hamilcar glider with its nose door open, showing two troopers of 6th Airborne Armoured Reconnaissance Regiment securing their Tetrarch light tank. (Photo: Imperial War Museum)

84. A view of the interior of a Hamilcar, showing the steel fastenings being connected to the rear of the tank. (Photo: Imperial War Museum)

Baptism of Fire

At eleven o'clock on the morning of the 17th February 1944 Lieutenant General F. A. M. 'Boy' Browning, Commander Airborne Troops, arrived at Major General Richard Gale's headquarters to brief him on the task which the 6th Airborne Division was to carry out during 'Operation Overlord'.

Gale recalled afterwards his feeling of controlled excitement:

"Our great moment had arrived. I was now to be told what we had been so impatiently wanting to know. All our training; all our endeavours; all our beliefs were at last to be put to the test. We, had tried to think of every contingency. We, the whole team, had studied, laboured, pondered and deduced. We knew what we could do and what we wanted. We knew just how far the bow would stretch."

However, when Lieutenant General Browning had outlined the entire operational plan and had given full details of the division's tasks, Gale was dismayed although he hid his feelings at the time.

The plan called for one of the division's parachute brigades and one anti-tank battery to be placed under the command of 3rd Infantry Division which would be assaulting from the sea. The parachute brigade's task was to seize two bridges over the Caen Canal and the River Orne at Benouville and Ranville respectively, both bridges being about fifteen miles north of Caen itself. The limitation on the size of the force was due to the number of aircraft available for the operation. Gale detailed Brigadier James Hill's 3rd Parachute Brigade for the task. Hill immediately realised that parachute troops would not be ideal for the *coup de main* party for the bridges, due to the scattered nature of their drop. He requested that a company of gliderborne troops be placed under his command for this task and General Gale readily agreed.

As well as being bitterly disappointed that his division was not to be committed to battle in its entirety, Gale was also very worried that one parachute brigade would not be sufficient for the task. This argument obviously impressed others because a few days later, on the 23rd February, the decision was taken to allocate Nos. 38 and 46 Groups RAF to the operation and thus the whole of the division would be committed under the command of 1st British Corps.

A vastly relieved divisional commander and a small group of his staff immediately commenced the planning for the operation, ensconsing themselves at Headquarters 1st Corps in Ashley Gardens, London, where it was co-located with General Browning's Headquarters, Airborne Troops. This group consisted of Gale himself, Lieutenant Colonel Bobby Bray his GSO 1, Major Gerry Lacoste the GSO (2 Intelligence), Captain Nick Pratt the GSO3 (Air), Lieutenant Colonel Shamus Hickie the AA & QMG, Lieutenant Colonel M. McEwan the ADMS, Lieutenant Colonel Jack Norris the CRA, Lieutenant Colonel Frank Lowman the CRE and the headquarters' chief clerk. Later, the more detailed planning was carried out at The Old Farm at Brigmerston House near Milston, a village located between Netheravon and Bulford in Wiltshire. Each element of the division, including the 1st Special Service Brigade which would be under command, and Nos. 38 and 46 Groups RAF had its own planning cell there. During the final stages, the planning staff moved to Scotland to co-ordinate plans with 3rd Infantry Division.

85. 19 May 1944. Their Majesties pay a visit to the division. *Left to right:* Major General Gale, HM Queen Elizabeth, HM King George VI, Colonel Reggie Parker (Deputy Commander 6th Airlanding Brigade), Lieutenant Colonel Jack Norris (CRA 6th Airborne Division) and Brigadier The Honourable Hugh Kindersley (Commander 6th Airlanding Brigade). (Photo: Imperial War Museum)

The Plan

In essence, the overall Allied invasion plan called for an assault on the coast of Normandy in the area between the Cherbourg Peninsula and the River Orne, the Americans on the right and the British 2nd Army on the left. The British assault was to be carried out by two corps: 1st Corps on the left and 30th Corps on the right. 6th Airborne Division was to come under command of Lieutenant General Sir John Crocker's 1st Corps. Its role was to cover the left flank of the British assault, which was bounded by the Caen Canal and the River Orne, and to dominate the area east of Caen whose features themselves dominated the British left flank.

The division was given three primary tasks: firstly, the capture of the bridges at Benouville and Ranville and the establishment of a bridgehead to hold them; secondly, the destruction of a coastal battery at Franceville Plage (known as the Merville Battery) prior to seaborne forces coming within its range; and thirdly, the destruction of the bridges over the River Dives at Varaville, Robehomme, Bures and Troarn in order to delay any movement by enemy forces from the east.

Two secondary tasks allotted to the division consisted of the following: firstly, the mopping up and securing of the area between the River Orne and Dives, including the capture of the towns of Sallenelles and Franceville Plage as well as the clearing of the coastal strip between these towns and Cabourg at the mouth of the River Dives; and secondly, after securing a firm base east of the River Orne, to operate against any enemy reserve formations trying to move towards the covering position from the east and south-east.

The task which Gale had been allotted was formidable, and involved seizing an area of twenty-four square miles and holding it. To do this, he had one airborne division and a brigade of commandos.

Gale's initial plan was governed by the fact that the aircraft resources of Nos. 38 and 46 Groups RAF were insufficient to permit the transportation of the entire division in one airlift. He had to decide, therefore, which of his brigades and divisional troops were to be flown in and which were to be transported by sea. The tasks of seizing the bridges at Benouville and Ranville and the destruction of the Merville Battery required speed and surprise for them to be successful. These essential factors could not be guaranteed in a parachute operation. Moreover, the troops seizing the bridges had to be capable of resisting German counter-attacks which would include armour. This meant that some of the division's anti-tank assets would have to be landed as soon as possible.

With these factors in mind, Gale decided that 6th Airlanding Brigade and its more heavily armed units would carry out the operation to capture the two bridges, whilst the neutralising of the Merville Battery and other more dispersed tasks to the east were given to 3rd Parachute Brigade. 5th Parachute Brigade, together with the 6th Airborne Armoured Reconnaissance Regiment and other divisional troops, would be brought in on a second airlift. Gale's headquarters, together with elements of the division's artillery and anti-tank units, would land after 6th Airlanding Brigade.

Enemy forces in 6th Airborne Division's planned area of operations consisted of the 711th and 716th Infantry Divisions, possibly two squadrons of armour and a number of infantry and artillery units formed from training schools. Both divisions were classified as low category formations whose efficiency was assessed, in comparison to a first class division, as being forty per cent in static defence and not more than fifteen per cent in a counter-attack role. The 711th Infantry Division, which was located east of the River Orne with its headquarters at Pont Leveque, numbered some thirteen to fourteen thousand men and was equipped with a number of anti-tank guns and approximately sixty infantry, field and medium artillery pieces. It had been reported as being equipped with French Renault 35 tanks. Artillery in the 716th Infantry Division consisted of twenty-four gun-howitzers, twelve medium howitzers and a number of anti-tank guns. Its

86. HM The King and Queen Elizabeth inspect the medical equipment of a member of 224th Parachute Field Ambulance whilst Lieutenant General 'Boy' Browning takes a personal interest in the man's pack. (Photo: Imperial War Museum)

armour comprised a few obsolete German and French tanks.

However, a major threat was posed by the 12th SS (Hitler Jugend) Panzer Division which, with its 21,000 men and Mk V Panther tanks, was deployed thirty miles to the south-east at Lisieux. Likewise, the 21st Panzer Division, which also numbered some twenty thousand men and was fully equipped with Panthers, was based in the Rennes area and was also considered a threat by Gale and his planners. Finally, the 352nd Infantry Division, also fully manned and well-equipped, was situated within striking distance as well. The intelligence staff estimated that it could be ready for operations in the Caen-Bayeux area by H + 8 hours and that 12th SS Panzer Division could arrive east of Caen by H + 12 hours.

On the 18th March, Major General Gale issued orders to his brigade commanders. 6th Airlanding Brigade would land shortly after midnight on the 5th June and was to capture intact the bridges over the Caen Canal and the River Orne; these were to be secured before dawn. Subsequently the brigade was to establish defensive positions to the east and south-east, and was to hold a small bridgehead on the west of the Caen Canal pending the arrival of 3rd Infantry Division. 3rd Parachute Brigade was to silence the Merville Battery by not later than one-and-a-half hours before the seaborne landings were due to take place, destroy the bridges over the River Dives and deny the Bois de Bavent ridge to the enemy. 5th Parachute Brigade and the major element of the divisional troops were to land on the evening of D-Day. 1st Special Service Brigade was to seize the towns of Sallanelles and Franceville Plage and was to clear as much as possible of the coastal area between these two towns and Cabourg. One airlanding battalion, the airlanding light regiment less one battery, and the balance of divisional troops would come by sea.

In April, however, intelligence produced by aerial reconnaissance showed that the Germans had erected anti-glider defences in the form of poles and pits on the landing and dropping zones selected by Gale and his staff. Initially it was feared that the division's plans had been compromised but further evidence showed that all open areas along the entire French and Belgian coasts had been similarly obstructed. These defences posed a problem and it was agreed amongst the planners that a mass glider landing was out of the question until the landing zones had been cleared.

Gale thus decided to modify his plans. Accordingly, the task of capturing the bridges at Benouville and Ranville was now allotted to 5th Parachute Brigade in place of 6th Airlanding Brigade. The *coup de main* operation itself was still to be carried out by a gliderborne force consisting of a reinforced company, comprising six platoons, which was placed under the command of 5th Parachute Brigade. The brigade was to land shortly after the capture of the bridges and would clear the landing zones after securing the area of Benouville, Ranville and Le Bas de Ranville. The tasks of 3rd Parachute Brigade and 1st Special Service Brigade remained unaltered and 6th Airlanding Brigade was to land on the evening of D-Day.

Now that each brigade's tasks had been confirmed, training became even more intense. 7th Parachute Battalion, which would relieve the *coup de main* force at the two bridges, went with the gliderborne company to Devon where it exercised and rehearsed on two similar bridges spanning the River Exe and a canal nearby. Meanwhile 13th Parachute Battalion and some sappers trained on Salisbury Plain, practising landing zone clearance with explosives.

In 3rd Parachute Brigade, 9th Parachute Battalion had been given the task of silencing the Merville Battery whilst 1st Canadian Parachute Battalion was to destroy the bridges over the River Dives at Varaville and Robehomme, after which it was to hold the centre of the Bois de Bavent ridge at Le Mesnil. 8th Parachute Battalion was tasked with blowing the bridges over the Dives at Bures and Troarn and subsequently denying the dense woods along the southern part of the ridge to the enemy. A dummy battery, complete with gun emplacements, minefields, anti-tank ditch

87. An officer of 3rd Parachute Squadron RE explains the mysteries of sapper demolitions equipment to HM The King, Queen Elizabeth and Princess Elizabeth. On the right is Brigadier James Hill, Commander 3rd Parachute Brigade. (Photo: Imperial War Museum)

and barbed wire defences, was constructed and similar bridges were found in the South of England. Most of the preparatory training was carried out by night and in wooded country. Nothing was left to chance. Brigadier James Hill, when addressing the battalions immediately prior to D-Day, issued these prophetic words: *"Gentlemen, in spite of your excellent training and very clear briefing do not be daunted if chaos reigns — it undoubtedly will!!"*. This warning was to stand many soldiers in very good stead, particularly as only Hill himself, Lieutenant Colonel Alastair Pearson and Major 'Tim' Roseveare of 3rd Parachute Squadron RE had seen a shot fired in anger before and the average age of those in the brigade was around twenty-one years. They did not know what to expect!

Throughout other parts of the division the tempo of training was intensified for all units, including divisional troops. The gunners of 53rd Airlanding Light Regiment RA went to Wales to carry out battery and regimental shoots with their American 75mm pack howitzers whilst those of 3rd and 4th Airlanding Anti-Tank Batteries RA trained assiduously with their 6 and 17-pounder anti-tank guns. Troopers of the 6th Airborne Armoured Reconnaissance Regiment worked with their Tetrarch light tanks whilst signallers of the 6th Airborne Divisional Signals concentrated on perfecting the techniques of operating the division's vital radio and line communications. Meanwhile, the pilots of the six gliders who would carry the *coup de main* force to capture the bridges over the Caen Canal and the River Orne were undergoing concentrated training by day and night, as were their comrades who would fly in the divisional headquarters, 6th Airlanding Brigade and elements of divisional troops during the rest of D-Day.

The division's administrative staff, under Lieutenant Colonel Shamus Hickie, was also under pressure grappling with the seemingly endless problems involved in the supply of weapons, ammunition, equipment, fuel, rations and water, as well as the organisation of casualty evacuation and other aspects of logistical support for all the division's units with their individual requirements. In addition to the load carried by each soldier and glider, all Halifaxes, Stirlings and Albemarles being employed as parachute and tug aircraft would carry in their bomb bays containers full of ammunition and equipment. These would be dropped after each aircraft's parachutists had jumped or its glider had been released. Some would contain plasma and drugs because field surgical teams from both parachute field ambulances would be dropped in the first waves. Once the planned link-up with 1st Corps had been achieved, further supplies and logistical support would be moved up by road.

On the 19th May, the division and No. 38 Group RAF were visited by King George VI who was accompanied by Queen Elizabeth and Princess Elizabeth. It was a great day for the division which was able to demonstrate its skills to the Royal visitors who watched a mass landing by gliders at Netheravon and a drop by 1st Canadian Parachute Battalion. The Queen and Princess Elizabeth spent a considerable amount of time talking to hundreds of men of the division as they walked through its ranks after the initial parade.

The division was also visited by General Bernard Montgomery. Wearing a red beret given to him by a previous commander of 1st Airborne Division, the Commander-in-Chief addressed the men of each brigade after gathering them round his jeep. He spoke to them of the coming invasion, of his confidence in them, and for the need for them to have confidence in themselves and their commanders. Subsequently he sent the division a signal in which he expressed his approval at what he had seen that day. This was reinforced by a letter from General Browning, by then Commander 1st Airborne Corps, from which the following extract is taken:

"...to confirm our conversation last night, I should like to congratulate you on the very fine appearance of your division, not only the type of officers and men, but also the turnout and the state of weapons and equipment.

88. Brigadier Hill explains the finer points of the PIAT to HM The King whilst Queen Elizabeth talks to a sniper. Lieutenant Colonel Shamus Hickie, AA & QMG 6th Airborne Division, stands next to Princess Elizabeth. (Photo: Imperial War Museum)

It showed a standard which I have always hoped airborne forces would attain and maintain; whetever anyone else thought I, at any rate, was fully satisfied . . .''

To those who knew General 'Boy' and his very high standards, this was praise indeed.

The preparations of 'Operation Overlord' culminated in a four-day test exercise, set up by General Browning, which took place between the 21st and 25th May and during which the 'enemy' was provided by elements of 1st Airborne Division and 1st Polish Parachute Brigade. Although very few members of the division were aware of it, this was the final rehearsal. On the 25th May, the division moved into airfield transit camps which were surrounded by barbed wire and guarded by armed sentries. Only those on special duty were allowed to go in or out.

It was at this point that all was revealed concerning the division's tasks for the invasion, with detailed briefings for company and platoon commanders taking place. Highly detailed and realistic models of objectives, supported by accurate maps and air photographs, were used to ensure that each officer taking part in the individual operations knew exactly what was required of him and his men. On the 30th May, commanding officers briefed the men of their battalions after which, during the next two days, company and platoon commanders gave their orders. Included in these were outline details of the division's tasks, so that each soldier was aware not only of his own role but also of the background to it and the reasons for it.

Originally, take-off for the airborne invasion was scheduled for the evening of the 4th June. On the morning of the 3rd June, battalions paraded in full battle order and moved in transport to the launching airfields. Containers were loaded aboard aircraft whilst parachutes were drawn and fitted. Just before lunch, however, a signal postponing the operation for twenty-four hours was received by all units. On the following morning of the 5th June a further signal was received, confirming that take-off would be later that day.

That evening the troops of 3rd and 5th Parachute Brigades departed from their transit camps for their launching airfields. The first of them to take off were the men of the 22nd Independent Parachute Company whose task it was to mark the dropping zones. Meanwhile, the *coup de main* force for the assault on the Caen Canal and River Orne bridges was already airborne and heading for its objectives in its six gliders.

It was a clear sky and the moon shone as the aircraft carrying the two parachute brigades took off. They were followed by the tugs and gliders carrying Major General Richard Gale's headquarters and divisional troops, including 4th Airlanding Anti-Tank Battery RA, the 17-pounder troop of 3rd Airlanding Anti-Tank Battery RA and artillery forward observation parties.

89. General Montgomery, Lieutenant General Browning and Major General Gale watching a demonstration of a jeep being loaded into a Horsa glider. (Photo: Imperial War Museum)

90. Queen Elizabeth is seen here talking to Corporal 'Jungle' Jones of 22nd Independent Parachute Company. Before enlisting, Corporal Jones was a physical training instructor in the Metropolitan Police. (Photo: Imperial War Museum)

91. HM The King and Lieutenant General Browning pause in front of men of 1st Canadian Parachute Battalion.
(Photo: Imperial War Museum)

92. HM The King shakes hands with Major Don Wilkins of 1st Canadian Parachute Battalion as Lieutenant Colonel George Bradbrooke, the Commanding Officer, looks on.
(Photo: Imperial War Museum)

93. HM The King shaking hands with The Reverend J. O. Jenkins, chaplain of 12th Parachute Battalion. On the right is Brigadier Nigel Poett, Commander 5th Parachute Battalion.
(Photo: Imperial War Museum)

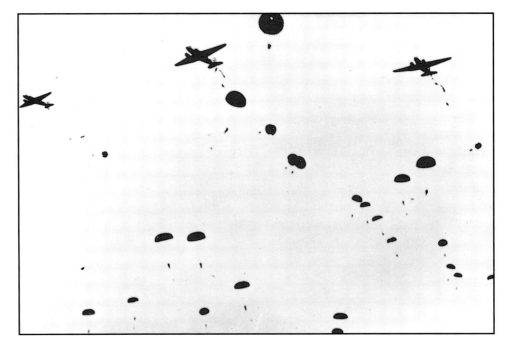

94. Troops of 3rd Parachute Brigade being dropped by Dakotas at the start of an exercise.
(Photo: 1st Canadian Parachute Battalion Association)

95. Members of 1st Canadian Parachute Battalion landing on a DZ during an exercise.
(Photo: 1st Canadian Parachute Battalion Association)

96. The Machine Gun Platoon of 1st Canadian Parachute Battalion moving off the DZ.
(Photo: 1st Canadian Parachute Battalion Association)

97. Brigadier Hill (*far right*) talking to *left to right:* Captain Robert Macdonald, Captain Peter Griffin, and Major Jeff Nicklin – all of 1st Canadian Parachute Battalion. In the background is Major Bill Collingwood, Brigade Major of 3rd Parachute Brigade.
(Photo: 1st Canadian Parachute Battalion Association)

98. Two brothers serving in 1st Canadian Parachute Battalion, Lieutenants Philippe and Maurice Rousseau. Photographed at Ampney Down transit camp before embarking for D-Day.
(Photo: 1st Canadian Parachute Battalion Association)

99. Sergeant Peter Kowalski and 'Johnny Canuck', 1st Canadian Parachute Battalion's mascot which jumped into Normandy with the Battalion
(Photo: 1st Canadian Parachute Battalion Association)

100. General Montgomery inspecting officers and men of 13th Parachute Battalion. He is accompanied by the Commanding Officer, Lieutenant Colonel Peter Luard. Behind is Brigadier Nigel Poett.
(Photo: Imperial War Museum)

101. *Below:* General Montgomery talking to Major John Marshall, Second in Command of 8th Parachute Battalion. The Commanding Officer, Lieutenant Colonel Alastair Pearson, is standing beside General Montgomery.
(Photo: Imperial War Museum)

102. *Above right:* General Montgomery inspects a jeep fitted with stretchers and a Vickers K machine gun. *Left to right:* Major General Kenneth Crawford (Director of Air at the War Office), General Montgomery, Brigadier Edward Flavell and Lieutenant General Browning. The gauntlets worn by General Montgomery were 'purloined' during his visit by a member of 22nd Independent Parachute Company as souvenirs.
(Photo: Imperial War Museum)

103. General Montgomery in conversation with The Reverend J. C. Hales. On the general's left is Lieutenant Colonel M. McEwan, ADMS 6th Airborne Division. On the extreme right of the picture is Major H. J. Darlington, DAAG 6th Airborne Division.
(Photo: Imperial War Museum)

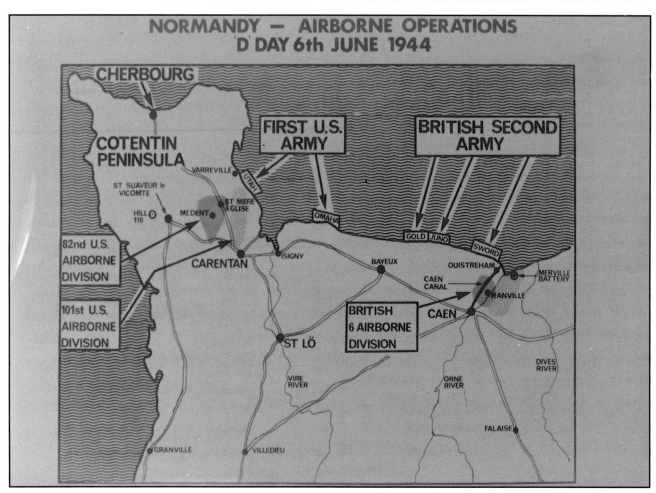

104-105. The assault on Europe begins.
(Photos: Imperial War Museum)

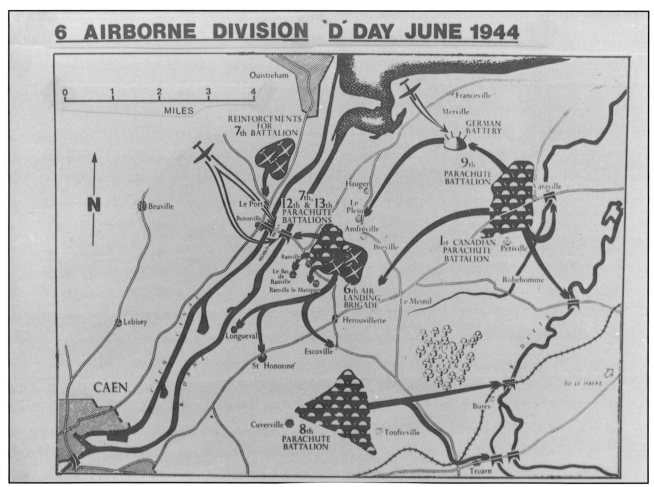

106. Preparing for the 'off'. Troops of the 2nd Battalion The Oxfordshire & Buckinghamshire Light Infantry load a jeep aboard a Horsa.
(Photo: Imperial War Museum)

107. A 6-pounder anti-tank gun is man-handled aboard a Horsa glider in preparation for the airborne invasion of Normandy by men of the 2nd Battalion The Oxfordshire & Buckinghamshire Light Infantry.
(Photo: Imperial War Museum)

108. Sappers of 249th Field Company RE load bicycles aboard a Horsa.
(Photo: Imperial War Museum)

109. Lieutenant Bob Midwood of 22nd Independent Parachute Company briefs the men of his pathfinder 'stick'.
(Photo: Imperial War Museum)

110. Major General Gale addresses officers and men of his division. (Photo: Imperial War Museum)

111. Men of a parachute unit prepare their equipment. In the background are the Stirling bombers from which they will jump into Normandy. (Photo: Airborne Forces Museum)

112. Men of one of the two parachute brigade signals sections fit their parachutes with the aid of an RAF NCO. (Photo: Imperial War Museum)

D-Day - Airborne Assault on Normandy

5th Parachute Brigade

The first member of 5th Parachute Brigade to land on DZ 'N' was the brigade commander, Brigadier Nigel Poett. A man who always led from the front, he had jumped in with the pathfinders of 22nd Independent Parachute Company so that he would be well placed to be in control in the event of Major John Howard's gliderborne assault on the Caen Canal and River Orne bridges being unsuccessful.

Poett later described his landing in Normandy:

"I was very well dropped. When I landed, it was in absolute and complete blackness. There was not a soul in sight and not a sound apart from the noise of the aircraft going away. I could see the exhausts of the aircraft and knew the direction in which they were flying, which was towards Ranville. I moved up the line in the direction in which they were heading, and met a private soldier from my defence platoon. A few seconds later, the attack on the bridges went in and we could see the flashes and hear the sounds. I immediately headed for the bridges, not waiting for anyone else, where I expected to meet my wireless operator who was an officer. Unfortunately, he had been killed on the DZ."

In fact, Brigadier Poett's radio operator was Lieutenant Gordon Royle of 6th Airborne Divisional Signals. Shortly after landing he encountered a number of enemy with a machine gun. He was killed whilst attacking them single-handed.

On reaching the River Orne bridge, Poett found that all had gone well. Howard's company had seized and secured both their objectives, and had already beaten off a German counter-attack. As he was being briefed by Lieutenant Tod Sweeney, the commander of No. 5 Platoon, he heard the sound of the aircraft bringing in his brigade. In addition to 7th, 12th and 13th Parachute Battalions, this also included FOO parties from 53rd Airlanding Light Regiment RA, 591st Parachute Squadron RE (less one troop) and 225th Parachute Field Ambulance.

After watching the arrival of 7th Parachute Battalion at the bridges, Brigadier Poett went off to meet 12th and 13th Parachute Battalions who were already heading for Le Bas de Ranville and Ranville respectively. After seeing them, he went to his brigade headquarters which he reached soon after dawn.

The commander of 5th Parachute Brigade's signal section was Captain Guy Radmore of 6th Airborne Divisional Signals. He later recalled vividly his landing in Normandy:

"We took off just after dark in a Stirling. I remember opening the hatch and seeing Normandy and then some flak. We jumped from five hundred feet and it seemed a very short time before being on the ground. I had a kitbag and also my walking stick — the latter on a separate line. I carried a .45 Colt pistol and a Sten gun, with some clothes line coiled up inside my jumping smock in case I got caught up in a tree.

The scene on the ground was like Epsom Downs on Derby Day, with people from various units muddled up. The challenge was "V" and the answer "For Victory". It was an exhilarating and confusing moment, planes flying in and parachutes coming down. I had gathered some men of different units when we heard a vehicle. We were about to engage it when I realised it was our two attached naval signallers who, never having had any parachute

113. Major Ted Lough, DAQMG of 5th Parachute Brigade, with members of the brigade headquarters at RAF Fairford prior to embarkation for Normandy. On the extreme right of the picture, half-hidden, is Captain Guy Radmore who commanded the brigade signals section.
(Photo: Airborne Forces Museum)

training, had dropped with us to work the sets communicating with the battleship HMS Warspite and the monitor HMS Roberts. I asked them what the hell they thought they were doing and they replied,

"In the Navy no one taught us how to march and so we knocked off these Germans and this Volkswagen. We are driving to the RV."

The RV was in a quarry a mile north of Ranville, on the east bank of the River Orne.

I then met Maurice Dolden, our intelligence officer. We both thought we had been dropped in the wrong place and for a moment, as we could hear no sound from the bridges, contemplated gathering up as many men as we could and advancing on the bridges. However, remembering General Gale's instruction to do what we had to do, we discarded this idea. We then found a signpost and I said to Maurice,

"There are no umpires on this exercise, so let's cheat."

He climbed on my shoulders and shone his torch on the signpost. At that moment, we heard the hunting horn of 13th Parachute Battalion which was its rallying call.

We arrived at the RV at 0300 hours and the first person I met was Leonard Mosley of the Daily Mirror who had started to type his report. As dawn broke, brigade headquarters moved down to a farm a few hundred yards south of the Orne bridge where we dug in and opened up communications."

7th Parachute Battalion

7th Parachute Battalion's advance party had dropped with the pathfinders on to DZ 'N' but had taken a long time to rally. As a result, no one was able to reach the battalion's RV location at Le Hom, near the River Orne bridge, and mark it before the main drop came in. Despite the fact that the dropping of the brigade went well, the battalion was scattered. This was due largely to the fact that each man was very heavily laden with equipment and this led to slow exits from aircraft and subsequent dispersing of sticks.

One of the advance party, Lieutenant Rogers, was equipped with a green Aldis lamp which was intended to signal the location of the battalion RV. As the main drop came in he started to flash it from where he was at that time, still some distance from the RV location. A number of men saw the lamp and moved towards it, amongst them the Commanding Officer, Lieutenant Colonel Geoffrey Pine Coffin. By the time they reached the RV some seventy men had joined them. By 0230 hours, only forty per cent of the battalion had arrived and few of the containers with the mortars, machine guns or radios had been found.

The sound of Major John Howard's whistle could be heard signifying the successful capture of the two bridges, and Lieutenant Colonel Pine Coffin decided to move off from the RV to the bridges without any further delay, leaving his second in command, Major Eric Steele Baume, to collect any stragglers. C Company, under Captain Bob Keene, set off at the double and was followed by Major Nigel Taylor's A Company which turned left over the bridges and took up positions in houses in the southern part of Benouville. B Company moved into positions in the wood and hamlet of Le Port at the northern end of Benouville, indulging in some skirmishing with a small number of enemy who were summarily dealt with.

By dawn the battalion had established its defensive position. However, Lieutenant Colonel Pine Coffin still had only some two hundred of his own men and seventy men of Major John Howard's D Company 2nd Battalion The Oxfordshire & Buckinghamshire Light Infantry, plus their attached sappers, who were holding the eastern end of the Caen Canal bridge. Moreover, he still had none of his mortars or medium machine guns.

B Company, under the command of Major Roger Neale, was positioned in Le Port with its platoons located in some of the houses and on a wooded spur betwen the village and the canal bridge. Initially the company came under fire from the church nearby but this was dealt with by a well-placed PIAT bomb, fired

114. Paratroops putting on camouflage cream as part of their preparations before emplaning. (Photo: Imperial War Museum)

by Corporal Killean, which decapitated the church tower and silenced any opposition.

Shortly afterwards, at about 0700 hours, some enemy light tanks appeared and halted in full view of one of C Company's platoons which was positioned as an outpost at the Chateau de Benouville. The tank commanders and their crews proceeded to dismount and assemble in a group at the head of the column. No sooner had they done so than the platoon opened fire, hitting some of the tank crewmen and scattering the others back to their vehicles. The concentrated small arms fire from the platoon and heavy bombardment from Allied bombers and warships offshore sent the German column heading away across the fields towards the coast.

A Company, which was occupying the southern part of Benouville, was deployed with a platoon under Sergeant Villis in the houses on either side of the main road on the southern edge of the village, with Lieutenant David Hunter's platoon positioned in a farm just to the west of the road. Lieutenant Bill Bowyer's platoon, meanwhile, was located in some houses on the eastern side of the village. Bowyer himself had tragically been mortally wounded earlier on when the company suddenly encountered an enemy motorcyclist coming round a corner. In the ensuing excitement with everyone opening fire, Bowyer's batman had accidentally shot him as he fired at the motorcyclist who was by then lying on the ground.

Throughout the morning, the enemy probed A Company's defences. The company came under fire from self-propelled guns at close range and Sergeant Villis's platoon eventually had to be withdrawn into the centre of the village itself. Meanwhile, Lieutenant David Hunter's platoon was occupied with dealing with groups of enemy infantry trying to carry out a flanking movement to its right. Later in the morning, enemy infantry and armour reached the southern edge of the village but A Company prevented them from advancing any further. At one point, however, a German Mark IV tank did manage to reach the centre

of the village from the rear but this was knocked out and set on fire with Gammon bombs.

In the middle of the morning, three figures were spotted strolling casually along the road from Ranville towards the canal bridge. These turned out to be General Gale, Brigadier Poett and Brigadier Hugh Kindersley, Commander of 6th Airlanding Brigade, who had landed with the divisional advanced headquarters so as to be fully *au fait* with the situation by the time his brigade arrived.

As Gale and his two companions reached the bridge and headed for 7th Parachute Battalion's headquarters, two patrol craft were spotted approaching the bridge. When they were about one hundred yards away, a platoon at the bridge opened fire whilst one of Major John Howard's men used a PIAT to hole the leading craft and stop its engine. This vessel was captured whilst the other made its escape.

Throughout the rest of the morning, 7th Parachute Battalion was subjected to probing attacks by the enemy who were operating in about company strength and sometimes supported by troops of tanks. The enemy also attempted to infiltrate the battalion's positions but was thwarted by active patrolling. However, the battalion was hampered by the lack of radios and thus the situation became somewhat obscure at times, much to the Commanding Officer's concern.

At midday, the first sign of relief for the battalion came with the sound of pipes which heralded the arrival of Brigadier The Lord Lovat's 1st Special Service Brigade. Bypassing the enemy, the commandos pushed through and linked up with 7th Parachute Battalion at about 1330 hours. Their arrival, however, did not bring any respite for the battalion which continued to be subjected to enemy action.

During the late afternoon A Company bore the brunt, at one point being cut off from the battalion, with fighting taking place at very close range. The company commander, Major Nigel Taylor, had been wounded in the thigh during fighting in

115. Gunners of the 17-pounder troop of 3rd Airlanding Anti-Tank Battery RA listen to a final briefing on the evening of 5th June. Also listening are the two pilots of their glider and the aircrew of the tug aircraft. Behind them is the Hamilcar containing their 17-pounder anti-tank gun and tractor. Graffiti on the glider's fuselage bears testimony to their high morale. (Photo: Imperial War Museum)

the morning but continued to command his company whilst propped up by a window in a house. During the afternoon he was eventually forced to hand over command to his second in command, Captain Jim Webber, who had also been wounded but was able to carry on. By the middle of the afternoon, A Company was down to twenty men. Despite its heavy casualties, it held out in Benouville for seventeen hours. All of its officers were either killed or wounded.

At 2115 hours the 2nd Battalion The Royal Warwickshire Regiment, who were the leading troops of 3rd Infantry Division's 185th Infantry Brigade, reached the bridges. Even then, the relief of 7th Parachute Battalion was not a simple affair as it was still in contact with the enemy. Eventually it was achieved by an attack to relieve the battalion's forward company and to permit the evacuation of the wounded. By 0030 hours on the 7th June, the Warwicks had taken over the battalion's positions and thus enabled it to withdraw over the bridges to a position in reserve on the western edge of the dropping zone.

Major General Gale later commented:

"This ended a great day for the 7th Parachute Battalion. They had fulfilled their task. They had held the west bridgehead and had had twenty-one hours continous and hard fighting. The men were tired but well satisfied and proud of their achievements. Casualties had amounted to sixty killed and wounded."

12th Parachute Battalion

12th Parachute Battalion was dropped, together with 13th Parachute Battalion, at 0050 hours and was scattered. Its RV location was at a quarry below the road between Ranville and Sallenelles near the River Orne and approximately half a mile north of the bridge. The first man to arrive at the RV was the Commanding Officer, Lieutenant Colonel Johnny Johnson, who was accompanied by Major Gerald Ritchie who commanded A Company, and Captain Jerry Turnbull who was the second in

command of B Company. The Regimental Sergeant Major was also with them.

Most of the battalion, however, had landed in some woods and orchards on the eastern side of the dropping zone and it was about three-quarters-of-an-hour before some of it began to assemble at the RV. The situation was not helped by the fact that an enemy armoured vehicle opened fire every time the battalion's Intelligence Officer started to flash his torch as the signal for the RV. He was the only other officer from battalion headquarters who had reached the RV. The second in command, Major Ken Darling, and the adjutant, Captain Paul Bernhard, had been dropped in error on one of 3rd Parachute Brigade's dropping zones, whilst the Signals Officer, together with his signallers, and Headquarter Company commander, Major George Winney, had been dropped some distance away by a pilot who had mistaken the River Dives for the River Orne. All of them eventually rejoined the battalion a few days later.

By the time it moved off from the dropping zone, the battalion numbered no more than sixty per cent of its full strength. However, it moved swiftly to seize its objective which was the area of the village of Le Bas de Ranville and by 0400 hours the troops were digging in. A Company was deployed in the area of the road junction to the east of the River Orne bridge whilst B Company was the forward left company, positioned on the southern edge of Le Bas de Ranville. C Company was located on the rising ground to the south of the village, facing towards Caen with its right flank on the canal. It had a twelve-man standing patrol deployed in a hedgerow about three hundred yards in front of the main company position.

The enemy reaction was swift in the form of heavy mortaring mixed in with some artillery fire. The 125th Panzer Grenadier Regiment attacked Ranville but was beaten off after losing a number of men who were taken prisoner and a tank which was destroyed. This was then followed by a further attack. During both attacks, the battalion bore the brunt of the fighting but suc-

116. Four 'stick' commanders of 22nd Independent Parachute Company synchronise watches before emplaning for Normandy on the night of 5th June. *Left to right:* Lieutenants Bob de La Tour, Don Wells, John Vischer and Bob Midwood. (Photo: Imperial War Museum)

117. Gunners of 4th Airlanding Anti-Tank Battery RA enjoying a mug of tea before embarkation on the night of 5th June.
(Photo: Imperial War Museum)

ceeded in beating the enemy off. 4th Airlanding Anti-Tank Battery RA accounted for three self-propelled guns and a tank. By 1300 hours the fighting had died down.

During the fighting in Ranville one particular episode stood out. C Company's standing patrol, commanded by Captain John Sim, was attacked by enemy infantry supported by two self-propelled guns. He later recalled what happened:

"My particular task was to command a forward screen in a hedgerow some three hundred yards from C Company's position. It had been planned that I was to have a section from No. 4 Platoon, two LMGs, two PIATs, a 17-pounder and a 6-pounder anti-tank gun, a Forward Observer Bombardment (FOB) party who were going to direct the fire of a cruiser lying offshore and a wireless set for my use. The flanks of my position were to be covered by the fire of machine guns from a position in the rear.

By first light my party, less the 17-pounder anti-tank gun, the two PIATs and my wireless set, was dug in and well camouflaged. The FOB party was busily engaged in ranging the cruiser's guns on likely targets while one of my snipers scored a hit on a man inspecting a container some four hundred yards away. At about 10am we spotted some men who appeared to be positioning a gun on a hill towards Caen. My FOB directed fire on to them and they vanished. Then came a long wait without a movement to be seen.

At about 11am we were surprised to see a company of about fifty men straggling across our front from the left flank. They appeared to be some of our own men as they were wearing parachute-type steel helmets and camouflaged smocks. They were about three hundred yards away across a large open field and I thought that perhaps B Company, on my left, was sending out a patrol in force. However, I soon changed my mind when they changed direction and advanced in line towards us. I asked the FOB to direct the cruiser's guns on them and then switch to the

woods behind. A little while later he informed me that this could not be done as they were firing on a priority target.

Meanwhile the enemy continued to advance, knee deep in long grass. Only my sniper was active, further down the hedgerow, as our plan was not to open fire until the enemy had come to within fifty yards of us where there was a barbed wire cattle fence. We watched and waited as the enemy came closer and closer. When they had reached the fence, I fired a Verey light straight at them and my men opened fire. The enemy went to ground in the long grass. Simultaneously, two self-propelled guns lumbered up from behind a ridge to our front and opened fire while on the move. They stopped seventy yards away from us, a sitting target for our 6-pounder anti-tank gun, but no gun opened fire. Shortly after, a soldier crawled up to me on hands and knees and saluted! He was sorry but the 6-pounder could not fire as the breechblock had slipped and must have been damaged in the glider landing. I could not be angry with him for not telling me earlier as he was so apologetic but the knowledge that I had no weapon with which to engage the self-propelled guns was rather frightening.

We were by now suffering casualties rather quickly. The man on my right was dead. Another of my men, while crawling up to me moaning and groaning, slumped over before he could reach me and lay still. I noticed that the FOB had been badly wounded.

Meanwhile the enemy, under the covering fire of the self-propelled guns, were crawling round to my right flank. I sent up two red Verey lights in their direction, a pre-arranged signal to my company commander that I was being attacked from that direction. I hoped that he would get the 3-inch mortars into action and do something to help me. No response, however.

As so often happens in action, all fire suddenly ceased and silence reigned for a bit. I felt fogged and mentally dulled, incapable of realising that I was in danger.

118. Men of a parachute field ambulance sharing a last-minute cigarette with their aircrew. (Photo: Imperial War Museum)

Peeping through the thick hedge, I saw a German soldier standing up in another hedge running at right angles to ours. I ordered my batman to have a shot at him, which he did. The self-propelled guns had quietened down — one of them was only firing spasmodically into our position. To my amazement, I saw the hatch of one open and a German officer, splendidly arrayed in polished jackboots, stiff cap and Sam Browne, leisurely climb down and light a cigarette. He was allowed two puffs only. I don't think we killed him as we did not find his body later.

Again we were subjected to fire but this time by mortars, the bombs airbursting in the hedgerow trees. Most uncomfortable — and we could do little but keep our heads down and hope for the best while the hell lasted. Again that sudden silence. One of my sergeants came to me and informed me that there were only four of us left alive and asked me what we were to do. The question, I'm ashamed to say, made me very aware of my personal danger and I decided that, rather than wait in the ditch to be killed, it was worth the risk to dash back to our company position and perhaps live to fight another day. We could do no more good where we were in my opinion.

The four of us — my sergeant, my batman, a sniper and myself, — made use of a shallow ditch which ran alongside a ditch into the main position. We covered each other, leapfrog fashion, running a few yards, crawling, firing and so back to our company; the Germans firing wildly at us most of the time. Soon after we had evacuated the forward position, it was subjected to 3-inch mortar fire and was reoccupied by another section from C Company, Lieutenant Gordon Medd's platoon, the Germans having had enough and withdrawn. The FOB, who had been badly wounded in the thigh, and two other badly wounded men were taken away by stretcher-bearers, the remainder lay dead at their posts.''

The two German self-propelled guns had in fact followed up

on Sim's withdrawal but both were knocked out by a 6-pounder firing from B Company's position. Nothing further took place until 1700 hours when the standing patrol reported enemy movement in an area known as the "Ring Contour". Later that evening Lieutenant Colonel Johnson decided to mount an attack on the Ring Contour. A Company sent a platoon forward under cover of artillery fire from the guns of 3rd Infantry Division across the river. However, it came under very heavy fire and was forced to withdraw.

It was shortly afterwards, at 2100 hours, that British and Germans alike looked up at the sound of a large number of aircraft and were spellbound by the sight of over five hundred transport aircraft and gliders bringing in the troops of 6th Airlanding Brigade.

13th Parachute Battalion

13th Parachute Battalion was dropped at 0050 hours and, like both the other battalions in the brigade, was scattered. By the time it moved off from its RV, it numbered no more than sixty per cent of its full strength. Its task was to secure Ranville and, along with 12th Parachute Battalion, to cover both the bridges from the good approaches to the south-east, between the River Orne and the wooded ridge of the Bois de Bavent.

A Company, under Major John Cramphorn, was tasked with protecting and assisting the sappers of 591st Parachute Squadron RE who were responsible for clearing the anti-glider poles from the landing zone on which Major General Gale's divisional advance headquarters, 4th Airlanding Anti-Tank Battery RA, the 17-pounder troop of 3rd Airlanding Anti-Tank Battery RA, FOO and FOB parties attached to the division from 3rd Infantry Division, a section of 286th Field Park Company RE and elements of RASC would land at 0330 hours. The company managed to complete its task with half-an-hour to spare, doing so at 0300 hours despite being mortared and coming under machine gun fire. At 0335 hours the gliders landed.

By dawn the battalion had cleared and secured Ranville which was normally garrisoned by a company from the 21st Panzer Division. However, during the night the main part of this company was away from its billets. The battalion encountered a number of defensive positions on the northern edge of the village, overlooking the dropping zone, as well as groups of enemy troops in various houses. These were all dealt with by 0400 hours. When A Company arrived from its clearing of the LZ for the gliders, it was put to work laying a minefield to the east of the village.

During the day, four self-propelled guns advanced from the direction of Herouvillette but all were knocked out by 6-pounders. In the afternoon the Germans mounted a company attack on Ranville from the same direction but this was beaten off.

3rd Parachute Brigade

The divisional plan called for two sticks of pathfinders to be dropped on to each of the two dropping zones which had been allocated to 3rd Parachute Brigade as follows:

Dropping Zone 'V' — 1st Canadian and 9th Parachute Battalions
Dropping Zone 'K' — Headquarters 3rd Parachute Brigade and 8th Parachute Battalion

One member of 22nd Independent Parachute Company who dropped into Normandy that night was Sergeant Matt Wells who later described what happened when he and his stick jumped from their Albermarle:

"We had taken off from Harwell in one of two Albemarle aircraft destined for Varaville in France. Our stick commander was Lieutenant Don Wells and our job was to drop on DZ 'V' and set up a Eureka beacon and lay out marker lights to bring in the 9th Parachute Battalion.

It was a very tight fit in the aircraft because there was very little room inside and we were carrying a lot of equipment. The chap at the front was right up against the bottom of the aircraft's middle gun turret and it was a bit difficult for him when it traversed. When the time came for the hatch to be opened, we had to squeeze up towards the front so as to give the stick commander enough room to open it. There was no RAF dispatcher and so we dispatched ourselves when the green light came on.

I landed in some sort of orchard which was flooded to a depth of about two or three feet. The first things that struck me were the eerie silence and the searchlights that were sweeping the sky. I had just got up out of the water and taken off my harness when there was a loud splashing noise coming through the water towards me. As I prepared for the worst, five or six cows came out of the darkness. I decided that they had obviously been disturbed by some of us, so I went around and along a hedge until I came to a gate. I climbed over this and as I did so, someone came marching along the lane in which I now found myself.

I challenged whoever it was with the password "Punch". He replied "Judy". It was Corporal Frank Knowles from my stick. We had obviously been scattered so we set off in the same direction from which the cows had come and met up with the others who were in the process of laying out the DZ marking aids. We had been allowed thirty minutes to find the correct DZ. Under the conditions prevailing at that time, we could have done with ten minutes longer."

As it was, things began to go wrong from the start. Nearly all the radar beacons and lights for DZ 'V' were lost or damaged, whilst the pathfinder team intended for DZ 'K' was dropped on DZ 'N' which was allocated to 5th Parachute Brigade — not realising that they were on the wrong drop zone, the pathfinders set up their beacons and lights which indicated DZ 'K'. This resulted in fourteen aircraft, carrying Headquarters 3rd Parachute Brigade and 8th Parachute Battalion, dropping their passengers on to DZ 'N' instead of DZ 'K'. Some time later, 5th Parachute Brigade's pathfinders, who had themselves been wrongly dropped

119. Paratroops board their aircraft on the night of 5th June. (Photo: Imperial War Museum)

some distance away, arrived on DZ 'N' and set up the correct beacons and light signals

3rd Parachute Brigade's advance party consisted of elements of brigade headquarters and of each battalion, and a company of 1st Canadian Parachute Battalion which was responsible for clearing obstructions from DZ 'V'. Their delivery also proved somewhat chaotic: of the fourteen Albemarles carrying them, two aircraft dropped only three and nine men respectively, six men made their exit from a third aircraft as it crossed the coast and only four jumped over the dropping zone; a fourth Albemarle, under fire, was forced to make a second run and thus dropped its troops late; two more aircraft reported technical problems, one losing time whilst flying along the coast to find the correct approach point and the other being forced to return to base after being hit by anti-aircraft fire whilst on its seventh approach to the dropping zone which it could not find. Major Bill Collingwood, the Brigade Major, was travelling in this aircraft and was waiting to jump when it was hit. He was knocked through the hole and remained suspended beneath the fuselage, hanging by his static line which had become wound round his leg. Despite the fact there was a sixty pound kitbag attached to his leg, he was eventually pulled back into the aircraft. He eventually arrived in Normandy during the evening, having flown in by glider with 6th Airlanding Brigade.

There were twenty-six aircraft which carried the main body of 3rd Parachute Brigade which, in addition to 1st Canadian, 8th and 9th Parachute Battalions, also included FOO parties from 53rd Airlanding Light Regiment RA, a section of 4th Airlanding Anti-Tank Battery RA, 3rd Parachute Squadron RE, one troop of 591st Parachute Squadron Re and 224th Parachute Field Ambulance.

Nine of these aircraft dropped their troops in the marshy areas on either side of the River Dives, two or three miles from the dropping zone, and the remainder were scattered over a wide area.

Brigadier Hill landed about half a mile south of Cabourg in four feet of water alongside the submerged bank of the River Dives. He recalls what happened subsequently:

"It took me four hours to reach dry land adjacent to my brigade DZ. The country in question had been wired prior to flooding and there were deep irrigation ditches which could not be seen and in which many drowned. I was able to collect other soldiers in the same predicament and they were saved by fastening themselves to one another by their toggle ropes. Early in the proceedings I heard a small exchange of shots only to find it was one member of my bodyguard shooting the other through the leg! Being a professional soldier, I had a large number of tea bags sewn into the tops of my trousers and regrettably spent four hours making cold tea.

Upon arrival on dry land I sent for a company commander of 1st Canadian Parachute Battalion who told me of the Canadians' success in clearing the DZ for those who eventually arrived. They had captured the enemy command post and were now engaged in mopping up Varaville. As the time was about 0600 hours I decided to proceed to Sallenelles to see how 9th Parachute Battalion had fared at the Merville Battery. I collected some forty-two very wet stragglers, amongst whom were a Royal Navy Bombardment Officer and rating, as well as an Alsatian messenger dog and its handler, and I then proceeded down a narrow lane which ran parallel to the coasts. I remember the sight of the naval bombardment which opened up prior to the landings and which had to be seen to be believed. It was the greatest and noisiest firework display of all time!

Suddenly I heard a noise which I recognised and shouted to all the men to get down. There were no ditches in the road, only a hedge and then water. My party found itself in the middle of an attack by low flying aircraft coming in from the sea and using anti-personnel bombs. I threw myself to the ground and lay on top of Lieutenant Peters, the Mortar Officer of 9th Parachute Battalion. I looked around and knew I had been hit. The lane was covered in dust and the smell of cordite and death prevailed. In the middle of the track I saw a leg and thought it must be mine but then realised it belonged to the officer on whom I was lying

and who was now dead. I myself had been saved worse injuries by my water bottle, which was smashed to pieces, and my spare underwear which I carried in the tail of my jumping smock. I found that there appeared to be only two survivors capable of getting to their feet — myself and my defence platoon commander. An immediate problem then arose: what do you do? Do you look after the many wounded and dying or press on? There was, of course, only one answer — to press on. The two of us therefore, injected the wounded with our own morphia and took the morphia from the dead and handed it to those who needed it most. I will never forget the cheer that was given to us as we left by those who were soon to die! I eventually turned up at the first aid post of 9th Parachute Battalion and an officer told me that the battalion had successfully dealt with the battery and, although only eighty strong, was now trying to dislodge the enemy from the Sallenelles feature.

'Doc' Watts, 9th Parachute Battalion's Medical Officer, unwisely told me that I looked bad for morale to which I replied that so would he if he had spent four hours in cold water and then had much of his left backside removed! No doubt to keep me quiet, and to assist in temporary patching up operations, Doc Watts put me out for a couple of hours. Being a good soldier, he then produced a lady's bicycle and a soldier to push it and I wobbled off on a two-mile bicycle ride to see the Divisional Commander who had now established his HQ in Ranville.

On my arrival, General Richard Gale said:

"Well, James, I am happy to tell you that your brigade has succeeded in all its objectives".

This was marvellous news! The ADMS, Colonel McEwan, then seized me and said I must leave for the Main Dressing Station for an operation. This I refused to do unless he guaranteed to drive me personally to my brigade headquarters after I had been operated on. This was agreed. It was about 1200 hours and the last thing I knew was a heavy artillery concentration coming down on Ranville.

When I awoke, McEwan was as good as his word and sat me on the back seat of his jeep and, with his driver, we set off for my brigade headquarters at Le Mesnil. As we were leaving Ranville, six Germans crossed the road ahead of us. The ADMS, to my amazement, pulled up his jeep, took a revolver out of the jeep pocket and with his driver set-off in hot pursuit of the Germans, no doubt wishing to take them prisoners. However, three minutes later they sheepishly returned and they continued on their mission to Le Mesnil which was reached at 1600 hours in the afternoon. I found that Alastair Pearson had temporarily taken over the brigade and had been shot through the hand, but it took more than this to render him hors de combat. *After briefing me, Alastair then returned to his battalion.*

On taking stock I found that I had no Brigade Major. He had been blown out of the door of his aircraft by enemy fire and hung suspended with a sixty-pound kit bag attached to his leg before they could pull him in as the aircraft limped back to Odiham in England. Although his leg was pretty well dislocated and stuck out sideways, he was able to get a lift over in a glider the same evening with the air landing brigade and arrived at my headquarters at Le Mesnil at 0900 hours the next morning. However, the Brigade Major must have two legs that work so he was taken to the Main Dressing Station some forty-eight hours later; it is of such stuff that good Brigade Majors are made.

Neither did I have my DAA QMG. Major Alec Pope was dropped some fifteen miles east of the River Dives and with a party of men he had refused to surrender and died fighting.

There was no Roman Catholic padre. Before the battle I had given Padre McVeigh a shillelagh for self-defence and when he had been dropped wide he was taken prisoner. He got fed up with being interrogated by six Germans and set about them with his shillelagh and escaped. He was in due course recaptured but the Germans refused to accept he was a priest, stripped him of his dog collar and he spent the rest of the war in the toughest prisoner-of-war camp on the Baltic.

Nor was there a Commando Liaison Officer — Peter Haig Thomas, for three years stroke of the Cambridge boat and Olympic oarsman, was killed within half-an-hour of landing and lies buried in the village church at Bavent.

This perhaps was not an auspicious way to start the Normandy campaign.''

The Attack on The Merville Battery

The advance elements of 9th Parachute Battalion, consisting of reconnaissance and rendezvous parties, had been dropped on DZ 'V' with no problems and they had reached the battalion RV point without difficult. Major Allen Parry and his men set out the lights marking the company locations whilst Major George Smith and CSMs Harold and Miller set off towards the battery which was a mile away. Shortly afterwards, RAF Lancaster bombers carried out a raid on the battery but missed it; most of their bombs fell to the south, nearly hitting Smith's party.

The aircraft bringing the main body of the battalion were by now approaching the French coast. Unfortunately, due to the fact that most of the pathfinding equipment for DZ 'V' had been damaged, there were only a few lights marking the dropping zone when the aircraft arrived. Consequently, few of the pilots saw them and visibility was further worsened by smoke from the bombing raid blowing across the zone. As a result, only a few sticks landed on DZ 'V' whilst others dropped into the Dives marshes and some on the high ground between Cabourg and Dozule.

By 0250 hours the Commanding Officer, Lieutenant Colonel Terence Otway, had assembled one hundred and fifty of the five hundred and fifty men of his battalion. None of the eleven gliders, bringing in jeeps, anti-tank guns and trailers had appeared. Moreover, the battalion's 3-inch mortars, the sappers, the field ambulance section and the naval bombardment parties were all missing. However, bearing in mind that the battery had to be destroyed by 0530 hours, Otway decided to press on.

After following a route skirting the northern edge of the village of Gonneville, Otway and his men made their way to a crossroads where they met Major George Smith. He and his two warrant officers had cut their way through a wire fence and, making their way through a minefield to an inner wire fence, had managed to locate some enemy positions. A taping party, commanded by Captain Paul Greenway, had successfully cleared and marked four lanes through the minefields, locating and disarming several tripwires.

Otway split his force into four assault groups but decided to use only two of the breaches in the wire. It was now 0430 hours. As the battalion was redeploying, six enemy machine guns from outside the battery position opened fire, three from either flank. The one Vickers medium machine gun with the battalion engaged the enemy guns on the left whilst a party of an NCO and six men engaged those on the right as they made their way to the main entrance of the battery.

It was at this point that two of the three gliders carrying the fifty-eight strong assault group commanded by Captain Robert Gordon-Brown suddenly appeared, flying in low over the battery. Both aircraft came under fire and were seen to be hit. One glider, piloted by Staff Sergeant Bone, flew on into the darkness, eventually landing in a field two miles to the south. The other, flown by Staff Sergeant Kerr, touched down and was heading for a large hedge at the edge of the minefield. Kerr suddenly spotted a minefield warning sign and managed to haul his glider up over the hedge and a lane behind it, streaming his arrester parachute and crashing into an orchard beyond. The platoon inside, commanded by Lieutenant Hugh Pond, made a somewhat dazed exit only to hear the sound of men approaching. Quickly deploying into positions on either side of the lane, Pond and his men opened fire as enemy troops approached.

At that point, Lieutenant Colonel Otway launched his attack. Bangalore torpedoes were detonated and the four assault groups went in. Having penetrated the battery's defences, they had to fight their way to the gun casemates, coming under fire from three machine guns as they did so. These were silenced by a Bren gun team under Sergeant Knight. Once they reached the casemates, Otway's men proceeded to neutralise the German gun crews and to silence the guns with Gammon bombs.

One of the assault groups was commanded by Sergeant Harold

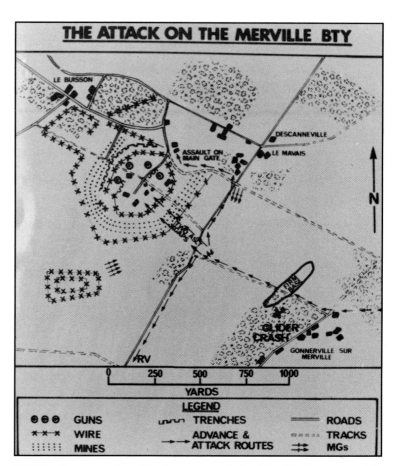

THE ATTACK ON THE MERVILLE BTY

LE BUISSON

DESCANNEVILLE

LE MAVAIS

ASSAULT ON MAIN GATE

GLIDER CRASH

GONNERVILLE SUR MERVILLE

RV

| 0 | 250 | 500 | 750 | 1000 |

YARDS

LEGEND

⊕ ⊕ ⊕	GUNS	⌒⌒⌒	TRENCHES	═══	ROADS
✳ ✳ ✳	WIRE	→	ADVANCE & ATTACK ROUTES	═ ═ ═	TRACKS
:::::::	MINES			⇥	MGs

120-121. A map and aerial photograph of the Merville Battery — 9th Parachute Battalion's objective. (Photo: Airborne Forces Museum)

Long who afterwards vividly recalled the attack on the guns: *"The assault was all hell let loose. The wire had been cut for us by an advance party and, firing from the hip and throwing grenades, we went forward to the guns. Our attack was a complete surprise to the Germans but they soon recovered and gave a very good account of themselves. But in the end we overcame them, taking some prisoners. A few got away; the rest were killed or wounded. We lost about eighty killed and wounded in the battle, so by that time we were very weak. No explosives had arrived but we had to silence the guns. We damaged and destroyed them by any means we could.*

We then withdrew andd moved to higher ground before the Navy, in the form of HMS Arethusa, *used its guns to shell the battery. We had no smoke signals to let them know we had been successful.*

Anyone who came through that battle was very lucky. By the end of it, out of six hundred and forty men who left England, only about seventy or eighty of us were on our feet and in one piece. You have to have been through something like that to understand what it was really like."

It was 0500 hours and the guns had been silenced. 9th Parachute Battalion had achieved its objective but at a very heavy cost. Out of the force which had attacked the battery, only about eighty were unscathed; about sixty-five were killed, wounded or missing. Consequently, Lieutenant Colonel Otway decided to attack and seize the village of Le Plein on the Bavent ridge. At 0600 hours he and his men moved off. After being mistakenly bombed by high flying RAF bombers, they reached a crossroads between Le Plein and the neighbouring village of Hauger where the leading company, B Company, came under fire. Major George Smith led a company attack on the village, forcing a platoon of German troops back into Le Plein and into the church, killing about fifteen of them in the process. As the battalion was in the process of clearing and securing a number of houses at the north end of the village, an enemy platoon counter-attacked but met the battalion's one and only Vickers machine gun which proceeded to wreak havoc at close range, killing twelve enemy and forcing the remainder to withdraw.

A platoon of B Company, commanded by Lieutenant Halliburton, attacked a large house near the church from the rear. Surrounded by a six-foot wall, it appeared to be the main enemy defensive position. As the leading section of the platoon crossed the wall it came under fire and Haliburton, who had been in the lead, was killed. The platoon was forced to withdraw.

9th Parachute Battalion was now very weak in numbers, its strength being less than a hundred men. Lieutenant-Colonel Otway decided to set up defensive positions in the Chateau d'Amfreville and await the arrival of the commandos of 1st Special Service Brigade. On moving into its new positions, the battalion found a hoard of German rations, which were duly shared out, as well as a car and some horses which were commandeered. The early afternoon saw the welcome arrival of No. 6 Commando which took up positions within the village.

8th Parachute Battalion

Meanwhile, Lieutenant Colonel Alastair Pearson's 8th Parachute Battalion, which was tasked with destroying the bridges at Bures and Troarn, had also been scattered during its drop. The plan called for the battalion to secure and hold Troarn, with one company providing cover for the sappers of 3rd Parachute Squadron RE who would blow the bridges at Bures. However, when the Commanding Officer reached the battalion RV at a track junction near Touffreville at 0120 hours, he found only thirty men plus a jeep and trailer belonging to the engineer squadron. By 0330 hours, this number had increased to eleven officers and a hundred and thirty other ranks but there was no news of the rest of the sappers who had dropped with the battalion.

Pearson decided to send a small force to destroy the bridge at Bures whilst he waited at a crossroads a mile north of Troarn until he had enough men with which to attack the town. At 0400 hours his group moved off to the crossroads which were in heavily-wooded terrain east of the main road between Troarn and Le Mesnil. On the way Pearson set up an ambush which comprised two PIAT detachments under the command of a junior NCO, Lance Corporal Stevenson, to cover the battalion's rear.

On reaching the crossroads, Pearson dispatched a patrol to reconnoitre the two bridges at Bures, one of which was a steel girder railway bridge and the other a similar but shorter one carrying a trackway. At 0630 hours No. 2 Troop of 3rd Parachute Squadron RE, under the command of Captain Tim Juckes, reached the bridges. By 0915 hours both had been destroyed, the smaller trackway bridge having been blown by the troop's No. 3 Section which was commanded by Lieutenant John Shave. Having completed their task, No. 2 Troop joined up with 8th Parachute Battalion.

Meanwhile, more men of the battalion were arriving including Lieutenant Thompson, some fifty men of A Company and the majority of the machine gun and mortar platoons. He and his men had earlier met Major Tim Roseveare and some of his sappers from 3rd Parachute Squadron RE on their way to blow the bridge at Troarn. Roseveare had ordered Thompson to set up a firm base at a road junction whilst he went forward to deal with the bridge. Thompson had done so but had made contact with the PIAT ambush party whilst personally reconnoitring the local area, and had thus learned of the battalion's whereabouts.

Not long afterwards, six enemy vehicles drove into the PIAT ambush and were destroyed. The enemy, subsequently identified as being from the 21st Panzer Division, withdrew on foot towards Troarn.

Pearson sent out patrols to reconnoitre the areas to the north and west of Troarn. He had received no confirmation of the Troarn bridge having been blown so he dispatched Captain Tim Juckes and his sappers, together with No. 9 Platoon of B Company under the command of Lieutenant Brown, to check whether the bridge had been destroyed and, if so, to further increase any damage if possible.

Brown's platoon and the sappers made their way to the outskirts of Troarn, heading for the bridge where they came under fire from a house near the church. After a brief skirmish they captured a small number of Germans, who turned out to be members of a 21st Panzer Division reconnaissance unit, and a machine gun. Soon afterwards they came under fire again from enemy troops positioned in other houses near the church. After Brown's platoon had cleared these with great spirit, taking more prisoners in the process, Juckes and his sappers went forward and inspected the stone bridge in which they found a gap had been blown. This they correctly assumed to be the work of Major Roseveare. Placing further charges, they increased the gap to a width of seventy feet. Having completed their task, and having been plied with food and wine by local townspeople, the small force returned to the battalion.

1st Canadian Parachute Battalion

1st Canadian Parachute Battalion, which had been tasked with destroying the bridges at Varaville and Robenhomme, found itself with the majority of its troops dropped some distance from DZ 'V'. C Company had departed from England as part of the advance group along with brigade headquarters, elements of the 22nd Independent Parachute Company and a stick of 9th Parachute Battalion. The company second in command, Captain John Hanson, found himself and his stick some ten miles from the drop zone. Lieutenant John Madden, a platoon commander in the company, and his stick found themselves on the opposite side of the River Orne and only twelve hundred yards from the Normandy beaches. Corporal Dan Hartigan landed within five hundred yards of the drop zone, landing in an apple tree in a French villager's back yard. Eventually, those elements of C Company who had reached the drop zone area headed for Varaville where they were to attack and neutralise the garrison, whilst the pathfinders set up the two serviceable Eureka beacons and other navigational aids to guide in the main force.

When the rest of 1st Canadian Parachute Battalion arrived, A Company was dropped over a wide area and some of its men linked up with elements of C Company who were preparing for the assault on Varaville. The rest of A Company were covering the withdrawal of 9th Parachute Battalion. When Lieutenant

Jack Clancy reached A Company's RV, he found only two or three men waiting there. When no one else arrived, he decided to reconnoitre the nearby village of Gonneville-sur-Merville but found no signs of the enemy. On returning to the RV, he met one officer and twenty other ranks who had arrived in his absence. Taking them under command, he led them along the pre-arranged route towards the Merville Battery. On the way, Clancy's small force met no enemy but had to take rapid evasive action from the heavy bombing of Gonneville-sur-Merville by the RAF.

After clearing a chateau of some enemy who had been firing on 9th Parachute Battalion, which by then had completed its task of destroying the Merville Battery, and after acting as a rearguard for the battalion's withdrawal, Clancy and his men finally reached 1st Canadian Parachute Battalion's positions at Le Mesnil at 1530 hours.

B Company had also been dropped over a wide area, two platoons landing in marshy flooded terrain two miles from the drop zone. One stick, under the command of Lieutenant Philippe Rousseau, was dropped several miles to the north-east near Villers-sur-Mer. Five sticks landed in the flooded areas near Robehomme which were criss-crossed with large drainage ditches, many of which were up to seven feet in depth. Several men were forced to jettison their equipment to avoid drowning, whilst others were unable to free themselves of their heavy loads and were drowned.

Lieutenant Norman Toseland, the commander of No. 5 Platoon in B Company, was one of the few to land on firm ground. After joining up with another member of his platoon, he met Sergeant Joe LaCasse who had a small number of men with him and together they headed for the Robehomme bridge which was one of the battalion's objectives. With the assistance of a French girl who acted as a guide, they made their way to the bridge, encountering a number men from other units. As he headed for the objective. Toseland collected some ten men from his own platoon and others from 8th and 9th Parachute Battalions, as well as some engineers.

When they reached the Robehomme bridge, they met Major Clayton Fuller who had landed in the River Dives nearby. By 0300 hours the sappers tasked with blowing the bridge had not arrived. However, Sergeant Bill Poole of No. 3 Troop of 3rd Parachute Squadron RE, who was one of the sappers who had joined up with Lieutenant Toseland, collected all the plastic explosive carried by infantrymen for making Gammon bombs. This amounted to some thirty pounds in all. Sergeant Poole attempted to blow the bridge but, with the limited amount of explosive available to him, only managed to weaken it. At about 0600 hours, however, Lieutenant Jack Inman and five sappers of No. 3 Troop arrived with two hundred pounds of explosive charges and the bridge was duly destroyed.

The Commanding Officer, Lieutenant Colonel George Bradbrooke, landed in a marsh west of the River Dives. However, he quickly headed for the battalion's RV which was beside the drop zone. When he arrived, he met his second in command, Major Jeff Nicklin, together with Lieutenant R. Weathersbee who was the Intelligence Officer and Lieutenant John Simpson, the Signals Officer. Also at the RV were a number of men from 8th and 9th Parachute Battalions and an anti-tank detachment of the 2nd Battalion The Oxfordshire & Buckinghamshire Light Infantry whose glider had landed in the wrong location. Shortly afterwards, a small number of men from Headquarter Company and a section of 224th Parachute Field Ambulance also appeared.

Deciding he needed information as to C Company's progress with its task at Varaville, Lieutenant Colonel Bradbrooke sent Lieutenant Weathersbee and two men to find out and report back on the situation. Meanwhile, he led the rest of his small force, complete with the anti-tank detachment, towards the crossroads at Le Mesnil. On the way he and his men came under fire and had to clear enemy troops out of houses along the road before they could continue. After an attack carried out by Headquarter

122. "Normandy, here we come!" Paratroops in obvious high spirits give a thumbs-up during the night flight to France.
(Photo: Imperial War Museum)

Company personnel, the enemy withdrew and the crossroads was reached at 1100 hours. Here Bradbrooke set up his battalion headquarters.

C Company, meanwhile, had been undertaking the four tasks allocated to it with a fraction of its normal strength of over one hundred men.

The company had been tasked with clearing the enemy garrison from Varaville, neutralising a 75mm gun emplacement at a road junction near the Chateau de Varaville just east of the town, the demolition of the bridge over the River Divette and the destruction of a radio transmitter station which was also near Varaville. Even for a full strength company this was a formidable task. As it was, when the company commander, Major Murray McLeod, arrived at his company RV at 0030 hours, he found only a small number of his men. He himself, along with several others, had been on the drop zone when the RAF Lancasters bombing the Merville Battery had flown over the DZ on to which some of them had emptied their bomb loads. McLeod, along with everyone else on the DZ at the time, had been left badly shocked.

By 0030 hours, McLeod's group numbered only fifteen men and could muster only one PIAT, three Sten guns, eight rifles and his own pistol. Nevertheless, he led his small group off to take on the enemy force at Varaville. As he did so, he met a small group from No. 9 Platoon, led by Private Rudko who had survived the RAF's bombing of the drop zone. Despite that fact that they were still somewhat badly shocked, they were unhurt and were in possession of all their equipment.

. With just twenty-five minutes left before the drop of 3rd Parachute Brigade's main force was due to take place, McLeod and his men made their way in the dark to Varaville. Passing through the village without being detected, they came to the chateau gatehouse which was some distance from the chateau itself and which overlooked the enemy defensive positions. McLeod could see that these consisted of a long trench fortified with concrete and earthworks, with machine gun positions located at intervals. At each end of the trench was a bunker. Unbeknown to McLeod, a 75mm gun was located in a concrete emplacement to the rear of the trench.

Entering the gatehouse, some of McLeod's men searched it and found that it was being used as a barracks housing a total of ninety-six men. McLeod positioned his men around the gatehouse. His one other officer, Lieutenant 'Chug' Walker, placed twelve men in a shallow ditch which would have been the position for the machine guns giving covering fire if all had gone according to plan.

McLeod, accompanied by Private Thompson, went up to the second floor of the gatehouse where, shortly afterwards, they came under fire from the 75mm gun. An attempt was made to neutralise the gun with the group's one and only PIAT but this failed. Before a second attempt could be made, the gun opened fire on the gatehouse, setting off the bombs beside the PIAT operator, Corporal Oikle, and killing Lieutenant Walker. McLeod himself was mortally wounded.

At that point the company's second in command, Captain John Hanson, arrived with two more men which brought the total in the force to some thirty. Although the PIAT had been lost, there was now a machine gun. This was augmented shortly afterwards when Corporal Hartigan, accompanied by Private Mallon, arrived with his 2-inch mortar. They both managed to reach cover just in time as enemy machine guns opened fire on the road.

At 0830 hours the enemy showed a white flag and requested that they be permitted to send out their wounded. Captain Hanson, who had assumed command after McLeod had died in his lap shortly after his arrival, gave permission. Shortly afterwards, a massive explosion was heard away to the south-east and Hanson and his men realised that other members of the company, under Sergeant Davies, had succeeded in demolishing the Varaville bridge and thus had achieved one of their objectives.

123. Troops of 6th Airlanding Brigade pose for a last-minute picture before taking off for Normandy in the early evening of 6th June. (Photos: Imperial War Musuem)

At 1000 hours, Corporal Hartigan managed to work his way into a position from which he could bring down effective fire with his 2-inch mortar on the German positions. He fired four high explosive bombs, followed by several smoke bombs, all of which hit their target. A few minutes later, a white flag was waved from one of the bunkers and the Germans, totalling some forty-three men, surrendered. The battle for Varaville was over.

Quickly occupying the German positions, the Canadians waited for an enemy counter-attack but none came. In mid-afternoon they were relieved by commandos of 1st Special Service Brigade. Hanson and his men, taking their prisoners with them, departed on their three-mile march to Le Mesnil where they would join the battalion. On several occasions they came under fire, and two sections had to be detached each time to deal with the problem. At 1800 hours, Hanson and his men reached Le Mesnil and rejoined their unit.

Headquarters 6th Airborne Division

The gliders carrying the divisional commander and his advance headquarters took off after the aircraft carrying the two parachute brigades. Major General Gale was travelling in glider No. 70, flown by Major Billy Griffiths, and was accompanied by his ADC, Captain Tom Haughton, Major David Baird his GSO 2, his signaller, his personal escort, his driver and Rifleman Grey who was Captain Haughton's batman. The party numbered twelve in all. Also in the glider was the general's radio-equipped jeep and two motorcycles.

Major General Gale described his flight to Normandy and the subsequent landing:

"In the glider we all wore Mae Wests, and taking our places we all fastened ourselves in and waited for the jerk as the tug took the strain on the tow-rope. Soon it came and we could feel ourselves hurtling down the smooth tarmac. Then we were airborne and once again we heard the familiar whistle as the air rushed by and we glided higher and higher into the dark night.

I suppose all men have different reactions on these occasions. I went to sleep and slept soundly for the best part of an hour. I was woken up by a considerable bumping. We had run into a small local storm in the Channel. Griffiths was having a ticklish time and the glider was all over the place.

Between the glider and tug there is an intercommunication line, so that the two pilots can talk to one another. In this bumping we received, the intercommunication line broke; the only means of speech contact from the tug to the glider or vice versa was lost. The problem of cast-off would have to be solved by judgement. Griffiths merely said, "The intercom has bust."

Only a few minutes after that he said, "We will be crossing the French coast shortly." We were flying at about five thousand feet and we soon knew the coast was under us, for we were met by a stream of flak. It was weird to see this roaring up in great golden chains past the windows of the glider, some of it being apparently between us and the tug aircraft. Looking out I could see the canal and the river through the clouds; for the moon was by now fairly well overcast and the clear moonlight we had hoped for was not there. Nevertheless here we were.

In a few moments Griffiths said, "We are over the landing zone now and will be cast off at any moment." Almost as soon as he had said this we were. The whistling sound and the roar of the engines suddenly died down: no longer were we bumping about but gliding along on a gloriously steady course. Away went the tug aircraft with Crawford in it back to England. Round we turned, circling lower and lower; soon the pilot turned round to tell us to link up as we were just about to land. We all linked up by putting our arms round the man next to us. We were also, as I have said, strapped in. In case of a crash this procedure would help us to take the shock.

I shall never forget the sound as we rushed down in our final steep dive, then we suddenly flattened out, and soon with a bump, bump, bump, we landed on an extremely rough stubble field.

124. A Horsa glider is pulled into position by a tractor and positioned behind its Stirling tug aircraft. In the background other Horsas are also being towed forward. (Photo: Museum of Army Flying)

Over the field we sped and then with a bang we hit a low em-
bankment. The forward undercarriage wheel stove up through
the floor, the glider spun round on its nose in a small circle and,
as one wing hit one of those infernal stakes, we drew up to a
standstill. We opened the door. Outside all was quiet.

...About us now the other gliders were coming in, crashing
and screeching as they applied their brakes. It was a glorious
moment.

In the distance from the direction of the bridges we could now
hear bursts of machine gun fire. Except for the arrival of more
and more gliders around us, all seemed to be still. It was eerie.
Had Ranville been cleared of the enemy? Were the bridges taken?
Were they intact and safely in our hands? How was Terence Otway
and his gallant battalion faring at the Merville Battery? We could
still hear intermittent fire from the direction of the bridges?

Whilst they were attempting to unload the glider the passing
moments seemed like hours. It was still dark and this unloading
was proving to be more difficult than we had anticipated. The
crash we had had, though not serious, resulted in the nose being
really well dug into the ground and the problem of getting the
jeep out was defeating us. Eventually we had to give it up: and
so on foot we set out for Ranville."

Shortly afterwards, as dawn was breaking, General Gale met Brigadier Poett who informed him that the bridges had been captured by the *coup de main* operation which had worked perfectly and that 7th Parachute Battalion was now on the west bank. He also told him that 13th Parachute Battalion was in Ranville whilst 12th Parachute Battalion was holding Le Bas de Ranville.

Meanwhile the rest of divisional headquarters had deployed from the twenty gliders in which it had arrived. By 0430 hours, it was moving off the LZ in its jeeps and trailers and by 0600 hours was set up in the Chateau de Heaume in Le Bas de Ranville. One key member of the headquarters who was missing, however, was Lieutenant Colonel Bobby Bray, the GSO 1 Operations. Together with an officer from 6th Airborne Divisional Signals, he had landed in his glider near Varaville. Whilst heading west to rejoin the headquarters, the two men had a lucky escape when fired upon by a lost section of 9th Parachute Battalion.

The headquarters itself was set up with the operations staff and signals element in the stables whilst the CRE, Lieutenant-Colonel Frank Plowman, shared a copse behind the main house with the ADMS, Colonel McEwan, and the AA & QMG, Lieutenant-Colonel Shamus Hickie. Meanwhile the CRA, Colonel Jack Norris, and his gunners dug themselves into positions in a nearby orchard. The headquarters was guarded by military policemen of the 6th Airborne Division Provost Company and the headquarters defence platoon.

At 0700 hours the Allied air and sea bombardment of the assault benches began. This was the signal for radio silence to be broken and the signallers immediately busied themselves with establishing communications. At the same time, 4th Airlanding Anti-Tank Battery RA and the 17-pounder troop of 3rd Airlanding Anti-Tank Battery RA deployed to positions in support of

12th and 13th Parachute Battalions, whilst the sapper section of 286th Field Park Company RE now moved out with its small bulldozer, brought in with the section in its single glider, to clear the landing zone of obstacles and gliders which might obstruct the arrival of 6th Airlanding Brigade.

Later in the morning, after returning from his visit to 5th Parachute Brigade, Major-General Gale started to receive news of 3rd Parachute Brigade and in particular the details of 9th Parachute Battalion's assault on the Merville Battery. This was a relief to him because he had until then not received any news of their progress and was becoming anxious.

6th Airlanding Brigade

The arrival of 6th Airlanding Brigade on the evening of D-Day was by all accounts an awe-inspiring sight. At 2100 hours, the noise of hundreds of aircraft could suddenly be heard and the sky was filled with two hundred and fifty tug aircraft towing two hundred and twenty Horsas and thirty Hamilcars. Casting off at a height of about eight hundred feet, the gliders turned and came swooping down on the landing zones.

Into Landing Zone 'N' went the brigade headquarters and the 1st Battalion The Royal Ulster Rifles, whilst the 2nd Battalion The Oxfordshire & Buckinghamshire Light Infantry, minus its six platoons already holding the bridges, flew into Landing Zone 'W'. With them came A Company of the 12th Battalion The Devonshire Regiment, the 6th Airborne Armoured Reconnaissance Regiment, 211th Airlanding Light Battery RA, 249th Field Company RE and two sections of 195th Airlanding Field Ambulance which were each attached to the two infantry battalions.

Major Napier Crookenden of the Cheshire Regiment was the Brigade Major of 6th Airlanding Brigade. He describes here his departure from England and his subsequent landing in Normandy:

"I had spent the night before D-Day at Headquarters 1st Airborne Corps at Moor Park. Brigadier Hugh Kindersley had landed at 0330 hours with divisional headquarters and it was my job to receive the ''off'' from Corps Headquarters and to launch the brigade at 1840 hours from its airfields in the Midlands. I only received this at about 1200 hours and, after sending out the necessary signals, drove off to Brize Norton in Oxfordshire. At Slough I saw a newsboy selling copies of the Evening Standard with the headline ''SKYMEN IN EUROPE'' and bought up his whole stock. My main contribution to D-Day was the delivery of those papers to most of my friends in the parachute brigades scattered round the bridgehead before midnight.

Brigade headquarters and the Royal Ulster Rifles took off from Brize Norton on time at 1840 hours. An hour before take-off, the battered and dirty figure of Bill Collingwood, the Brigade Major of 3rd Parachute Brigade, appeared in the Officers Mess, where we were eating bacon and eggs, and asked for a lift. He had got stuck and injured in the aperture of his Albemarle air-

125. A Stirling tug aircraft lines up on the runway and takes the strain on the tow-rope as it prepares to take off on the evening of D-Day.
(Photo: Imperial War Museum)

craft on jumping early that morning and had been forced to land back in England. We fixed him up with a spare glider for his 'stick' and he was able to rejoin his brigade that night. The only other incident was the collision between our second signals glider and the corner of a hangar on take-off — a serious loss which I only discovered after landing at the other end.

The flight itself was smooth and uneventful. In my glider was the DAAG from divisional headquarters, my batman/driver, two signallers, a jeep and trailer and a No. 22 Radio Set. Shortly before 2100 hours, we sighted the French coast and could soon pick out the mouth of the River Orne and Ouistreham. Spread out to our right we could see the invasion fleet, and the muzzle flashes from the guns of the bombarding ships were clearly visible. Over the land were masses of smoke and haze. Our tug and glider stream ran in down the line of the Orne, turned through a hundred and eighty degrees and landed on LZ's 'N' and 'W'. There was a little light flak coming up and I could see one of the tug aircraft ahead of us going down on fire. LZ 'N' was already covered in gliders and parachutes, and one glider on the ground was burning with a column of black smoke.

Our glider pilot released from the tug at about eight hundred feet and made a steep diving turn towards the LZ. We were all strapped in by now and we put our arms round each other's shoulders and lifted our legs off the floor, ready for the landing. In a few seconds we were down, bumped twice, broke off a wing on an anti-landing pole and stopped. We got the tail off without difficulty, unloaded the jeep and trailer and were moving off to our RV in Le Bas de Ranville a few minutes after landing. Our first impressions were how like our briefing models and photographs the countryside was, and how like an exercise the whole thing seemed.

The Brigadier met us at the brigade headquarters RV. This was to be our location for some days and here he briefed the commanding officers on the situation. The battalion seconds in command had also taken off with divisional headquarters early that morning but their glider's tow-rope had parted and they had landed near Worthing. However, they all got back to their battalions before take-off. Our whole brigade landing in the evening was successful and we had fewer casualties than on any previous exercise.''

Major Charles Russell, whose 210th Airlanding Light Battery RA was to land by sea the next day but who was in command of the FOO and FOB parties which would be attached to 5th Parachute Brigade, tells how he arrived:

''Coming over the coast the flak floated lazy and remote, until a bright little explosion in the middle of the glider was followed by a sharp rap on the sole of my left foot. I had the defenceless feeling of a man on a single-bar latrine and the idea of landing lost its terrors. A heavy jarring bounce as we touched down, a pause and then blackout. We had run into an unloading glider and everything had gone for six. Dusty moonlight showed through jagged edges and I crawled out. Nothing of the two Horsa gliders stood higher than six feet. Two men were killed, three with broken arms or legs; jeep, trailer, motorcycles and wireless were all 'written off', and five hundred cigarettes lay in the debris at map reference 115745. The Officer Commanding FOO and FOB had arrived with his party to support 5 Para Brigade and to liberate Europe and did not feel confident of success...''

The German reaction to the brigade's landing was swift. Mortar fire came down on the village of Ranville and on the divisional headquarters. The CRA, Colonel Jack Norris, was hit and badly wounded in the throat and the GSO (2 Intelligence), Major Gerry Lacoste, was also wounded. On the landing zones the casualties were light from small arms and mortar fire being directed on to them. A 6-pounder anti-tank gun and its jeep were hit as they were being driven off the LZ, whilst the Royal Ulster Rifles only sustained one casualty. On Landing Zone 'W' one glider, carrying men of the Oxfordshire & Buckinghamshire Light Infantry, was hit by anti-aircraft fire and broke up over the LZ. Only three of its six passengers survived and they were all badly injured. An hour-and-a-half later, however, the 2nd Battalion The Oxfordshire & Buckinghamshire Light Infantry was ready to moved from its assembly point north of Benouville and the 1st Battalion The Royal Ulster Rifles landed almost at its RV in Le Bas de Ranville.

The 6th Airborne Armoured Reconnaissance Regiment had encountered problems on landing. Two Tetrarch light light tanks had been destroyed when their Hamilcar gliders had collided on landing. Subsequently, on leaving their gliders, the remaining Tetrarchs had been immobilised when their bogies and sprocket wheels had become entangled in the rigging lines and canopies of parachutes lying on the landing zones. It took their crews some time to disentangle them with the aid of blowtorches before they could move off the landing zone to the regiment's harbour area. This had been reconnoitred and secured on the previous night by the Harbour Party which had dropped with the pathfinders of the 22nd Independent Parachute Company and which had lost its commander, Lieutenant Belcher, plus a complete 'stick' through enemy action. Despite this setback, the regiment could claim to have made history as the first unit in the British Army ever to have flown its tanks into action.

211th Airlanding Light Battery RA landed at 2130 hours without sustaining any casualties and its 75mm pack howitzers were in action north of Ranville half-an-hour later. It too had just made history as being the first battery of the Royal Artillery ever to fly into action against an enemy.

Brigadier Hugh Kindersley assembled his brigade headquarters in an orchard in Les Bas de Ranville where it had begun to dig in. The headquarters itself consisted of the brigadier's staff and the signals detachment which manned the forward and rear link radio nets. When mobile, this group was mounted in six jeeps with trailers. Attached to it to provide protection was a defence platoon equipped with four 20mm Hispano-Suiza cannon which were towed by jeeps. Also attached was the battery commander from 53rd Airlanding Light Regiment RA with his forward observer officers (FOOs) and their signallers, together with the

126. A Halifax tug aircraft takes off from RAF Tarrant Rushton, its Horsa already airborne behind it. (Photo: Imperial War Museum)

Forward Observers Bombardment (FOB) who directed the guns of the Royal Navy's warships lying offshore.

The brigade commander held an orders group at 2230 hours, only an hour-and-a-half after the first gliders had touched down. Lieutenant Colonel Jack Carson, of the 1st Battalion The Royal Ulster Rifles, was ordered to capture the villages of Longueval and Sainte Honorine on the following morning, whilst Lieutenant Colonel Michael Roberts, of the 2nd Battalion The Oxfordshire & Buckinghamshire Light Infantry, was ordered to take Escoville at the same time.

By midnight on D-Day 6th Airborne Division had thus undergone its baptism of fire and was fully deployed in Normandy, apart from its seaborne element which would arrive on the following day. 3rd Parachute Brigade was deployed over a four-mile front with 9th Parachute Battalion at Le Plein in the north, 1st Canadian Parachute Battalion and Brigadier James Hill's brigade headquarters at Le Mesnil in the centre, and 8th Parachute Battalion in the southern part of the Bois de Bavent and Bures. 5th Parachute Brigade was holding Le Bas de Ranville and Ranville with 12th and 13th Parachute Battalions respectively, with 7th Parachute Battalion as its reserve on the western edge of DZ 'N'. 6th Airlanding Brigade had two of its battalions deployed and ready to move out on operations to extend the division's bridgehead on the following morning. 1st Special Service Brigade, which was still under command of the division, was holding the villages of Hauger, Le Plein and Amfreville which were to the north and north-east of DZ 'N'.

All that remained to arrive by sea on the following day were the 12th Battalion The Devonshire Regiment (less one company), 53rd Airlanding Light Regiment RA (less one battery), 3rd Airlanding Anti-Tank Battery RA (less one troop), 2nd Airlanding Light Anti-Aircraft Battery RA, 195th Airlanding Field Ambulance (less two sections) and other divisional troops.

Major-General Gale summed up his feelings that night:

"I thanked God for the courage of the troops: they were splendid. Quiet in their strength and great in their skill, they lived up to the traditions of the British Army. The light of God was in their eyes."

127. A Horsa in the 'high tow' position behind its Halifax tug aircraft. In bad weather and poor visibility, the glider pilot would position his aircraft in the 'low tow' position, using his tow-rope as a guide in maintaining his glider in the correct position.
(Photo: Imperial War Museum)

128. A Hamilcar glider in tow behind a Halifax on its way over England to Normandy on the evening of D-Day.
(Photo: Museum of Army Flying)

Holding The Bridgehead

6th Airlanding Brigade

As dawn came on the 7th June, the 6th Airborne Division was ready for its next move. In the northern end of Les Bas de Ranville men of the 1st Battalion The Royal Ulster Rifles were making ready to move out that morning for their advance on Longueval, whilst in Ranville the 2nd Battalion The Oxfordshire & Buckinghamshire Light Infantry prepared itself for its attack on Escoville.

1st Battalion The Royal Ulster Rifles

At 0900 hours the Royal Ulster Rifles moved off along the eastern bank of the River Orne towards Longueval. C Company, under the command of Major Bob Hynds, and the Machine Gun Platoon under Lieutenant Harry Morgan, remained dug in on the Ring Contour feature to provide fire support for the battalion. In addition, the battalion's second in command, Major John Drummond, was also with C Company, and with him was a Forward Observer Bombardment who was in contact with HMS *Arethusa* which was lying offshore. The other three rifle companies were to carry out a right flanking attack, the battalion's 3-inch mortars providing additional support from a baseline position south of Ranville.

In the event, Longueval was found not to be held by the enemy and it was secured without any opposition. Lieutenant Colonel Carson thus decided to press on and attack Ste Honorine without delay. D Company, under Major Tony Dyball, and Battalion Headquarters would remain in Longueval whilst A and B Companies, commanded respectively by Major Charles Vickery and Major Gerald Rickord, would carry out the assault.

By now, C Company was under intense fire from mortars and from 88mm self-propelled guns of the enemy's 200th Assault Gun Battalion which were causing severe casualties. The forward observer from the 3rd Infantry Division artillery supporting the battalion could not reach the company's position because of the heavy fire and the Forward Observer Bombardment was unable to contact the cruiser HMS *Arethusa* to call for fire support from her. Thus the battalion's own mortars were its only support.

Moreover, the zero hour for the attack on Ste Honorine had been delayed but notification of this had not been passed to C Company, the mortars or machine guns. Consequently the fire plan had gone ahead as planned. As a result, by the time A and B Companies advanced from their start line across open ground towards the village, the machine guns and mortars were running low on ammunition. At the same time, those on the Ring Contour observed seven enemy 75mm self-propelled guns moving from the north-east towards Ste Honorine. Unfortunately, the warning radioed to Battalion Headquarters in Longueval did not get through.

The two rifle companies advanced under cover of smoke and managed to penetrate the German positions to a certain extent but they suffered heavy casualties from heavy machine-gun fire and self-propelled guns. Contact between the two companies and Battalion Headquarters was lost and both companies were forced to withdraw back to Longueval. Lieutenant Colonel Carson decided to withdraw C Company and the Machine Gun Platoon from the Ring Contour and to concentrate his battalion in defensive positions in Longueval. The attack on Ste Honorine had cost A and B Companies dear, with one officer and five ORs killed, six officers and sixty-four men wounded and one officer and sixty-seven men missing. Approximately twenty of the missing personnel rejoined the battalion during the next few days. C Com-

pany had lost one officer killed and twenty men wounded.

2nd Battalion The Oxfordshire & Buckinghamshire Light Infantry

Meanwhile the 2nd Battalion The Oxfordshire & Buckinghamshire Light Infantry was also having a tough time. At 0430 hours the battalion had advanced on Herouvillette with C Company, commanded by Major Johnny Granville, in the lead. However, the village was found to be clear of the enemy which had withdrawn towards Escoville. At this point, the enemy shelled the village and the road junctions leading to Escoville and Ste Honorine but the battalion proceeded with occupying Herouvillette and by 0830 hours was ready to advance on Escoville.

Patrols from A and B Companies were sent forward to reconnoitre Escoville itself which was a distance of about a thousand yards to the south of Herouvillette. The terrain between the two villages consisted of small fields bordered with very thick hedges of the type for which the Normandy 'bocage' countryside is well known. The patrols discovered that there was no enemy in Escoville itself but that there were several snipers in its vicinity.

At 1000 hours the battalion advanced, leaving C Company in Herouvillette to form a firm base. As it advanced, the battalion met increasing opposition but by 1100 hours A, B and D Companies had reached their objectives and were digging in. Major John Howard's D Company took up position in houses on the southern edge of the village, with A Company, commanded by Major Gilbert Rahr, on its right flank. Lieutenant Colonel Michael Roberts had intended to locate his battalion headquarters in the Chateau d'Escoville but an enemy self-propelled gun decided to select the chateau as a target and thus he had to choose an alternative location.

Attempts to bring forward the battalion's 6-pounder anti-tank guns were unsuccessful because of heavy and accurate shellfire. The village was dominated by high ground to the south and east which afforded the enemy forward observers an excellent view. Meanwhile, all three companies were suffering increasing casualties from heavy artillery and mortar fire. At 1500 hours enemy infantry, supported by armour, reached the village and began to bring heavy fire to bear. With none of the battalion's 6-pounder anti-tank guns forward with them, and with all attempts to communicate with Battalion Headquarters being unsuccessful, the three companies were hard pressed. During the next hour, they became heavily engaged in actions at close quarters and in house-to-house fighting. It rapidly became apparent that Escoville could not be held without severe casualties and without the battalion's 6-pounders to counter the enemy armour.

At this point, the Commanding Officer ordered a withdrawal and C Company moved forward to a position forward of Herouvillette to cover the three companies as they moved back. However, elements of A and D Companies became cut off in Escoville and were saved by a counter-attack led by B Company's commander, Major J. S. R. 'Flaps' Edmunds.

The battalion then proceeded to adopt defensive positions in Herouvillette, expecting an enemy counter-attack which did not transpire. It had so far suffered several casualties which numbered seven officers and eighty other ranks. Lieutenant Colonel Roberts was evacuated that evening, having been injured in a collision between his own glider and another just before landing. He had insisted on carrying on but by the evening was unable to walk. The battalion's second in command, Major Mark Darell Brown, assumed command.

That afternoon at 1700 hours, the 12th Battalion The Devonshire Regiment arrived at Les Bas de Ranville and relieved 12th Parachute Battalion which was now under the command of 6th Airlanding Brigade and which withdrew to a rest position near the Chateau de Ranville. The Devons dug in on the southern edge of the village with two companies in reserve. During the night, they were attacked by enemy aircraft which dropped anti-personnel bombs causing casualties amongst B Company, killing three men and wounding sixteen.

The following morning, the 8th June, initially proved to be a relatively quiet one for 6th Airlanding Brigade. At 1100 hours, however, the Devons were subjected to mortar and artillery fire which continued until 1830 hours. The day was also marred by a tragic incident when the Reconnaissance Platoon of the 1st Battalion The Royal Ulster Rifles suddenly found itself at the receiving end of a salvo of shells fired by artillery of 3rd Infantry Division. Attempts to stop the shelling by radio proved fruitless and so Captain Robin Rigby, the platoon commander, swam the River Orne in an attempt to contact the nearest unit to stop the firing. He remembers the ensuing events well:

"We were being shelled by a Canadian medium regiment which we could see from the top of a hill where we were sited fairly well forward but we couldn't get through to anybody on the wireless. They could see us moving about and for some reason stonked us. They'd caused two or three casualties in my platoon and we were already fed up with being shelled by our own troops, so I asked the Commanding Officer if I could swim the river and the canal. It seemed all right, because there didn't seem to be any Jerries around. I swam the canal and the river quite easily; they were quite long swims but I managed them all right. When I got to the other side, I found the Essex Regiment — I think it was the Essex Regiment. I found their Commanding Officer and told him that I was trying to stop the guns shooting at us. After we'd sorted things out and the shelling had stopped, he then asked me if I wanted to go back via the bridge, because the Germans were between me and the river. I decided, however, to go back the way I had come. I was fairly lucky because at that time I had a pair of civilian trousers on and if I had been pinched, I would have been in trouble. I was in uniform but I'd taken my trousers and boots off because they were a bit heavy to swim in. I'd pinched these civilian trousers and I also tried to pinch a bicycle from a Frenchman but he wouldn't give it to me. Going back, I got to the river and I could see the canal on the other side. At that point I saw some Jerries down on the tow path, two of them were on motorbikes. I swam the river very fast and had reached the canal bank when one of the motorbikes started coming down the road. I got a bit worried and crossed the canal at record speed. My Commanding Officer meantime had sent some of our chaps with a Bren gun down to the bank of the canal and they knocked off the chap on the motorbike who had obviously come down to investigate me. After that I went back to my platoon's position — we'd stopped the trouble and the guns didn't fire again."

That evening an enemy infantry platoon was spotted preparing to attack the Royal Ulster Rifles' battalion headquarters. It was engaged with small arms by the Adjutant, Captain Bob Sheridan, and Regimental Sergeant Major Griffiths, together with some clerks and men of the battalion's defence and intelligence sections. The Germans were beaten off, at which point they came under fire from B Company and were forced to withdraw.

Later that evening, an enemy Mark IV tank commenced shelling the Royal Ulster Rifles' battalion headquarters from a position on the high ground north-east of Longueval. A request for help to Headquarters 6th Airlanding Brigade resulted in the brigade commander, Brigadier Hugh Kindersley, setting off with a small force of two M10 75mm self-propelled guns, which were on loan from 3rd Infantry Division, and two jeeps containing two Bren gun groups. After moving to a position on a hill a few hundred yards north of Longueval, the Brigadier's force spotted two enemy tanks which withdrew after being unsuccessfully engaged with two rounds fired by the brigadier himself from one of the M10s.

129. Hamilcar gliders landing on LZ 'N' on the evening of D-Day, bringing in the light tanks of 6th Airborne Armoured Reconnaissance Regiment. (Photo: Airborne Forces Museum)

The following day, the 9th June, Headquarters 6th Airlanding Brigade received a message at 1000 hours from divisional headquarters that the Germans were withdrawing from Ste Honorine. An observation post of the Devons, located on the reverse slope of the Ring Contour feature, confirmed enemy movement out of the village. A reconnaissance patrol, commanded by Lieutenant L. A. Salt, was sent out by the Devons to obtain further evidence of the enemy's movements. Cover was provided by a fighting patrol, commanded by Lieutenant R. A. Vickery, which was accompanied by Lieutenant Colonel Dick Stevens, the Devons' commanding officer. When Lieutenant Salt's patrol approached the top of the Ring Contour, however, it was met by heavy mortar and machine gun fire and was forced to withdraw under cover of smoke laid down by A Company. The latter had rejoined the battalion during the evening of the previous day, after being under command of 13th Parachute Battalion, and had relieved B Company as one of the forward companies.

On the strength of the reports received from the Devons, Brigadier Hugh Kindersley decided to attack Ste Honorine again. The Royal Ulster Rifles were detailed for the task, whilst 12th Parachute Battalion moved down to Longueval to take over its defence and to protect the start line for the attack.

Whilst carrying out a preliminary reconnaissance, two platoons of the Royal Ulster Rifles' D Company, led by Major Tony Dyball, encountered and ambushed an enemy platoon on the Ste Honorine-Colombelles road. Another patrol, under Captain Ken Donnelly, spotted enemy infantry and armour in the town whilst the observation post on Ring Contour reported more infantry and armour moving back into the town from the east. Consequently, on learning that no artillery support for the attack was available, the brigade commander cancelled the attack. Both the Royal Ulster Rifles and 12th Parachute Battalion were concentrated in Longueval which was now coming under heavy artillery and mortar fire. After some confusion 12th Parachute Battalion was ordered to return to its positions in reserve near the bridges whilst the Royal Ulster Rifles remained in defence of Longueval.

12th Battalion The Devonshire Regiment

At 1900 hours that evening, extremely heavy artillery and mortar fire was brought to bear along the whole southern front from Ranville to Herouvillette by the Germans. Headquarters 6th Airlanding Brigade suffered shellbursts amongst its trenches and the Devons' observation post on Ring Contour was knocked out by a direct hit. At 2000 hours a strong attack was launched against the battalion. The enemy managed to penetrate the Devons' position but were subsequently beaten off by a counter-attack.

At 2030 hours the enemy laid down smoke across the Ring Contour and shortly afterwards three companies of infantry, supported by tanks, appeared opposite the position of the Devons' A Company. No. 7 Platoon, under Lieutenant Dick Whiteway, and No. 8 Platoon, commanded by Lieutenant Jack Hobbs, opened fire at a range of three hundred yards. The battalion's Vickers medium machine guns also joined in and the FOO with A Company called down artillery fire from the guns of 3rd Infantry Division. Despite the heavy fire which was now causing them heavy casualties the enemy infantry, subsequently identified as the 125th Panzer Grenadier Regiment, continued to advance over open ground until they were only fifty yards from the Devons' positions. Finally they broke and fled.

2nd Battalion The Oxfordshire & Buckinghamshire Light Infantry

The 9th June proved to be an active day for the 2nd Battalion The Oxfordshire & Buckinghamshire Light Infantry who had spent the previous day fortifying Herouvillette. During the morning, C Company had advanced into Escoville after patrols had reported the village to be unoccupied by the enemy. The company had reached the Chateau d'Escoville without incident but had come under mortar and artillery fire when it moved into the southern part of the village. Enemy infantry, supported by armour,

advanced into the village and started to move round the company's flanks. At the same time, a self-propelled gun opened fire on the chateau.

At 1600 hours more enemy troops, with armoured cars in support, also arrived at the village. Thirty minutes later C Company was ordered to withdraw to Herouvillette which it did without difficulty. However, patrols remained behind in Escoville to monitor the enemy's movements and at 1730 hours these reported a build-up of enemy infantry and armour which was assumed to be in preparation for an attack on Herouvillette.

At 1830 hours, the battalion came under heavy mortar and artillery fire. This was followed by an attack by Messerschmitt 109 fighters which strafed the village. Shortly afterwards, the enemy attacked from the direction of Escoville. Infantry of the 192nd Panzer Grenadier Regiment, supported by tanks and self-propelled guns, advanced on Herouvillette. However, the battalion had worked out its defensive fire plans well, the Vickers guns of the Machine Gun Platoon and the 6-pounders of the Anti-Tank Platoon being well-sited with good fields of fire. Moreover, the battalion was able to call down a very heavy concentration of artillery fire on Escoville and its northern outskirts from the field and medium regiments on call to 6th Airborne Division.

However, the enemy continued its advance and reached a point within a hundred yards of C and D Companies' positions before they were driven back by the intense volume of fire. At 2130 hours they withdrew, leaving behind a total of six Mark IV tanks and two armoured cars destroyed. Two tanks and two self-propelled guns had also been destroyed by guns of 3rd and 4th Airlanding Anti-Tank Batteries RA which had been in support.

Headquarters 6th Airborne Division

Divisional Headquarters also took its fair share of punishment due to the fact that it was only five hundred yards behind the positions of the Devons. The Commander Royal Artillery, Lieutenant-Colonel Jack Norris, had earlier been severely wounded in the throat whilst watching the landing of 6th Airlanding Brigade on the evening of the 6th June. Major Gerry Lacoste, the GSO 2 (Intelligence) had also been wounded on D-Day and had to be evacuated. His post was taken over by one of his intelligence officers, Captain Freddie Scholes of the Intelligence Corps, but he was unfortunately killed later.

3rd Parachute Brigade

9th Parachute Battalion

On the 7th June, 9th Parachute Battalion left its location in Chateau d'Amfreville in Hauger to rejoin 3rd Parachute Brigade south of Breville. Its new positions would be in the area of the Chateau St Come, extending across the road between Breville and Le Mesnil to include a villa called the Bois de Mont. The planned route had been across country, bypassing Breville to the west. However, those in the lead somehow made an error and the battalion found itself marching through Breville, fortunately without encountering any enemy. By 1330 hours the battalion had reached its new location and started digging in. Shortly after it had arrived, the Germans reoccupied Breville.

After discussion with Brigadier Hill concerning the weak strength of the battalion, it was decided to hold the Bois de Mont and endeavour to deny the chateau area by patrolling. Lieutenant-Colonel Terence Otway therefore altered his battalion's positions so that they centred on the villa of the Bois de Mont itself, the villa being situated in a clearing surrounded by trees. Almost opposite the gates of the villa was the entrance to the three hundred yard long drive to the small chateau which was a stud farm. Beyond the chateau were stables and outbuildings. Opposite the chateau drive gates was a narrow lane, lined by trees and with deep ditches on either side of it, which ran along the northern edge of the Bois de Mont towards the west and the drop zone.

Brigade headquarters and 1st Canadian Parachute Battalion

were located one thousand yards away to the south at Le Mesnil, whilst 8th Parachute Battalion was in the Bois de Bavent and holding the southern edge of the ridge. 5th Parachute Brigade was holding Ranville and the two bridges, whilst 6th Airlanding Brigade was covering the southern approaches from Herouvillette and Le Bas de Ranville. 1st Special Service Brigade meanwhile held Le Plein and Amfreville.

A Company was positioned along either side of the chateau drive whilst B Company was located along a sunken lane which ran along the northern edge of the Bois de Mont wood, overlooking open ground towards Breville. C Company defended the southern and western sides of the position and was the battalion's counter-attack force. The Machine Gun Platoon's Vickers guns were positioned in the road ditch near the gates to the chateau's drive, covering both ways along the Breville-Le Mesnil road. Battalion Headquarters and the Regimental Aid Post were located in the Bois de Mont villa itself.

On the following day, the 8th June, a patrol under Lieutenant Dennis Slade reconnoitred the Chateau St Come but found it unoccupied. It did, however, find a German payroll amounting to the equivalent of some five hundred pounds and this was promptly appropriated for the battalion's funds. Other signs of recent occupation by the enemy were evident in the form of items of uniform and equipment strewn about. At about midday, a German patrol encountered A Company and was beaten off. Later in the afternoon, attacks against A and B Companies were carried out by the 857th Grenadier Regiment but all these were driven off easily. Regimental Sergeant Major Cunningham played a key role in these actions, leading his own small counter-attack force of a Vickers machine gun, a Bren group and some members of the Anti-Tank Platoon, which he moved swiftly to areas in the battalion's perimeter where a threat was being posed. On several occasions he exposed himself without any regard for his own safety, at one point standing on top of a bank in full view of the enemy whilst directing the fire of his men.

That night, the battalion received two 3-inch mortars, three Vickers machine guns and more ammunition. All the battalion's mortars had gone astray during the drop and had been sorely missed, as had the members of the Mortar Platoon of whom nearly all were still missing. However, within a very short space of time, Sergeant Hennessy of the Mortar Platoon had trained some replacements to a very creditable standard. Sergeant McGeever, meanwhile, had formed a new Machine Gun Platoon and had mounted one of his guns on a jeep for use as a mobile fire support vehicle.

At first light on the 9th June, the battalion was subjected to heavy mortar fire. This was followed by a strong attack by enemy infantry against A Company and part of B Company on either side of the road. Both companies waited until the enemy troops were fifty yards away before opening fire. Heavy small arms fire, together with 2-inch and 3-inch mortars bringing down defensive fire, wreaked havoc amongst the German infantrymen who broke and fled into the woods near the chateau. A subsequent attack, which took place about an hour later, also met the same fate.

Later in the morning the battalion received a report that brigade headquarters was under threat. Lieutenant Colonel Otway quickly gathered together a force of some thirty men from his battalion headquarters and C Company, under the command of Lieutenant Christie, together with a fire support group of two light machine gun groups, equipped with two captured MG 42s, under Major George Smith. Leading them rapidly through the wood to the south-east they were able to trap the enemy between themselves and the Brigade Headquarters Defence Platoon. Between them, nineteen of the enemy were killed and one prisoner was taken. Regrettably, Captain Wilkinson, the Brigade Intelligence Officer, was killed in this action.

During the afternoon A Company again came under threat when two platoons of enemy infantry started to infiltrate through the wood to the east and south of the company's position. A platoon of C Company led by Major Eddie Charlton, who was the battalion's second in command, and Lieutenant John Parfitt,

carried out a counter-attack. Unfortunately they encountered two machine guns and Major Charlton, Lieutenant Parfitt and five others were killed. Their bodies were recovered that night by a patrol.

That afternoon saw some air activity in the form of some Focke Wulf 190 fighter bombers which were engaged by the 40mm Bofors guns and 20mm Hispano Suiza cannons of 2nd Airlanding Light Anti-Aircraft Battery RA. Later, RAF Stirling bombers dropped supplies and 6-pounder anti-tank guns to the north of Ranville.

Very early on the morning of the 10th June, a section under the command of Sergeant Frith, with Lance Corporal Watkins as his second in command, was sent into the chateau to check on any enemy activity. After searching the chateau itself, which was found to be empty, the section came under fire from a machine gun in buildings which it had already searched. Private Pattinson was hit in the leg but was rescued by Lance Corporal Watkins.

Just after dawn, Captain Robert Gordon-Brown rejoined the battalion, bringing some thirty men with him. This increased the battalion's strength to two hundred and seventy all ranks, still a very low figure. However, despite the fact that everyone was extremely tired, morale was very high. Rations were adequate and it was only 3-inch mortar bombs which were in short supply.

Throughout the rest of the day, the battalion saw plenty of action. A weak attack on A Company at 1100 hours was easily dealt with. Shortly afterwards, after a platoon of A Company had been redeployed forward about fifty yards into a ditch north-east of the chateau drive gates, about fifty enemy troops commenced digging in along the ditch beside the Breville road in full view of two of the battalion's Vickers guns. At a range of five hundred yards, they were in perfect enfilade. Joined by two Bren groups from B Company, the machine gunners had a field day and virtually wiped out the entire German force. Shortly afterwards, A Company's recently deployed forward platoon ambushed a German patrol at a range of ten yards, virtually annihilating it.

During the morning, the enemy had reoccupied the chateau and by early afternoon were there in force. A company of infantry advanced down the drive, supported by two self-propelled guns which opened fire on A and B Companies. Due to the fact that supplies of 3-inch mortar ammunition were now running very low, some of the Anti-Tank Platoon's PIATs were used as makeshift mortars. Combined with the fire of some of A Company's Bren light machine guns, this measure proved effective in breaking up the enemy infantry. At that point, Sergeant McGeever's jeep-mounted Vickers machine gun engaged one of the self-propelled guns which had suddenly appeared to the north of the chateau. To the amazement of all those watching, the self-propelled gun suddenly exploded and stopped.

Shortly afterwards, two companies of enemy attacked B Company from the north. It was a strong attack as they were supported by mortars, and they were only driven off by the battalion's mortars, which had now been resupplied with ammunition, and by B Company's light machine guns.

At this point, Lieutenant Colonel Otway called for supporting fire from HMS *Arethusa* via the Forward Observer Bombardment who was located at brigade headquarters. Fifteen minutes later, as the salvos of 6-inch shells thundered in five hundred yards to the front of the battalion's positions, Captain Paul Greenway stood in full view of the enemy and shouted corrections to the Commanding Officer who transmitted them by radio to the FOB. Despite the fact that the Germans suffered heavy casualties from this shelling, their leading troops managed to reach B Company's positions where they received a further mauling which few survived. Those taken prisoner, including the commanding officer of the 2nd Battalion 857th Grenadier Regiment, spoke of their battalion as having been destroyed, and of their regiment having met the same fate during the fighting in Ranville and Amfreville.

Late that night, after 2300 hours, Major Ian Dyer led C Company forward to occupy the chateau. After some skirmishing with small groups of enemy, he and his men succeeded in doing so.

During the rest of the night enemy patrols probed the company's position and kept the company busy whilst the rest of the battalion was left undisturbed.

On that same day, the commander of 1st Corps. Lieutenant General Sir John Crocker, had decided to extend the bridgehead to east of the River Orne. 51st Highland Division crossed the bridges to take over the southern half of the sector from 6th Airborne Division.

That night saw the arrival of the 5th Battalion The Black Watch at an assembly area a short distance south-west of 9th Parachute Battalion. Detached from 153rd Infantry Brigade and now under command of 3rd Parachute Brigade, it had been tasked with attacking and capturing Breville from the south-west on the following day, the 11th June, in order to dislodge the Germans from their vantage point on the ridge overlooking Ranville. The chateau, currently held by C Company, was a vital element in any successful attack on Breville from the south as any assault from that direction would be vulnerable to counter-attack through the area to the north of the chateau. Breville itself was occupied by a strong force of enemy infantry and self-propelled guns.

The commanding officer of the Black Watch battalion arrived at Lieutenant Colonel Otway's battalion headquarters to plan his attack. His main assault would approach Breville from the south-west after heavy artillery and mortar fire had been laid down on the village by the guns of 51st Highland Division and the mortars of the two battalions. Before dawn, a company of the Black Watch took over the chateau from C Company, whilst Captain Hugh Smyth took out a reconnaissance patrol along the road towards Breville to check the ground over which the Black Watch attack would approach.

When the attack went in, the leading companies of Black Watch had to cross two hundred and fifty yards of open ground from the village. As they did so, the supporting artillery and mortar fire lifted. They were immediately subjected to heavy mortar and machine-gun fire which caused several casualties amongst the Highlanders. At the same time, the enemy also laid down a heavy mortar bombardment on the area to the south-west through which the Black Watch reserve companies were moving at the time. Heavy casualties were suffered amongst them as well and the attack quickly ground to a halt. The Highlanders withdrew to 9th Parachute Battalion's positions, reorganising in the Bois de Mont before taking up positions around the chateau. The two battalions quickly formed a combined defence of the area of the chateau and the Bois de Mont, the link between the two units being halfway down the chateau drive.

1st Canadian Parachute Battalion

The 7th June had found 1st Canadian Parachute Battalion being resupplied with much needed mortars, to replace those missing in the drop, and a large quantity of ammunition. This resupply proved particularly fortuitous as the mortars proved to be a decisive factor on the following day when a strong attack was made on the battalion's positions at the Le Mesnil crossroads by enemy infantry of the 857th and 858th Grenadier Regiments who were supported by self-propelled guns and tanks. These had formed up in a column along the road leading to Le Mesnil in the apparent belief that the battalion did not possess mortars. Before they were in a position to assault, the battalion's mortars opened fire and caused heavy casualties amongst them.

However, the enemy pressed home an attack on B and C Companies, supported by a single Mark IV tank which advanced between them and caused heavy casualties before being driven off by PIATs. As the tank withdrew, the enemy infantry following it came under heavy fire and fled when B Company counter-attacked with a bayonet charge, withdrawing to a fortified farmhouse some two hundred yards down the road.

This enemy position was heavily defended with machine guns and surrounded by a low wall. From it the Germans could threaten the crossroads with harassing fire and sniping. At 0900

130. Gliders on one of the LZs north of Ranville. (Photo: Imperial War Museum)

hours, some time after the attack on the crossroads had been beaten off, B Company was ordered to attack and clear the enemy from the farmhouse.

Led by Captain Peter Griffin, two platoons reinforced by some Headquarter Company personnel carried out the task. Whilst Captain Griffin and one-and-a-half platoons carried out a frontal assault through an orchard, taking the enemy by surprise and forcing them to withdraw to the farmhouse itself, the remainder of his force moved into a position to protect his flank. As Lieutenant Norman Toseland led his group in a bayonet charge on a hedgerow, he and his men came under heavy fire. He and Privates Davies and Hughes fought their way through the orchard. Before they could reach the hedgerow, however, Davies and Hughes were wounded and Privates Sachro and Turner were killed, as were Corporals Evans and Hume.

On the left flank, Sergeant Huard was killed immediately, Corporal Bastien and Private Shwaluk falling after him. Privates Lanthier, Oxtoby and Lockyer were hit by machine gun fire a short distance from the hedgerow which was cleared as Captain Griffin's frontal assault group attacked the farmhouse and nearby outbuildings.

A further assault on other outbuildings was halted when Captain Griffin and his men discovered a large number of enemy troops and armoured vehicles in the farmyard. Almost immediately, enemy mortars opened fire on the farmhouse and an enemy counter-attack ensued, supported by a tank. As Griffin's assault group withdrew, his flank protection party opened fire on the enemy counter-attack force which was caught in a crossfire. In this withdrawal two men, privates Geddes and Noval, between them killed or wounded almost half the enemy counter-attack force which was estimated at being fifty strong.

Due to the strength of the enemy, B Company had to withdraw. The action had cost it dear, with eight men killed and thirteen wounded. However, the farmhouse was subsequently abandoned and thereafter enemy activity was limited to sniping from the hedgerows. Enemy snipers were gradually eliminated by patrols and individual members of the battalion, some of whom became expert at doing so.

6th Airborne Division adopted a policy of 'static offensive' at this time. This involved heavy patrolling by day and night, harassing the enemy whenever possible. This ensured that the Germans were kept off-balance as far as possible, not knowing when or where to expect trouble and having to deploy large numbers of troops who had to be constantly on their guard. On a number of occasions, patrols encountered enemy patrols and some fierce fire fights took place. This also had the beneficial effect of maintaining an aggressive spirit and high morale amongst members of all units in the division.

One such patrol was carried out in broad daylight on the 9th June by 1st Canadian Parachute Battalion. A platoon of C Company moved out through B Company's positions and set off for the village of Bavent. Its mission was to determine the strength of the enemy in the village and surrounding area and to pinpoint the number and positions of the guns located in the village itself; the platoon was to attack the village in such a way as to cause the enemy to retaliate with all their weapons. No. 1 Section was tasked with entering the village and generally causing a commotion. Meanwhile, three men would draw the enemy's fire by running across an open field in full view of the village whilst the rest of the platoon would give covering fire from a ditch. One member of this patrol was Corporal Dan Hartigan who describes here what happened:

"It was a bright sunny morning as we slithered along hedgerows parallel to the Le Mesnil-Varaville highway and passed beneath a rough planked bridge over a shallow brook or anti-tank ditch with a foot or two of water in the bottom of it. We turned right towards Bavent once we were beyond our own B Company positions and followed this shallow waterway towards the town. Thick hedges arched over the water so it gave us good cover, provided the enemy didn't have machine guns posted to fire straight down its length. It turned out that the route was clear. As we neared the town, we became over-confident because of the lack of ac-

tivity by the enemy, and came up out of the watery trench into the fields a little way from its hedges. All was still quiet. Now we became totally over-confident and, shouldering our arms, prepared to walk right into what we now thought to be an unoccupied town.

The enemy waited until they could see the whites of our eyes — maybe seventy-five feet out from the hummock or low stone wall which surrounded our side of Bavent — before an MG42 machine gun blasted away at us from point blank range. The gun crew didn't have the right stuff and missed us completely. Just ahead was a huge crater, put there by one of the RAF's blockbusters. Our section, Sergeant Morgan's, was in the lead. We ended up in this crater with all of us going in head first, feet first, upside down and sideways — all tangled up. It took a moment or two to regain some form of composure for we all knew we had been mercifully reprieved from a literally bloody and sudden death by a bungling enemy soldier. Sergeant Morgan, though, remained alert and was definitely made of the right stuff. The forward edge of the crater, where he had swiftly positioned himself, was only about thirty or forty feet from where the gun had fired. He threw a couple of phosphorous smoke grenades, followed by a Gammon Bomb, and ordered us forward.

Private Colin Morrison and I tore up a slight rise on the right edge of the town, with his Bren light machine gun and my 2-inch mortar and rifle, to give covering fire from the rear right flank. Morgan took the remaining six men of our section (Private Middleton had been lost on the drop on D-Day) right into the houses after the enemy. The town, far from being undefended, was crawling with enemy troops. Machine-gun and rifle fire came from everywhere. One surprising thing was that the enemy, well within range of Morrison's and my weapons and positioned on upper floors and balconies, were obviously afraid to withdraw by way of the streets and could be seen scrambling over the rooftops of houses. These became our best targets and, for a fleeting moment or two, we made the most of the opportunities offered.

As Sergeant Morgan led the rest of the section up the main street towards the first enemy occupied house, Private Gilbert Commeau was stitched across the chest by an enemy machine gun and died immediately on the road. Sergeant Morgan got the section into the houses, leaving one man by the door of each to warn of any impending trouble. At the first house he leapt through the entrance, followed by Private Eddie Mallon, and shot two enemy soldiers before they knew what was happening to them. On entering another house he met his opposite number, a German sergeant, pointing a Schmeisser machine pistol at him. Both men fired, the German falling and Sergeant Morgan receiving two 9mm bullets in his lower abdomen.

After Morrison had sprayed the rooftops with his Bren, harassing the retreating enemy scrambling over the rooftops, an enemy machine gun returned his fire. Since our cover was not particularly good, we had to back off to a less exposed position from where we used my 2-inch mortar.

Sergeant Moshier McPhee, our platoon sergeant, had found a German 2-inch mortar near the position from where the MG42 had blasted away at us at the start of the action. It was the regular infantry type with a heavy baseplate and a bipod. There was a good supply of bombs for it in a dug-out nearby. However, someone had attempted to destroy the weapon by apparently detonating a grenade in its barrel. We could only assume that it had been done by the enemy when Sergeant Morgan had thrown his grenades and Gammon bomb. Anyway, the barrel of the mortar had a hole in the side of the barrel about eight to ten inches from the muzzle. Sergeant McPhee, cool as always, experimented with this weapon whilst under a considerable volume of fire. Although he found that its range was severely limited, he had Privates Murray and Makelki passing him ammunition whilst he proceeded to rain a heavy shower of bombs down on to the town. I can remember laughing, when Morrison and I returned to the patrol's firm base, because each time Sergeant McPhee fired there came a sheet of flame and smoke out of the hole in the side of the barrel.

Our platoon commander, Lieutenant McGowan, decided that he was not going to let Jerry off the hook. He already had a pretty good idea of the number of enemy in Bavent, having judged it from the strength of the reaction to our assault. He called forward the three men designated to draw the enemy's fire, Privates Saunders, Sauder and Swim, and sent them galloping across the open fields in front of the town to a copse which was about two hundred and fifty yards from the main enemy positions. The enemy took the bait and spewed out a torrent of fire across the fields. The worst of it was that these three men then had to do the same thing to get back. Anyone who watched this spectacle never forgot it. All three did get back but we all knew that miracles were happening on that day.''

Another patrol into Bavent was carried out that night by C Company. Twelve men, accompanied by a party of fourteen sappers, infiltrated through enemy positions into the village. The plan called for the sappers to place demolition charges in houses and on some heavy mortars located at the far end of the village whilst the C Company patrol engaged the enemy. In the event, all went according to plan and the patrol withdrew in small groups, with the loss of one man killed and one wounded, as the enemy responded with machine guns firing wildly in several directions.

On the 10th June, a strong German attack broke through Breville and advanced on Ranville where it was beaten off. However, the enemy had forced a wedge between 3rd Parachute Brigade and 1st Special Service Brigade. Brigadier James Hill then realised that he was confronted by 346th Infantry Division, which was a high calibre formation, and that 21st Panzer Division was active in the bridgehead area to his rear.

On the same day, 1st Canadian Parachute Battalion was posed with a serious threat when two enemy battalions moved on to the glider landing zone north-west of the Le Mesnil crossroads. The 2nd Battalion 857th Grenadier Regiment, a combined force of 1st and 2nd Battalions 858th Grenadier Regiment and several companies of the 744th Grenadier Regiment, supported by tanks and armoured cars, launched an attack at a point between 1st Canadian and 9th Parachute Battlions. This was broken up by heavy fire from artillery and machine guns, and the enemy were prevented from reaching the Canadian positions. However, during the afternoon, two further attacks were launched to the north of the battalion's positions.

On the 12th June, at 1200 hours, the entire front of 3rd Parachute Brigade was subjected to heavy shelling and mortar fire. This was followed at 1500 hours by an attack on 1st Canadian Parachute Battalion's positions by an enemy battalion. At the same time, a strong force supported by six tanks and self-propelled guns advanced on 9th Parachute Battalion and the 5th Battalion The Black Watch.

Within a short space of time, all the Black Watch anti-tank guns had been destroyed and nine of the battalion's Bren carriers were also hit. The centre of the fighting began to take place around the chateau, the Germans desperately trying to seize it from the Black Watch who doggedly held on despite heavy fire from tanks and self-propelled guns. However, the pressure began to tell and gradually the enemy started to force the Highlanders from other positions back towards the Bois de Mont. At one point a platoon of the Black Watch, which was under fire and had lost its platoon commander and some of its NCOs, began to look as though it might be beginning to lose its nerve. The situation was saved by Captain Hugh Smyth, of A Company of 9th Parachute Battalion, who jumped out of his trench and walked up the drive. Strolling round their positions, he talked to the Highlanders and restored their confidence before returning to his company.

At this point in the battle the enemy started to switch their attention to 9th Parachute Battalion, A and B Companies coming under heavy fire from tanks and self-propelled guns. The battalion's mortar platoon, under Sergeant Hennessy and Corporal Gower, operated their 3-inch mortars continually, dropping their bombs three hundred yards away in the woods whilst enemy shell and mortar fire burst around them. More enemy infantry, supported by two tanks, now appeared opposite B Company. One tank was hit by two PIAT bombs but remained unscathed, responding by knocking out two machine-gun posts astride the road leading to Breville. It was hit again by a PIAT which damaged it and forced it to withdraw. At this point the enemy infantry, who had managed to advance to within very close range of A and B Companies, also decided to withdraw back into the woods around the cheateau.

Lieutenant Colonel Terence Otway now signalled to brigade headquarters that he would not be able to hold out for long because the battalion was now very weak in numbers and very low on ammunition. Brigadier Hill takes up the story:

131. Glider No. 70 in which Major General Gale and his advance headquarters flew into LZ 'N' in the early morning of 6th June.
(Photo: Imperial War Museum)

"Realising that Colonel Otway would not have sent this signal unless the situation was serious, I immediately went to Colonel Bradbrooke to ask him if he would let me have what reserves he had available at his headquarters. At that moment Bradbrooke himself was hard pressed and for the first time in the operation in his sector, the Le Mesnil/Troarn road had been crossed by enemy tanks which were shooting up his right hand company headquarters which was in a small sawmill. However, he felt that they could cope with this situation and let me take Major Hanson and some forty Canadians who were the only ones left in his reserve company. A young Red Indian, Private Anderson, aged eighteen, informed me that he would act as my bodyguard. We set off across the four hundred yards which separated the brigade headquarters defence platoon from 9th Parachute Battalion. I remember seeing Padre Nicol of the Black Watch, a great tall figure, quietly walking up and down whilst calming his young soldiers who had fallen back across the road. I thought to myself, "Here is a great man in anybody's army." And so it was to be, for the Padre later became Moderator for the Church of Scotland.

I took the Canadians up through the wood to the north-east of 9th Parachute Battalion where a shambles reigned. It appeared to be occupied by Germans and Black Watch. At the end of the wood a Mark IV tank was cruising up and down but the men had no weapons to deal with it. At that time Private Anderson was shot through the arm but refused to leave the field. I then handed over the party to Major Hanson with instructions to work his way on to the chateau. When they got there they found that a gallant section of the Black Watch was still holding out in one of the outhouses and they drove out many weary Germans who retreated.

A great defensive victory had been won by 9th Parachute Battalion, the Canadians and the Black Watch."

8th Parachute Battalion

Meanwhile Lieutenant Colonel Alastair Pearson's 8th Parachute Battalion, which was in the Bois de Bavent, had been dominating its area with vigour from its base near the road junction southeast of Escoville. Despite the fact that the battalion had lost about half its strength during the drop on the 6th June, it had been patrolling ceaselessly and aggressively at night and lying up by the day.

The battalion was deployed in thick forest through which movement was impossible except via the network of tracks which ran through it. The road runs through the forest and, from a point south of Le Mesnil through to Troarn this was dominated by the battalion.

Visibility and fields of fire within the forest were very limited, being no more than a few yards. The road running through the forest and the main tracks within it were under constant mortar fire from the enemy. The battalion soon learned to avoid track junctions which were deathtraps and Pearson's men became adept at leaping into their trenches at the sound of enemy mortar bombs arriving. Initially, casualties had been caused by mortar bombs exploding in the branches of trees above. However, overhead cover was soon constructed and this helped to reduce the risk of head wounds caused by flying steel fragments and wooden splinters.

Conditions in the forest were grim because everything was permanently wet through with rain, the foliage of the trees being so thick that the sun could not penetrate it. Trenches soon became sodden and the mud slimy and slippery. To make matters worse, the forest was infested by large mosquitoes which plagued all members of the battalion, their bites causing skin sores when scratched. Lieutenant Colonel Pearson himself was a sick man, suffering from a wound and covered in boils and sores.

Despite these grim conditions, however, the battalion's confidence was unshaken and its morale was as high as ever. At night Pearson's men went out on patrols, sometimes entering Troarn and Bures from which the battalion had withdrawn previously on the arrival of strong enemy forces.

5th Parachute Brigade

On the 7th June, A Company of 12th Parachute Battalion, which was on the high ground south of Le Bas de Ranville, was attacked by seven tanks supported by approximately a hundred and fifty infantry. The crew of the company's only anti-tank gun was knocked out, as was a section of one of the platoons. The day was saved by Private Hall who ran across to the gun and proceeded to destroy three tanks in rapid succession, putting the enemy force to flight as he did so.

On the same day, 13th Parachute Battalion came under attack from three enemy self-propelled guns which tried to break through A Company's position but were destroyed in the process. On the following day, the 8th June, the battalion beat off another attack and destroyed six tanks.

Before dawn on the 10th June, B Company of 13th Parachute Battalion detected a large force of enemy in the wooded areas south-east of Breville. A reconnaissance patrol from C Company was sent out and returned to report that the enemy were forming for an attack. At 0900 hours the enemy force moved off, crossing DZ 'N' and heading for the two bridges. At a very close range of fifty yards, 13th Parachute Battalion opened fire and caused heavy casualties. C Company then counter-attacked with a bayonet charge. At this point, 7th Parachute Battalion opened fire with its machine guns and mortars as the remaining enemy troops withdrew in confusion into three areas of woods at Le Mariquet along the road between Ranville and Le Mesnil. The total number of enemy killed was in excess of four hundred and over a hundred prisoners were taken.

During the morning of the 10th June, Headquarters 6th Airborne Division had been receiving reports from the two parachute brigades and 1st Special Service Brigade that they were all heavily engaged by enemy forces attacking from Breville. The Germans were attacking in two directions: north-west against 1st Special Service Brigade in and around Le Plein, and south-west across the landing zone towards Le Mariquet which was held by 13th Parachute Battalion.

Major General Gale had already decided that he needed armoured support from 1st Corps and this arrived in the early afternoon in the form of B Squadron of the 13/18th Royal Hussars which was put under his command. Its initial task was to support 5th Parachute Brigade in a counter-attack to clear the enemy from the three woods into which they had been driven by 7th and 13th Parachute Battalions.

The squadron leader, Major Anthony Rugge-Price, rendezvoused that afternoon with the Commanding Officer of 7th Parachute Battalion, Lieutenant Colonel Geoffrey Pine Coffin, on the edge of DZ 'N'. Both appreciated that the use of artillery or mortar fire support was out of the question because of the risk to 13th Parachute Battalion, and to 3rd Parachute Brigade which was located to the left and beyond the objectives. The task of clearing the woods would be carried out by A and B Companies. A troop of four Sherman tanks would precede them, remaining on the open ground of the drop zone to the left of the paratroops' axis of advance, and would lay down fire into the trees for two minutes before signalling the companies to advance by firing smoke. A second troop of Shermans would advance in reserve behind the leading troop, whilst the squadron's reconnaissance troop of five Honey light tanks would move along on the left flank, covering the Breville ridge.

The tanks encountered problems during the attack. One of the reserve troop's tanks was hit by enemy fire from the DZ. As fire was going down on the second wood, the reconnaissance troop leader's tank became entangled in the rigging lines of parachutes lying on the drop zone. Immobilised, it was almost immediately hit by a self-propelled gun and set on fire. Meanwhile, the leading troop leader's tank was also set ablaze and the troop came under fire from a self-propelled gun. At that point the squadron leader's tank was also hit and burst into flames. The squadron started to withdraw but another Sherman and Honey were hit. Another Sherman was immobilised by parachute rigging lines entangling themselves in its tracks, immediately being knocked out by

132. Men of the 1st Battalion The Royal Ulster Rifles move off from LZ 'N'. (Photo: Imperial War Museum)

a self-propelled gun.

The two parachute companies, meanwhile, had been successful in clearing the enemy infantry, subsequently identified as a battalion of the 857th Grenadier Regiment, out of the woods. B Company cleared the first two woods, its commander narrowly escaping being shot as he emerged from a hedge in front of Lieutenant Colonel Pine Coffin who was leading A Company up to the third and final wood. Fortunately, Pine Coffin had omitted to cock the German MP38 machine pistol that he was carrying at the time. The third wood was being cleared as the tank squadron ran into trouble. A Company moved through B Company and completed the task. By the end of the afternoon, a further hundred prisoners had been taken and twenty more enemy soldiers killed, for the loss of ten men of 7th Parachute Battalion wounded. Unfortunately the 13th/18th Royal Hussars' squadron had suffered badly, losing one officer and nine men killed and one officer and four men wounded. The squadron had also lost three Sherman and two Honey tanks destroyed.

The Battle of Breville

On the afternoon of the 12th June, Major General Gale decided that the security of the division's front depended on removing the enemy from Breville once and for all. Due to the fact that 3rd Parachute Brigade was by now exhausted and weak in numbers, he had little choice but to use his reserve to carry out this task: the understrength 12th Parachute Battalion which numbered only three hundred men, D Company of the 12th Battalion The Devonshire Regiment and a squadron of the 13th/18th Royal Hussars. However, for artillery support he had available to him four field regiments and one medium regiment. In addition, Gale decided to use the 22nd Independent Parachute Company to deal with any enemy counter-attack.

Gale decided to mount an attack on Breville that evening, thus catching the enemy off-guard whilst still recovering from the day's fighting. He directed that the attack was to go in at 2200 hours and that it would be mounted from a start line on the outer eastern edge of Amfreville which would be secured by No. 6 Commando.

Having received his orders for the attack, the Commanding Officer of 12th Parachute Battalion, Lieutenant Colonel Johnny Johnson, had to draw up his plans very rapidly because of the very limited amount of time available. C Company would seize the first objective which was the crossroads. The Devons' D Company would follow C Company and then swing to the left on reaching the village. A Company would pass through C Company and advance to secure the south-eastern part of Breville. B Company would be following up as the battalion's reserve.

Between the start line and the outskirts of the village were four hundred yards of open terrain. In order to provide cover for the companies as they advanced over this open ground, one troop of the 13th/18th Royal Hussars would move down on their right flank and knock out a known enemy strongpoint which was about two hundred yards from the village.

Captain John Sim, by now second in command of B Company of 12th Parachute Battalion, takes over the story:

'A whole German battalion was concentrated behind Breville and all indications pointed to the probability that they were going to attack at first light next morning and drive through to the bridges. This had to be prevented at all costs. Breville was held at that time by at least two companies of the enemy, plentifully supplied with light automatics, mortars and self-propelled guns. Standing on high ground, it overlooked the bridges and was an ideal starting point for an attack. We had to get our attack in fast and time for reconnaissance was all too short.

At 8pm we were ordered to prepare for battle and the company commanders were whisked away for orders and a quick recce. At eight thirty-five the battalion moved off, up the hill, towards Amfreville. To our surprise, on arrival, we filed into the church, a large solid building standing in the middle of the village green. The men sat in the pews talking in subdued whispers and sucking sweets. Others gazed at the gaily painted effigies of saints and at the elaborate gilded cross on the altar. The time dragged by, then the platoon commanders were called for and some sergeants and corporals filed out. We continued to sit and wait. Soon there was a scurry and bustle. Quick orders were given and the battalion filed out of the church in the order of C Company, A Company, B Company and Headquarter Company.

On the steps of the church the Padre handed out copies of the division's paper called 'Pegasus'. In the order in which we had advanced from the church, we lined up along the side of the road with the head nearest to Breville. Our company commander (I was now with B Company, having been sent there on reorganisation of the available officers) had just sufficient time to inform us that we were going to attack Breville and hold it, that our artillery would fire on the village for twenty minutes and that we were to be supported by a squadron of Sherman tanks. The advance was to be made in four waves in the order C Company, A Company, a company of the 12th Battalion The Devonshire Regiment and B Company. Headquarter Company was to arrive later. For a little while we had time to look at 'Pegasus' and to study a small sketch showing the amazing Russian advances in the East.

With a crash, the show commenced and the attackers moved off down the road to Breville. It was 9.50pm. Shells whistled over our heads and the noise was colossal. Trails of white smoke from smokeshells appeared overhead. Then we came under very heavy gun and mortar fire. We hurriedly took cover in the narrow ditches beside the road, many of us had to be content with lying in the open hugging the walls of houses. It was not until ten past ten that the fire slackened and we were able to move on to our start line...''

As it crossed the start line, C Company almost immediately lost both its remaining officers and its company sergeant major. However, it continued to advance under the command of Sergeant Warcup whilst still suffering casualties from the fire of self-propelled guns. By this time, Breville was ablaze. There was no enemy small arms fire from the village itself but German shells and mortar bombs continued to rain down. The unearthly din was reinforced by the noise of the machine guns of the Sherman tanks of the 13th/18th Royal Hussars firing tracer to guide the assaulting companies. By the time C Company reached the village, it was only fifteen strong.

Corporal Ron Dixon, who was a member of the Signals Platoon of 12th Parachute Battalion, accompanied C Company into the attack. His memories of the action are very vivid:

''I went into the attack carrying on my back a No. 68 radio set. I was with the advance company crossing the open fields into Breville. It was as though hell had been let loose — mortars, shells, airbursts, machine guns all firing at once. There was no cover until we got to the village itself. ''Take cover!'' I heard called. I saw a slit trench and dived in and landed on top of a bloke who I thought was one of our lads until he spoke. ''Prisoner'', he said, ''Prisoner,'' and handed me a Luger. I was speechless. I then heard, ''Attack! Attack!'' I said to the Jerry. ''Sorry chum, you stay here.'' I got out of the slit trench and followed a sergeant and a number of our lads to the houses in Breville. A number of us were sheltering against the wall of a chateau when a shell or mortar bomb dropped amongst us, killing three and injuring the remainder. I picked myself up and, to my amazement and relief, found that I hadn't been scratched...''

As A Company crossed the start line the company commander, Captain Paul Bernard, was wounded and the whole of No. 2 Platoon, including Lieutenant James Campbell, was killed or wounded. Company Sergeant Major Marwood took over command of the company but he was killed as it entered Breville. Captain Bernhard slowly followed after his company, passing the company commander of C Company, Major C W 'Steve' Stephens, who was lying wounded by the road and urging his company on into the village, Bernhard found No. 3 Platoon in the village square. Shortly afterwards its platoon commander, Lieutenant Brewer, was killed and Sergeant Nutley took over command of its remaining nine members. Whilst he led them forward to clear the chateau, Sergeant Murray and the other members of No. 1 Platoon reached the cheateau garden which was their objective.

D Company of the Devons had been the next company to cross the start line. As the supporting artillery barrage started at 0950 hours the company, under its second in command Captain John Warwick-Pengelly, was moving forward past the church in Le Plein on its way to the start line where it would meet its commander, Major John Bampfylde. At that moment a shell exploded in the middle of the company, wounding several men. Nevertheless, the company pushed on and headed towards Amfreville along a narrow sunken lane. As it did so, it encountered wounded members of 12th Parachute Battalion crawling or limping back from the direction of Breville. As the Devons struggled forward, they met their battalion's Support Company commander, Major Eddie Warren, whose company was not involved in the action but who had been asked by Bampfylde to help by bringing D Company on to the start line.

When Warwick-Pengelly and the two leading platoons of D Company reached Amfreville and the start line in an orchard, they found Bampfylde who told his second in command to gather in any stragglers as quickly as possible because the company would be advancing on Breville immediately. Warwick-Pengelly found a dozen men of the company and, after bringing them up to the start line, was told by Bampfylde to clear the right-hand side of the road into Breville. This he and his men did, killing an enemy machine gun crew which was attempting to set up its weapon and clearing two Germans out of the houses as they advanced. At that point, Warwick-Pengelly himself was wounded in the leg but still managed to shoot an enemy soldier climbing out of the window of a house nearby. Shortly afterwards he was hit again by a burst from a self-propelled gun.

Major Eddie Warren had meanwhile collected a dozen men of the Devons and had led them over the start line after D Company. As he did so, he came across a group of bodies on the ground, two of which he recognised as being those of Lieutenant Colonel Johnny Johnson and Major Bampfylde. As D Company had crossed the start line a salvo of shells, suspected to be from the supporting artillery of 51st Highland Division, had fallen short and one had exploded in the middle of a group of senior officers consisting of Johnson, Brigadier Hugh Kindersley and Brigadier The Lord Lovat, the commander of 1st Special Service Brigade, who were all standing near the start line. Both Kindersley and Lovat had been badly wounded.

By now, a troop of the 13th/18th Royal Hussars on the right flank had worked its way forward to the crossroads, whilst some of the squadron's other tanks on the left had moved to the north-eastern outskirts of the village. These were unable to bring fire to bear on some enemy strongpoints which were still holding out.

B Company of 12th Parachute Battalion was the last to cross the start line. Captain John Sim continues the story:

''When we were in position, our company commander signalled us to advance. Between us and the burning, dust-hazed village was a large open field in which were four Sherman tanks blazing away with tracer at the houses. Steadily and in line we advanced up to the tanks and, as they were still firing, we halted and waited for them to cease fire. Behind and to the left, a black pillar of smoke poured out of one of the Shermans. When the tanks switched their fire over to the left of the village and into the dark shadows of a wood (by this time it was getting dark) B Company advanced again.

Without any fuss or bother, we moved into Breville and took up defensive positions in an orchard. There were masses of German trenches in the orchard. Dead Germans lay around and the ground was littered with arms and ammunition. Our men quickly found themselves trenches, as they had been trained to do, so as to be ready for the counter-barrage. For about ten minutes it was hell in that orchard, as shells and mortar bombs rained down. Then it ceased suddenly. While the church and some houses continued to blaze and with the eerie wails of an air raid siren to cheer us up, we waited for the counter-attack; everyone now in the possession of a captured enemy automatic. The Germans, however, had had enough.''

B Company had by then been joined by Colonel Reggie Parker, the Deputy Commander of 6th Airlanding Brigade. He was a former Commanding Officer of 12th Parachute Battalion and had been standing near Lieutenant Colonel Johnson when the latter had been killed. Although wounded in the hand, he had now come forward and taken command of his old battalion.

It was now 1045 hours and it was almost dark. The remnants of C Company, under the command of Sergeant Warcup, had secured the crossroads whilst the eighteen remaining men of A Company, under Sergeants Nutley and Murray, occupied the south-east corner of the village. In the north-east corner, twenty men of the Devons' D Company had secured their objective which was an orchard.

What happened next added to the heavy casualties already suffered by 12th Parachute Battalion and the Devons. As Colonel Parker, accompanied by Captain Hugh Ward who was a Forward Observation Officer from 53rd Airlanding Light Regiment RA, was walking along the road towards C Company, he called for defensive fire to forestall any enemy counter-attack. Despite the fact that the message to HQRA 51st Highland Division was clearly sent, there was a misunderstanding at the gun end. Immediately, the village was subjected to yet another heavy bombardment of artillery fire which caused heavy casualties. During the shelling, Captain Ward was killed and it was his signaller, Gunner Allsop, who on his own initiative ordered the guns to cease fire. When the shelling stopped, it was found that Major Harold Rogers, the commander of B Company, had been mortally wounded and that nine more men of 12th Parachute Battalion had been hit. Captain Paul Bernhard had also been wounded again and Captain John Sim had received a wound in the arm. Rogers

died shortly afterwards and Bernhard was evacuated to 225th Parachute Field Ambulance's MDS at Le Bas de Ranville.

Major Eddie Warren went forward from the village square, where he had taken cover during the shelling, and took command of the remnants of the Devons' D Company which had lost some thirty-five killed and wounded. He immediately reorganised them and set them to digging defensive positions. By the following morning, the company numbered five officers and sixty-five men.

At 0200 hours, a troop of the 13th/18th Royal Hussars moved into Breville and took up positions alongside C Company at the crossroads. Later, in the early morning, the 22nd Independent Parachute Company, under the command of Major Nigel Stockwell, arrived in the village as reinforcements. During the morning, there was the very welcome sight of the 1st Battalion The Royal Ulster Rifles marching up the road from Ranville in high spirits to relieve the now desperately depleted 12th Parachute Battalion and its attached company of Devons.

Breville had been taken but at a very heavy cost. Nine officers and one hundred and fifty-three men of 12th Parachute Battalion and D Company of the 12th Battalion The Devonshire Regiment were killed in the battle. Out of the five hundred and fifty men of 12th Parachute Battalion who had jumped into Normandy on the 6th June, only Headquarter Company and an understrength company of fifty-five men remained. All the battalion's officers,

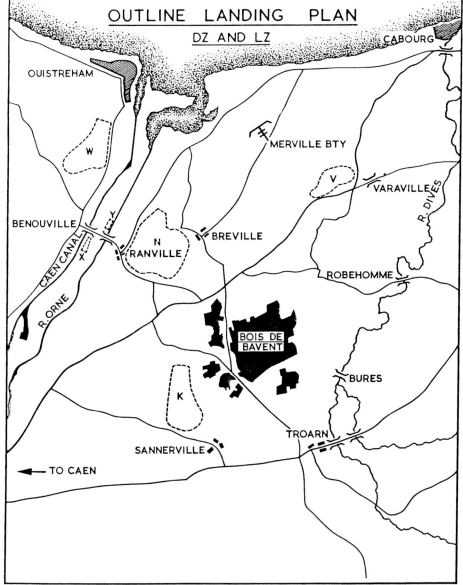

Time	DZ/LZ	Unit
0050	N	* Adv party 5 Para Bde Gp
	V	* Adv party 3 Para Bde Gp
	K	* Adv party 8 PARA
	X&Y	D Coy Gp 2 Ox & Bucks LI
		* Pathfinders also dropped
0200	N	5 Para Bde Gp
	N	Adv party HQ 6 Abn Div
	V	3 Para Bde Gp less 8 PARA
	K	8 PARA
0320	N	HQ 6 Abn Div, A/TK btys and engineers eqpt
0430	Merville Bty	Det 9 PARA
2100	N	HQ 6 Airlanding Bde 1 RUR 6 Abn Div Armd Recce Regt
2100	W	2 Ox Bucks LI less one coy A Coy 12 Devons +6 Airlanding Bde sp elms.

INTENDED ORDER OF LANDING
6th JUNE 1944

including the Commanding Officer, and all its warrant officers had been killed or wounded. On the enemy side, seventy-seven German soldiers died during the battle for the village.

During the following night of the 12th June, 152nd Infantry Brigade of 51st Highland Division crossed over the River Orne. At 0400 hours on the morning of the 13th June, the 5th Battalion The Cameron Highlanders attacked and captured Longueval. At 0915 hours, the Germans counter-attacked and recaptured it. At 1800 hours that evening, the 7th Battalion The Argyll & Sutherland Highlanders entered 6th Airborne Division's area and moved into Ranville. During the night of the 13th June, 51st Highland Division took over responsibility for the southern part of the bridgehead from 6th Airborne Division.

14th June to 16th August

The division's front now stretched nine thousand yards from a point in the Bois de Bavent due east of Escoville to the sea. To hold it, Major General Gale now had only nine weak battalions and 1st Special Service Brigade who had all been fighting ceaselessly for eight days and nights. The total strength of his force numbered less than six thousand men. As a result, and in order to be able to pull one brigade out at a time for rest and to provide him with some form of reserve, Gale was given 4th

Special Service Brigade, commanded by Brigadier B W Leicester RM, which comprised Nos. 41, 46, 47 and 48 Commandos Royal Marines.

3rd Parachute Brigade was the first to be withdrawn because it was particularly tired and had suffered particularly heavy casualties. 5th Parachute Brigade took over the southern part of the front, up to and including Le Mesnil, whilst 6th Airlanding Brigade was deployed along the rest of it to Breville. One of its battalions was located in depth behind. 1st and 4th Special Service Brigades covered from Breville to the coast.

On the 14th July, Major General Gale received a letter from the Commander-in-Chief, General Montgomery, notifying him of the award of fifty-five decorations for gallantry to members of the division: ten Distinguished Service Orders, twenty Military Crosses, three Distinguished Conduct Medals and twenty-two Military Medals. Two days later, the Commander-in-Chief visited the division and personally decorated the officers and men concerned.

On the 18th July, Operation Goodwood took place and 6th Airborne Division witnessed an armoured battle that commenced from its bridgehead. At 0745 hours, a large formation of armour, consisting of the 7th, 11th and Guards Armoured Divisions, advanced on a front of a thousand yards behind a rolling artillery barrage down a corridor that had already been subjected to three

INT – EST OF EN SIT

ASTRIDE THE ORNE

PLANNING WAS CARRIED OUT ON THIS INFO IN LATE APR / EARLY MAY 44

EN DEPLOYMENT AS AT 28 APR 44

INTELLIGENCE ESTIMATE OF ENEMY STRENGTH

Unit	Notes
716th Inf Div	Eight bns, incl two Russian each 1000 strong, 24 gun-how, 12 med how, one anti-tank sqn. Believed to be low category div of limited fighting value.
711th Inf Div	13,000 troops, 20 anti-tank gns, 60fd/med guns, 35 tanks. Important coastal bty at Merville. Fire support available from coastal btys at Le Havre. This division well situated to counter attack 6th Airborne.
352nd Inf Div	Little known but believed to be counter-attack formation. If deployed in counter-attack role could be operating in Caen area by H+8.
12 SS Pz Div (Hitler Jugend)	Believed to be well up to strength of 21,000. Unknown number of Panther tanks. Operational role assumed to be north of Lisieux or east of River Seine. Expected to be ready to operate SE of Caen by H+12 if ordered.
21 Pz Div	In late April situated further west than shown on map, moved into Caen in May on anti-invasion exercise on night 5/6 June 1944.

89

hours of concentrated bombing by the Allied air forces. From their positions, members of the division watched in awe as the tanks advanced and waves of bombers struck at targets further forward. The battle raged for two days, the three armoured divisions encountering increasingly stiff opposition, and finally came to an end on the afternoon of the 20th July when bad weather and heavy rain turned the ground into a quagmire. During these two days, the division came under some retaliatory fire from German mortars and artillery but this did not cause any severe casualties.

During this period the bridgehead was expanded and 49th Infantry Division, commanded by Major General Sir Evelyn Barker, moved up to take its place in between 6th Airborne Division and 51st Highland Division.

For the next two months, until the 16th August, 6th Airborne Division was employed in static defence. "Static" is perhaps a somewhat misleading word to describe the division's activities during that period because it was in fact far from being static as such. From the very start of this new phase of operations the division adopted a policy of aggressive patrolling, seeking out the enemy wherever it could and inflicting the maximum damage at every opportunity.

The Bois de Bavent, previously the hunting ground of 8th Parachute Battalion and now belonging to Lieutenant Colonel Geoffrey Pine Coffin's 7th Parachute Battalion, saw much of this type of action. The battalion was much assisted in its tasks by a local poacher, called Barriere, whose knowledge of the area was encyclopaedic. The battalion's intelligence officer, Lieutenant Bertie Mills, with Barriere's assistance, produced a large scale map of the battalion's area on which all information was plotted. To this was added all topographical information brought back by patrols.

The battalion's snipers also waged a continual war against the enemy and caused them to be on their guard at all times. Each day saw them return with yet more 'kills' to their credit.

In late June, Lieutenant-Colonel Pine Coffin decided to carry out an attack on a farm called 'Bob's Farm'. B Company, commanded by Major Bob Keene, was given the task.

The company moved up to the start line and had shaken out into assault formation when one of the platoon commanders, Lieutenant Poole, spotted a platoon of enemy infantry a short distance away which was obviously preparing to attack in the opposite direction. Without any more ado, B Company immediately went into the attack and charged through an orchard into the farm. As they pushed through it, Keene and his men came under heavy fire and were forced to withdraw back into the farm itself. The company suffered fifteen casualties, including two of its platoon commanders, Lieutenants Poole and Farr, who were both wounded. In addition, Company Sergeant Major Durbin had been killed; having already been wounded, he continued to man a Bren gun until fatally wounded. However, greater damage had been inflicted upon the enemy which had lost thirty men killed, a number wounded and nine taken prisoner by B Company.

Bob's Farm was also subsequently raided by seven men of the 22nd Independent Parachute Company. Tasked with capturing some prisoners, they were led on this mission by Lieutenant Bob de Latour who was one of the two surviving officers of the company. The original company commander, Major Francis Lennox-Boyd, had been killed during the drop and the company second in command, Captain Andrew Tait, had subsequently been killed during a raid into Breville soon after D-Day. Two other officers, Lieutenants Don Wells and Bob Midwood had subsequently been wounded. The two remaining officers were de Latour and Lieutenant John Vischer who was the company's Intelligence Officer.

The patrol was successful in making its way right inside the enemy positions and in silently taking some prisoners. Unfortunately the alarm was raised whilst the patrol was withdrawing and in the ensuing action Lieutenant de Latour was fatally wounded.

Lieutenant Colonel Pine Coffin decided to attack Bob's Farm once more. On the 10th July, B Company again attacked it in the early afternoon. However, it was not successful and had to withdraw with difficulty under heavy mortar and machine gun fire. Sergeant Lucas covered the company's withdrawal by engaging the enemy machine guns with his Bren gun. Support was, however, forthcoming from the whole of 53rd Airlanding Light Regiment which had fired five thousand rounds by the time the action ended.

135. Troops of 6th Airlanding Brigade hitch a trailer to their jeep before moving off from the LZ. (Photo: Imperial War Museum)

The Supporting Arms

The men of all the division's supporting arms units had rendered sterling service in providing support for the parachute and airlanding brigades since landing on D-Day. In many instances they had been required to fight as infantry whilst still carrying out their specialist roles. The fact that they were able to do both equally well paid tribute to the high standards of training and professionalism within the division.

53rd (Worcestershire Yeomanry) Airlanding Light Regiment RA

The gunners of 53rd Airlanding Light Regiment RA not only fired in support of their own division but also in support of 51st Highland Division during its attacks on Ste Honorine on the 23rd June and Colombelles on the 9th July.

One of the main problems that had plagued the 6th Airborne Division since D-Day was the German use of mortars. These had become a deadly menace and had caused a steady flow of casualties amongst all units. By the 21st June, it had been decided by the division's new CRA, Lieutenant Colonel 'Chubby' Faithfull, that the airlanding light regiment would also adopt a counter-mortar role. This involved the forward observers listening for the sound of an enemy mortar and taking a bearing on it. This information was then passed to the batteries who would locate the likely position of the mortar by use of cross-bearings. The Commanding Officer of 53rd Airlanding Light Regiment RA, Lieutenant Colonel Tony Teacher, later commented:

"So, instead of finding the usual friendly face of a No. 1 at his gun, I would, on my daily round, now discover the same face at an OP: some little upper-storeyed room in a mortared or shelled home in a village such as Breville. To find him I would pick my way slowly through the debris of the shattered house and mounting the staircase would come upon the No. 1, comfortingly staunch and cheerful, quietly listening. It is odd to recall how so often on those visits there appeared to be a complete stillness around: nothing stirred. Even nature seemed to be listening with a quiet intentness. Then would be heard the "pop" of the enemy mortar as it fired and with it, seemingly, a moment or two when we could relax as we recorded the sound and discussed it in low voices. And then I would leave with a quiet word to the signaller, sitting with his wireless set at the bottom of the stairs amongst the shambles of a ruined home."

One particular episode during counter-mortar operations concerned 210th Airlanding Light Battery RA's target "Revenge". The Royal Ulster Rifles' battalion headquarters was located in a house near to the crossroads at Le Mesnil. It was an unpleasant and dangerous location which was a constant target for enemy mortars. In order to alleviate matters for the Ulstermen, 210th Battery initiated target "Revenge" in which targets were selected so that the shells would pass directly overhead of the battalion headquarters. As soon as a mortar bomb landed in its area, all in the battalion headquarters location would shout "Revenge!" and the FOO's signaller would transmit "Revenge" to the guns. A salvo of six shells would then be fired in rapid response.

Much was known about the enemy's pattern of behaviour at night as a result of information obtained from prisoners. This led to the frequent use of harassing fire, based on the HF Target List. On most nights, as fire from the main gun positions might have betrayed their locations, some of the guns under their Nos. 1 would go forward to temporary positions from which they fired at intervals during the hours of darkness. This type of harassing fire proved to have a distinctly deteriorative effect on enemy morale.

During the period up to the 22nd July, the regiment provided FOOs for both parachute brigades and the two Special Service brigades. The Commanding Officer visited most of them daily and found the forward observers' knowledge of their local situations invaluable.

The regiment's gun positions also had their share of action. On occasions they were bombed and strafed by low-flying Messerschmitts sweeping down the Orne valley early in the morning or just before last light. In addition, they were shelled by enemy artillery on two occasions during this period.

6th Airborne Armoured Reconnaissance Regiment

Since its arrival in Normandy on the evening of D-Day and during the period of operations since, the 6th Airborne Armoured Reconnaissance Regiment had been almost constantly employed. Initially it had been deployed with 8th Parachute Battalion in the Bois de Bavent where it had set up a number of OPs watching the area bordered by Troarn, Caen, Ranville and Escoville. It had provided invaluable information for the divisional commander, acting as his eyes and ears in the forward areas. As well as using 'B' Squadron's Bren carriers and Dingo scout cars, the regiment deployed patrols mounted on bicycles deep into enemy-held areas. These obtained information on enemy dispositions, including vehicle parks and armour FUPs, which resulted in successful air strikes and bombardments by the cruiser HMS *Mauritius*.

Ten days after the landing the regiment was withdrawn into reserve. However, A Squadron was called back almost immediately and was employed with its Tetrarch light tanks dug-in in support of the battalions of 5th Parachute Brigade. During operations in early July, the regiment captured a self-propelled 20mm anti-aircraft gun which it proceeded to use with good effect when Troopers Davies and Walden claimed a Messerschmitt 109 and a Focke Wulfe 190, both unconfirmed kills.

When A Squadron was eventually withdrawn at the beginning of August, it was sent to a tank replacement unit where it exchanged its light tanks for twelve Cromwell Mk IV cruiser tanks. After a crash conversion course lasting a few days, it was again operational. On the squadron's return, the regiment was subsequently deployed south of Troarn.

Royal Engineers

The sappers of all the division's engineer units had been kept busy since their arrival in Normandy. Headquarters Royal Engineers had sent in a four-man advance party with 591st Parachute Squadron RE, consisting of the CRE himself, Lieutenant Colonel Frank Plowman, his Intelligence Officer and two sappers. Lieutenant Colonel Plowman landed in Herouvillette, some twelve hundred yards south of the drop zone but, after climbing over a series of garden walls in a bid to avoid enemy patrols and armoured vehicles, reached the squadron's RV location at 0230 hours.

The rest of Headquarters Royal Engineers travelled in two gliders. Of these only one, bringing in a sergeant physical training instructor, a lance-corporal and a draughtsman, arrived at 0330 hours together with divisional headquarters. The second glider, containing the Adjutant and three sappers, was missing and was reported to have been hit by flak. Subsequently, Lieutenant Colonel Plowman established his headquarters alongside the advanced divisional headquarters in Le Bas de Ranville at about 0600 hours. Lieutenant Lockey was borrowed from 591st Parachute Squadron RE to fill the combined posts of Adjutant and Intelligence Officer, although Captain Dixon, the second in command of 286th Field Park Company RE, arrived to take over as Adjutant three days later. However, on D-Day itself the CRE's staff at that point consisted only of himself, one officer and five other ranks. At 0600 hours all the division's sapper units, with the exception of 3rd Parachute Squadron RE, reverted to under command CRE.

3rd Parachute Squadron RE

Shortly after landing, the commander of 3rd Parachute Squadron RE, Major J. C. A. 'Tim' Roseveare, had discovered that he was on DZ 'N' instead of DZ 'K'. Within a few minutes he had met Lieutenant David Breeze and a section of No. 1 Troop who were joined shortly afterwards by other sappers (who had managed to collect some of the special thirty-pound explosive charges designed to demolish the bridges) and a team from one of the parachute field ambulances with a jeep and trailer.

Roseveare decided to press on towards Troarn, rather than look for 8th Parachute Battalion, and led his small force through German-occupied Herouvillette and Escoville without being spotted. Three miles from the Troarn bridge, he met a group from the battalion. Deciding to send his main party of sappers on foot to the bridge at Bures under the command of Lieutenant Juckes, Roseveare commandeered the medical team's jeep and trailer and, loading it with all the explosives and Lieutenant David Breeze's section of sappers, he drove at high speed for Troarn.

On the outskirts of the town Roseveare and his men ran into a barbed wire barrier, positioned across the road, which became tangled round the vehicle's front axle. After a few minutes spent cutting the wire free, the small group drove on to the edge of the town where the Germans were alerted by Lieutenant Breeze shooting a German soldier on a bicycle who blundered into the sappers. Roseveare drove through Troarn at breakneck speed, followed by heavy small arms fire. Whilst going downhill out of the town Sapper Peachey, who was sitting on the trailer with a Bren gun, was thrown off, injured and captured.

Arriving at the bridge, Roseveare and his sappers placed some of their charges across the road crossing the bridge and positioned the trailer containing the rest of the explosives in the centre of the bridge itself. Shortly afterwards, they detonated the charges and blew a fifteen-foot hole in the bridge roadway. Heading north along a track along the river, they abandoned the jeep and trailer when the track ended and set off on foot towards 3rd Parachute Brigade's headquarters at Le Mesnil.

Other elements of the squadron which landed in the Ranville area came into contact with enemy troops almost immediately on landing. There were many instances of sappers being initally cornered but managing to fight their way out to eventually rejoin the squadron.

Once the squadron had reformed at Le Mesnil where it had rejoined 3rd Parachute Brigade, it remained under the command of the brigade for a few days where it was employed in the infantry role. In addition, it laid minefields and carried out demolitions tasks. In one instance a section of the squadron, supported by a platoon from one of the battalions in the brigade, infiltrated behind enemy lines and blew two craters in the road leading out of Breville. As they withdrew, they heard the satisfying noise of an enemy half-track vehicle falling into the first crater.

Lieutenant John Shave was in command of a section of No. 2 Troop which, on the 9th June, was dug in with C Company of 9th Parachute Battalion. He takes up the story:
"During a lull in our first battle, I was ordered to take my section two miles down the Troarn road to be attached to 8th Parachute Battalion. At low strength, the battalion held the end of a salient spread from the Bois de Bures on the left, across the Troarn road and to the edge of the escarpment falling away to the right. We dug in on part of the battalion perimeter where our first task was to booby trap a wood in front of the platoon on our right. We spent the day of the 10th June laying trip wires connected to charges of plastic explosives in this wood.

On the following day, the 11th June, we lifted the mines which we had laid on D-Day in order to allow the 1st Battalion The Gordon Highlanders to pass through as the initial move by 51st Highland Division to extend the salient. During the night, along with a platoon of 8th Parachute Battalion, we patrolled through the Bois de Bures to crater the Bures-Bavent road which was the only route open to the Germans on our side of the River Dives.

In the depth of the woods we encountered sustained machine-gun fire and the platoon commander ordered a withdrawal. Angered by this incident, Lieutenant Colonel Alastair Pearson led us out in company strength on the following night, cleared up the enemy and held the road whilst my sappers and I cratered it over a culvert. During that day we had also removed the booby traps laid earlier as the platoon on our right was disturbed by straying cattle setting off the charges. We also suffered a serious casualty when Corporal Dick Powell was badly wounded by mortar fire and had to be evacuated. His loss was a great blow to us all and I promoted Sapper Hurst to be my second in command.

Patrols ordered for the night of the 13th included sapper reconnaissance of the River Dives to discover what the Germans were doing about crossings. Accompanied by Sapper Martin, I ventured through the woods to Bures. The railway bridge was as we had left it on the 6th June. Following the river, we disturbed some cows which alerted a German patrol. Leaving Martin with orders to return to the battalion if I ran into trouble, I swam the river near the road bridge. To avoid the steep reed-covered bank, I climbed up the broken steelwork of the bridge where I was greeted by indistinct shapes and a shout of "Hande hoch!" I ducked down and fed them the 36 Grenade that we all carried. In so doing, I fell back into the water and was able to escape. Whilst running back to the woods, I was fired upon by what later turned out to be the crew of a self-propelled gun laagered up on the road. We measured its track width on the following night when we repeated the patrol. On this occasion, with two others, I approached close enough to the Troarn bridge to be able to hear and see, in the moonlight, that it was being rebuilt with timber."

On the 10th June, the squadron was relieved of its infantry tasks and came under command of CRE at divisional headquarters.

136. Troops of 6th Airlanding Brigade digging in around Ranville.
(Photo: Imperial War Museum)

591st Parachute Squadron RE

No. 2 Troop of 591st Parachute Squadron RE had jumped in two sticks with 9th Parachute Battalion for the assault on the Merville Battery. One of them, under Captain Jackson, had been widely scattered in the drop. One by one they had been hunted down and captured by the enemy, but not without putting up a very stiff fight. The other stick, under Lieutenant Hinshelwood, had dropped between Varaville and Robehomme, also being widely scattered. They joined up with C Company of 1st Canadian Parachute Battalion and took part in the action at Varaville after which they withdrew to 3rd Parachute Brigade's positions at Le Mesnil. Six members of the troop, travelling in the gliders carrying 9th Parachute Battalion's assault group, suffered varying fortunes. One glider was forced to turn back soon after taking off, one was forced to crash-land half a mile from the battery after being hit by flak and the third crash-landed in the orchard just outside the battery's perimeter. In the event, 9th Parachute Battalion carried out the destruction of the battery without sapper support.

Nos. 1 and 3 Troops had dropped north of Ranville, none of their sticks landing on the drop zone but within reasonable distance of it. They had been met by small arms fire from several directions but some of them succeeded in reaching their RV south of the DZ. Here they met A Company of 13th Parachute Battalion which had been tasked with helping them to clear the landing zone on which divisional headquarters and other elements of the division would be landing at 0330 hours. Under the command of Captain Fergie Semple they worked frantically, clearing the anti-glider defences and any other obstructions. By 0215 hours they had cleared two strips for the Horsas and by 0330 hours they had completed two for the Hamilcars. At 0355 hours the first gliders landed. In the event, few of the glider pilots used the cleared strips but touched down from a variety of directions, swerving past each other and crashing through poles on the uncleared parts of the landing zone. Casualties to men and equipment were surprisingly light.

By 0500 hours on D-Day, the squadron had taken up positions in Bas de Ranville. Its strength was very weak, most of its number still missing. No word had been received of the squadron commander, Major Andy Wood, whose complete stick was missing. The second in command, Captain Davidson, and several members of Nos. 1 and 3 Troops were also missing after having been dropped wide of the drop zone. Moreover, one of the section commanders, Lieutenant Thomas, and several sappers had been wounded as they landed.

Later that day, Captain Davidson appeared with two sappers. It transpired that they had landed in the Amfreville area and, after meeting up with two members of one of the parachute battalions, had been attacked by a section of enemy infantry whilst trying to establish their whereabouts. They had been cornered for an hour, during which one of the infantrymen had been killed and the other wounded, before being forced to surrender because of the serious condition of the wounded man. After being taken into Amfreville, they were forced to lie flat on their faces in the village square whilst a battle between enemy troops and commandos of 1st Special Service Brigade raged around them. Eventually, after the commandos had taken the village, they were released.

During the rest of D-Day, Nos. 1 and 3 Troops completed their allocated tasks by laying an anti-personnel minefield amongst the forward defences around Ranville. That night it suffered two more casualties when two sappers were wounded whilst checking the minefield.

Major Andy Wood, meanwhile, had been taken prisoner along with Lieutenant Bartlett and two sappers. Their aircraft had been hit by flak shortly after crossing the coast. As it rapidly lost height, the leading members of the stick jumped. Of these only Wood, Bartlett and the two sappers survived, despite the fact that their parachutes had only just deployed. The rest of the stick were still in the aircraft as it caught fire and flames spread down the fuselage. One man jumped to his death with his parachute on

fire whilst others desperately struggled to rid themselves of the explosive charges that each of them carried. When the aircraft crashed, Lieutenant Shinner and three sappers managed to struggle free from the blazing wreckage whilst behind them the remaining nine wounded sappers lay trapped and screaming. As Shinner, who had a shattered arm, desperately fought to free his men, enemy troops arrived and machine-gunned the wreckage until the screams ceased.

The period immediately after D-Day saw the squadron fighting as infantry and carrying out many sapper tasks such as laying minefields as part of the defence of the Ranville area, fortifying the divisional headquarters, constructing shell-proof command posts for the brigade headquarters and digging in the tanks of 6th Airborne Armoured Reconnaissance Regiment. During this time the squadron was reinforced by the arrival of No. 2 Troop who returned from their adventures in Varaville and Le Mesnil. However, on the 17th June, Lieutenant Wharton was killed and Lieutenant Little was seriously wounded whilst trying to salvage equipment from the middle of an enemy minefield near Ouistreham, thus decreasing the squadron's already heavily depleted officer strength.

On the 21st June, No. 3 Troop moved to the Le Mesnil area in support of 5th Parachute Brigade and almost immediately found themselves under mortar fire. Their tasks in this area consisted of laying small anti-personnel minefields and occasionally disposing of bombs. The troop was subsequently relieved by No. 1 Troop under the command of Captain Harboard who was shortly afterwards wounded in the chest by a shell splinter. Two days later, Lance Sergeant Fosters was wounded by a sniper whilst reconnoitring a position for a machine gun to deal with the sniper concerned. These incidents were typical of what proved to be a period of constant danger and acute discomfort in this forward area.

249th Field Company RE

A detachment of thirty men of No. 2 Platoon of 249th Field Company RE, commanded by Captain Jock Neilson with Lieutenant Bence as his second in command, had landed with the *coup de main* force. They had been tasked with checking the two bridges for explosives and disconnecting any wiring that they found. The sappers were divided equally between the six gliders of the *coup de main* force, each group of five having been carefully briefed as to the searching of the bridges. They were equipped for this task with scaling ladders, hand axes, small crowbars and four small inflatable assault boats.

Within a few minutes of landing, as the assault went in on the canal bridge, the sappers were searching for possible demolition charges but found none. On receiving a message that only one glider had landed by the River Orne bridge, Captain Neilson led a group of sappers to the bridge and searched it. He had just declared it clear of demolition charges when Lieutenant Bence and his sappers arrived, their glider having landed five hundred yards away. Captain Neilson and his detachment then took up defensive positions and played their part in repelling enemy counter-attacks during the rest of D-Day and the following day.

The rest of the platoon landed by glider at 0325 hours on D-Day, bringing with it rafting equipment for the 6-pounder anti-tank guns of 4th Airlanding Anti-Tank Battery RA which landed at the same time. This equipment was stockpiled on the east bank of the River Orne for use in the event of the bridges being subsequently destroyed. The platoon then joined Captain Neilson and his detachment by the bridges where they assisted in their defence.

The remainder of the company landed with the division's seaborne element at 0915 hours on D-Day. However, the enemy was still in possession of the assembly area to which the company had been directed. As a result, the company had to clear and capture the area, taking some prisoners in the process. By the time it had done so, and its vehicles had eventually landed on the following afternoon, it was not until about 1200 hours on D+2 that the company finally reached 6th Airborne Division's assembly area. The following day found the company setting up water points in Ranville and Le Bas de Ranville.

286th Field Park Company RE

A detachment of 286th Field Park Company RE landed by glider at 0335 hours on D-Day. It was equipped with two airborne bulldozers and its task was to assist in the clearing of the LZ for the landing of 6th Airlanding Brigade and divisional troops that evening at 2100 hours. After initial problems in unloading, the two machines were carrying out their allotted tasks by 0445 hours. By the end of eight hours, they had cleared all glider debris and had filled in all holes. During this time, the LZ was under occasional mortar and shell fire, as well as sporadic sniping.

At 1200 hours on D-Day a single glider landed, bringing in a fitter and carpenter from the company's workshops platoon, together with a jeep and trailer containing a hundred Mk V anti-tank mines. At 1900 hours on D+2, the stores detachment arrived in the division's assembly area with 249th Field Company RE.

6th Airborne Divisional Signals

Accompanying the division's two parachute brigades were the leading elements of 6th Airborne Divisional Signals, including Lieutenant Colonel 'Pigmy' Smallman-Tew and Captain Tony Windrum, the Adjutant. With them were men of No. 1 Company and the two signals sections which supported the two brigade headquarters. These were commanded by Captains John Wilkes and Guy Radmore respectively.

5th Parachute Brigade Signal Section landed at 0100 hours, intact but scattered from a point half a mile east of the Pont Tournant down to Ranville itself. However, it was able to establish radio communications quickly. By 0330 hours, all but ten of its number had made their way to brigade headquarters, some of them having experienced some encounters with the enemy on their way. Unfortunately the second in command of the section, Lieutenant Gordon Royle, was killed soon after landing. He had jumped from the same Albemarle as Brigadier Nigel Poett whom he was accompanying as a radio operator. Separated from the brigadier on landing, he encountered a group of enemy troops shortly afterwards whilst on his way to the RV. He engaged them single-handed but was killed in the process. The gliderborne element of the section also suffered mishap when one of its four gliders failed to appear.

3rd Parachute Brigade Signal Section had also been scattered during the drop and its commander, Captain John Wilkes, had landed in the marshes of the River Dives and had been taken prisoner. In addition, about eighty per cent of the section's equipment had been lost and consequently communications could not be established immediately. However, the section was later rallied and reorganised by Major 'Lucky' Fenton, commander of No. 1 Company, who had landed with the advance divisional headquarters and whose glider had crash-landed in a minefield. It was he who supervised the establishment of communications at about 1235 hours. Subsequently, the second in command of the section, Lieutenant D. W. A. Smith, arrived to take over after having spent ten hours extricating himself from the marshes, canals and woods of the Dives valley. A large number of the section had been cut off after landing and had to go into hiding, with the aid of members of the French Resistance, until they were able to exfiltrate from behind the enemy lines and rejoin the section.

The advance party of two sticks of No. 1 Company, which provided the infrastructure for divisional headquarters, had been dropped eight miles apart but had landed safely and had sustained only a few casualties. One of these was Regimental Sergeant Major Carr who was injured when he struck one of the anti-glider poles on the drop zone. Badly injured, he lay unseen in the standing corn on the DZ until the next day. Whilst there, he gave assistance to an NCO and signaller who were also lying injured and unable to move.

The main gliderborne element of the unit landed with Major General Gale and his advance divisional headquarters at 0335

hours. By 0700 hours most of this group had reached the headquarters location and radio communications were rapidly established. The rear link to England was opened within fifteen minutes and the artillery signal section established communications with 3rd Division's artillery, only to find that it was still at sea on board the invasion fleet.

6th Airlanding Brigade Signal Section arrived safely with the brigade at 2100 hours that evening. The following evening, on the 7th June, the unit's seaborne element arrived with the heavy vehicles and equipment which by then were urgently needed. This included the line party whose glider had been forced to ditch in the Channel. Fortunately they had been picked up by a vessel from the invasion fleet.

At both divisional and brigade levels, the signals sections dug themselves in quickly. Due to the shell and mortar fire which continued daily from D+1, all radios had to be sited underground and all trenches and command posts had to be roofed with sufficient overhead protection. Despite such precautions, three officers and twenty men were killed at the unit's headquarters in the first two weeks. Meanwhile, salvage of lost equipment remained an important task and this was carried out whenever possible. In addition, the unit provided some one hundred and fifty men to assist in the protection of the divisional headquarters. During the period following D-Day, many of the seventy-two missing members of the unit made their way back through enemy lines.

The work of the linesmen and dispatch riders was particularly demanding and dangerous. Whatever the weather or hour, they were to be found repairing broken field telephone lines and carrying signals in areas which were under almost continuous mortar and shell fire. It was under such circumstances that one member of 5th Parachute Brigade Signal Section, Corporal Waters, earned his subsequent award of the Military Medal for laying and maintaining his line across the canal and river bridges under fire. His section commander, Captain Guy Radmore, tells what happened:

'At about 1300 hours on D-Day, we heard the sound of Lord Lovat's piper. In the meantime, my party had started to lay the line from Brigade Headquarters across the two bridges. They had all three been wounded from machine gun fire from the Chateau de Benouville to the south-west of the canal bridge. Corporal Tom Waters, who with his wireless detachment was in reserve, on his own initiative threw three smoke grenades and got covering fire from one of our Bren guns. He then proceeded to rescue the wounded before, under intense enemy fire, taking the line across the bridges to 7th Parachute Battalion which was resisting powerful counter-attacks in Le Port. He then spent all day maintaining it.''

On the 25th June, Headquarters 6th Airborne Division moved its location to the Ecarde escarpment. The Signal Security Section was employed very successfully on interception of enemy radio communications. The enemy countered by resorting to jamming and deception, the latter ploy requiring operators to be particularly alert. Enemy stations frequently requested information and on one occasion had almost been successful in impersonating one of the commanding officers in the division. Attempts were made to intercept line circuits in the division's area and ambushes of enemy intercept parties had to be carried out. Captain Guy Radmore again:

''Corporal Waters, who had now taken over the lines, said he thought that the Germans were cutting them by hand. Subsequently he went out and lay up for a while. Some time later he came back wearing a pair of jackboots and carrying a German helmet. I met him on the road looking very pleased with himself. He had seen a German creep out of a ditch with a pair of wire cutters and had shot him.''

On the 22nd July tragedy struck when the Commanding Officer, Lieutenant Colonel Smallman-Tew, was killed whilst taking a newly joined officer, Lieutenant Much, to his post at 3rd Parachute Brigade Signal Section. His jeep suffered a direct hit from a shell near Escoville. Shortly afterwards, Lieutenant Colonel E. S. Cole arrived from England to take over command of the unit.

Royal Army Medical Corps

224th Parachute Field Ambulance

Most of 224th Parachute Field Ambulance, which dropped with 3rd Parachute Brigade, was dropped in or around Varaville. Two men landed on the drop zone but at least two sticks landed eight miles away.

The brigade commander's plan had called for the Main Dressing Station (MDS) to be located at Le Mesnil, the Commanding Officer's party and the MDS main party being dropped with brigade headquarters. In the event, the Commanding Officer, Lieutenant Colonel D. H. Thompson, landed a considerable distance from the DZ; after three weeks of attempting to get back through enemy lines, he was eventually captured and taken prisoner.

One of those who landed several miles from the DZ was Major Alastair Young, the second in command. Shortly after landing, he met a small party from 9th Parachute Battalion with whom he joined up. After travelling a short distance, they came upon a party from the field ambulance. At about 0300 hours, Young and his men decided to separate from the 9th Parachute Battalion group and headed north, picking up five more men from their own unit. After reaching the drop zone where they treated some casualties, they arrived at 1st Canadian Parachute Battalion's RV where they met Lieutenant G. C. A. Philo RASC and twelve more men of the field ambulance.

In the early hours of the morning, Young and his men reached Le Mesnil where they were joined at 1100 hours by Lieutenant D. J. C. Cunningham and the Reverend A. L. Beckingham. Here they opened up the MDS at midday. Shortly afterwards, one of the unit's dental surgeons and anaesthetists, Captain Chaundy, and three members of the unit arrived. However, two thirds of the field ambulance were still unaccounted for and there was no news of the section attached to 9th Parachute Battalion for the assault on the Merville Battery.

Meanwhile, Regimental Sergeant Major Green and five other members of the unit had landed south-east of Varaville. Initially they could not establish their own position and struggled through swamps and ditches towards the sound of fighting for three hours before reaching the scene of action at just after 0400 hours. Here they waited until dawn when the RSM recognised the silhouette of Varaville Church from the briefings prior to the operation. On going forward on his own to reconnoitre the area, RSM Green came to a chateau where he met Captain Nelson, Lieutenant (QM) Horder and fourteen other members of the unit who had set up an Advanced Dressing Station (ADS). He returned to his own party, meeting *en route* Major Darling who was also from the field ambulance. After directing him to the chateau, the RSM returned to his own group and led them towards the chateau.

However, when RSM Green and his group arrived at the chateau, they found the ADS abandoned. They did not know that a German patrol had appeared on the scene and had taken Major Darling and the ADS party prisoner. When the RSM and his group arrived, there were sixteen wounded who were being cared for by Private Harris who had been absent on an errand when the German patrol had appeared. Leaving his group of five with Harris, the RSM moved on to Le Mesnil where he reported to the MDS that evening.

Meanwhile, Lieutenant R. Marquis's No. 2 Section, which had been allocated to 8th Parachute Battalion, had been dropped a considerable distance from the drop zone. Marquis and his men had found themselves near Dozule and he had decided that they would head straight for Le Mesnil as they would not be able to reach the battalion before it had completed its two primary tasks of blowing the bridges at Bures and Troarn. At 0400 hours, they reached Robehomme where they met a force of one hundred and fifty men of B Company of 1st Canadian Parachute Battalion, commanded by Captain Peter Griffin, plus some men from 8th and 9th Parachute Battalions, together with some engineers who had been cut off from the division. On the evening of 7th June, Lieutenant Bob Mitchell of 1st Canadian Parachute Battalion

made his way through the enemy lines with orders for the force to make its way to Le Mesnil. At 2330 hours Captain Griffin's force moved out and, after a couple of skirmishes with the enemy, reached Le Mesnil at 0330 hours.

No. 3 Section, commanded by Captain I. F. B. Johnson and allocated to 9th Parachute Battalion, landed well away from the drop zone in the marshes east of the River Dives and north-east of Robehomme. By 0230 hours, Johnson had managed to assemble his ten men and some members of the battalion in a wood. In the absence of any other officers, he assumed command. Realising that it would be impossible to reach the battalion which would by then be fully committed to its task of destroying the Merville Battery, he decided to take his men to Le Plein, which was 9th Parachute Battalion's secondary objective. Moving across country he made his way via Robehomme where he encountered B Company of 1st Canadian Parachute Battalion to whom he handed over the infantrymen in his group. Here he set up an ADS where he was later joined by Lieutenant Marquis and No. 2 Section.

225th Parachute Field Ambulance

At 0120 hours on D-Day, the men of 225th Parachute Ambulance jumped from their aircraft. By 0230 hours most of its personnel had reached the unit's RV despite being under mortar fire. Following 12th Parachute Battalion, Lieutenant Colonel Bruce Harvey and his men moved off to Le Bas de Ranville. By 0400 hours the MDS had been set up in the chateau and at 0430 hours the first casualties began to arrive.

At dawn, the Commanding Officer went off to find No. 3 Section, commanded by Captain D. J. Tibbs. He found it treating casualties in the church at Ranville where a Regimental Aid Post (RAP) had been set up. Despite the fact that they were constantly under fire, and regardless of the six casualties caused amongst their own number, Tibbs and his men continued searching for and treating casualties.

The situation was similar at the ADS, in a large ditch near the Caen Canal bridge, where Captain Jacobs was treating casualties under the fire of enemy snipers. There were some fifteen wounded and several dead when Lieutenant Colonel Harvey arrived.

Elsewhere, No. 2 Section under Captain Wagstaffe had set up an ADS alongside A Company of 7th Parachute Battalion at Benouville, whilst Captain D. R. Urquhart had established his ADS near the bridges and was looking after the casualties from D Company of the 2nd Battalion The Oxfordshire & Buckinghamshire Light Infantry and the other companies of 7th Parachute Battalion.

137. Lance Corporal L. Barnett *(left)* and Lance Corporal A. Burton *(right)* of 6th Airborne Division Provost Company dug in at a crossroads. (Photo: Imperial War Museum)

The entire field ambulance was under constant mortar fire and sniping throughout D-Day. Its field surgical teams worked ceaselessly due to the number of casualties. However, because of the situation, it was not possible for many of the wounded to be evacuated to the MDS but by 2100 hours contact had been established with 8th Field Ambulance of 3rd Infantry Division and the evacuation of casualties to the Field Dressing Station on the invasion beaches began that night. The bridge on the evacuation route came under heavy mortar fire, however, and so 8th Field Ambulance set up a Casualty Clearing Post (CCP) at a nearby farm and the evacuation continued.

Throughout the night and the following day, the 7th June, the fighting continued to be fierce with the MDS under fire all day. By 1700 hours it had treated a total of three hundred and eighty casualties and the wounded were still arriving.

195th Parachute Field Ambulance

195th Airlanding Field Ambulance arrived in ten Horsa gliders in the late evening of D-Day, along with the rest of 6th Airlanding Brigade. The Commanding Officer, Lieutenant Colonel Bill Anderson, and No. 3 Section landed on LZ 'N' and No. 4 Section and the MDS on LZ 'W'. By 2330 hours, the MDS was ready to move off after being met by Captain West who had parachuted in with 225th Parachute Field Ambulance the previous night. He guided the MDS party to Le Bas de Ranville where it was to be based for the night. Meanwhile, No. 3 Section had departed for Longueval with the 1st Battalion The Royal Ulster Rifles and No. 4 Section had moved off with the 2nd Battalion The Oxfordshire & Buckinghamshire Light Infantry for Herouvillette.

The following morning, by 1100 hours, the MDS was established and operational in Le Mariquet. It was located in a large house which had been used previously by the enemy as a regimental headquarters. By midnight on the 7th June, it had received a total of one hundred and fifty-four casualties and had carried out twenty-three surgical operations.

On the following day conditions started to become very difficult. Evacuation of the wounded had taken place in the morning, commencing at 0700 hours. That evening the MDS itself came under direct attack from enemy mortars and received a direct hit which resulted in three men being killed. Conditions became even more difficult and the operating theatre had to be moved into the building's basement. The total number of casualties admitted that day was one hundred and two, with twenty-eight operations being performed. On the following day, the 9th June, the MDS received a direct hit. Despite this, it handled one hundred and fifty-six casualties and carried out eleven operations.

Despite the difficulties caused by being constantly under fire, all three field ambulances managed to operate their Main Dressing Stations. On a number of occasions, the MDS were in very close proximity to the enemy who were encountered at close range on a number of occasions by medical orderlies evacuating casualties. By the 19th June, 224th Parachute Field Ambulance had treated eight hundred and twenty-two casualties and performed one hundred and twelve operations, whilst by the end of the month 195th Airlanding Field Ambulance had admitted one thousand six hundred and eighty-seven cases and had carried out one hundred and twenty-seven operations.

The period until the middle of July saw 224th Parachute Field Ambulance relocated at Ecarde, although still providing medical support to 3rd Parachute Brigade. 225th Parachute Field Ambulance was moved to a new location in a quarry in the forward area. From here it would receive casualties resulting from attacks carried out by 5th Parachute and 6th Airlanding Brigades, as well as from patrol activity throughout the bridgehead. 195th Airlanding Field Ambulance's MDS, meanwhile, remained until the beginning of August at Le Mariquet.

Royal Army Service Corps

The other supporting arms units within the division played their part to the full from the moment they arrived in Normandy. 716th Light Composite Company RASC had a supply dump operating by 0600 hours on D-Day, from which units were able to draw ammunition, mines, defence stores and medical supplies, having recovered approximately sixty per cent of the containers dropped. Once the link-up with 3rd Infantry Division had been achieved, 6th Airborne Division RASC provided a smooth flow of supplies forward to the three brigades and divisional units. The only problem encountered was that of ammunition for the 75mm pack howitzers of 53rd Airlanding Light Regiment RA. Consumption of ammunition by the eight guns of 211th Airlanding Light Battery RA ranged from 1,500 rounds on 7th June to 2,500 rounds on the 9th June. Anxiety was caused by the guns using every round that could be supplied, this problem being compounded by the fact that 6th Airborne Division was the only formation in the British sector which used the 75mm pack howitzer.

Royal Army Ordnance Corps & Royal Electrical & Mechanical Engineers

6th Airborne Division Ordnance Field Pack RAOC deployed a detachment which operated in close proximity to the divisional maintenance area, providing ordnance support in the shape of spares for vehicles and weapons. The Advanced Workshops Detachment of 6th Airborne Division Workshop REME carried out its work of repairing the division's vehicles and weapons, as did the REME light aid detachments attached to the three brigades and divisional units.

Corps of Military Police

6th Airborne Division Provost Company performed its tasks despite the fact that it had suffered a number of casualties, resulting in its members being heavily overworked. The company's problems were also compounded by its lack of transport.

Glider Pilot Regiment

No account of the role played by those supporting the brigades of 6th Airborne Division would be complete without coverage of the glider pilots. Theirs was a particularly demanding dual role: that of flying in men, weapons and equipment, frequently under fire, and of subsequently playing their part in operations after landing.

On D-Day, the gliderborne elements of 6th Airborne Division were flown in by squadrons of Nos. 1 and 2 Wings of the Glider Pilot Regiment.

Those gliders bringing in stores and equipment, shortly before the arrival of the parachute brigades, had landed on the main dropping and landing zones in bad conditions made worse by a pall of smoke and dust caused by the heavy bombing carried out by the RAF beforehand. Half of those tasked with landing north of Petiville managed to do so. Only one third of those aircraft that should have landed between Touffreville and Cuverville were successful, the rest landing on another LZ. A third group of seventy-two gliders (sixty-eight Horsas and four Hamilcars) led by Lieutenant Colonel Iain Murray DSO, Commanding Officer of No. 1 Wing, was due to land between Ranville and Amfreville. Of these, forty-seven Horsas and two Hamilcars were successful in landing successfully. Of the rest, five had to turn back and land in England whilst three were forced to ditch in the sea and fifteen were lost.

Out of the two hundred and fifty-eight gliders which took off from England carrying 6th Airlanding Brigade on the evening of D-Day, only ten failed to reach the landing zones in Normandy. On their arrival, only one Horsa failed to land safely after being hit by flak in mid-air. Two Hamilcars, carrying light tanks of the 6th Airborne Armoured Reconnaissance Regiment, collided on landing. These were the only casualties amongst a very large number of aircraft.

Once they were on the ground, the glider pilots were formed into a unit designated 'Force John'. By the evening of D-Day, a total of ninety-three had assembled and were dug in, defending the landing zone from the south-west.

The philosophy of glider pilot training, as laid down by the Commander Glider Pilots, Colonel George Chatterton, was based on the concept of the "total soldier". This required the glider pilot to master a very wide range of skills and to be capable of performing a variety of roles. The success and value of this training is well illustrated by the performance of one glider pilot during an action involving enemy armour that took place on the edge of the landing zone. A member of "Force John", Captain B. Murdoch, was acting as a loader for a 6-pounder anti-tank gun crew when the layer was killed. Murdoch immediately took over and he and the gun crew succeeded in destroying four out of the five tanks attacking them.

A further illustration is an account which concerns the crew and passengers of one of the fifteen Horsas which failed to appear between Ranville and Amfreville. Piloted by Major J. F. Lyne, this glider was hit by flak and its tow-rope broken as it crossed the French coast. It was in cloud at the time and began to descend. As it came out of the cloud, the Horsa was hit by flak again, damage being caused to the jeep that it was carrying but with none of the personnel on board being injured. Continuing his descent, Major Lyne searched for a landing place in the darkness until, when he was at a very low height, he spotted an orchard and successfully crash-landed his Horsa into it. He suffered a broken foot whilst his second pilot received cuts on his face.

Without any idea of their whereabouts, Lyne and his second pilot, together with their five passengers, moved off but shortly afterwards spotted some enemy troops and were forced to hide. They lay up in a field until day, after which they met a farmer who gave them directions to the River Dives. After swimming the river, they encountered a platoon of B Company of 1st Canadian Parachute Battalion, together with a small force of members of 8th and 9th Parachute Battalions and some engineers,

near Robehomme which was subsequently surrounded by enemy troops. After three days, however, this small force succeeded in making its way through the enemy positions to Ranville.

Forty-eight hours later, Lyne and his small group made their way into the Bois de Bavent. By now they were all exhausted by the strain of fighting their way through swamps, swimming streams, struggling through thick and tangled undergrowth and hiding in ditches. Finally they reached a road but enemy troops appeared and Lyne and his men immediately engaged them, wiping out with grenades two trucks full of infantry and a car carrying four officers.

After another engagement, Lyne and his men finally reached the landing zone. They were all exhausted, having marched a distance of forty-five miles from the spot where their glider had crash-landed.

Others had similar experiences, making their way back to the landing zones through enemy-held territory. Glider pilots fought in a number of capacities: as infantry, mortarmen, anti-tank gunners, signallers, motorcyclists or drivers. It was Major Billy Griffiths DFC, a well known Test cricketer before the war and second in command of No. 1 Wing, who set up the defence of Major General Gale's advance divisional headquarters. He and his pilots were soon in action against enemy patrols and snipers whilst equipment and vehicles were being unloaded.

On D+2, the 8th June, orders came through for the withdrawal of all glider pilots back to England. Under the command of Lieutenant Colonel Iain Murray, they made their way back to the invasion beach-head from where they were taken across the channel by the Royal Navy. Of the seven hundred and eight glider pilots who had flown three hundred and fifty-four gliders into Normandy two days earlier, six hundred and fifty-two returned. Relatively speaking, their casualties had been light: two officers and thirty-two senior NCOs killed; one officer and twenty-three senior NCOs wounded; and one officer and twenty-one senior NCOs taken prisoner.

138. Stirling bombers drop supplies on DZ 'N' on the 7th June. (Photo: Imperial War Museum)

The Advance To The Seine

Operation "PADDLE"

On the 7th August, Major General Gale received orders from the Commander 1st Corps, Lieutenant General Sir John Crocker, to prepare for a withdrawal by the Germans and to plan for a follow-up.

One problem facing Gale, however, was the woeful lack of transport in his division which would make any rapid pursuit of the enemy somewhat difficult. Moreover, the division's own artillery was an odd assortment consisting of its own airlanding light regiment, two field regiments and a heavy anti-aircraft regiment being used in the ground role as field artillery. These units were augmented by a battery of 25-pounders from the Belgian Brigade under Colonel Pirron which, together with the Princess Irene of The Netherlands Brigade, was now under command of the division. The division was also short of bridging equipment, a vital component in any pursuit operation.

However, General Gale was determined that the division should overcome any such difficulties. He was well aware that two months of static defensive operations had resulted in an abundance of pent-up energy amongst his troops and he was determined to exploit it to the full.

The overall operational plan was for 1st Canadian Army to break out of the bridgehead, move south-east from Caen towards Falaise and then turn eastwards towards the River Seine as the German forces withdrew. The main axis of 1st Corps' advance would be through Lisieux which was some fifteen miles from the coast. In order to facilitate the Canadians' advance, pressure on the enemy's right flank would have to be constantly maintained. It would be 6th Airborne Division's task to exert and maintain such pressure. To carry out this task, the division still had 1st and 4th Special Service Brigades under command, as well as the Belgian and Dutch brigades.

The division's final objective was the mouth of the River Seine. In order to reach it, a number of river crossings would have to be carried out. Due to the fact that these would have to be effected near estuaries, the rivers would obviously be wider, deeper and often tidal. The three main rivers to be crossed were the Dives, the Touques and the Risle. The Dives lay in a broad and marshy valley, its strength as an obstacle increased by the derelict Dives Canal running alongside it. In the middle of the valley was a large island with the river on its western side and to its east the Dives Canal and large areas of swamps. To the east of the Dives valley was a line of hills which dominated it. The Touques and the Risle lay in narrower valleys with marshy water meadows.

There were two routes which led to the Seine. The first went from Troarn through Dozule, Pont Leveque, and Beuzeville to Pont Audemer; the distance by road measured approximately forty-five miles. The second ran along the coast through Cabourg, Trouville and Honfleur. The terrain along both routes was similar: undulating ground with hills covered in woods and scrub, between which were pastures divided by very thick hedges.

Major General Gale decided to opt for the inland route through

139. Tea up! (Photo: Imperial War Museum.)

Troarn and Pont Audemer, despite the fact that this would mean crossing an eight thousand yard wide valley of marshes and streams as well as the double obstacle of the River Dives and the Dives Canal. His reason for choosing this route was influenced by the division's shortage of sappers and bridging equipment which meant that only one route could be maintained. The route via Troarn and Pont Audemer would pose less bridging problems, being further away from the estuaries and the sea, and would also keep his division's axis closer to that of 49th Infantry Division on his right.

In essence, Gale's plan was for the main part of the division to push forward on its main route via Troarn and Pont Audemer whilst 6th Airlanding Brigade, with the Belgian and Dutch brigades under command, would mop up enemy positions along the coastal areas. 3rd Parachute Brigade would move to Bures, crossing the river there and moving on to the island in the middle of the Dives Valley. 5th Parachute Brigade would then follow on to the island, whilst 4th Special Service Brigade would remain at Troarn and hold the area to the south of the town, both brigades being prepared to exploit any gains made by 3rd Parachute Brigade and to open up the main axis of advance. Meanwhile, 1st Special Service Brigade would take Bavent and Robehomme, preparing to cross the river at Robehomme if able to do so. 6th Airlanding Brigade, with the Belgian and Dutch brigades, would take the coastal area between Franceville Plage and Cabourg and was to cross over at Cabourg if possible.

It was Gale's intention that the momentum of the advance would be such that the enemy would have little or no time to prepare defensive positions east of the River Dives.

17th — 26th August

During the night of the 17th August the enemy, as had been ex-pected, began to withdraw under observation from the division's patrols. At 0300 hours on the 18th August, 3rd Parachute Brigade commenced its advance and by 0600 hours the whole division was on the move. By 0700 hours, 8th and 9th Parachute Battalions had taken Bures without meeting any opposition and at 0800 hours 1st Canadian Parachute Battalion commenced moving through the Bois de Bavent where they encountered mines and booby traps left behind by the enemy. Meanwhile, 4th Special Service Brigade had advanced towards Troarn and St Pair, whilst 1st Special Service Brigade moved towards Bavent and Robehomme.

6th Airlanding Brigade

6th Airlanding Brigade, now commanded by Brigadier Edward Flavell who had replaced Brigadier Kindersley after the latter had been evacuated after being severely wounded at Breville, commenced its advance on two roads. Initially on the left was the 12th Battalion The Devonshire Regiment which was supported by 210th Airlanding Light Battery of 53rd Airlanding Light Regiment and which was moving along the Breville-Merville road. On the right was the 2nd Battalion The Oxfordshire & Buckinghamshire Light Infantry which was advancing along the Le Mesnil-Varaville road with 212th Airlanding Light Battery in support. The 1st Battalion The Royal Ulster Rifles were moving up in reserve.

12th Battalion The Devonshire Regiment

At 0700 hours on the 17th August B Company, commanded by Major W. F. Barrow, moved through D Company at the start of the first bound on the axis of the advance towards Cabourg. By 0925 hours, after having cleared a roadblock and some mines,

140. A knocked-out enemy self-propelled gun. (Photo: Imperial War Museum)

141. The northern edge of Breville seen from an enemy anti-tank gun position which overlooked 12th Parachute Battalion's line of attack.
(Photo: Airborne Forces Museum)

B Company had reached a point some five hundred yards short of the end of the first bound when it came under heavy fire from light machine guns and mortars from an enemy delaying position astride the road north of the Longuemare crossroads. During this action Major Barrow was wounded, although he remained with the company until evacuated to 195th Airlanding Field Ambulance's MDS later in the day. The enemy resistance was eventually overcome by some very accurate shooting by 210th Airlandding Light Battery RA together with support from the battalion's mortars and a troop of Belgian armoured cars.

The 1st Battalion The Royal Ulster Rifles moved through to take over as leading battalion in the brigade whilst the Devons withdrew into brigade reserve and reoccupied their previous positions in the Breville area. Here the battalion remained until the afternoon of the 20th August when it moved to a location at Troarn. At 0200 hours the following morning, the 21st August, it moved by vehicle and then on foot to a concentration area with the 2nd Battalion The Oxfordshire & Buckinghamshire Light Infantry following behind. The weather was very bad and there was no moon, this resulting in difficult conditions. By 0630 hours, however, the Devons had deployed in the concentration area and the Oxfordshire & Buckinghamshire Light Infantry arrived shortly afterwards.

At 1000 hours, the battalion crossed the start line of the advance with C Company in the lead. No opposition was encountered until the early afternoon when D Company, which was now leading the battalion, came under machine-gun and mortar fire. There then ensued some very heavy fighting in and around the hedgerows in A Company's area and some casualties were suffered. Both companies were too close together for mortar or artillery support to be used and there was insufficient time before dusk for an attack to be mounted on the enemy positions. The battalion thus remained in its positions at the end of the first bound of the brigade's advance whilst preparing for an attack

on the following day.

At 0300 hours the following morning, the 22nd August, C Company carried out a flanking move to Branville with orders to carry out a reconnaissance, prior to an attack at first light, to discover whether the enemy had withdrawn and occupied the village. At 0530 hours, it arrived at Branville and discovered several enemy asleep in their positions. These were captured without any resistance. At the same time, six members of one of the division's parachute units, who had been hidden by the local French people, were liberated. At 0800 hours, Brigadier Flavell ordered the battalion to occupy Branville with two companies and B Company was duly dispatched to join C Company.

1st Battalion The Royal Ulster Rifles

At 1300 hours on the 17th August, the 1st Battalion The Royal Ulster Rifles had moved through the Devons near Gonneville and the 2nd Battalion The Oxfordshire & Buckinghamshire Light Infantry at Descanneville to take over as leading battalion of the brigade. The battalion advanced with a close pursuit force deployed forward. This consisted of C Company with under command the Reconnaissance Platoon, the Pioneer Platoon and one section of 249th Field Company RE. As the battalion moved forward, the enemy could be heard exploding demolition charges on the road ahead. When it reached Le Petit Homme, the Reconnaissance Platoon was within eight hundred yards of the enemy when the road was suddenly cratered in its path. At this point, B Company was left in the Le Petit Homme area to cut off any enemy retreating from Franceville Plage. The Belgian brigade, meanwhile, was operating on the company's left in the Merville and Franceville Plage area.

At the same time the rest of the battalion was continuing its advance along the coast road. Due to the fact that the entire area was heavily mined and because speed was of the essence, the

142. A Sherman tank of the 13th/18th Royal Hussars on the edge of Breville on the 13th June. (Photo: Airborne Forces Museum)

companies remained on the roadway itself and progress was rapid without any resistance being met. However, on the outskirts of Cabourg they met stiff opposition and all attempts to outflank the enemy failed due to the lack of room to manoeuvre. The battalion had been ordered to pursue the enemy without becoming heavily engaged and Lieutenant Colonel Carson thus decided, in view of the fact that the light was failing, to concentrate the battalion in the area of Le Homme and Les Panoramas.

The battalion dug in and on the following morning, the 18th August, a patrol was sent out to reconnoitre the area for a possible right flanking attack. The Reconnaissance Platoon also moved forward and was engaged by the enemy, suffering several casualties. The patrol reconnoitring the right flank subsequently returned and reported that an attack from that direction would not be feasible because of minefields, enemy strongpoints and areas of flooded ground.

At this juncture, the Commanding Officer decided to try and force an advance with the support of tanks. However, the attempt failed and the plan was abandoned when the leading tank struck a mine and was put out of action whilst bypassing a crater in the road.

Orders were at that point received from brigade headquarters for the battalion to remain in its location and maintain contact with the enemy without becoming heavily engaged. During the afternoon and evening, it was subjected to sporadic shelling and mortar fire which was largely ineffective. The Reconnaissance Platoon was withdrawn back into the battalion's area and B Company was recalled from Le Petit Homme. C Company was located as forward centre company in Les Panoramas, with B Company on its left and A Company on its right. D Company was in reserve to the rear whilst Battalion Headquarters was located in some buildings at the eastern end of Le Homme.

The following day, the 19th August, was relatively quiet apart from some occasional enemy shell and mortar fire. A patrol

was sent out during the night, under the command of Lieutenant O'Hara Murray, and was engaged by the enemy at close range but suffered no casualties.

The next day, the 20th August, was very different. From early morning the battalion was subjected to increasingly heavy artillery fire. In the early afternoon the battalion received orders to move to Le Plein after being relieved by the Belgian brigade. The Belgians arrived earlier than expected and the relief operation was carried out with difficulty under fire. One of the Royal Ulster Rifles' 6-pounder anti-tank guns was destroyed and its crew killed by a direct hit from a shell, whilst a Belgian Bren carrier was blown up by undiscovered mines beside the same crater where the tank had been put out of action earlier.

By midnight the battalion was concentrated at Le Plein and in the early morning of the 21st August moved by transport to a concentration area east of Troarn. That night, it moved to a lying up area at Lieu St Laurent where it arrived at 2130 hours.

2nd Battalion The Oxfordshire & Buckinghamshire Light Infantry

The 16th August found the 2nd Battalion The Oxfordshire & Buckinghamshire Light Infantry occupying positions at Le Mesnil. That night, A Company reported that enemy positions to its front were no longer occupied and, as a result of this information, prearranged plans for an immediate advance were put into action.

C Company moved off as the leading element of the battalion with orders to secure Varaville and then move north to cut off some enemy who were reported to be withdrawing in the path of the Devons in the Breville area. A number of machine gun positions, obviously left behind to delay any pursuit, were encountered whilst artillery and mortar fire came down on some of the crossroads on the battalion's line of advance. B Company encountered some enemy in Descanneville whilst A and D Companies were preparing to mount a two-company attack, supported by artillery, when the enemy withdrew.

On the night of the 17th August, the battalion was consolidated with A and B Companies at Descanneville whilst C and D Companies were located at Gonneville and Merville respectively. Battalion Headquarters was positioned in the Merville Battery, the scene of 9th Parachute Battalion's assault during the early hours of D-Day. Although the area in the general vicinity was cratered by bombing, the gun emplacements themselves were intact and the area of the battery itself was heavily mined.

The battalion remained in the Merville area until the 20th August when it marched south to Troarn. On reaching the brigade concentration area east of the town, it joined up with the Devons for the night march which was undertaken in very bad weather conditions.

The following day, the 21st August, found the battalion advancing with the rest of the brigade and taking its turn in the lead. Only minor opposition from the enemy was encountered but the welcome from the local people in all the villages was tumultuous.

3rd Parachute Brigade

3rd Parachute Brigade crossed the river at Bures, having been delayed until the late afternoon whilst 3rd Parachute Squadron RE constructed a bridge to replace that which it had demolished on D-Day. By dusk the entire brigade was across the river, by which time 1st Canadian Parachute Battalion had encountered the enemy at Plain-Lugan whilst 8th Parachute Battalion was on the outskirts of Goustranville which it eventually took after some heavy fighting.

On the following day, the 18th August, the brigade advanced to Goustranville where it encountered stiff resistance and at the same time came under artillery fire from the heights of Putot. In view of the fact that the island was under constant observation, any attack could only be carried out under cover of darkness. Thus General Gale decided on a leap-frog attack in which 3rd Parachute Brigade would move forward and secure the railway line east of the canal, which would be the start line for the second phase. 5th Parachute Brigade would then move through for the attack on the enemy positions on the heights of Putot.

At 2200 hours, the brigade crossed its start line with 1st Canadian Parachute Battalion in the lead. Thirty-five minutes later, C Company had taken the northernmost railway bridge which was found to have been blown but was considered usable by infantry. The next bridge to the south was found to have been destroyed, as was the third bridge to be taken. The southernmost bridge was captured intact by A Company. By midnight, 1st Canadian Parachute Battalion had taken two well-fortified positions manned by two companies of enemy infantry of the 744th Grenadier Regiment and had captured a hundred and fifty prisoners.

9th Parachute Battalion then moved through the Canadian positions on its way to take the railway station at Dozule. By 0100 hours on the 19th August it had reached the outskirts of Dozule itself where it came under artillery fire which caused casualties. By 1100 hours fifty-four casualties had been suffered and the battalion's RAP itself had been hit.

5th Parachute Brigade

At 0400 hours, meanwhile, 5th Parachute Brigade had crossed the canal by the southernmost bridge and had advanced towards the village of Putot-en-Auge. 7th Parachute Battalion's task was to secure the spur immediately east of Putot-en-Auge then 12th Parachute Battalion would commence its task of taking the village. It would be an extremely difficult operation as the enemy were well dug-in and were obviously prepared to put up a stout resistance.

13th Parachute Battalion, which was due to cross the canal and move up behind 9th Parachute Battalion to 5th Parachute Brigade's start line, initially tried to cross via the blown railway bridge. However, by the time it arrived at the bridge, the water level had risen and a crossing was by then impossible. Lieutenant Colonel Peter Luard then led his battalion to a small bridge which had been discovered earlier by a patrol of 1st Canadian Parachute Battalion. There the battalion halted under cover and waited in reserve.

7th Parachute Battalion, meanwhile, had encountered problems with the thick and impenetrable hedges which constantly held up its advance and forced detours to be made. Moreover, the enemy was very alert, their sustained fire machine guns firing on fixed lines at frequent intervals whilst flares constantly lit up the countryside. However, the enemy's use of tracer enabled the battalion to pinpoint the machine guns' fixed lines and thus to avoid them. In addition, the area between the canal and the railway, which was the battalion's start line, had not been completely cleared and several enemy positions and a number of anti-tank guns were encountered and had to be neutralised. At one stage, fifty enemy were spotted by the battalion which at that moment was hidden behind a hedge. These were successfully ambushed and heavy casualties caused. By the time the battalion reached and crossed its start line, however, it was an hour late and dawn was breaking.

B Company, commanded by Major B. R. Braithwaite, came under machine gun fire whilst advancing up a hedgerow and was pinned down. Behind it, the battalion's other two rifle companies were advancing across the start line and there was a risk of all three companies becoming concentrated in a dangerously small area in full daylight. A section was dispatched to locate the machine gun causing the problem and to deal with it. In so doing, it captured the weapon and its crew.

At that point, troops were seen advancing in extended line towards the battalion across the next field on its left. Initially, in the early light of dawn, it was assumed that these were men of 13th Parachute Battalion who were due to pass through. However, as they approached, it was realised that they were enemy troops. The battalion immediately adopted positions in the hedgerow which totally concealed it from the advancing infantry. The Commanding Officer, Lieutenant Colonel Geoffrey Pine Coffin, decided that he would try and capture them. Accordingly, a Bren group was deployed to a flank to cover them whilst the Intelligence Officer, Lieutenant Bertie Mills, who spoke German, called out and ordered the enemy troops to lay down their arms when they were only some twenty-five yards from the hedgerow.

Surprise was total and the German troops stood motionless in astonishment. Unfortunately one of their number acted rashly by dropping to the ground and opening fire with a machine gun. The battalion retaliated by returning fire and causing devastating casualties at such close range. After fifteen minutes, those Germans still alive had surrendered; only three escaped. The battalion then continued its advance without encountering any further problems and took its objective, the spur east of the village, whilst 12th Parachute Battalion occupied Putot-en-Auge itself.

13th Parachute Battalion was now advancing on its objective which was a prominent feature known as Hill 13 and which was located just beyond Putot-en-Auge. After waiting three hours in the open under constant fire, the battalion now had to cross a thousand yards of open terrain. Lieutenant Colonel Peter Luard here gives an account of his battalion's attack:

"Obviously, speed was the only way to cross the open space and I called my company commanders and issued my orders. B Company, commanded by Major Reggie Tarrant, was to lead, followed by Battalion Headquarters, then Major John Cramphorn's A Company and finally C Company which was commanded by Major Nobby Clark. I said that it was my opinion that the Germans would not expect us to do anything so mad, and that by the time we had started, and they had given the necessary orders to engage, we had a fool's chance, and a good one, of getting away with it. In any case, we had no real alternative as

143. Knocked-out self-propelled guns, together with a wrecked car and a captured gun at Breville. (Photo: Airborne Forces Museum)

there was no cover.

So off we went. The distance was about three quarters of a mile, of which the middle two hundred yards was the most hazardous.

We were all very fit young men and there is no doubt that everyone knew that the speed they made was likely to save their lives. And they moved. The whole battalion was across, except for the last four men, before the Germans realised the danger and opened fire. There were a couple of casualties, neither serious, and I lost my waterbottle but had not the slightest intention of looking for it!

Major Reggie Tarrant and his company went straight up the hill with A Company, under Major John Cramphorn, supporting them. I remember so well seeing them storming into the Germans, using the bayonet and getting right to the top of the hill. Then — suddenly — they were counter-attacked and a well-sited machine gun opened up, seriously wounding Major Tarrant and killing Lieutenant Bibby, who was leading his men with the utmost gallantry, and killing many others. The leading platoons were almost all killed or wounded and the supporting platoons fell back to join us on the intermediate ridge. What had happened was that a fresh German battalion had arrived to reinforce the hill position and they had caused the damage. Had we been just a little earlier, and been able to have organised ourselves on the hilltop, it would have been more difficult for them. But it was not so.

The Germans counter-attacked very well and I remember lying with the men of A Company in the grass on the reverse slope of the ridge and hearing bullets singing through the grass all around us. There was no fear; we just felt that as the enemy came into view, they would be welcome to everything we had.

At that moment I heard a voice coming from a Bren carrier saying: "We must have immediate fire. We are being counter-attacked." It was Colonel Mitchell of the 'Gunners' talking to his regiment. He had crossed the open ground and there he was, cool and calm. His support was marvellous! The fire from his guns was so accurate that it stopped the Germans about a hundred yards from him. Realising that the initiative might now be

with us again, I told C Company to make a flanking attack to the right. Off they went with Major Clark leading them but the re-entrant up which they had to go was well covered by the enemy and they could make no progress.

On reporting to Brigade Headquarters, I was told to hold where we were. This was no difficulty as on the intermediate ridge we were in a commanding position, and in any case the enemy counter-attack had failed. B Company had lost many men and casualties had been suffered by the other companies. The battalion had been on the move and in action for forty-eight hours, almost without let-up, and was very tired.

So we stayed where we were. I had a company commanders meeting and in the middle of it, I was so tired that I went to sleep as I was actually talking. They left me sleeping, and left word that I was not to be disturbed. I woke up two hours later and the rest of the meeting was resumed, with my apologies."

Despite this setback, the attack on Putot-en-Auge had been a great success. The enemy had been driven back from all except one of a series of well-prepared positions and the division had captured one hundred and sixty prisoners, two 75mm field guns, four 20mm mortars and a considerable number of machine guns.

3rd Parachute Brigade

The following day, the 21st August, 3rd Parachute Brigade commenced its advance towards Pont L'Eveque. It met stiff opposition on the way, particularly at the village of Annebault where the enemy infantry were supported by armour. 8th Parachute Battalion was tasked with clearing the village, initially being held up by a single 88mm gun. Unfortunately, a number of casualties were suffered in Battalion Headquarters when a rocket from a 'Nebelwerfer' scored a direct hit on it, killing a number of soldiers. However, after some very heavy fighting, the battalion succeeded in taking and clearing the village.

5th Parachute Brigade

That night, 5th Parachute Brigade moved through 3rd Parachute

Brigade and continued to advance until it reached the town of Pont L'Eveque on the River Touques at midday on the following day, the 22nd August.

Pont L'Eveque itself is built on both banks of the river which flows through it in two channels which are two hundred yards apart. Alongside the eastern channel is a railway line which is situated on an embankment, whilst on either side of the valley are wooded hills which dominate it.

Lieutenant Colonel Peter Luard's 13th Parachute Battalion was tasked with infiltrating into the town and securing a bridgehead across both channels of the river. Meanwhile 12th Parachute Battalion was to effect a crossing south of the town and to secure both the railway embankment and the feature of St Julien which controlled the approach from the south. The battalion was now commanded by Lieutenant Colonel Nigel Stockwell who had taken over from Lieutenant Colonel W. A. B. Harris MC who was wounded shortly after assuming command on the death of Lieutenant Colonel Johnny Johnson at Breville.

At 1500 hours that afternoon, A Company of 12th Parachute Battalion advanced under the cover of smoke, laid down by the guns of the 150th and 191st Field Regiments RA which were in support, across open ground towards two fords over which it would cross the river. All went well to begin with and the company had advanced some four hundred yards before it came under fire. Once it appeared to those watching that A Company, which was commanded by Captain J. A. S. Baker, had reached the fords, Major E. J. O'B. Croker's B Company started its advance. Unfortunately, however, A Company had missed the fords and was unable to inform the Commanding Officer because the company commander's radio set had been hit and rendered useless. Whilst his company took cover in ditches on the west bank, Captain Baker and nine men swam the river and succeeded in dislodging the enemy from the railway embankment but soon found that they were running low in ammunition.

By this time, the cover provided by the smoke was lessening and B Company was pinned down in a hedgerow by machine guns and shellfire from the St Julien feature to the south and from the high ground east of the river. One of its platoon commanders, Lieutenant Bercot, was killed just before reaching the river with his platoon. More smoke was called for and was laid down on the St Julien feature, the railway embankment and the railway station. This enabled B Company to move further forward to some dikes but here it was pinned down again. At this point, Captain Baker decided that the position of himself and his men on the railway embankment was becoming extremely precarious as they had now run out of ammunition and the rest of A Company could not cross over to join them. Reluctantly, Baker and his small group withdrew back to the west bank.

It was at that stage in the battle, with 12th Parachute Battalion's two leading companies pinned down between the start line and the river, and with the enemy once more in possession of the railway embankment from which all approaches were dominated, that Brigadier Poett realised that there was no chance of success being achieved in daylight and thus ordered the attack to be broken off. From 1700 hours until dark, A and B Companies were forced to remain in their very exposed positions with no smoke from the supporting artillery and cut off from the rest of the battalion. It was only after dusk that the two companies were able to gradually withdraw, having lost one officer and fifteen men killed as well as approximately fifty wounded.

13th Parachute Battalion meanwhile had managed to penetrate the town and cross the bridge spanning the western channel of the river. However, it had been unable to clear the main street which led to the bridge crossing the eastern channel, having encountered determined resistance from enemy troops in well-prepared positions. Moreover, the enemy had set fire to several houses in the town, the majority of which were of wooden construction, and the effects of this inevitably hampered the battalion's advance. At this juncture four Cromwell tanks of No.1 Troop of A Squadron of 6th Airborne Armoured Reconnaissance Regi-

ment came forward in support, having crossed the first channel via a ford constructed by sappers using an armoured bulldozer. They engaged several targets and gave covering fire from near the church. They accounted for three enemy and destroyed one pillbox. Unable to cross the river, however, they were in positions vulnerable to enemy anti-tank guns and to the risk of catching fire from the blazing ruins of buildings around them. Shortly afterwards, one of the Cromwells was hit by a 20mm anti-tank gun and was set on fire. The troop, which was commanded by Captain R. de C. Rennick, was then withdrawn.

At 1900 hours, Lieutenant Colonel Luard was ordered by Brigadier Poett to consolidate his positions in the town. During the evening Lieutenant Colonel Bobby Bray, the GSO 1 at divisional headquarters, came forward to 5th Parachute Brigade's headquarters to discuss the situation with Brigadier Poett. It was agreed that 12th Parachute Battalion should withdraw from its positions south of Pont L'Eveque into brigade reserve and that 7th Parachute Battalion would assume responsibility for the western and southern approaches to the town.

On the morning of the 23rd August, Brigadier Poett and Lieutenant Colonel Luard carried out a reconnaissance. By then a patrol under Captain F. H. Skeate had managed to cross the eastern channel of the river, without meeting any opposition, via the single remaining intact girder of one of two bridges which had been blown by the enemy as 13th Parachute Battalion was just about to reach them on the previous day. It appeared to Poett that there was now a better chance of establishing a bridgehead on the far bank and he ordered Lieutenant Colonel Luard to carry out a crossing as quickly as possible.

Using the steel girder, B Company was soon across the river but shortly afterwards met stiff opposition from the enemy. Lieutenant Colonel Luard then ordered Major John Cramphorn's A Company to assist B Company whilst C Company was kept in reserve and set up a firm base at the eastern end of the girder, keeping an eye on the battalion's left flank. Lieutenant Colonel Luard set up his advance battalion headquarters to the north-east of the girder bridge. There then ensued some vicious street fighting in which the battalion had to fight hard for every yard of ground because the enemy were in well-prepared positions and were giving a very good account of themselves. At midday the battalion's second in command, Major Gerald Ford, returned from visiting A and B Companies and reported that they were held up and that the enemy was attempting to infiltrate their positions.

Brigadier Poett realised that the bridgehead on the far bank was too weak for the attack to have any chance of success. He therefore ordered the battalion to withdraw back across the river through a firm base set up by 7th Parachute Battalion.

The withdrawal itself was carried out with utmost skill and with great steadiness on the part of A and B Companies. Fortunately, it was discovered that, by using a rope, it was possible to wade the river in one particular spot. Amongst the wounded was one badly injured man who was being carried on a door whilst being given covering fire by Major A. R. Clark MC who was using a .45 pistol to shoot at an enemy machine-gun position.

At dawn on the following day, the 24th August, patrols from 7th Parachute Battalion discovered that the enemy had quietly withdrawn from the town during the night. Brigadier Poett ordered Lieutenant Colonel Pine Coffin to follow up immediately, the battalion using the Pont Audemer road as its axis.

7th Parachute Battalion pushed forward with all haste across the river and on to the high ground to the east of Pont L'Eveque, soon being followed by the other two battalions.

5th Parachute Brigade advanced without meeting any opposition until it reached a point east of the line of the railway at Bourg. Here it encountered some resistance but despite this the high ground at Bourg was taken and held without any problems. At this point Major General Gale ordered Brigadier Poett to limit any further action by his brigade to patrolling, whilst 1st Special Service Brigade moved through.

144. Troopers C. Davies and L. Walden of 6th Airborne Armoured Reconnaissance Regiment with a captured 20mm anti-aircraft gun mounted on a half-track. The two men claimed a Messerschmitt 109 and a Focke Wulf 190 with this gun. (Photo: Imperial War Museum)

6th Airlanding Brigade

1st Battalion The Royal Ulster Rifles

Meanwhile, 6th Airlanding Brigade had succeeded in capturing Vauville and Deauville on the 22nd August. The 1st Battalion The Royal Ulster Rifles had been relieved at their positions outside Cabourg by units of the Belgian brigade and had moved to Troarn via a concentration area at Le Plein. On the night of the 21st August, the battalion moved again to a lying-up area at Lieu St Laurent. Early the following morning, Lieutenant Colonel Carson was ordered to put his battalion at thirty minutes notice to move. At 1130 hours, the battalion moved forward through the Devons and the Oxfordshire & Buckinghamshire Light Infantry on its way to take up a position on a spur near Vauville. Whilst *en route*, it received orders to continue its march to take Deauville and the hill behind it.

After receiving reports that Deauville was clear of the enemy, the battalion's Intelligence Officer went forward into the town where he received a tumultuous welcome as the first Allied soldier to enter it. On his return, he reported that all the bridges over the River Touques had been blown and that the enemy still held Trouville. At that point the Commanding Officer received orders for the battalion to move on as fast as possible to secure the central bridge, which had been reported as being intact, and to establish a bridgehead on the far bank.

When the battalion entered Deauville, it found elements of the Belgian brigade in the eastern and southern parts of the town. Lieutenant Colonel Carson set up his battalion headquarters in the former German commander's residence whilst B Company occupied the area of Vieux Deauville. D Company's area turned out to be in full view of the enemy and thus had to be relocated.

A Company, whose objective was the Touques railway station, encountered problems when taking over from a Belgian company because of the exposed nature of the area. C Company came under fire from enemy artillery and the company headquarters received a direct hit. The company commander, Major E. F. Johnston, who had taken over from Major Bob Hynds when the latter was wounded in early July, was killed and one of his platoon commanders, the company sergeant major, two radio operators and several riflemen were wounded. In the absence of the company second in command, who was on a reconnaissance task at the time, Sergeant Redpath organised the evacuation of the wounded with the assistance of some French civilians.

The following morning, the 23rd, a small reconnaissance patrol managed to cross the river Touques in an assault boat but discovered the enemy in positions on the far side. The Commanding Officer decided that the crossing would have to take place further upstream opposite the village Bonneville sur Touques. The battalion subsequently withdrew from Deauville and moved to the area of La Poterie, A Company suffering several casualties during the withdrawal. That afternoon a patrol from No.10 Platoon, under Lieutenant O'Hara Murray, crossed over the river and made its way towards the church at Bonneville sur Touques. However, it came under heavy fire from the area of the railway and was forced to withdraw. The Commanding Officer then learned that a strong enemy force of between one and two thousand men was positioned along the railway and that this was the enemy's main line of defence east of the Touques.

In view of the strength of the enemy, a crossing at this location was obviously out of the question. The battalion was therefore withdrawn to an area between Glatigny and La Poterie, out of range of enemy mortars. During the night, four reconnaissance patrols were sent across the river in assault boats. All four penetrated the enemy-held area to a depth of about a thousand yards and all made contact with the enemy. On the following morning, the 24th August, the battalion received news that the 2nd Battalion The Oxfordshire & Buckinghamshire Light Infantry had crossed the river and that the Belgian brigade had occupied Trouville. The Commanding Officer was then ordered to cross the river as quickly as possible and to occupy Bonneville sur Touques and St Philibert. By 1230 hours, the battalion had crossed the river and was in possession of Bonneville sur Touques. By 1615 hours, it had reached St Philibert.

2nd Battalion The Oxfordshire & Buckinghamshire Light Infantry

On the 22nd August the battalion was the leading unit when members of the French Resistance appeared with news that the enemy had withdrawn to the far banks of the River Touques. Two patrols of the Reconnaissance Platoon in jeeps were dispatched to verify this report whilst the Intelligence Officer, Lieutenant Dick Osborne, was sent to Deauville to check on the situation concerning the coastal route. Both he and the Reconnaissance Platoon patrols returned to report that the Resistance information was accurate and that all the bridges over the river had been destroyed.

That night the battalion was ordered to carry out a crossing of the river at Touques. The following morning, the 23rd August, Major John Howard's D Company moved up on to the high ground which overlooked the river, suffering some casualties from shellfire in the process. However, the company then swam across the river and established a small bridgehead on the far bank. Captain Charles Mason, the Reconnaissance Platoon Commander, was tasked with finding a suitable crossing place for the battalion and its vehicles. This was a difficult task because the river was some thirty feet in width, ten feet deep and fast flowing. The banks of the river were steep and covered in slippery mud. Added to these problems was the fact that the only approach to the river was via the road which led to the bridge which had already been blown by the enemy.

The problem of transporting the men of the battalion across the river to the east bank was solved by the discovery by D Company of a boat which, with the aid of some local people, was used as a ferry. The vehicles were subsequently ferried across by improvised rafts built by the battalion's pioneers, also with the help of some local inhabitants. On the following day, the 24th August, whilst it was engaged in this task, the battalion was visited by the commander of 1st Corps, Lieutenant General Sir John Crocker, and Major General Gale who were much impressed at the way in which it had overcome a considerable obstacle.

Once across the river, the battalion entered Touques to an enthusiastic welcome from the town's inhabitants. The following morning it continued its advance at the head of the brigade, moving through St Philibert, La Correspondence, Petreville and Malhortie. At 1130 hours, a report reached the battalion that an armoured car of the Belgian brigade's reconnaissance unit had been engaged and knocked out just before the bridge at Malhortie. It was also reported that the enemy was holding the bridge itself and the high ground to the east near the village of Manneville La Raoult.

Brigadier Edward Flavell was with the battalion when this report arrived and ordered Lieutenant Colonel Roberts to take the crossing over the river as quickly as possible. At 1300 hours, Major 'Flaps' Edmunds and B Company successfully attacked the enemy positions at the bridge, capturing it intact but encountering opposition from further enemy positions to the east.

Major Johnny Granville's C Company, meanwhile, had been carrying out a right flanking attack in order to link up with B Company and, if possible, to advance round the village of Manneville La Raoult up to the line of a road which ran in a north-south direction to the east of the village. The flanking movement itself took longer than expected because of the difficult terrain and it was not until 1600 hours that the two companies linked up. Major Granville decided to advance towards Manneville La Raoult but when the company was about three hundred yards from the village, it came under fire. No.21 Platoon, under Lieutenant Freddy Scott, dealt with this problem, causing the enemy to withdraw. C Company then moved on to its objective, capturing some enemy horse-drawn transport and stores on the way, and by dusk had established itself in new positions. Unfortunately, however, the company could not inform the battalion of its success as all its radio sets were out of action: the FOO's signaller had fallen down a railway embankment whilst the mortar fire controller's signaller had fallen into a stream, added to which the company headquarters' set became unserviceable.

Lieutenant Colonel Roberts, being unable to communicate with C Company but hearing the sounds of action, ordered A and D Companies to attack Manneville La Raoult. The village was taken and cleared by D Company after a tough fight during which the enemy brought down mortar and artillery which caused casualties on both sides. However, D Company occupied the village by dusk, capturing a number of prisoners and some transport. That night, the 1st Battalion The Royal Ulster Rifles moved through C Company on its way to Berville sur Mer.

The following day, the 26th August, the battalion advanced on the village of Foulbec. By 1900 hours, it had consolidated in the area of the village whilst under sporadic mortar fire from the enemy which had withdrawn and had blown the bridge. The battalion's mortars contented themselves by responding accordingly.

6th Airborne Division

The enemy's efficient use of demolitions on roads and bridges had caused delays and problems for the vehicles of the division's supporting arms elements following up behind the brigades. Initially it became necessary for some communications and command vehicles, some artillery forward observers and four anti-tank guns to make a detour south and cross the River Touques via a bridge constructed by the sappers of 49th Infantry Division. Eventually, however, the division's own sappers were able to construct a Class 9 bridge capable of accommodating men on foot, jeeps and trailers. Subsequently two Class 40 bridges were also erected and thus the airlanding light regiment's pack howitzers, the 6 and 17-pounders of the anti-tank batteries and the Cromwell tanks of 6th Airborne Armoured Reconnaissance Regiment could also again participate in the advance.

The division was now advancing on a ten-mile wide front. On its left were 6th Airlanding Brigade and the Belgian Brigade moving on a twin axis towards the towns of Honfleur and Foulbec, whilst the rest of the division advanced along the road towards Pont Audemer. It was not until its leading elements reached the town of Beuzeville that the division once again met stiff resistance from the enemy on the southern axis of its advance.

Beuzeville is the junction of five roads: one from the north, one from Pont Leveque to the west, one from Pont Audemer to the east and two from the south. The town itself is large and sprawling, surrounded by rolling countryside and cider apple orchards.

On the morning of the 25th August, 1st Special Service Brigade was held up short of Beuzeville. 3rd Parachute Brigade and 4th Special Service Brigade were tasked with moving through and clearing the enemy from the town. Initially some heavy losses were sustained when some troops were heavily mortared whilst moving up along a sunken lane from the south towards the town as part of a flanking movement. It was during this action that the support given by A Squadron of 6th Airborne Armoured Reconnaissance Regiment proved particularly valuable.

1 Troop of A Squadron was under — command of 8th Parachute Battalion as it attacked a farm to the south of the town. In support of one of the battalion's companies, the troop's four Cromwells advanced to a position from which they were able —

145. Major John Cramphorn, commanding A Company 13th Parachute Battalion, debriefs three men of his unit who landed in Troarn instead of on DZ 'N'. They avoided capture with the help of members of the French Resistance but it was not until after the fall of Caen that they could rejoin their battalion. *Left to right:* Company Sergeant Major McParlan, Major Cramphorn, Private Bardsley and Lance Corporal West. (Photo: Imperial War Museum)

to provide covering fire for the company's advance into the farm. The leading tank, confronted by an obstacle, continued to fire on a suspected 20mm gun emplacement while the troop leader, Captain R. de C. Rennick, advanced to try and find a way around the obstacle. At this point Captain Rennick was wounded in the head by machine gun fire and Sergeant Cressy, the troop sergeant, took over command until the troop was recalled by the commanding officer of 8th Parachute Battalion, Lieutenant Colonel Alastair Pearson. However, the action was successful and the farm was taken and occupied.

No.1 Troop was then ordered to attack another farm and to destroy a 75mm gun positioned in it. As it advanced, the leading tank, commanded by Corporal Miller, came under fire. The tank's gunner, Trooper Williams, immediately returned the fire and knocked out the enemy gun. After being recalled, the troop was tasked with shelling a forest with some sixty enemy located in it. Just as the wood was being cleared, Lieutenant K. T. Robertson arrived to take over command.

The troop's next task was in support of a platoon of 8th Parachute Battalion which was to occupy some high ground. The four tanks preceded the platoon up a track and reached the objective without meeting any opposition. On the objective, however, the two leading Cromwells came under fire from a machine gun which was subsequently knocked out. The platoon then occupied the position whilst the troop moved into positions to deal with any counter-attack.

Later in the day a patrol from 8th Parachute Battalion moved down a track leading to the town and came under fire from a machine gun, suffering casualties. The troop provided covering fire for stretcher-bearers recovering the wounded and then moved down the track for a mile, with a platoon in support, to

clear it. During this task, two more machine guns were silenced.

The troop then moved to support another company of 8th Parachute Battalion, putting down fire on a house suspected of containing enemy. After this had been carried out, and the house cleared by the company, the troop took up a defensive position with the battalion. Later, fire was directed at an enemy roadblock six hundred yards away but the failing light prevented observation of the results, although a large flash was seen. At 2230 hours that night, the troop returned to the squadron harbour area.

That evening, Major General Gale received orders from Lieutenant General Crocker with regard to operations for the following day. Crocker's orders laid down boundaries for 6th Airborne Division's operations and these excluded Pont Audemer which would be on the axis of advance of 49th Infantry Division. However, Gale was convinced that his division was nearer to Pont Audemer and was certain that his troops were in a better position than those of 49th Infantry Division to reach the town and seize the bridge over the River Risle, which was a major obstacle, before the Germans could blow it.

Gale gave the task of leading the race to the bridge to the Dutchmen of the Princess Irene of The Netherlands Brigade, commanded by Lieutenant Colonel A. C. de Ruyter Van Stevenick, which was put under command of 5th Parachute Brigade. On the morning of the 26th August, mounted on the Cromwells of A Squadron of 6th Airborne Armoured Reconnaissance Regiement, the Dutch brigade raced for Pont Audemer but unfortunately arrived too late. The enemy had blown the bridge twenty minutes beforehand. Shortly afterwards, 7th Parachute Battalion arrived after a high-speed march and occupied the town whilst the Dutch brigade took up positions on the high ground overlooking the river.

Meanwhile, the units of 6th Airlanding Brigade had been heading rapidly for the town of Berville sur Mer beyond Honfleur. By 0800 hours on the 26th August, it had become apparent that the enemy had withdrawn and the advance developed into a race between the Belgian brigade and the Devons. The Belgians overtook the Devons, only to discover that the Royal Ulster Rifles had arrived before them. Upon the arrival of the brigade, the Belgians remained in Berville whilst the Oxfordshire & Buckinghamshire Light Infantry were deployed in Foulbec on the right and the Royal Ulster Rifles on the left in the area of the hamlet of La Judee.

It was the gunners of 53rd Airlanding Light Regiment RA who fired the last rounds of the division's operations in Normandy. The regiment's war diary relates what happened:

"C Company of the 2nd Battalion The Oxfordshire & Buckinghamshire Light Infantry had on 26th August taken up a position on the heights to the west of Foulbec. An OP was established on the hillside with a good command of the demolished bridge over the River Risle. Enemy movement was seen in the neighbourhood of a house about two thousand yards away on the far side of the river.

212 Battery engaged the area around the house during daylight, firing about two hundred rounds. As a result of this, the enemy were soon crawling where a few hours before they had been walking. On 27th August, further movement was seen in the same area and fire was brought down several times. By 1700 hours, the house had received several direct hits.

OC 212 Battery, Major W. C. Knox Peebles, himself at the OP with the FOO, was the first to observe a white flag — a white sheet hung out of a top storey window — waving in the breeze; two more quickly appeared. C Company was asked to provide a fighting patrol. A jeep, trailer and MMG with an officer and four men were soon ready. In anticipation of any possible treachery, a No.68 set and a Verey pistol were taken so that fire could be called for.

As soon as the OP party and patrol reached the river, they received a setback as they found a thirty-foot gap in the bridge, a strong-flowing deep river and neither boat nor raft. They approached the bank cautiously and waited. Presently a solitary Hun appeared on the other side with a white bandage wrapped round his steel helmet. From him they gathered that six more were still in the house; the remainder had fled. It therefore seemed imperative to get across the river.

So the infantry officer and the FOO, Captain H. H. Thomson, stripped down to their battledress trousers and vests and, carrying a Sten gun apiece, attempted to swim the river. After a struggle both officers, with only one Sten gun, reached the other side. Boots and socks were flung across the gap and two semi-clothed officers were marching up the road with the Hun a few paces ahead of them. They reached the house and target area and found an anti-tank gun, sited to cover the bridge and road, and the layout of a company position. At the house they took seven prisoners, of whom three were wounded, without any difficulty. Everywhere there were signs of precipitous flight. Two dead were lying outside an outhouse and a car, complete but without any petrol, stood in the roadway loaded with three officers' kit. The remains of a handcart which had received a direct hit were strewn about in the ditches. Clothing, equipment and arms of all kinds were lying about in the slit trenches and outhouses. The prisoners made clear by signs that the artillery fire had been too much for them."

The following day, the 27th August, 6th Airborne Division was ordered to concentrate in the area between Honfleur and Pont Audemer. The division's task in the Normandy campaign was complete and it was to return home during the early days of September. It had been fighting continuously for almost three months and had suffered four thousand four hundred and fifty-seven casualties: eight hundred and twenty-one killed, two thousand seven hundred and nine wounded and nine hundred and twenty-seven missing. In the ten days of fighting since the 17th August, it had liberated four hundred square miles of enemy occupied territory and captured over one thousand prisoners.

On the day before the division's entry into Pont Audemer, Major General Gale had received the following signal, via Lieutenant General Sir John Crocker, from Lieutenant General H. D. G. Crerar, Commander of 1st Canadian Army under whose command 1st Corps had operated since the Canadians had taken over responsibility for the sector east of the Orne at the end of July:

"Desire you inform Gale of my appreciation of the immense contribution 6th Airborne Division and all Allied contingents under his command have made during recent fighting advance. The determination and speed with which his troops have pressed on in spite of all enemy efforts to the contrary have been impressive and of the greatest assistance to the Army as a whole."

146. General Montgomery in conversation with Major General Gale and Brigadier Poett after the former had been decorated with the American Order of Merit and the latter with the Silver Star by General Omar Bradley at General Montgomery's Headquarters in early July 1944. (Photo: Imperial War Museum)

From The Ardennes To The Maas

The closing days of 1944 found 6th Airborne Division re-equipped and reinforced after its ordeal in Normandy. Many of its units had suffered grievous losses by the time they returned to England in early September 1944; 1st Canadian Parachute Battalion, for example, had lost twenty-four of the twenty-seven officers, and three hundred and forty-three of the five hundred and sixteen other ranks, who had parachuted into Normandy on D-Day. Consequently, many new faces had appeared in the division's camps in Wiltshire.

There had also been a number of changes in command appointments at all levels. Major General E. L. Bols DSO replaced Major General Gale as divisional commander on the 19th December, but 3rd and 5th Parachute Brigades were still commanded by Brigadiers James Hill and Nigel Poett whilst Brigadier Edward Flavell remained in command of 6th Airlanding Brigade.

Amongst the battalions' commanding officers, however, there were several newcomers. 8th Parachute Battalion was now commanded by Lieutenant Colonel George Hewettson who replaced Lieutenant Colonel Alastair Pearson after the latter had been forced to hand over his command because of ill health. 9th Parachute Battalion was commanded by Lieutenant Colonel Napier Crookenden, who had previously been Brigade Major of 6th Airlanding Brigade, whilst Lieutenant Colonel Jeff Nicklin had assumed command of 1st Canadian Parachute Battalion on the departure of Lieutenant Colonel George Bradbrooke who had moved to a staff appointment in early September.

In 5th Parachute Brigade, Lieutenant Colonels Geoffrey Pine

Coffin and Peter Luard still commanded the 7th and 13th Parachute Battalions respectively but Lieutenant Colonel Ken Darling now commanded 12th Parachute Battalion. In 6th Airlanding Brigade, the 1st Battalion The Royal Ulster Rifles was still led by Lieutenant Colonel Jack Carson whilst the 2nd Battalion The Oxfordshire & Buckinghamshire Light Infantry was now commanded by Lieutenant Colonel Mark Darell-Brown DSO. The 12th Battalion The Devonshire Regiment was commanded by Lieutenant Colonel Paul Gleadell who had succeeded Lieutenant Colonel Dick Stevens.

Since its return from Normandy, units of the division had undergone intensive training in street fighting and had practised assault river crossings over the Thames. It was generally acknowledged within the division that its next task was likely to be part of a push across the Rhine into Germany.

However, within a very short space of time, all was changed very rapidly. On the 16th December 1944, the Germans launched a series of powerful counter-attacks against General Omar Bradley's 12th Army Group with the objective of seizing Antwerp. Under the cover of the noise of salvos of VIs roaring low overhead towards Liege and Antwerp, fourteen German infantry divisions moved through the Eifel forests before dawn. In front of them, on a sector of one hundred miles width in the Ardennes, were a mere four divisions of the US VIII Corps comprising the 4th, 28th, and 106th Infantry Divisions, and the 9th Armoured Division.

The German plan was designed to prevent an Allied invasion of

147. The first in a sequence of photographs taken during operations in the Ardennes. Here a patrol moves down a road through snow-covered countryside. (Photo: Imperial War Museum)

Germany by disrupting the build-up of reserves of troops and equipment and by generally disrupting any Allied preparations. At the same time, it was designed to provide a breathing space which would permit the regrouping and re-equipping of German forces for the defence of Germany.

The German offensive involved the use of three armies comprising a total of no less than seventeen infantry, parachute and Panzer Grenadier divisions to be committed behind a spearhead of *Wehrmacht* and SS armoured divisions. These armies consisted of the following: 6th SS Panzer Army in the north, with the objectives of capturing Monschau and Butgenbach and subsequently opening up the road leading north-west to Eupen and Verviers; 5th Panzer Army, tasked with capturing the key cities of St Vith and Bastogne, subsequently advancing westward to the River Meuse and Namur; and 7th Army in the south where it was to cross over the river line into the Ardennes between Vianden and Echternach and subsequently provide a flank guard north of Luxembourg and Arlon.

At 0530 hours, two thousand guns started shelling the American positions between Monschau and Echternach. As they did so, German infantry advanced with five panzer divisions close behind.

The Americans were taken totally by surprise. The 28th Infantry Division, in the River Our sector, was attacked by five German divisions and was completely overwhelmed whilst two regiments of the 106th Infantry Division in the Schnee Eifel were outflanked and encircled the following morning, the 17th December, by units of 5th Panzer Army which had moved west across the River Our. On the southern flank 4th Infantry Division held its ground whilst in the north the US V Corps put up a stout resistance against 6th SS Panzer Army and stopped the German attack at Monschau. However, the 1st SS Panzer Division attacked the junction between VIII Corps and V Corps, overrunning the armoured unit in that location and penetrating some six miles by the evening of the 16th December.

The American troops fought back hard but VIII Corps was outnumbered. Despite this , however, the Germans did not reach all their objectives on the first day. At higher levels of US command, the full extent and scale of the German thrust was not appreciated and information from the front was both confused and scarce. Consequently, reactions were slow and it was not until the late afternoon of the 16th December that the 7th and 10th Armoured Divisions were committed to the Ardennes as reinforcements. Moreover, General Eisenhower's reserves, the 82nd and 101st Airborne Divisions, were not even alerted for possible deployment from their locations at Rheims until the evening of the 17th December.

On the 20th December General Eisenhower, the Supreme Allied Commander, placed Field Marshal Montgomery in command of all Allied forces north of the German breakthrough. By this time the operations of the US 1st Army consisted of a number of individual delaying actions. Divisions moved up as reinforcements and became involved in the battle as they arrived, as opposed to being deployed in accordance with any plan. Before assuming command, Montgomery had already familiarised himself throughly with the situation in the Ardennes. During the next few days, despite renewed German attacks which were heavier and more sustained than expected, he laid his plans to head the enemy off away from the direction of their final objectives and force them to advance south-west.

6th Airborne Division, meanwhile, had received orders on the 20th December to move to Belgium. On the following day, advance parties left for Tilbury Docks and on the 22nd December the main body of the division moved from its camps in Wiltshire. On Christmas Eve, units of the division reached a transit camp at Ostend.

On the 26th December, the division was concentrated in an area between Dinant and Namur. By this time the German advance had been halted and the Allies had gone over to the offensive.

On the 29th December, the division was ordered to prepare to advance against the very tip of the German salient. 5th Para-

148. The patrol halts whilst its commander observes a wood a few hundred yards away across open ground.
(Photo: Imperial War Museum)

149. Two members of the patrol observe closely the terrain in front of them. (Photo: Imperial War Museum)

150. *Below:* The patrol moves forward from the road, a sniper and Bren gunner covering the movement of the remainder.
(Photo: Imperial War Museum)

chute Brigade advanced on the right of the division towards Grupont whilst 3rd Parachute Brigade occupied the area of Rochefort. However, the enemy were putting up a very stiff fight and it was decided that an attack would be mounted by 13th Parachute Battalion against the village of Bure in order to facilitate the capture of Grupont. Major Jack Watson, commanding A Company, takes up the story:

"My Commanding Officer, Lieutenant Colonel Peter Luard, sent for me to brief me on the task. His plan was to spend one night in Pondrome and move in transport to Resteigne where we would march to Tellin. It was very cold, well below freezing, and there was ice on the roads but the men were in very good form. We marched to a wood overlooking Bure which was our first objective.

This was the furthest point that the enemy's armour had reached during their offensive. It was the battalion's task to drive the Germans out of Bure.

We were the left assault company with B Company on our right and C Company in reserve. We were to attack Bure itself whilst B Company, commanded by Major Bill Grantham, secured the high ground. We formed up and were ready for H-Hour at 1300 hours. It was a bloody cold day and it was snowing heavily. Moving up to the start line was very difficult because of the very thick snow which was three or four feet deep in places.

We reached the start line and looked down on the village which was silent. However, the enemy knew that we were there and were waiting for us. As soon as we broke cover, we came under heavy fire — I looked up and saw the branches of the trees above me being shattered by machine gun fire and mortar bomb splinters. The enemy had set up sustained fire machine guns on fixed lines and these pinned us down before we had even left the start line. This was the first time that I had led a company attack and after a few minutes I had lost about a third of my men. We were held up for about a quarter of an hour because of the dead and wounded amongst us but we had to get going.

We were some four hundred yards from the village and so, as quickly as I could, I got a grip of my company and gave the order to advance. Whatever happened, we had to get into the village as quickly as possible. On the way we suffered more casualties, including my batman. One of my men was hit by a bullet which ignited the phosphorous grenades that he was carrying. He was screaming at me to shoot him. He died later.

We reached the village and took the first few houses, in one of which I installed my company headquarters. At this stage I was unaware that B Company was also suffering badly in its attempt to take the high ground, having come under fire from tanks and artillery. Bill Grantham had been killed on the start line, along with one of his platoon commanders, Lieutenant Tim Winser, and Company Sergeant Major Moss. His company second in command and one of the other two platoon commanders had been wounded. The only surviving platoon commander, Lieutenant Alf Largeren, led the remainder of B Company to their objective. Unfortunately he was killed later in the day whilst clearing a house in which there was an enemy machine gun position.

Once the company was in the village, it was very difficult to find out exactly what was happening. I got my platoon commanders together to make sure that their platoons were secure and to give them orders for moving forward to start clearing the rest of the village. It was a most peculiar battle because we would be in one house, with my company headquarters and myself on the ground floor, when my radio operator would suddenly tell me that there were enemy upstairs. In other instances, we were upstairs and the enemy were downstairs!

We were suffering heavy casualties as we advanced, clearing each house in turn. Eventually we reached the crossroads in the middle of the village by the old church. I had kept the Commanding Officer informed as to our progress and he decided to move C Company up to support us. However, by that time the enemy had decided to send in some of their Tiger tanks and they

151. The patrol comes under fire from an enemy mortar as it crosses the open ground towards the treeline. (Photo: Imperial War Museum)

were now firing at us, demolishing some of the houses in the process. I moved from one side of the road to the other, drawing their fire. One of the tanks opened fire on me and the next thing I knew was that the wall behind me was collapsing. At that point one of my PIAT teams came running up and opened fire on the tank, destroying its tracks. They were extremely brave.

The battle went on like this all day. The enemy counter-attacked but we managed to hold them. They forced us back and then we in turn advanced again. It became very difficult to keep the men awake because they were exhausted and had not eaten a hot meal all day. During that night, the fighting continued non-stop with us firing at the Germans and them firing back and shelling us. When we had told Battalion Headquarters that we were up against armour, C Squadron of the Fife & Forfar Yeomanry was sent forward to support us. A troop approached the village first but the leading tank was blown up by a mine. The remaining tanks then tried to approach from another direction and reached the village but one was knocked out. Three tanks stayed with us during that night but by the following morning all of them had been knocked out. The problem was that the Shermans were no match for the Tigers and by the end of the battle sixteen of them had been put out of action. We were also reinforced by C Company of the 2nd Battalion The Oxfordshire & Buckinghamshire Light Infantry, under Major Johnny Granville, because my own company was by then down to one platoon in strength.

The following day, the 4th January, Colour Sergeant Harry Watkins suddenly and miraculously arrived out of the blue with a hot meal. How the hell he ever found us I do not know because we were still scattered amongst the houses along the main road in the centre of the village. He brought us a stew which was more than welcome and we managed to organise the men into small groups to have their meal and then return to their positions in the houses.

At one point one of our medics, Sergeant Scott of the Royal Army Medical Corps, went forward in an ambulance to rescue some casualties. One of the Tiger tanks, which had been in action against us all day, came up alongside him and the commander popped his head out of the turret and said, ''Take the casualties away this time but don't come forward again, it is not safe.'' Needless to say, Sergeant Scott took the hint.

During the following day, the 5th January, we were subjected to five further counter-attacks which were supported by enemy armour. However, by that time we had a field regiment and a medium battery in support and started giving the enemy a hard time too. They responded to our shelling by trying to blast us out of Bure with their own artillery. Luckily, however, most of my men had experienced heavy shelling in Normandy and thus knew what to expect.

I instructed Major Johnny Granville to move his men forward beyond my own positions in order to find out what was happening. As his company advanced, the enemy counter-attacked again with two Tiger tanks in support. However, we beat them off and then everything went quiet. At that point I decided that it was now high time that we secured the other half of the village, along with C Company and Major Granville's company, and cleared the Germans out of all the houses. This we did, with much hand-to-hand and close-quarter fighting going on all day.

By about 2100 hours that night we had finally taken the whole village, with my company overcoming the last enemy position. We established ourselves in defensive positions but that same night received orders to withdraw. We later discovered that 7th Parachute Battalion had made an approach from a different direction and, meeting little opposition, had taken Grupont. As a result, we ourselves did not have to go any further. In the very early hours of the following day, the 6th January, I assembled my very tired and very wet company and withdrew to Tellin. The battalion had suffered casualties which totalled seven officers and a hundred and eighty-two soldiers. Of these, about sixty-eight men had been killed, of whom about half were from my

152. The patrol advances through the wood. (Photo: Imperial War Museum)

company. They were buried in a field in Bure by our padre, The Reverend Whitfield Foy, a few days later.''

The gunners of 53rd (Worcestershire Yeomanry) Airlanding Light Regiment RA had also been active since the division's arrival in the Ardennes. The regiment's guns had been in action on the 26th December, firing from positions two miles west of Dinant in support of 6th Airlanding Brigade. On the 29th December the regiment's dispositions had been adjusted, with 2llth Airlanding Light Battery in support of 5th Parachute Brigade on the line of the River Lesse from Houyet west towards the village of Furfooz and moving into action at Boisseilles, east of the River Meuse, on the 30th December. The rest of the regiment remained in support of 6th Airlanding Brigade until the 2nd January when it moved its positions to Buissonville in support of 3rd Parachute Brigade. The following day, two regimental concentrations were fired from positions at Havrenne.

The sub-zero temperature and terrain covered with thick snow made operations, and particularly patrolling, somewhat hazardous. An illustration of the problems encountered is that of a patrol of 22nd Independent Parachute Company which was sent out on a reconnaissance task to locate the enemy in the area of a wood near the town of Marloie, which is situated between Namur and the border with Luxembourg. The leading member of the patrol was wounded after treading on an anti-personnel mine. The patrol commander, a corporal, tried to rescue the injured man but also trod on a mine and was wounded. Help eventually arrived in the form of five medical orderlies, of whom two were also wounded when they trod on mines. Eventually a medical officer arrived. After ordering everyone else to remain where they were until the arrival of some more men with mine detectors, he made his way into the minefield to the nearest wounded man and stopped the bleeding. He then went to each of the other wounded in turn, carrying out emergency first aid. Shortly afterwards, Sergeant Lou Carrier and another sergeant from 22nd Independent Parachute Company arrived with mine detectors and a party of stretcher-bearers.

After clearing a path through the minefield, they made their way to the medical officer who was by then supporting one of the wounded in a sitting position. On sweeping the area round the two men, the rescue party found a mine where the sitting man's shoulders would have been if he had laid down, and two more by the medical officer's feet.

The wintry conditions also made life extremely difficult for men of the 6th Airborne Divisional Signals. Linesmen found themselves going out to repair the same lines broken twenty times in a day, whilst dispatch riders had to abandon their motorcycles and take to their feet to deliver signals. Radio technicians frequently had to work in the open, repairing equipment with frozen fingers. Most of the unit's radio equipment was mounted in jeeps or open trailers and was thus susceptible to the freezing temperatures.

Life in the Ardennes did, however, have its lighter moments as is illustrated by this account from Captain Guy Radmore, the commander of 5th Parachute Brigade's Signals Section.

''We had arrived at Namur after a difficult drive through cold, fog and snow and then had moved to the high ground above the Meuse, just to the east of Dinant. Conditions were very bad with snow and ice. On New Year's Eve our new Brigade Major, Michael Brennan, and I decided to celebrate the New Year. He had been second in command of the South Staffordshires in the Sicily invasion where his glider had come down in the seas. He was a charming man, a hunting parson's son.

We went to the Chateau Royal d'Ardennes, a sort of Gleneagles-type of luxury country hotel. We arrived and, to our astonishment, were greeted by a receptionist and a head waiter in a tail coat. Having organised a bath and a bottle of wine, we enquired as to how long ago the Germans had left and were told, ''They went through the garden ten minutes ago.''

By the end of January, 6th Airborne Division had been withdrawn to Holland where it was located near the River Maas

153. The sniper covers the patrol commander as he moves forward to the far edge of the wood. (Photo: Imperial War Museum)

in the area of Venlo and Roermond. A vigorous programme of patrolling was carried out, this being made particularly hazardous due to the requirement for patrols to cross the river which was very wide and in full flood. Small assault craft had to be used and these were swept along by the strong current, making it extremely difficult to land at any pre-determined spot on the far bank.

The enemy, in the form of the German 7th Parachute Division, were also very active and had sewn mines thickly on the banks on their side of the river.

Their positions consisted of an extensive system of trenches and defences which extended along a low ridge overlooking the valley from Venlo in the north to Roermond in the south. Moreover, the enemy had opened a dam on the upper River Roer, releasing a large quantity of water which in turn raised the level of water in the low area between the Roer and Maas.

Despite these difficulties, however, the division continued to keep up the pressure on the enemy forces facing it. On the 29th January, 1st Canadian Parachute Battalion sent out a two-man patrol, consisting of Lieutenant Don Proulx and Sergeant R. MacLean, on a twenty-four hour mission. The two men were tasked with escorting an artillery forward observer party, under the command of Captain Boss, across the Maas and taking it behind enemy lines to a location where an observation post would be established. Artillery fire would then be directed on to targets on the main road and railway line which ran parallel to the river. The forward observers were equipped with a new type of radio which could not be detected by enemy radio direction-finding equipment.

The patrol departed well after last light and made a successful crossing of the river. On the far side it disembarked from its assault boat and waded up a small stream for about a hundred yards before reaching higher ground. After crawling past an enemy-occupied house, two German soldiers were encountered in a trench. These were dispatched silently with fighting knives

and the patrol continued on its way through the night to its intended OP location which was two miles away.

By dawn the patrol was in position and the radio set up and operational.

Lieutenant Proulx and Sergeant MacLean installed themselves nearby in an abandoned gun pit. The position of the OP afforded a very clear view of the main road and railway line whilst providing good cover for the observers. Consequently, effective artillery fire was brought down on enemy troops and transport in a series of barrages throughout the day. However, the weather was bad with a steady downpour of rain and snow and, as dusk was approaching, Captain Boss decided to return to his base.

The route back to the rendezvous with the assault boat was slow and without incident, the patrol making a wide detour of the enemy-occupied house. When the river bank was reached, however, the enemy suddenly opened fire and the patrol was forced to take cover in the stream, with everyone being forced to crawl down it to the river with only their heads above water until they reached the RV point about a hundred yards away. Once clear of the area, the patrol could hear shouting from the enemy positions after which all was quiet. When it was deemed safe to continue, a signal was sent for the boat to cross and the patrol was picked up safely half-an-hour later.

By the middle of February the flood conditions were making patrolling conditions even more hazardous for both sides, the water level of the Maas rising even further. Conditions on the front became relatively quiet, the main battle by then being to the north. 1st Canadian Army had already crossed the Maas and, having cleared the Reichswald Forest by the 13th February, was only a day's march away from the town of Emmerich on the banks of the Rhine.

Patrol operations by the division nevertheless continued. During the latter half of February, Lieutenant Eric Burdon of C Company 1st Canadian Parachute Battalion led a reconnaissance patrol across the Maas to a small village on the far bank to discover the

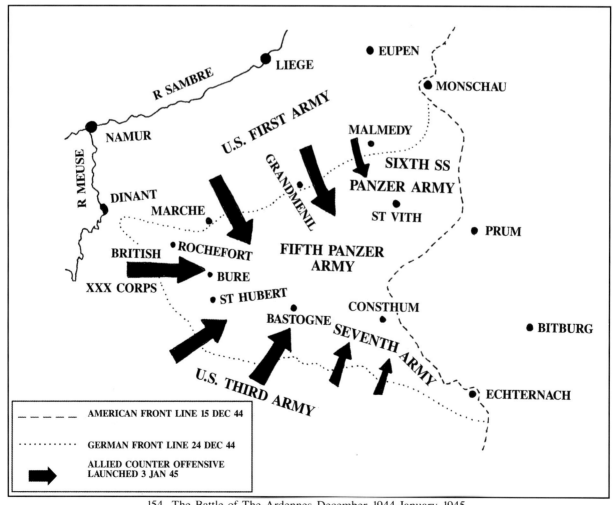

154. The Battle of The Ardennes December 1944-January 1945.

number of enemy in that particular area. The plan called for Lieutenant Burdon, Sergeant Saunders and other members of their platoon to establish a firm base on the outskirts of the village whilst another officer, Lieutenant Brown, and one soldier entered the village to discover the strength of the enemy.

After this task had been successfully carried out, Lieutenant Burdon studied the movements of the enemy troops and noticed that some of them regularly left a house at the edge of the village, moved down a short length of destroyed railway line to another house about a hundred yards from the village and later returned. On returning to his platoon's positions Lieutenant Burdon reported this information to his company commander, Major John Hanson, who decided to send Burdon and a small group of men back to the same area on the next night with the task of capturing a prisoner.

On the following evening Lieutenant Burdon and his patrol crossed the river and headed for a large drainage ditch, some ten feet in width and six feet in depth, which had previously been spanned by a small railway bridge which had been destroyed by shellfire. The ditch was now crossed via a wide plank of wood. From his study of enemy movements the previous day, Burdon knew that each time a German soldier left the village and walked to the lone house across the plank, another soldier would return to the village via the same route a few minutes later.

Burdon positioned his patrol in the ditch by the plank and waited, the lack of a moon and the overcast sky making it a dark night. As soon as an enemy soldier had crossed the ditch, Burdon's men removed the plank and waited. Sure enough, a few minutes later, they heard the sound of someone approaching the ditch from the direction of the lone house and seconds later a very startled enemy soldier found himself falling into the ditch and into the arms of a group of Canadian paratroopers. He was immediately subdued and rapidly bundled back down the ditch to the river and the waiting boat which then ferried the patrol and its captive back to the other side of the Maas.

During the third week of February, 6th Airborne Division was withdrawn back to England to prepare for its coming role in a major operation which would take place in the latter part of the following month: Operation 'Varsity' — the crossing of the Rhine. The seaborne 'tail' of the division was left behind in Belgium, the intention being that this element would rejoin the division once it had landed in Germany. The three brigades, together with those divisional troops also taking part in the operation, returned to their bases in Wiltshire to start preparing for an airborne assault on Germany.

155. Sapper Marshall of 249th Field Company RE searches for mines along the verge of a road in the Ardennes. (Photo: Imperial War Museum)

156. Field Marshal Montgomery with senior officers of 6th Airborne Division during his visit in the Ardennes in January 1945. *Back row, left to right:* Lt Col Napier Crookenden (CO 9 Para Bn), Lt Col Paul Gleadell (CO 12 Devons), Lt Col Gerald Ford, Lt Col Michael Roberts (GSO 1 Ops HQ 6 Abn Div), Maj Archie Bookless (Adjt 8 Para Bn). *Centre row left to right:* Lt Col Ken Darling (CO 12 Para Bn), Lt Col Geoffrey Pine Coffin (CO 7 Para Bn), Lt Col Jeff Nicklin (CO 1 Cdn Para Bn), Lt Col Peter Luard (CO 13 Para Bn). *Second and front rows, left to right:* Brig Edward Flavell (Comd 6 Aldg Bde), Maj Gen Eric Bols (Comd 6 Abn Div), Brig James Hill (Comd 3 Para Bde), Field Marshal Montgomery, Brig Nigel Poett (Comd 5 Para Bde). (Photo: Imperial War Museum)

159. *Above:* A member of 5th Parachute Brigade Signals Section operating two ten-line field telephone exchanges in a cellar at Venlo, on the Mass.
(Photo: Imperial War Museum)

160. *Above right:* Sergeant Davies, the cipher NCO, and a signaller of 5th Parachute Brigade Signals Section in a defensive position around the brigade headquarters near Venlo. The radio in the trench is a No. 76 Set, which was used for CW rear link communications.
(Photo: Imperial War Museum)

158. *Opposite page. bottom:* Field Marshal Montgomery talking with the three brigade commanders during his visit. *Left to right:* Major General Eric Bols, Field Marshal Montgomery, Brigadier Edward Flavell, Brigadier James Hill and Brigadier Nigel Poett. On the extreme right of the picture is Lieutenant Colonel Napier Crookenden, Commanding Officer of 9th Parachute Battalion.
(Photo: Imperial War Museum)

161. *Right:* two linemen of 5th Parachute Brigade Signals Section checking a junction at Heldon, in Holland.
(Photo: Imperial War Museum)

Operation 'Varsity'

By the middle of January 1945, the Germans had been routed in the Ardennes and Hitler's final gamble in trying to prevent the eventual invasion of Germany had failed. His losses had been huge, about forty thousand men killed or wounded and over fifty thousand taken prisoner by the time his forces had withdrawn over the Rhine.

The Allies, on the other hand, despite their heavy losses had nearly four million men under arms in North West Europe. Their armies were once again at full strength with effectiveness and morale at very high levels.

Field Marshal Montgomery had produced a plan for a crossing of the Rhine north of the Ruhr, between Wesel and Emmerich, and for the establishment of a secure bridgehead from which his divisions would subsequently advance into northern Germany. Two armies, General Simpson's 9th US Army and General Miles Dempsey's 2nd British Army, would carry out the crossing. Montgomery later summed up his plan as follows:

"My intention was to secure a bridgehead prior to developing operations to isolate the Ruhr and to thrust into the northern plains of Germany.

In outline, my plan was to cross the Rhine on a front of two armies between Rheinberg and Rees, using the 9th American Army on the right and 2nd Army on the left. The principal initial object was the important communications centre of Wesel. I intended that the bridgehead should extend to the south sufficiently far to cover Wesel from enemy ground action, and to the north to include bridge sites at Emmerich: the depth of the bridgehead was to be made sufficient to provide room to form up major forces for the drive to the east and north-east."

The codename given to this operation was 'Plunder' and the date set for it was the 24th March. The forces available were the XIII, XVI and XIX US Corps of the 9th US Army and the 8th, 12th and 30th British Corps, 2nd Canadian Corps, and XVIII US Airborne Corps which were all under command of 2nd Army.

XVIII US Airborne Corps, commanded by Major General Matthew Ridgway, comprised 17th US Airborne Division, under Major General William 'Bud' Miley, and 6th Airborne Division. Both divisions were to be dropped by day east of the Rhine after the main crossings had commenced and would be supported by artillery on the western side of the river. The codename for this airborne operation was 'Varsity'.

On the other side of the northern Rhine, the German forces defending the area where the Allies would cross consisted of the 1st Parachute Army. This formation was commanded by Generaloberst Schlemm who was a veteran of German operations in Crete, Russia, Italy and the bitter fighting that had taken place in the Reichswald. 1st Parachute Army consisted of the 2nd Parachute Corps, 86th Infantry Corps and 63rd Corps. Generaloberst Schlemm's corps reserve was 47th Panzer Corps. 2nd Parachute Corps consisted of the 6th, 7th and 8th Parachute Divisions, each consisting of between three and four thousand men only but still effective as fighting formations. 86th Infantry Corps comprised mainly 84th Infantry Division, a very weak formation numbering just over fifteen hundred men, whilst 47th Panzer Corps consisted of 116th Panzer and 15th Panzer Grenadier Divisions.

The total number of armoured vehicles available to 1st Parachute Army was estimated at being between a hundred and a hundred and fifty, with 116th Panzer Division reported as having up to seventy tanks and 15th Panzer Grenadier Division credited with fifteen tanks and between twenty and thirty self-propelled guns. A heavy anti-tank battalion was also reported as having possibly arrived in the area.

Enemy artillery in the area where the airborne landings would take place was reported as totalling fifty field or medium guns. Anti-aircraft artillery, however, was estimated at a hundred and fifty-three light and a hundred and three heavy guns. By the third week of March, however, these figures had increased to seven hundred and twelve light and a hundred and fourteen heavy weapons, indicating that the enemy were definitely anticipating an airborne operation of some sort to be launched against them.

The terrain over the area on which XVIII US Airborne Corps was to land was flat, forming part of the Rhine flood plain. It

162. Final briefings being given with the aid of a model.
(Photo: Imperial War Museum)

163. Officers and NCOs study air photographs as part of their final familiarisation with their objectives.
(Photo: Imperial War Museum)

possessed one single dominating feature in the form of an area of high, heavily wooded ground called the Diersfordterwald which overlooked the area where 2nd Army's 12th Corps would cross the river. The main road connecting Wesel to Rees and Emmerich ran through the Diersfordterwald, to the east of which the ground was open and flat, consisting of fields bounded by small ditches and wire fences. Along the east of XVIII US Airborne Corps' area was the River Issel which varied between thirty and fifty feet in width and thus formed an obstacle to armour. An unfinished autobahn also ran along the eastern edge of the area whilst all the roads entering it converged on the village of Hamminkeln.

The Outline Plan

The task allocated to XVIII US Airborne Corps was firstly the seizing and holding of the Diersfordterwald and the ground north of Wesel up to the River Issel, and secondly the defence of the bridgehead against counter-attacks. The lessons of Normandy, and subsequently Arnhem, had been well learned because the entire corps would be flown in one lift and would be dropped in daylight on top of its objectives. Both divisions would be dropped or landed within range of the supporting guns on the west bank of the Rhine in order that artillery support would be immediately available after the landings had taken place. In addition, the planned link-ups with ground troops would take place on the first day of the operation.

6th Airborne Division would drop and land on the northern part of the area at 1000 hours on the 24th March, with the tasks of seizing the high ground east of Bergen, the town of Hamminkeln and certain bridges over the River Issel whilst also protecting the northern flank of XVIII US Airborne Corps. It was then to make contact as soon as possible with 17th US Airborne Division, which would be on its right, and with 12th Corps which would be crossing the Rhine and moving up to its rear and on its left flank.

17th US Airborne Division would land on the southern part of the 'Varsity' area at the same time, seizing the high ground to the east of Diersfordt and other bridges over the Issel. It was also to protect the southern flank of XVIII US Airborne Corps whilst establishing contact with 6th Airborne Division on its left, with 1st Commando Brigade which would be on its right after seizing Wesel the night before and with 12th Corps which would be to the rear and on its right flank after crossing the Rhine.

An early link-up and provision of armoured support would be effected by elements of 6th Guards Tank Brigade. A squadron of the 3rd Tank Battalion Scots Guards would cross the Rhine on D+1 to link up with 6th Airborne Division, whilst the remainder of the battalion plus the 4th Tank Battalion Grenadier Guards and the 4th Tank Battalion Coldstream Guards, both of whom would be supporting 17th US Airborne Division, would cross as soon as the situation permitted.

6th Airborne Division

Once detailed orders had been received from Major General Ridgway at Headquarters XVIII US Airborne Corps on the 25th February, Major General Bols and his staff set to work. On the 2nd March the divisional commander verbally issued his provisional plan. This was followed on the 6th March by verbal orders and on the 12th March the divisional operation order was issued. A final co-ordinating conference was held on the 14th March, commanding officers and heads of supporting arms having been briefed on the 9th March. Subsequently, company commanders were briefed on the 18th March and platoon commanders and their equivalents on the 21st March.

3rd Parachute Brigade would drop on to DZ 'A' at the north-west corner of the Diersfordterwald and seize the Schneppenberg feature. It was then to clear and hold the western side of the forest and the road junction at Bergen. In addition, it was to patrol out to, and if necessary hold, the area of the railway line which ran through the north-east of the forest. Contact with 5th Parachute Brigade was to be established as soon as possible.

Meanwhile 5th Parachute Brigade would drop on DZ 'B' north-west of Hamminkeln and was to clear and secure an area on either side of the main road leading from the drop zone to Hamminkeln. It was to patrol westwards and was to hold the area immediately east of the railway line whilst linking up with 3rd Parachute Brigade.

6th Airlanding Brigade, now commanded by Brigadier Hugh Bellamy DSO, was tasked with landing in company groups as close as possible to individual allocated objectives. Each battalion was allotted its own landing zone within which the exact location for every company was carefully planned. Headquarters 6th Airlanding Brigade and the 12th Battalion The Devonshire Regiment would land on LZ 'R' south-west of Hamminkeln, the battalion being tasked with the capture of the town. The 2nd Battalion The Oxfordshire & Buckinghamshire Light Infantry would land on LZ 'O' north of Hamminkeln and would take and secure the road and rail bridges over the River Issel between Hamminkeln and Ringenberg. Meanwhile, the 1st Battalion The Royal

164. Members of No. 2 Platoon, A Company 8th Parachute Battalion pose in front of the aircraft which will fly them over the Rhine and drop them beyond it.
(Photo: Mr J. Enstone)

165. A group of officers of 8th Parachute Battalion. *Left to right:* Maj Archie Backless (Adjt), Lt Col George Hewetson (CO), Maj John Kippen (OC B Coy), Maj John Tilley (Bn 2i/c), Maj Bob Flood (OC A Coy) and Maj John Shappee (OC C Coy).
(Photo: Imperial War Museum)

Ulster Rifles would land on LZ 'U' south of Hamminkeln and would seize and hold the bridge over the Issel on the main road from Hamminkeln to Brunen and the area around it.

Headquarters 6th Airborne Division, Headquarters Royal Engineers, two batteries of 53rd (Worcestershire Yeomanry) Airlanding Light Regiment RA, the light tank squadron and the 4.2-inch mortar troop of 6th Airborne Armoured Reconnaissance Regiment, three troops of sappers and certain other supporting arms elements would land on LZ 'P' north-east of the Diersfordterwald near Kopenhof where the main divisional headquarters would be established on arrival.

An impressive amount of artillery support had been allotted to 6th Airborne Division. In direct support would be three field regiments and two medium regiments. On call would be two further medium regiments, whilst a battery of American long range artillery would be available for harassing fire tasks. 3rd Parachute Brigade would be supported by the three field regiments whilst 5th Parachute and 6th Airlanding Brigades, which would be beyond the range of field guns, would each be supported by a medium regiment and by the division's own airlanding light regiment. 2nd Forward Observation Unit RA, which had been newly formed for this role, would provide all the forward observer parties and fire control for the supporting artillery on the western bank of the Rhine, as well as fire liaison parties at the gun end of each supporting battery.

In order that there would be no risk to the aircraft bringing in 6th and 17th US Airborne Divisions, a major limitation had to be placed on the supporting artillery to the west of the Rhine with regard to the preliminary bombardment of German positions. The softening bombardment, carried out by nine field regiments, eleven medium regiments, one heavy regiment, four heavy batteries, one heavy anti-aircraft regiment, one super-heavy battery and three American 155mm battalions, would commence one hour and forty minutes before the time of the drop (P-100) and would cease forty minutes beforehand (P-40). An anti-flak

bombardment, designed to neutralise the enemy anti-aircraft defences, would be carried out by eleven field regiments, eleven medium regiments, two heavy regiments, one super-heavy regiment, one heavy anti-aircraft regiment and three US 155mm battalions. This would take place from thirty minutes prior to the drop (P-30) up to the time of the drop (P-Hour), guns ceasing fire as the leading aircraft crossed the line of the gun areas. All firing was to cease on commencement of the fly-in so as to avoid any risk of aircraft inadvertently being hit by artillery fire. There was a risk, of course, that this breathing space would give the enemy a chance to recover as the drop was taking place. However, it was firmly laid down that no gun was to fire along or across the route taken by any aircraft during the fly-in or fly-out.

The division would be flown in by aircraft of Nos. 38 and 46 Groups Royal Air Force, which would provide all the tug aircraft for towing the division's gliders, and of IX US Troop Carrier Command which would drop all the paratroops. The total number of machines required to lift both 6th and 17th US Airborne Divisions was some two thousand seven hundred and forty aircraft and gliders.

Early in March two full-scale divisional exercises were conducted in the area of Bury St Edmunds. Designated "Mush I" and "Mush II" they were intended to practise the division in operations behind a major enemy defensive line. Although it was not divulged at the time, they were in fact rehearsals for Operation 'Varsity'.

On the 19th and 20th March, all units of the division taking part in the operation moved into secure transit camps. Here commanding officers gave out orders as Lieutenant Colonel Napier Crookenden, Commanding Officer of 9th Parachute Battalion, later recalled:

"We set up our models and air photos in a specially guarded room and I gave out my orders to the company commanders. We were to drop last on Drop Zone 'A' after the 8th and 1st Canadian Parachute Battalions and, while they secured the landing

166. Men of 8th Parachute Battalion prepare their equipment whilst waiting beside their aircraft. (Photo: Imperial War Museum)

area, we were to move southwards to attack and capture the highest part of the Diersfordterwald and the Schneppenberg, destroying several batteries of German guns on the way.

Then the whole battalion crowded into the same room, all six hundred of them, and I explained to them our drop and our tasks in some detail. It was both an exhilarating and a sobering experience, talking to so many men of such quality and realising how intently each one of them was following my words and their tasks, as the plan unfolded. I must have spoken for twenty minutes or more with hardly a sound, a cough or a movement from the men. Afterwards each company and each platoon took its turn in the briefing room and each man had to confirm, on the model in front of his own platoon, his rendezvous, his task and the objectives of his company and of the battalion.''

One particular briefing undoubtedly designed to be a morale booster was that given by Brigadier James Hill to 1st Canadian Parachute Battalion and other units in 3rd Parachute Brigade: ''Gentlemen, the artillery and air support is fantastic! And if you are worried about the kind of reception you'll get, just put yourself in the place of the enemy. Beaten and demoralised, pounded by our artillery and bombers, what would you think, gentlemen, if you saw a horde of ferocious, bloodthirsty paratroopers, bristling with weapons, cascading down upon you from the skies? And you needn't think, just because you hear a few stray bullets flying about, that some miserable Hun is shooting at you. That is merely a form of egotism. But if by any chance you should happen to meet one of these Huns in person, you will treat him, gentlemen, with extreme disfavour.''

On the night of the 23rd March, three and a half thousand Allied artillery pieces opened fire against the enemy positions on the eastern bank of the Rhine in the sector where the crossing would take place. The Germans had already been pounded by heavy bombing which had commenced on the 21st February, 3,471 bombers unleashing 8,500 tons of bombs on roads, railways and airfields whilst another 2,090 bombers dropped a further 6,600 tons on enemy barracks and positions. In addition, Allied fighter aircraft carried out sweeps over the area east of the Rhine, attacking convoys, anti-aircraft batteries and, on one occasion, the headquarters of 1st Parachute Army when Generaloberst Schlemm himself was severely wounded in the attack.

At 2100 hours on the 23rd March, units of 1st Commando Brigade crossed the Rhine in assault boats whilst RAF Lancaster bombers attacked the town of Wesel. At 2200 hours, 12th Corps commenced crossing near Xanten whilst at 2300 hours 30th Corps crossed over further north. By 0400 hours the US 9th Army had started to cross south of Wesel and by dawn 21st Army Group had established a number of bridgeheads on the east bank.

Meanwhile, in England, 6th Airborne Division was preparing to emplane and by 0530 hours each 'stick' was waiting beside its Dakota or glider. When dawn came, it broke clear and bright. At 0730 hours the first aircraft started taking off and soon the entire vast armada of transport aircraft, gliders and tugs was airborne and heading towards Germany. For many members of the division it would be their first parachute jump or glider landing into action, and for some their first encounter with the enemy. As the aircraft carrying the division crossed the Ruhr, they met heavy bombers on their way back to England after softening up targets on the ground. Some of them were limping along, trailing black smoke from damaged engines.

Over Belgium, the division's aircraft turned north-east and joined the column of aircraft carrying 17th US Airborne Division. The two streams of aircraft, each nine wide, flew side by side as they headed towards the Rhine.

3rd Parachute Brigade

3rd Parachute Brigade's drop went according to plan, although it was nine minutes early. The order of landing was 8th Parachute Battalion, Brigade Headquarters, 1st Canadian and then 9th Parachute Battalions, a troop of 3rd Parachute Squadron RE and 224th Parachute Field Ambulance. Enemy anti-aircraft fire was only light when the leading aircraft arrived but intensified as the drop continued and as the enemy recovered from the preliminary artillery bombardment which had ceased just before the aircraft crossed the Rhine.

Brigadier James Hill later recalled events during the landing of his brigade:

167. Officers of 13th Parachute Battalion. *Back row, left to right:* Lt Alf Lageren, Lt Dick Burton, Lt Geoff Otway, —?—, Lt Dixie Dean, Maj Nobby Clarke, Lt Col Peter Luard, Capt Claude Milman, Maj John Cramphorn, Maj Gerald Ford, Maj Bill Grantham. *Front row, left to right:* Padre W. Whitfield-Foy, Lt Joe Hodgson, Lt Ken Walton, Capt Leslie Golding, Lt Malcolm Town, Lt Harry Pollak, Capt Jack Watson. (Photo: Major J. Watson MC)

"As the great battle for the Rhine Crossing approached, everyone felt that it would mark the beginning of the end. I myself looked with amazement at the progress that had been made in airborne warfare since the days when I had led 1st Parachute Battalion in its drop in North Africa in October 1942 from thirty-two American Dakota aircraft whose crews had never dropped parachutists before and which were not equipped with radio communications equipment. On that occasion I had sat in the cockpit with the American commander. The Dakotas were flying in line astern and, aided by a quarter-inch to the mile scale French motoring map, the navigators located our DZs in Tunisia some four hundred miles away. On seeing the leading aircraft disgorge its load, the remainder followed suit.

Two-and-a-half years later the airborne armada, in which 3rd Parachute Brigade and the rest of 6th Airborne Division were travelling, comprised some five hundred and forty Dakotas flying low in tight formation, followed by thirteen hundred gliders and their tug aircraft in which 6th Airlanding Brigade and the divisional troops were riding into battle - some two thousand seven hundred and forty aircraft, all communicating with one another by radio.

By this time lessons from previous operations had been learned and I had the choice of dropping 3rd Parachute Brigade on a small DZ, measuring approximately a thousand yards by eight hundred yards, which was located in a clearing in a wood amongst enemy positions manned by German parachute troops. The alternative was a far more ideal DZ some three miles away but with the prospect of fighting all the way to our objective. The choice for me was simple — land on top of the objective and take the risks of a bad drop which in the event did not occur as the American pilots performed brilliantly, although they dropped us some nine minutes early.

Regrettably, one of the few soldiers to be dropped into the surrounding trees was Lieutenant Colonel Jeff Nicklin, the Commanding Officer of 1st Canadian Parachute Battalion, who was

immediately shot and killed before he could get down from where he was hung up.

Apart from the loss of a splendid battalion commander, I recall two other incidents. The first took place near my command post on the edge of the DZ where there was a small belt of trees. At the end of this was a spinney which was held by some Germans who immediately engaged our troops as they landed. I saw Major John Kippen, who was one of the best company commanders in my brigade, of 8th Parachute Battalion which was tasked with clearing the DZ. I told him to collect some men and eliminate the enemy position which he proceeded to do with considerable gallantry but was unfortunately killed in the process.

The second incident occurred when I was watching the approach of a Horsa which was obviously going to crash into the wood on the edge of which I was standing. It banked steeply and flew along the side of the wood until it caught its port wingtip in the trees twelve feet above the ground. To my amazement, I discovered that it contained, amongst other things, my batman, jeep, and wireless operator as well as a motorcycle. Regrettably, the pilot broke his legs but the other men in the aircraft survived."

8th Parachute Battalion

8th Parachute Battalion's initial task was to clear and secure the drop zone, and in particular to clear the enemy dug in around it. Its objectives were the triangular and hatchet-shaped woods protruding from the main woods to the south of the DZ and two small copses which commanded the open area of the DZ itself. Only four minutes had been allowed to complete this task. As soon as it landed, each company went straight into action against its own assigned objective. A Company, under Major Bob Flood, advanced on a small wood in the north-east corner of the DZ, which it took with little difficulty by 1030 hours, taking several prisoners in the process. C Company, commanded by Major John Shappee, together with Battalion Headquarters and the Mortar

168. A 'stick' relaxes beside its aircraft. (Photo: Airborne Forces Museum)

Platoon, occupied the triangular wood in the south-east corner where they found some well dug enemy trenches which they promptly took over.

B Company and the Machine Gun Platoon, however, were having a tough time. Their objective was the hatchet-shaped wood, on the southern side of the DZ, which was defended by two platoons of enemy paratroops. Unfortunately the company was somewhat disorganised on landing and thus started to assemble at the objective, which was also its RV location, in groups of two or three. Men coming across the DZ from the north found themselves under fire. Eventually the company commander, Major John Kippen, assembled about a platoon in strength and attacked through the narrow part of the woods from the south. However, this attack was beaten off and Major Kippen and the platoon commander were killed.

While B Company was attempting to take its objective, the rest of the battalion was still arriving. The Commanding Officer, Lieutenant Colonel George Hewetson, later described the events that took place:

"In the meantime, men were still coming in from the DZ. The stick of the Anti-Tank Platoon with the platoon commander had jumped to the east of the DZ, owing to a failure in the light signals in the aircraft. Returning to the DZ, they had a short sharp engagement in a house and captured an officer and fifteen men of a German signal unit together with their 3-ton lorry. This vehicle was invaluable later when the DZ had to be cleared.

The gliders began to arrive at 1100 hours. One of the first down, a 9th Parachute Battalion glider, overshot the LZ but although it was badly damaged there were no casualties. My second in command, Major John Tilley, had gone off to see Brigade Headquarters and B Company. I was standing on the edge of the wood, briefing my Intelligence Officer to keep in touch with Brigade Headquarters on the wireless, while I went down to see how B Company was faring and to see if it would be necessary to put in an attack with C Company. Two sergeants, one from 9th Parachute Battalion, were standing a few yards away.

Suddenly, with a terrific crash, a glider came through the trees and I found myself lying under the wheel of a jeep. I managed to crawl out from the wreckage to find the glider, one of the medical Horsas of 9th Parachute Battalion, completely written off. The crew had been killed and my Intelligence Officer and the two sergeants were also dead.

At about this time my second in command reported back from B Company. The wood had been taken by a platoon attacking from the north-east using 36 and 77 grenades and covered by the fire of the platoon which had earlier attempted an attack from the south. The last phase of the attack was a hand-to-hand fight down a trench, led by the platoon commander. A considerable number of the enemy had been killed and one officer and twenty six soldiers were taken prisoner."

At 1115 hours the battalion's Hamilcar glider arrived, bringing in a very welcome load of a Bren carrier, spare 3-inch mortars, Vickers medium machine guns and some radio sets. Shortly afterwards, the enemy began to bring down shell and mortar fire on the drop zone. However, the battalion continued to clear it of equipment and containers, almost completing the task by 1200 hours at which time it was ordered into brigade reserve. It subsequently moved off from the DZ, leaving one platoon from C Company to finish clearing equipment from the DZ and to guard the equipment dump. *En route* to its new position, the battalion encountered two 88mm guns, one of which was firing into the trees and causing casualties from shrapnel bursts. Both guns, however, were attacked and knocked out. Later in the day, at 1830 hours, the battalion was ordered to move again to a position covering the rear of divisional headquarters at Kopenhof.

1st Canadian Parachute Battalion

1st Canadian Parachute Battalion encountered machine gun fire as it jumped, and lost several men before they landed or when they became caught up in trees in the woods. The Commanding Officer, Lieutenant Colonel Jeff Nicklin, landed in a tree above

169. A group waits beside its Hamilcar glider. (Photo: Imperial War Museum)

170. Horsa gliders lined up at RAF Rivenhall with their Albemarle tug aircraft waiting to taxi forward in front of them to be hooked up. (Photo: Museum of Army Flying)

171-172. *Above:* A view from the cockpit of a Horsa *en route* for the Rhine. (Photo: Imperial War Museum) *Right:* A Horsa, carrying men of the 12th Battalion The Devonshire Regiment, photographed from the rear turret of a Stirling flown by Flight Sergeant R.S. Trout during the flight to the Rhine. (Photo: Mr R. S. Trout)

a machine gun position and was killed as he hung there in his parachute harness. When he failed to arrive at the battalion RV location, his second in command, Major Fraser Eadie, assumed command of the unit.

The leading element, C Company, jumped whilst 8th Parachute Battalion was still engaged in clearing the enemy from the vicinity of the DZ and encountered heavy machine gun fire on landing. Almost immediately, misfortune struck when the company commander, Major John Hanson, broke his collarbone on landing. To add to the company's woes, the aircraft carrying the company second in command, Captain John Clancy, was hit by flak over the drop zone. Clancy and two others, Lieutenant Ken Spicer and Private J. Cerniuk, managed to jump as the aircrew struggled to keep their blazing aircraft airborne. Clancy landed in an enemy occupied area and was captured whilst Spicer landed safely. Private Cerniuk, who was carrying the company headquarters radio set, descended under heavy machine gun fire which cut the rope from which the container carrying his radio set and Sten gun was suspended below him. Nevertheless he landed safely and, after a few encounters with enemy machine guns, later linked up with a unit of 15th (Scottish) Division.

The absence of both the company commander and the company second in command resulted in Sergeants Miles Saunders and Bill Murray taking command. Quickly organising a number of other members of C Company who had landed nearby, they carried out an attack which resulted in the enemy being cleared and the company's objective being taken, several enemy gun crews being neutralised in the process.

As the day continued, C Company was subjected to a considerable amount of mortar and shellfire. The enemy advanced in force into some woods near the company's positions and forestalled any attempts to reach the gliders on the drop zone.

Meanwhile A Company had landed at the eastern end of the drop zone and within thirty minutes over two thirds of its number had reached the RV. Major Peter Griffin decided to mount an immediate attack on a group of buildings which were designated for subsequent use by Battalion Headquarters. By 1130 hours these had been captured, although thirteen casualties were suffered.

Part of A Company's objective consisted of a group of houses.

When the attack went in on these, the enemy put up a fierce resistance and at one point the attack itself faltered. Seeing the problem, Company Sergeant Major Green quickly organised some covering fire and then went forward with an assault group to the first house. This was cleared after some vicious close quarter fighting, after which the other buildings were cleared of the enemy in a similar fashion until the entire objective had been captured. Later in the day, the enemy counter-attacked in an effort to recapture the area but they were beaten off. A heavy mortar concentration was then brought down on A Company's position, followed by a large enemy patrol moving up. This attack was also beaten off, with several enemy being taken prisoner.

B Company, which was commanded by Captain Sam McGowan, assembled at its RV and immediately put in an attack on a group of farm buildings and a wooded area which was one of its objectives and from which the enemy was already bringing fire to bear on the company. Under cover of its own Bren light machine guns, the company swept forward and quickly overran the enemy positions, flushing out bunkers and trenches with grenades. Company Sergeant Major Kemp led an attack on the farmhouse itself under very heavy fire. In less than thirty minutes the entire company objective had been taken and a number of prisoners captured.

Shortly afterwards, Sergeant A. Page took out a six-man patrol to reconnoitre the woods in the vicinity of the company's positions. He returned a short while later, escorting nearly a hundred prisoners who were promptly added to those already captured.

During the afternoon, it was learned that No. 5 Platoon had suffered very heavy casualties on the drop zone and Lieutenant Jack Brunnette, the platoon commander, was reported to have been killed. Nevertheless, the company consolidated its defences and proceeded to bring effective fire to bear on numbers of enemy troops who were moving around the company's area. By midafternoon the situation had quietened down and the area seemed clear of the enemy.

As the day wore on the intensity of the fighting slackened but the drop zone, which was littered with wrecked gliders and equipment, still continued to be an area of danger. Several casualties

173. Men of 6th Guards Tank Brigade watching 6th Airborne Division pass overhead. (Photo: Imperial War Museum)

were suffered and it was here that Corporal George Topham, a medical orderly of 1st Canadian Parachute Battalion, performed the action that was to result in his later being awarded 6th Airborne Division's only Victoria Cross. A wounded man was lying out in the open and two members of 224th Parachute Field Ambulance went forward to rescue him but were killed as they did so. Part of Corporal Topham's citation describes what happened next:

"Without hesitation, and on his own initiative, Corporal Topham went forward through intense fire to replace the orderlies who had been killed before his eyes. As he worked on the wounded man, he himself was shot through the nose. In spite of severe bleeding and intense pain, he never faltered in his task. Having completed first aid, he carried the wounded man steadily and slowly back through continuous fire to the shelter of a wood.

During the next two hours Corporal Topham refused all offers of medical help for his own wound. He worked most devotedly throughout this period to bring wounded in, showing complete disregard for the heavy and accurate enemy fire. It was only when all casualties had been cleared that he consented to his own wound being treated.

His immediate evacuation was ordered but he interceded so earnestly on his own behalf that he was eventually allowed to return to duty.

On his way back to his company he came across a carrier which had received a direct hit. Enemy mortar bombs were still dropping around, the carrier itself was still burning fiercely and its own mortar ammunition was exploding. An experienced officer on the spot had warned all not to approach the carrier.

Corporal Topham, however, immediately went out alone in spite of the blasting ammunition and enemy fire and rescued the three occupants of the carrier. He brought these men back across the open, and although one died almost immediately afterwards, he arranged for the evacuation of the other two who undoubtedly owe their lives to him.

This NCO showed gallantry of the highest order. For six hours, most of the time in great pain, he performed a series of acts of outstanding bravery, and his magnificent and selfless courage inspired all those who witnessed it."

9th Parachute Battalion

9th Parachute Battalion was the last to jump. Lieutenant Colonel Napier Crookenden later described the scene in his aircraft as it neared the final stages of the flight:

"There had been some singing in the early part of our three-hour flight but most men had gone to sleep or relapsed into the usual state of semi-conscious suspended animation. The yell of "Twenty minutes to go!" from the crew chief woke us up and sent the adrenalin pumping through our veins.

We were over the battle-scarred wilderness of the Reichswald and the terrible ruins of Goch when the order "Stand up! Hook up!" brought us to our feet. Each man fastened the snap-hook on the end of his parachute strop to the overhead cable, fixed the safety pin and turned aft, holding the strop of the man in front in his left hand and steadying himself with his right on the overhead cable. The stick commander, Sergeant Matheson, checked each man's snap-hook. We all checked the man in front and, beginning with the last man of the stick, shouted out in turn, "Number Sixteen okay — Number Fifteen okay!" and so on down to myself at Number One.

Just aft of the door stood the crew chief in his flying helmet and overalls, listening on the intercom for our pilot's orders. I was watching the red and green lights above the door and I am sure that the rest of the stick were too. The red light glowed, the crew chief yelled "Red on! Stand to the door!" and I moved forward, left foot first, until I was in the door with both hands holding the door edges, left foot on the sill and slipstream blasting my face.

Then the great, curving river was below me and seconds later, a blow on the back from the crew chief and a bellow of "Green on! Go!" in my left ear sent me out into the sunlight. Once the tumbling and jerking were over and my parachute had developed, I had a wonderful view of the drop zone right below me. I could see the double line of trees along the road to the west and the square wood in the middle of the DZ. The ground was already covered with the parachutes of the 8th and 1st Canadian Parachute Battalions and I could see them running towards their objectives. There was a continuous rattle of machine gun fire and the occasional thump of a mortar bomb or grenade and during my peaceful minute of descent, I heard the crack and thump of two near misses. It was clearly a most accurate and concentrated drop and I felt a surge of confidence and delight."

The battalion landed without any major mishap and after three quarters of an hour was almost fully assembled in the area of its RV. Shortly afterwards, it moved off with Major Alan Parry's A Company in the lead, followed by Battalion Headquarters, B and C Companies. As it headed for the Schneppenberg feature, the battalion encountered light opposition but this was easily dealt with by A Company which before long reached the Schneppenberg itself. B Company subsequently attacked a battery of 76mm guns, sited along the western edge of the woods, which were firing on units of 15th (Scottish) Division crossing the Rhine. Within a few minutes these had been silenced.

By 1300 hours 9th Parachute Battalion was in position on its final objective with A Company on the Schneppenberg, B Company astride the main road to the south-east and C Company in the wood to the south of the road. At 1530 hours, B Company sent out a patrol which made contact with the leading elements of the 1st Battalion The Royal Scots.

5th Parachute Brigade

Whilst 3rd Parachute Brigade was dropping with relatively few problems on Drop Zone 'A', 5th Parachute Brigade was encountering a rougher reception on Drop Zone 'B'. The order of drop was Brigade Headquarters, 13th Parachute Battalion, 12th Parachute Battalion and 7th Parachute Battalion.

In addition to the three battalions, the brigade group included 4th Airlanding Anti-Tank Battery RA, a detachment of 2nd Forward Observation Unit RA, a troop of 591st Parachute Squadron RE and 225th Parachute Field Ambulance. Heavy anti-aircraft fire was encountered and two aircraft were hit as they made their approach to the DZ. After dropping the brigade, the formation of Dakotas swung away to port for the flight home but met heavy anti-aircraft fire from units of the 7th Parachute Division in the area of Mehr to the west of the drop zone. Ten aircraft were shot down almost immediately, crashing on the east bank of the Rhine. A further seven were also brought down but these managed to crash-land west of the river. Seventy more aircraft were also damaged.

The drop zone also came under fire almost immediately after the drop began, whilst mortar and artillery fire was brought down on the battalions' RV areas.

Brigadier Nigel Poett was as usual jumping with the leading element of his brigade. With the rest of his 'stick', comprised of men of his brigade headquarters, he was standing at action stations in one of the leading Dakotas as it neared the battle already raging ahead.

'As we approached the Rhine, we could see ahead of us the battlefield covered by haze and the dust from the bombardment. At one thousand feet we passed over the administrative units and the supporting arms and then the crossing places themselves.

However, there was no time to interest ourselves in the troops on the ground, or in the craft upon the river, because the red light was on and, almost before we realised it, we were over

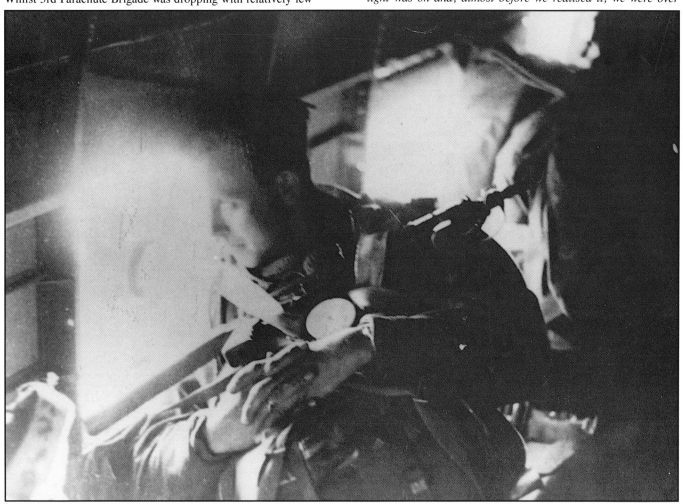

174. Sergeant Greenly of 22nd Independent Parachute Company seen here in the first Dakota to cross the Rhine. He was reputedly the first member of 6th Airborne Division to land east of the river. (Photo: Imperial War Museum)

enemy territory. We were being shot at and the aircraft bumped and shook. Then we were over the DZ, the green light was on and we were out.

As we dangled from our parachutes we tried, in the very short time available, to pick up the landmarks. These had seemed so very clear and simple on the sand models and in the air photographs, but now they appeared somewhat different as we came down rapidly amongst the firing and into the dust and smoke caused by the artillery bombardment which had finished more than ten minutes previously. Although this had been heavy, ten minutes was ample time for those enemy not knocked out to recover sufficiently to be a considerable threat to our parachutists as they swung in the air or disentangled themselves from their parachutes and got their bearings.

We felt very naked but this was where the battle experience of the brigade became evident. All three of my battalion commanders had taken part in the landings in Normandy. Together with our gunners, sappers and field ambulance, we had fought with the division in France, Belgium and Holland. Our officers and men all knew one another well and this was to prove an enormous advantage in this operation that was going to require a high standard of leadership right down to junior NCO level.

Assembly at RVs was always a tricky business and a landing in broad daylight, in an area covered by fire of enemy troops who were fully alert, meant that very rapid rallying and high standards of leadership on the DZ were essential. Moreover, the concentrated drop meant that the different sub-units of the battalions were inevitably mixed up. They had been shot at on their way down from the aircraft to the ground and they were under considerable harassing fire as they struggled out of their parachute harnesses, unfastened their kitbags, extracted their

weapons and got their bearings.

Although all three battalions had been dropped accurately, individual officers and men experienced considerable trouble in working out their exact positions. This period on the DZ was where most of our casualties occurred. Once enemy positions had been located and action taken to deal with them, the troops in them generally surrendered without putting up a serious fight. However, until they were spotted, they were extremely troublesome.

Just as our chaps were reaching their RVs, the gliderborne element of the brigade group began to approach its landing zone. To the south the gliders of 6th Airlanding Brigade also began to come in. This caused a considerable diversion of enemy artillery fire and provided a most welcome relief for us. It was, however, a most tragic sight to see gliders picked off in the air and on the ground. Their losses were very heavy and thus only a comparatively small proportion of our anti-tank guns and vehicles carrying the machine guns, mortars and ammunition reached the battalions at their RVs. There is no doubt that, had a strong enemy counter-attack developed later in the day, we would have been seriously embarrassed by these losses of anti-tank guns and ammunition reserves.

It was about one hour after the drop that our three battalions were sufficiently complete in their RVs to be able to report that they were ready to start on the second phase of the plan, the securing and consolidating of the brigade objective. Considering the circumstances of the landing, our casualties had not been unduly heavy. Our losses were approximately twenty per cent of those who had jumped. I lost my Brigade Major, Major Mike Brennan, and my Signals Officer, Lieutenant Crawford, on the DZ. My DAA & QMG, Major Ted Lough, was in a glider and also became a casualty when he was very badly wounded. As a

175. A Dakota and Horsa combination cross the Rhine. (Photo: Imperial War Museum)

result, my brigade headquarters had to be considerably reconstructed when we reached our RV.

One lesson I had learned in Normandy was that of wireless communications. On the night of D-Day I had lost the wireless team that jumped with me and I was without any proper communications throughout the whole night. This time, therefore, I and all my battalion commanders carried our own American walkie-talkie sets strapped inside our parachute harnesses. These radios were intended only to maintain control until proper communications had been set in the RV or on the final objectives but they proved to be a huge success.''

7th Parachute Battalion

7th Parachute Battalion's initial task was to establish itself at the northern edge of the drop zone, which was north-west of Hamminkeln, and to engage any enemy whilst 12th and 13th Parachute Battalions captured the brigade's objective which was the ground astride the road leading from the drop zone to Hamminkeln, thus preventing the movement of any enemy reserves through the area. The Commanding Officer, Lieutenant Colonel Geoffrey Pine Coffin, later gave an account of his battalion's landing and the events on the DZ:

"The drop was at 1010 hours and was from rather higher than we liked for an operational drop; it must have been from nearly one thousand feet. This would normally have been an advantage as it seems that one is in the air for longer than one expects and thus gets a good chance of spotting a landmark as one comes down, but in this case everyone was getting pretty anxious to get down quickly because it was far from healthy in the air. The German flak gunners weren't getting much success in shooting down the Dakotas so a lot of them switched and burst their shells amongst the parachutists instead; this was most unpleasant and we suffered a number of casualties before we even reached the ground. There was mortar bombing and shelling on the ground but it was a great relief to get there just the same.

The suddenness of the drop had the desired effect and we found the Germans slow to react. The battalion was in this position for five hours and during that time there was no really serious attack put in on us. There were various attacks on B Company's position by parties of about platoon strength or slightly more and, at one point, C Company took on a company that was working its way round towards them. However, it was A Company who came in for the worst time. They had arrived late and found their area was a very nasty spot. Their casualties were high and so were those of the mortars and machine guns who were with them.

The trouble came from a small wood seven hundred yards away. There was a troop of 88mm guns located there and they were commanded by an officer that one could not help but admire. When the drop took place it appears that the gun crews panicked and ran away but this officer managed to turn enough of them back to man one of the guns. He was, of course, in a hopeless position but he kept that gun firing and did an immense amount of damage before he was rounded up. Although A Company suffered badly, 12th Parachute Battalion and Brigade Headquarters got it worse. It was 12th Parachute Battalion that sent out the party that rounded him up; A Company, of course, should have done it but they were late getting in and it had to be done quickly. We got our share of it in Battalion Headquarters and had quite a few casualties, as well I know because I got a splinter in the face myself.''

In addition to its task in the area of the drop zone, the battalion had been given another which was the securing and holding

176. A Dakota on fire after crashing west of the Rhine. (Photo: Imperial War Museum)

of an important road and rail junction in an opening in a big wood between 3rd and 5th Parachute Brigades. Lieutenant Colonel Pine Coffin allocated one platoon from A Company for this task. The area to be held, however, was some three miles through territory probably held by the enemy as it was outside the areas of the landings. Pine Coffin had previously decided to send off a small reconnaissance patrol with a radio to check the route and surrounding terrain and then to dispatch the platoon if everythng was clear. Unfortunately, the officer who was due to command the reconnaissance patrol was killed on the DZ and, as the battalion had already lost more men than it could afford, Pine Coffin had no option but to send off the platoon without any preliminary reconnaissance. It was commanded by a Lieutenant Patterson, who was one of two Canadian officers who had joined the battalion in Normandy as non-jumping reinforcements, but who had stayed with it afterwards and subsequently qualified as parachutists.

Patterson's platoon reached the area between the two parachute brigades after several near encounters with the enemy. Subsequently it was attacked a number of times by the enemy who were beaten off each time. Patterson used somewhat unorthodox but highly successful methods in defending his position. If an attack was a weak one, the platoon would remain in its positions and defend itself as normal. If, however, it appeared the enemy were advancing in force, Patterson would withdraw his men from the position, move them unobtrusively to a flank and wait. As soon as the enemy had put in an assault on the empty trenches, the platoon would attack. This tactic was used successfully on a number of occasions and resulted in heavy casualties being inflicted on the enemy and a number of prisoners being taken.

The battalion took several hundred prisoners during the day. These were collected together until there was a substantial number

when they were sent back to the brigade headquarters under escort.

By 1500 hours, 5th Parachute Brigade's objective had been taken and 7th Parachute Battalion was ordered to start withdrawing at 1545 hours. The withdrawal itself proved difficult because B and C Companies were engaged in contact with the enemy at the time. However it was eventually achieved without any loss and the battalion moved to its next position which was in reserve. Casualties had been high, mainly caused by anti-aircraft fire during the drop and by artillery and mortar fire on the battalion's positions during the day. This was largely due to the fact that the battalion's task had required it to remain in the area of the drop zone which was inevitably a principal target for enemy artillery and mortars. Total casualties were ninety-two out of just over five hundred men dropped.

12th Parachute Battalion

12th Parachute Battalion, along with the other battalions in the two parachute brigades, knew that speed and surprise were going to be essential to the success of the operation. The Commanding Officer, Lieutenant Colonel Ken Darling, later described the measures he had taken beforehand to ensure that his battalion went straight into the attack as soon as possible after landing:

"We were dropping in broad daylight on top of the enemy positions and also on to our objective. The essence of the plan was rapid action, taking risks early, and rushing our objectives before the enemy could recover from the preliminary bombardment and the surprise of a mass landing of parachutists.

We were flown in by thirty-three Dakotas of the US Ninth Troop Carrier Command whose practice was to fly in tight formation

177. The painting by the late Lieutenant Geoff Ottway, showing Major Jack Watson MC, commanding A Company 13th Parachute Battalion, blowing his hunting horn whilst rallying his company on DZ 'B'. Unfortunately the painting, which was hung in the officers' mess, disappeared after the battalion's disbandment in 1946 and has not been seen since. (Photo: Major J. Watson MC)

178. A Horsa landing on LZ 'P'. (Photo: Imperial War Museum)

of V's of Vics which produced a tight concentration of parachutists on the ground. During the short time that we had for training and rehearsals in England before the operation, we paid great attention to parachuting techniques and especially the handling of kitbags. As a result, there were very few losses of equipment on the drop.

In addition, we took drastic steps to cut down weight on the man and this was an important factor in respect of movement and success. Entrenching tools and No. 75 Grenades were not carried; one man in two carried a toggle rope; no spare clothing, except socks, was taken and the time-honoured custom of every man being equipped with two No. 36 Grenades was abandoned.

Finally, because of the tight flight formation of the aircraft, the positioning of a platoon and its jumping order was determined by where we wanted the men on the drop zone rather than in the air. Thus a platoon could be allotted to, say, the last ten places in each of three aircraft (a Vic) with the platoon commander travelling in the middle Dakota, another platoon occupying the remainder of the same three aircraft.

All of these measures enabled the battalion to act with speed and they paid off handsomely."

Soon after landing, the majority of the battalion assembled at its RV point which was by a wood. Unfortunately, because of the poor visibility caused by smoke and a very thick haze, they had in fact made their way to the wrong location which was very similar in appearance to the correct one. This error was soon realised by Major Frank Bucher, the battalion's second in command, who then led the battalion across the drop zone to the correct RV.

As it moved across the DZ in one long line, the battalion came under heavy small arms fire and was shelled by 88mm guns which were in the vicinity. Casualties were suffered, these being collected by stretcher-bearers as the battalion continued its advance towards its objective.

The RV area itself was also under fire from 88mm guns located at very close range. Nevertheless, the battalion reorganised with men being dispatched to their respective company RV points. A Company, under Major Gerald Ritchie, was the first to take its objective, with No. 2 Platoon, commanded by Lieutenant C. E. Crook, clearing some enemy from a farm. Lieutenant Phil Burkinshaw's No. 1 Platoon attacked the 88mm guns and captured them and their crews without suffering any losses.

Major Steve Stephens' C Company meanwhile, was advancing on its objective. An assault group, led by Lieutenant T. Reed and Sergeant Wilson, cleared all buildings whilst the rest of the company followed up and secured the rest of the objective. Soon afterwards, a patrol from the company made contact with a com-

pany of the 12th Battalion The Devonshire Regiment which had just landed by glider.

B Company, under Major E. J. O'B. 'Rip' Croker, was having a tough time gaining its objective. A large group of enemy was located in several farm buildings which thus had to be cleared individually. Lieutenant Peter Cattell was in command of the assault group although he had already been slightly wounded. In the advance on one particular building Lieutenant Ginger Delaney was wounded, as was Lieutenant Cattell for the second time. At this point No. 4 Platoon arrived on the scene and, led by Sergeant Dobson, captured the rest of the company's objective. The remainder of the company under Captain Don Holmes, the second in command, then moved up. The company had suffered several casualties amongst its officers and senior NCOs; in addition to Lieutenants Cattell and Delaney, Lieutenant M. Mustoe, the commander of No. 6 Platoon, had been captured after dropping some distance from the DZ whilst Company Sergeant Major Warcup DCM BEM had been wounded on the drop zone.

The battalion now consolidated its positions and busied itself with digging in as quickly as possible. The Mortar Platoon, under Sergeant Walker, together with the Machine Gun Platoon, commanded by Lieutenant T. K. Russell, had been in action since an hour after landing and were now established in their respective positions. The Signals Platoon, under Lieutenant Jim Absalom, had been successful in bringing in virtually all its radios without damage and had quickly and efficiently established communications. The only problem facing the battalion was the problem of looking after the two hundred or so prisoners which it had taken during the capture of its objectives. Lieutenant Colonel Ken Darling later looked back on the end of that momentous day: *"Towards the evening, an eerie silence fell over the DZ which had been such a noisy battleground. Enemy resistance had been completely flattened and thus I was able to ride a horse, found on one of the farms nearby, around the battalion area. Special mention must be made of the sterling work of our medical staff: Captain Wilson, who was our Medical Officer, Corporal Houghton and the stretcher-bearers, and our most respected Padre, The Reverend Joe Jenkins, all of whom tended our casualties under fire. These amounted to twenty-one killed, forty-five wounded and twenty-five missing. Many of the latter rejoined the battalion later."*

13th Parachute Battalion

Like the rest of 5th Parachute Brigade, when 13th Parachute Battalion landed on the drop zone it found the entire area covered with smoke, dust and haze. This made identification of landmarks, and thus estimation of position, very difficult despite the fact that the battalion had been dropped with reasonable accuracy. Added to this problem was the considerable amount of small arms and artillery fire which was being brought down on the DZ at the time. Nevertheless, the battalion was assembled in its RV location by about one hour after the drop.

There were enemy troops dug in on the edge of the DZ and these caused casualties amongst the battalion which was very exposed as it moved across the open ground to its RV. The enemy positions were difficult to locate but once they had been pinpointed and attacked, the enemy troops surrendered without putting up any determined resistance.

Major Jack Watson, who was commanding A Company, describes the scene as he approached the drop zone, standing in the open doorway of the Dakota carrying him and the members of his 'stick':

"I was standing at the door over the Rhine and christened it by throwing an orange down. The next thing I noticed was the American dispatcher putting on his flak suit which was slightly worrying! Then I didn't see any more of him. As we got to the drop zone I could see where we were going. The thing that struck me most at the time was the amount of flak that was hitting the aircraft — the Germans really were pumping a lot of it into the Dakotas but that did not deter me.

"Red on! Green on! Go!" My batman, Private Henry Gospel, was behind me shouting, "I am right behind you, Sir!" and out we went!

It did not seem very long before I was on the ground and out of my harness. I threw away my helmet, put on my red beret and grabbed my Sten gun. The Commanding Officer had told us to put on our berets as soon as we had landed in order to "put the fear of God" into the Germans. As I moved off, I found myself with a platoon of Americans who had dropped on the wrong DZ and they now joined my company as we started to move off the drop zone towards the farm which was our objective. The most amazing thing was watching the whole battalion in the air in one go — in fact, the whole brigade. The entire division, in-cluding the gliders, was on the ground within forty-five minutes in what one would call a saturation drop.

Once we were on the ground we were immediately faced with the enemy. One of my platoons to my left captured a machine gun position and we started taking prisoners — the Germans were giving themselves up all over the place. Although there was a lot of firing going on, even 88mm guns being used in the ground target role, one seemed to be oblivious to what was happening because once one had landed, one was in action straight away. There was the objective and that is what we went for — wearing our red berets and shouting our heads off.

Like the Commanding Officer and all the company commanders in the battalion, I had a hunting horn. We each had our different calls to muster our men. I blew mine, calling my company as we went for the objective. My batman was still with me, saying, "Right behind you, Sir!" as we took the farm with no problems. We then secured all our objectives and it was all over. Whilst we were at the farm the Commanding Officer, Lieutenant Colonel Peter Luard, and the divisional commander joined us. We invited them for breakfast and my batman cooked us all bacon and eggs.

The ground was covered in mist and haze, which had been created by the bombardment from our guns, and it was very difficult to see. This caused a lot of problems for our gliders. I think that the saddest thing I saw was when we were moving towards our battalion objective, in the direction of Hamminkeln. There were glider pilots still sitting in their cockpits, having been roasted alive after their gliders had caught fire. One pilot and co-pilot were still sitting there with their hands on their control columns. A lot of people were lost like that. Although we lost a quite a lot of casualties in the air, it was nowhere near those of the gliderborne troops.

One of the major problems, as far as we were concerned, was that 3rd Parachute Brigade were the first to go in and they had been dropped about ten minutes too early. Consequently, the artillery bombardment had to be lifted so that, by the time that 5th Parachute Brigade and the remainder of the division arrived,

179. Troops of the American 513th Parachute Infantry on LZ 'P'. One of the Horsas which brought in the guns of 53rd (WY) Airlanding Light Regiment RA can be seen in the background. (Photo: US Army)

180. A gun detachment prepares to move off with its 20mm anti-aircraft cannon. (Photo: Imperial War Museum)

the enemy were able to recover and organise themselves. That is why there was such an awful lot of flak on my aircraft. However, it was all over and it was then a question of rooting the enemy out of all the buildings. They put up a resistance for the first few hours but once they could see it was the "Red Devils", as they called us, they started to give up."

6th Airlanding Brigade

The flight to Germany was peaceful and uneventful. However, as the fleet of gliders and tug aircraft approached the Rhine, a great pall of smoke rising from the area of the battle could be seen. Once across the river, enemy anti-aircraft fire became heavy and several gliders were hit, with casualties being suffered and equipment damaged. One of the glider pilots, Lieutenant Desmond Turner, later recalled what happened as he flew his Horsa carrying five men, a jeep and a trailer of the 1st Battalion The Royal Ulster Rifles towards the landing zones:

"We were flying at roughly two thousand nine hundred feet, to avoid slipstream. Three checkpoints were marked on our maps: points A, B and C which were all five minutes flying apart and with point C being the release point. Point A was easily seen but from then on nothing could be distinguished on the ground. The flak was extremely heavy and concentrated, and flying in position behind the tug became harder as the surrounding air was more than a little bumpy. As we could not see our own LZ or anybody else's, we remained on tow.

Suddenly we saw the autobahn below us and, as a result of previous careful study of air photographs, we knew where we were. We released and did a tight two hundred and seventy degree turn to port and saw the church spire of Hamminkeln in front of us. Owing to the immediate vicinity being rather crowded with gliders, we applied full flap and went down on to the LZ as briefed. Our passengers were none the worse after this unorthodox approach and proceeded to unload . . .'

Other gliders, however, were not so fortunate. The haze, smoke and heavy anti-aircraft fire made landing extremely hazardous. Some pilots were unable to pick up their bearings and several gliders landed in the wrong place. Some were hit by flak and were destroyed in the air whilst others crashed on landing or were set ablaze after being hit on touching down. All this added to a certain amount of chaos on the landing zones but, despite this, sufficient numbers of each of the three battalions were landed in the correct places. Most important of all, however, was the fact

that a high proportion of the *coup de main* parties, tasked with capturing the bridges over the Issel, were landed near their objectives.

On the ground, however, the brigade met stronger opposition than expected. All the farmhouses had been converted by the enemy into strongpoints and a number of armoured vehicles, including self-propelled guns, were encountered.

2nd Battalion The Oxfordshire & Buckinghamshire Light Infantry

Like all the units of 6th Airlanding Brigade, the 2nd Battalion The Oxfordshire & Buckinghamshire Light Infantry enjoyed a peaceful flight in its Horsas as it headed for the Rhine, as Lance Corporal G. Yardley relates in his account of his landing north of Hamminkeln:

"Some three hours flying time passed uneventfully as many such flights had in the past, except that once again in less than twelve months this was for real. Darkness turned into a lovely morning, clear sky and the promise of good weather. Now and again the sight of escort fighters gave the feeling of some security against attack by the Luftwaffe.

At last the Rhine came into view and as we approached it at about three thousand feet, the order was given to open the doors, one forward on the port side and one rear starboard. As I sat on the starboard side forward, I watched Ginger Belsham pull the forward door upwards and at that precise moment flak burst under the port wing, banking the aircraft over to starboard and almost throwing Ginger out of the door, only to be pulled back by the platoon commander, Lieutenant Bob Preston, and our platoon sergeant. This took about two seconds and allowed Ginger to live for another few minutes as he and sixty per cent of the platoon were soon to die.

The dropping and landing zones were shrouded in smoke and must have made target identification very difficult for the pilots. However, the gentle jerk of the tow-rope being cast off was felt, the nose went down and the landing procedure began, arms linked with each other and a silent prayer. The enemy were waiting for us and had prepared a concentration of ack-ack guns. Being the first in, our regiment took the full weight of the defences.

Through the heavy barrage of flak we descended, many lives being lost during those first few minutes, including that of one of our pilots, Sergeant Geoff Collins. Our other pilot, Staff Sergeant Bill Rowland, was wounded. One chap by the name of Shrewsbury, who sat opposite me, got a burst of machine gun fire through the back; the bullets passed between the heads of myself and Ted Tamplin, who sat on my right, through a gap of eight to ten inches.

With some of the controls damaged and no compressed air to operate the landing flaps, we flew across the landing zone, over the railway and the River Issel to crash head-on into a wood at ground level. At a speed of over seventy knots a fully loaded wooden glider the size of a heavy bomber becomes a pile of matchwood in one second flat. Whilst all this was going on No. 1 Glider, which was carrying No. 17 Platoon, had been badly hit by flak and was breaking up, spilling out men and equipment before crashing as we had done — except with them, there were no survivors.

This landing was typical of those which took place as the battalion landed on LZ 'O' north of Hamminkeln. During the landings, which only lasted ten minutes, the battalion lost almost half its total strength. Gliders made their approaches through thick smoke and heavy anti-aircraft fire, subsequently colliding as they touched down whilst others fell blazing from the sky. Amazingly, the battalion's Quartermaster, Lieutenant Bill Aldworth, took over the controls of his glider after both pilots had been killed and, despite the fact that he had no flying experience, landed the aircraft safely.

Lieutenant Colonel Mark Darell-Brown DSO, the Commanding Officer, was in a Horsa with his jeep and trailer together with men of Battalion Headquarters. The glider came under fire from a 20mm anti-aircraft battery in the area of Hamminkeln and was hit. The pilot, Squadron Leader V. H. Reynolds, put his aircraft into a dive and, as he did so, the co-pilot opened fire with his Sten gun through the front of the cockpit windshield. The glider landed beside the enemy guns and the Commanding Officer and his men disembarked at speed, attacking the German gunners and overpowering them. As they did so, other gliders were landing around them with varying fortunes.

Throughout the battalion's area all was confusion. Individual actions were taking place on and around each of the company objectives, whilst in the background the continual noise of ammunition exploding in burning gliders added to the din. As the battalion stormed the anti-aircraft batteries and overcame the gun crews, it came under fire from enemy machine guns and mortars on the landing zone at Ringenberg. At this point three enemy medium tanks and some motorcyclists drove over the LZ from the west, apparently withdrawing to the east. The tanks opened fire whilst on the move, setting fire to some gliders before wounded men still aboard them could be evacuated. However, they then encountered the 6-pounder anti-tank guns of the 1st Battalion The Royal Ulster Rifles which proceeded to knock one of them out.

Despite the severe setbacks which it had encountered, the battalion succeeded in taking all of its objectives by 1100 hours. B Company, under Major Gilbert Rahr, took up positions around the road bridge over the Issel whilst C Company, commanded by Major James Molloy, established itself in defence of the rail bridge. Major Harry Styles' A Company occupied the area of the road junction to the west whilst D Company, under Major John Tillett, was positioned in reserve to the west of the railway station. The Reconnaissance Platoon occupied the station itself.

However, the action had cost the battalion dear because it now numbered only two hundred and twenty-six all ranks and possessed only four of its twelve mortars and a few of its anti-tank guns. A hundred and three members of the battalion had been killed, mostly in the gliders. The wounded numbered over a hundred and several were in a very serious condition.

During the rest of the day there was little disturbance. However, during the evening C Company, which was guarding the railway bridge over the river, came under fire from an enemy machine-gun position. A fighting patrol, under Lieutenant John Stone, was sent out and this succeeded in silencing the enemy and capturing two prisoners. Shortly afterwards B Company, which was holding the road bridge, detected tanks moving up from

181. Gliders near the unfinished autobahn. (Photo: Imperial War Museum)

182. Men of 6th Airlanding Brigade prepare to head for Hamminkeln. Two prisoners are seated in the rear of the jeep.
(Photo: Imperial War Museum)

Ringenberg. This was followed soon after by some ineffective enemy artillery fire directed on to the company's positions.

At midnight enemy infantry, supported by tanks, attacked B Company. The anti-tank detachments engaged the tanks with their 6-pounders and scored hits but these proved ineffective against the tanks which were too heavy. The fighting continued in the dark and at one point one of the positions at the eastern end of the bridge was overwhelmed. This was then retaken by a counter-attack led by Lieutenant Hugh Clark MC. Two hours later another strong attack, again supported by tanks, was launched on the bridge and it became evident that B Company would not be able to repulse the enemy. On orders from the brigade commander, the bridge was therefore blown.

12th Battalion The Devonshire Regiment

The 12th Battalion The Devonshire Regiment landed on LZ 'R' and was tasked with taking and holding Hamminkeln, after first isolating the village by preventing any enemy movement in or out of it west of the main road running north and south. To support it, the battalion had 3rd Airlanding Anti-Tank Battery RA, minus three of its 17-pounders.

The Devons' task was to be carried out in two phases, the first being the isolation of the village and the second being the assault itself. In Phase 1, D Company with the Anti-Tank Platoon, less two detachments, would land as close as possible to the western side of Hamminkeln and would seize a crossroads nearby. Major John Rogers' A Company, with one anti-tank detachment, would land to the south and south-west of the village and isolate it from that area. B Company, with two 17-pounder anti-tank guns, would land to the west and isolate the village from the north and north-west. The Reconnaissance Platoon would land with B Company, subsequently sending out patrols which would link up with the Royal Ulster Rifles and prevent any infiltration by the enemy. C Company would be the battalion's reserve.

The second phase, the assault on Hamminkeln, would be carried out as soon as circumstances permitted. D Company, under Major Gerry Palmer, would clear the middle of the village and then take up positions covering the approaches to the east and south-east. A Company was to clear and hold the south of the village whilst B Company attacked and secured the north-east and north-west of it.

Lieutenant Colonel Paul Gleadell, Commanding Officer of the battalion, was flying in Horsa No. 188 flown by Major Maurice Priest. Private Jolly, his batman, was seated next to him on the forward starboard side of the aircraft. Opposite him sat Lieutenant Ronald Brixey, the battalion's Intelligence Officer, with Private Bray of the Intelligence Section and Private Tremeer, one of the Regimental Police.

As the battalion approached the Reichswald, visibility started to deteriorate. At last, the long winding ribbon of the Rhine appeared but nothing could be seen beyond it. Once over the river, visibility was even worse as the whole of the LZ was covered with a thick pall of smoke, dust and haze. However, the heavy anti-aircraft fire indicated that the glider was over the area of the battle.

Major Priest cast off and commenced his descent. At first all was quiet, in marked contrast with the last four hours on tow. Then, as the glider came closer to the ground, the sounds of battle could be distinctly heard.

The anti-aircraft and small arms fire was still heavy and the glider shuddered as a shell burst nearby. Priest signalled to his passengers that he was going to try a landing but the restricted view made him level up again with a sudden jerk. A burst, and then another, of bullets pierced the glider hull; the first struck the jeep, fortunately missing the petrol tank, and the second wounded Private Tremeer in the back. Again Priest tried a landing and again he levelled up, losing height all the while. A few seconds later he turned round and said, "I can't see a darned thing but I'll do the best I can for you." There was a crash, the floor boards were torn open and Gleadell and his companions found their feet being dragged along the ground for a few yards; at the same time, Private Tremeer was hurled forward against the cockpit.

The glider came to a halt with a crash and, after the door had been opened, Lieutenant Brixey quickly moved out to take up

183. A Bren carrier and motorcyclist beside a Hamilcar on one of the LZs. (Photo: Imperial War Museum)

a covering position with a Bren gun. Gleadell and his men had no idea where they were but they did notice that their glider had stopped inches short of a very large bomb crater. They were under fire from what appeared to be three different directions and a 20mm gun was also firing at them from the autobahn about a hundred yards away. Suddenly they heard shouting in English and saw a platoon of the Oxfordshire & Buckinghamshire Light Infantry who had been firing in their direction.

Lieutenant Colonel Gleadell takes up the story:
"There was no chance of extracting my jeep and so between us we carried our casualty towards our friends. We then realised that they were on the banks of the Issel astride the railway bridge, and that we had landed between them and the enemy from Ringenberg. Some Germans came out of a nearby copse and were rounded up. I was naturally anxious to get to Hamminkeln as soon as possible, so we left our casualty with the headquarters of that company of the Oxfordshire and Buckinghamshire Light Infantry and made our way south along the railway track. The sound of shellfire and machine guns, coming from all sides, was deafening and every now and then we came upon a glider blazing furiously, one or two with their crews trapped within and little one could do to extricate them. One glider, or what was left of it, had wrapped itself around a massive tree. The whole situation seemed chaotic and I wondered if we should ever get it unravelled. Every farmhouse appeared to contain a defended post and isolated battles were being fought all over the LZ and beyond.

The enemy were in greater confusion than we were. A number managed to concentrate in Hamminkeln, particularly on the north-east side. They consisted mostly of flak gunners, Lutfwaffe Regiment, Volksturm and parachutists. Three self-propelled guns, some tanks, armoured cars and half-tracks were cruising about the LZ and engaging troops who were deplaning.

I joined up with a platoon of D Company and we concentrated in the area of a road junction. After meeting some resistance, we eventually reached the northern edge of Hamminkeln. Contact was established by wireless with Battalion Headquarters and B Company, and so I gave the order for Phase Two to start at

1135 hours. The companies duly assaulted and the objective was taken by midday. Consolidation and mopping up were vigorously carried out in anticipation of the expected counter-attack and to eliminate the remaining flak positions. A German strongpoint of some forty men in a windmill was accounted for by one NCO."

A Company's commander, Major John Rogers, together with his company sergeant major and his batman, had tackled a tank and two half-tracked vehicles and had succeeded in knocking them out, after which they beat off an attack by another tank. Major Wallie Barrow, commanding B Company, was the sole survivor of a glider hit by anti-aircraft fire as it was about to land. Despite being wounded, he held out against the enemy for twenty minutes before being captured.

C Company, commanded by Major John Haythornthwaite, had landed slightly off-target and with only two platoons, the glider carrying Lieutenant Slade's platoon having been destroyed by a direct hit just after release whilst the company's fourth platoon had landed beside, and remained with, B Company. The company's task had been the clearing of the divisional landing zone but most of the enemy in the area had by then been cleared by troops of 17th US Airborne Division. Sporadic sniping and mortaring still continued, however, and C Company continued to suffer more casualties.

The battalion had reorganised and consolidated as planned at the end of the second phase of its task, Battalion Headquarters being located in the village school. Enemy activity during the afternoon was light, consisting mainly of sporadic shelling of Hamminkeln by two 88mm self-propelled guns and mortars. By the end of the day, the Devons had suffered casualties totalling a hundred and ten killed and thirty wounded.

1st Battalion The Royal Ulster Rifles

Despite the fact that the enemy had been surprised by the scale of the landings, the arrival of the 1st Battalion The Royal Ulster Rifles at LZ 'U' south-east of Ringenberg was greeted by heavy anti-aircraft fire. In addition, enemy armoured cars and self-propelled guns brought fire to bear on the landing zones, causing

184. Wrecked gliders lie strewn in and around Hamminkeln railway station. (Photo: Imperial War Museum)

a number of casualties.

The battalion plan was that D Company, under Major Tony Dyball, would land on LZ 'U1' and take the bridge over the Issel whilst A Company, commanded by Major Charles Vickery, would land on LZ 'U2' and seize the area of the station and the level crossing. The rest of the battalion would land on LZ 'U3' and would then move to take up defensive positions incorporating the objectives already taken.

D Company landed at 1025 hours on LZ 'U1', which was astride the Issel, with the company commander's glider touching down in the lead about a hundred and fifty yards from the bridge which was his objective. The Horsa landed heavily and some of its passengers were ejected somewhat forcefully through the wrecked nose of the aircraft. As it landed, the glider came under fire from a machine gun position at a range of seventy-five yards, one man being killed. Major Dyball takes up the story:

"As my wireless operator had been killed and the set having received part of the burst, I could not get in touch with any of my leading platoons. One good thing about the crash was that one of the wings had made a small trench in the ground, into which some seven of us crawled. In a matter of seconds we had a Bren in action and it silenced the machine gun but another started up some thirty yards to its left. I could still see no signs of my other platoons. I decided I would make a dash across the open and get into a small wood and see if I could contact anyone there.

The Bren covered me across and I contacted two glider pilots, two men from the Oxfordshire & Buckinghamshire Light Infantry and a few sappers. They had got into a good firing position covering the house that I wished to assault. I then moved the rest of my headquarters into a wood and we cleared it, killing two Germans. We then took up defensive positions. From where we were, a continuous trench ran up to the house and bridge. The Germans were still holding the house, although we could see a few retiring. A small party of enemy advanced towards us; we let them come until they were within twenty yards and then

threw a 36 grenade. Unfortunately it did not fall into the trench, though it exploded by its side. At once all hands went up. With two glider pilots and another two men, I went off down the trench towards the house. As we got to it, No. 21 Platoon arrived from the other side of the road in fine form, having cleared the house and captured twenty-five prisoners. About another twenty-five were also rounded up.

I then went across the bridge and found that No. 22 Platoon had done their job in clearing the houses. Although the platoon commander had been killed, the platoon sergeant, despite being wounded in the head, arm, leg and thigh, had led the platoon against strong opposition which was dug in. The bridge was in our hands and an all-round defence was quickly organised, consisting of four groups made up of the two platoons, Company Headquarters, some glider pilots, anti-tank gunners without their guns and a few men from the Oxfordshire & Buckinghamshire Light Infantry. Although it was originally planned to capture the bridge with four platoons, this was the force which actually did so — some fifty men in total.

During the attack five German self-propelled guns came down the road. One was hit at twenty-five yards range by a PIAT but it was not knocked out. However, they showed no fight and retired as quickly as they could. About fifty prisoners were taken and about twenty Germans were killed."

A Company, which was tasked with taking Ringenberg railway station and the area of a level crossing nearby, should have landed on LZ 'U2'. However, only two of its gliders succeeded in landing in the correct place. These brought in two platoons, commanded by Lieutenants Fred Laird and John Stewart respectively, which moved off immediately for their objectives where they discovered little or no opposition although the area was under fire from 20mm guns near Hamminkeln. However, they met a platoon of the 12th Battalion The Devonshire Regiment which was in a position about a hundred yards west of the railway and which had captured some fifty enemy troops who had been found sitting in a barn waiting to be taken prisoner.

185. Two members of an airlanding anti-tank battery start to dig in their 6-pounder anti-tank gun on the edge of one of the LZs.
(Photo: Imperial War Museum)

Lieutenant Laird organised the three platoons into a defence of the area of the level crossing. Not long afterwards Support Company, under Major Paddy Liddell, arrived with two Vickers machine guns. However, there was still no sign of the other two platoons of A Company nor the rest of the battalion.

The expected enemy counter-attack against A Company's two platoons did not materialise. Shortly after the area of the station and the level crossing had been occupied, three enemy self-propelled guns approached the direction of Hamminkeln and passed over the level crossing and the bridge over the river before disappearing to the east. The two platoons had no 6-pounders with them but a PIAT was fired at one of the self-propelled guns, damaging it but not knocking it out. All three were obviously intent on withdrawing as rapidly as possible because none of them engaged either of the platoons who were only a few feet from them by the road.

The rest of the battalion was by then landing on LZ 'U3'. It immediately came under a very heavy volume of fire from houses in the area designated as a concentration area for the battalion before it moved off to join A and D Companies. The glider carrying the Commanding Officer, Lieutenant Colonel Jack Carson, broke in half on landing and he was injured. When the Adjutant, Captain Robin Rigby, landed at 1030 hours, his glider touched down about eighty yards away from the enemy positions. The Horsa was badly smashed up and it was impossible to unload the jeep and equipment inside. Here he recalls the scene on the landing zone:

"I got everybody out of the glider into a ditch on the side of the road. Between ourselves and the houses a C Company glider was burning, the ammunition inside it exploding. About two minutes later, half a platoon of C Company came across the open ground towards us from the direction of the houses. On questioning these men I was told that they had crash-landed and that their glider had caught fire almost immediately. About two thirds of their platoon had got out alive and had moved towards the houses but had met considerable opposition and had been forced

to withdraw. Very shortly after this, another platoon of C Company and one from B Company arrived with twelve prisoners from the houses on the west side of the road. One or two men from B Company's headquarters were also with them but Major Ken Donnelly had been killed.

As this appeared to be the total sum of the battalion which had landed so far on this LZ, I decided to leave a small fire group in the ditch and to move round to the right and attack through the orchard. However, just as I was about to move, I saw Lieutenant Colin O'Hara Murray's platoon of B Company starting to advance through the orchard. I therefore had some 2-inch mortar smoke put down and put in an assault on the houses from where we were, going in at right angles to O'Hara Murray's line of attack.

Fire was spasmodic and a very half-hearted defence was put up, most of the Germans throwing their weapons away when we got to within forty or fifty yards them. Quite a lot of Germans were killed by grenades and Stens in and around the houses and barns, and in about fifteen to twenty minutes they had all been rooted out. The whole area appeared to be fairly clear so I sent B and C Companies to the position laid down in the original plan and put a few glider pilots that we had, about sixteen in all, in charge of the prisoners who numbered about a hundred.

By this time it was about 1115 hours and I established wireless communications with D Company and heard that they were on the bridge. However, I could not get in touch with A Company. I decided to wait until midday in case any more of the battalion should arrive, and very shortly two 6-pounders and some of the Machine Gun Platoon turned up. The machine gunners went to C Company and the two 6-pounders took up positions to cover the road running south from Hamminkeln. They had been in position for about two minutes when two armoured cars came up the road from the south. These were promptly knocked out and the crews taken prisoner.

Shortly after this the Liaison Officer and Signals Officer arrived with a 62 Set link to Brigade, accompanied by some

137

members of Battalion Headquarters and followed by our Medical Officer who had been collecting casualties on the LZ. Prior to this, we had been in touch with brigade headquarters via the FOO's set. As there appeared to be no sign of any more of the battalion on the LZ, I decided to move at 1215 hours along the original battalion route to the dispersal point from which B and C Companies would move to their positions as given in the original plan. As there was no sign of the Recce Platoon, one platoon of C Company acted as left flank guard and another platoon acted as rearguard, with the two anti-tank guns moving in bounds on the left flank. The right was by now safe as American gliders were landing on our immediate right during the move. Lieutenant John Wright joined the column en route *and we also met two platoons of the Oxfordshire & Buckinghamshire Light Infantry. On arriving at the level crossing, we met Major Paddy Liddell who had a platoon of A Company and two of our Vickers machine guns on the level crossing.''*

Battalion Headquarters was established in a wood south-west of the level crossing whilst B and C Companies moved into their respective areas and started digging in. The glider pilot squadron, in whose Horsas the battalion had flown and which was commanded by Major Peter Jackson, took over the defence of the station and level crossing area from A Company which moved to a new position covering the exits from Hamminkeln.

By the early afternoon, the fighting had died down and the battalion had secured all its objectives. Other elements of it rejoined during the day, having landed some distance away and having fought their way back to the battalion. These included Major Gerald Rickord, the second in command of the battalion, who assumed command in the absence of Lieutenant Colonel

186. Paratroop casualties hung up in trees.
(Photo: Imperial War Museum)

Jack Carson who was by now with the other wounded in a house near the railway, awaiting evacuation to 195th Airlanding Field Ambulance's MDS which was later established in the battalion's area.

The battalion had suffered heavy casualties which totalled sixteen officers and two hundred and forty-three other ranks. However, it had taken and held all of its objectives and was now in firm control of its area. During the rest of the day there was little enemy activity except for the appearance of three self-propelled guns which were seen off with the assistance of some RAF Typhoon fighter-bombers. However, the enemy were still occupying buildings to the east of the bridge and armoured vehicles were detected moving in the area of Ringenberg and in the wooded areas near it.

53rd (Worcestershire Yeomanry) Airlanding Light Regiment RA

The airlanding light regiment found itself with only about half of its twenty-four pack howitzers in action after landing. The first of the gliders bringing in 211th and 212th Airlanding Light Batteries RA landed on LZ 'P' at 1050 hours. By 1100 hours eleven pack howitzers were in action, together with one of the two 25-pounders flown in to fire coloured smoke for marking targets to be engaged by the 'cab ranks' of Typhoons on call for support.

Although the visibility was appalling and the anti-aircraft fire heavy, thirty-five gliders managed to land within a thousand yards of the LZ. Fourteen others landed sufficiently near that their gun detachments managed to rejoin the regiment within a few hours. Seven gliders landed to the west of the Rhine and arrived on the following day. However, twenty-two gliders had been lost; fifteen of these had landed some distance away from the landing areas and had been destroyed by enemy action, three had crashed when landing, three had been hit by anti-aircraft fire in mid-air and one had been destroyed on the LZ.

One glider, which crash-landed on LZ 'P', contained a gun detachment under the command of Sergeant Groom who later described what happened when he and his men arrived on the eastern side of the Rhine:

"My detachment consisted of Bombardier Mortibord and Gunners Smith, B. Fenton, J. Fenton, Rogers and Sheppard. Our actual flight was uneventful. Everyone was very impressed by the sight of the destruction and cratering caused by the bombing along the French coast. Then through the haze we caught sight of the Rhine and about then we cast off and started our descent. We flew into smoke and, coming out of it, found ourselves low over a wood. The glider just managed to clear the treetops but its undercarriage hit some power cables and was ripped off, the glider ending up on its nose. The intercom with the pilots had failed and the side door was stuck so we had to get out an axe and cut a hole in the side of the glider. All this took about an hour.

I dropped out on to the ground and found the pilots emerging from the front. The landing zone was a very vivid sight; there was a glider on fire about fifty yards away and the whole area was filled with drifting smoke in which shells burst continuously. There was also some mortaring going on. After a few minutes I got my detachment together and we tried to pull down the glider tail so that we could get the gun out. We were unsuccessful in this and it looked as if we should have to chop a hole in the glider big enough to get the jeep through. Then I saw Sergeant Thomas of 211th Battery with his gun moving off. I stopped him and we put a tow-rope round the tail of the glider and hooked it to a jeep; that did the trick and we got the gun out without any more trouble. The glider had in fact landed in its correct place on the landing zone and I was easily able to recognise the countryside from my briefing which had been excellent. I then drove to the rendezvous which I found without any difficulty, and there discovered Major Russell who showed me to my gun position.''

One of the gliders which had landed wide of the LZ was a Hamilcar carrying much needed ammunition for the pack howitzers. Once it had been located, the problem arose as to how the ammunition could be recovered. An initial attempt in daylight, led by the Commanding Officer, Lieutenant Colonel Robin Eden DSO, failed and resulted in one man, Bombardier Bawden, being mortally wounded. A second attempt, carried out during the night and with an infantry patrol in support, proved successful.

A limited amount of ammunition, based on two hundred rounds per howitzer, had been brought in by glider and this was earmarked for use in breaking up any enemy counter-attack. However, there was little risk of such a threat as the ceaseless artillery support from the field and medium regiments west of the Rhine ensured that the enemy was kept off-balance. Whilst the batteries held their fire, however, the crew of the 25-pounder was busy firing red smoke to mark targets for the RAF's Typhoons.

The regiment had suffered heavy casualties amongst its officers. Of its battery commanders, all three had been casualties. Major Charles Knox-Peebles, commanding 212th Battery, had been killed as he disembarked from his glider and Major George Culley MC, commanding 210th Battery, had also been killed in similar circumstances. Major Jim Craigie, commanding 211th Battery, was wounded but rejoined the regiment soon afterwards. Of the regiment's six troop commanders, only two had survived. One of those who was captured was Captain Keith Thomas, commander of B Troop of 210th Battery. The citation for his subsequent award of the Military Cross described what happened to him and the men who were with him:

"On March 24 Captain Thomas's glider landed about three miles east of the landing zone well outside the airborne perimeter. He organised his own and two other glider parties into a body which he was leading towards the landing zone when it was engaged at short range by automatic fire. Having twice crawled back to collect wounded and stragglers, he finally established his force in a house and organised its defence. Meanwhile the house had been surrounded by much greater numbers of enemy and from 1200 hours to 1800 hours was subjected to continuous small arms and mortar fire. Nevertheless the little force held out and even broke up an infantry assault on the house with heavy losses to the enemy largely owing to Captain Thomas's courage and leadership. He himself killed seven enemy for certain. It was only when all their ammunition was exhausted that Captain Thomas was compelled to surrender his force."

By the evening of the 24th March, the regiment's casualties totalled ninety-two. Two officers and seventeen other ranks had been killed, with one officer and two other ranks mortally wounded. Six officers and forty-four other ranks were wounded, whilst two officers and fifteen men were missing.

2nd Airlanding Anti-Tank Regiment RA

The gunners of 2nd Airlanding Anti-Tank Regiment RA had, like their comrades in the airlanding light regiment, suffered heavy casualties and only about half of the regiment's anti-tank guns were brought into action.

Closely followed by 4th Airlanding Anti-Tank Battery RA under Major Peter Dixon MC, 3rd Airlanding Anti-Tank Battery RA, commanded by Major Joe Woodrow, commenced landing on LZ 'P' at 1030 hours. One of its troop commanders was Lieutenant John Slater who vividly recalls his arrival on the LZ: *'As we crossed the Rhine the phrase 'fog of war' became a reality as the ground below was almost totally obscured by smoke. Our pilot cast off and the slipstream noise stopped abruptly, leaving us flying in almost complete silence. The peace was soon shattered, however, when we were engaged by German light flak — we discovered later that we had been hit at least twice in the undercarriage and the starboard wing. I remember our pilot*

187. A jeep ambulance of 224th Parachute Field Ambulance evacuates two casualties. (Photo: Imperial War Museum)

188. One of the first groups of prisoners, captured soon after the landings, being escorted to a PoW cage by a solitary NCO.
(Photo: Imperial War Museum)

saying "Christ! I'm getting out of this!" and we went into a very steep dive to the accompaniment of rending and tearing sounds from the starboard wing just behind me. Very disconcerting!

We hit the ground and the undercarriage collapsed immediately. The nosewheel came up through the floor and the glider filled with dust. We attempted to get out but the front port side door had jammed in the crash. The tail could not be dropped because the quick-release bolts had not been properly maintained and had seized up. We couldn't get out at the front because the nose was embedded in a ploughed field. It seemed hard to believe that only three hours earlier we were being given cups of NAAFI tea in England and now here we were in Germany, trapped in a glider in the middle of the enemy gun area!

After some fairly frantic chopping with an axe, our combined efforts resulted in our managing to open the door and we all got out. My most abiding memory of the first few moments on German soil is of a beautiful Spring morning, the smell of newly-turned earth and a lark singing overhead. My battery commander left immediately to try and reach Battery Headquarters and was briefly captured by German paratroops. However, he managed to escape and rejoin the battery.

We tried to salvage the load from the glider but soon came under mortar fire and moved to a farmhouse nearby. We found this occupied by a couple of German soldiers and two American fighter pilots who had just been shot down — one was badly wounded. Apparently the remainder of the German platoon who had been occupying the farm were in Hamminkeln for a bath parade and had left their heavy weapons behind.

We finally reached Battery Headquarters and soon discovered that both our battery and 4th Airlanding Anti-Tank Battery had suffered heavy casualties."

Both batteries had indeed suffered severe casualties. Out of the thirty-two anti-tank guns flown in, only three were in action one hour after landing and this figure had increased to only twelve guns after six hours. Of the eight officers and a hundred and fifty-four other ranks of 3rd Airlanding Anti-Tank Battery RA

who had taken off from England, one officer and twenty men had been killed and one officer and seventeen men wounded. In addition, ten men were missing. Major Peter Dixon MC was amongst those casualties of 4th Airlanding Anti-Tank Battery RA who had been killed.

The two batteries were amalgamated temporarily, under the command of Major Joe Woodrow, pending the arrival of reinforcements. No tanks were engaged immediately after the landings but an 88mm gun, which had been causing casualties amongst the gliders, was destroyed and a number of soft-skinned vehicles and buildings were shot up. Subsequently the regiment, which was commanded by Lieutenant Colonel Bill Allday, was joined by 6th Airlanding Anti-Tank Battery RA which crossed the Rhine together with the rest of the divisional troops.

6th Airborne Armoured Reconnaissance Regiment

Eight Locust light tanks, which had replaced the Tetrarchs used in Normandy, were flown in to provide initial armoured support whilst the rest of 6th Airborne Armoured Reconnaissance Regiment was due to rejoin the division with the rest of the divisional troops when they crossed the Rhine. The 4.2-inch mortar troop had flown in with the airlanding light regiment, being under command of the CRA for the initial phase of the operation.

One member of a crew of one of these Locusts was Trooper K. W. Dowsett who took off from RAF Woodbridge in a Hamilcar:

"Our ETA at the LZ was 1040 hours and as we approached we secured ourselves into our seats. The guns were loaded (37mm and .30 coaxial machine gun), the engine started and we were all set. I heard one of the glider pilots say, "Hang on, chaps. We're going in now." A very short time later we seemed to be going around and around and then, with an almighty crash, we came to a halt upside down suspended in our safety harnesses. It transpired later that, after casting off, we had glided down very close to a light flak position which took part of the Hamilcar's wing off. In the resulting crash both our pilots were

189. A Bren carrier of the 12th Battalion The Devonshire Regiment in Hamminkeln. (Photo: Imperial War Museum)

killed and the tank, propelled by its own movement, tore loose from the securing shackles and somersaulted through the air, landing upside down on its turret.

We eventually, with great difficulty, released our harnesses and were able to crawl out from under the tank. We were a pretty sore and sorry crew. My personal weapon was a Sten gun which, due to insufficient storage space inside the turret, was strapped to the outside — this was bent and totally unserviceable. A somewhat uninspiring descent into Germany — I didn't even have a weapon!

As the three of us lay alongside the wreckage, keeping our heads down and wondering when it would be practical to move on foot towards our RV, we heard the sound of tracks and thought this was the end for us. But, unbelievably, it was our commanding officer's Locust rattling up with the Commanding Officer himself, bedecked in his brightly coloured cavalry forage cap, sounding his hunting horn as he stood upright in the turret! We climbed on to the back of his tank and set off to the RV where defensive positions in the vicinity of divisional headquarters were being established.''

Of the eight tanks flown in, only four reached the RV and of these only two were completely fit for action. The others were either missing or out of action. During the rest of the day the two serviceable tanks were involved in engagements with the enemy and, with the support of a number of glider pilots and a platoon of the 12th Battalion The Devonshire Regiment, formed a strongpoint on the edge of the woods to the west of divisional headquarters.

Glider Pilot Regiment

A total of four hundred and forty-four Horsa and Hamilcar gliders took part in the operation, being flown by crews of No. 1 Wing of the Glider Pilot Regiment under the command of Lieutenant Colonel Iain Murray DSO.

The operational plan called for the gliderborne troops to be

landed on top of their objectives, the lessons of Normandy and Arnhem having been well learned. Moreover General Brereton, commanding 1st Allied Airborne Army, had insisted that the entire force of two airborne divisions should be transported in one lift.

The plan had also called for the total suppression of German anti-aircraft defences by bombing and artillery bombardment. In the event, this support in itself caused problems for the glider pilots through the smoke and dust which mingled to create a pall which hung over the entire area to a considerable height. Thus many pilots experienced great difficulty in locating their allotted landing zones. Despite these difficult conditions, however, many gliders delivered their passengers and loads to their objectives but few escaped unscathed. Some were shot to pieces in mid-air by anti-aircraft fire whilst others were hit as they touched down or crashed on landing. Unlike Normandy where the casualties amongst glider pilots had been light, this time the Glider Pilot Regiment suffered over a hundred killed, wounded or missing.

Headquarters 6th Airborne Division

Major General Bols established his main divisional headquarters by 1100 hours in a farm at Kopenhof without encountering any problem, his glider having delivered him to within one hundred yards of the headquarters location. Ten minutes after arriving, radio communications had been established with few problems as Lieutenant Colonel Peter Bradley, Commander Royal Signals, later recalled:

''The 'A' Command set was brought in and opened at 1100 hours. Immediate contact was made with 3rd and 5th Parachute Brigades who reported all well. The Commander was there at the time and I do not know which of us was the more excited and pleased when I reported the news to him. He had already seen the Commander of 6th Airlanding Brigade who had landed nearby and was in touch with his own brigade. The CRA and FOOs were

190. Brigadier James Hill, Commander 3rd Parachute Brigade, talks to men of 9th Parachute Battalion dug in on the edge of a wood. (Photo: Imperial War Museum)

191. A detachment of the Machine Gun Platoon of 9th Parachute Battalion. (Photo: Imperial War Museum)

through to our guns. And so within half an hour of the landing of the first divisional headquarters glider, the communications situation was highly satisfactory: the only communication not yet available was direct to XVIII US Airborne Corps, although that too was possible through RA channels.

At that time, apart from HQRA, the only wireless set available at divisional headquarters was the vital 'A' Command set that had come in with the GSO 1 and myself. OC A Section and the Signal Security Officer were the only signals officers that had arrived besides myself. There was a handful of men. The 'A' Command set was through to 6th Airlanding Brigade at 1128 hours. One of the FVCPs with its RAF crew was next to arrive and was through to the FCP on VHF soon after arrival, so air support was now available to the division — but to land fighter pilots by glider into the middle of an airborne operation is still unkind, to say the least of it!

By 1200 hours the Commander's Rover set was unloaded from its glider and, as he had no immediate requirement for it, it was put on to a lateral link to 17th US Airborne Division, though no communication was established until 1600 hours. As it transpired, the set and British crew with 17th US Airborne Division had met with a series of mishaps. The operators on either end of this link were brothers, so you can imagine the anxiety to establish communications.''

Rear divisional headquarters, however, had encountered problems from sniping and mortaring at its location on a farm west of the railway and about half a mile away from the main headquarters. That evening it moved and joined the main headquarters as there was insufficient manpower and resources to defend both separately.

On the night of the 24th March Major General Ridgway, Commander XVIII US Airborne Corps, accompanied by Major General Miley, Commander 17th US Airborne Division, visited the divisional headquarters. In his orders to Major General Bols,

General Ridgway stated that 6th Airborne Division would remain in the positions it was occupying, with the exception of 6th Airlanding Brigade which would be relieved by 157th Infantry Brigade of 52nd (Lowland) Division during the night of the 25th/26th March. 6th Airborne Division was to be ready to advance towards the east at dawn on the 26th March.

25th March

During the night of the 24th/25th March, the 2nd Battalion The Oxfordshire & Buckinghamshire Light Infantry was kept busy. The bridge held by B Company had been blown at 0230 hours to prevent the enemy from crossing and the enemy attack had petered out thirty minutes later. However, at 0400 hours, a small force of enemy infantry managed to infiltrate itself between A and C Companies. At 0445 hours it attacked C Company and overran one of the platoon positions, capturing a 6-pounder anti-tank gun and its detachment. SOS artillery fire was called down and A Company put in a counter-attack, whilst a company of the 12th Battalion The Devonshire Regiment moved up and took over A Company's positions at the road junction. The enemy withdrew in the face of the counter-attack and the battalion's perimeter was restored.

At 0530 hours, enemy armour was detected moving in the area of Ringenburg and two medium tanks were spotted. Air support was requested by the battalion via brigade headquarters and at 0700 hours two flights of Typhoons arrived overhead and succeeded in knocking out several tanks. One heavy tank, which was well situated in a hull-down position, escaped destruction and continued to trouble the battalion for the rest of the day.

Just after first light, a further attack was launched against 1st Canadian Parachute Battalion by infantry supported by tanks but this was beaten off.

At 0730 hours, in 6th Airlanding Brigade's area, two Panther

192. Brigadier Hugh Bellamy, Commander 6th Airlanding Brigade, talking to Major Eddie Warren of the 12th Battalion The Devonshire Regiment in Hamminkeln after its capture. (Photo: Imperial War Museum)

tanks with infantry aboard them attempted to retake the bridge over the Issel held by the 1st Battalion The Royal Ulster Rifles. As they approached at speed along the road, the leading tank was knocked out by one of the battalion's 6-pounders whilst the other was damaged by a 17-pounder positioned nearby. Later that morning the battalion was reinforced by a battery of self-propelled guns, a troop of these being positioned to protect each of the two bridges. At the same time, a squadron of amphibious tanks was sent forward to the area of Headquarters 6th Airlanding Brigade to provide armoured support if required.

During the afternoon, D Company of the 2nd Battalion The Oxfordshire & Buckinghamshire Light Infantry attacked some buildings to the north and north-west where movement had earlier been observed. These were successfully cleared. At 2040 hours A Company mounted another attack on a building to the north and engaged several parties of enemy. At midnight, a battalion of the Cameronians arrived to relieve the battalion which withdrew and by 0200 hours on the 26th March was concentrated in a farm on the western outskirts of Hamminkeln.

Meanwhile the rest of the division had a relatively quiet day as it prepared for the break-out and the start of what would be the final phase of its wartime operations — the advance to the Baltic.

193. A prisoner undergoes preliminary interrogation. (Photo: Imperial War Museum)

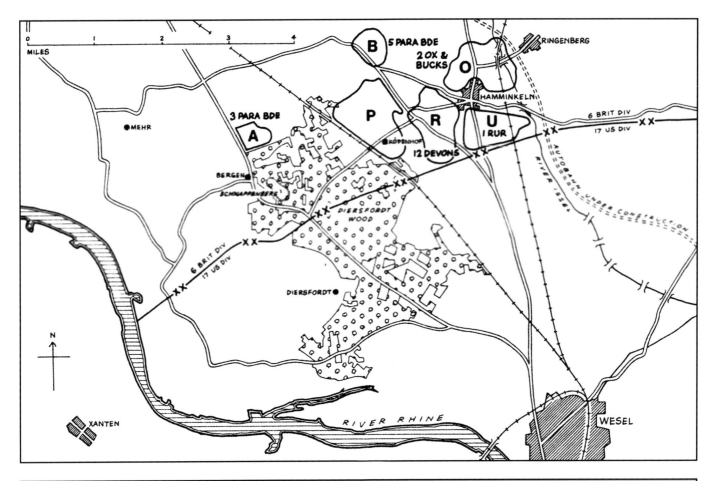

194. Prisoners being escorted through Hamminkeln by members of The Glider Pilot Regiment. (Photo: Imperial War Museum)

195. A posed photograph of a 6-pounder anti-tank gun of the 12th Battalion The Devonshire Regiment. In reality the gun would have been dug in and well camouflaged. (Photo: Imperial War Museum)

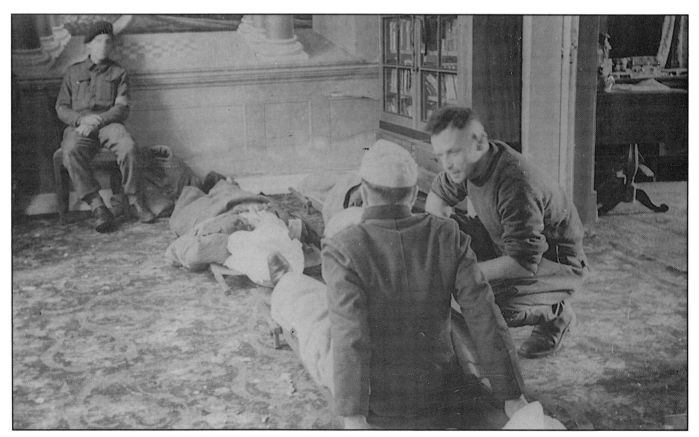

196. A British medical officer treating a German casualty. (Photo: Imperial War Museum)

197. Prisoners under guard on one of the LZs. (Photo: Imperial War Museum)

198. Major General Eric Bols and Brigadier James Hill in the divisional commander's jeep. In the rear of the vehicle are the general's ADC and his personal escort. (Photo: Imperial War Museum)

199. A glider pilot escorts a column of prisoners consisting mainly of *Luftwaffe* and *Volksturm* personnel. (Photo: Imperial War Museum)

200. Men of 224th Parachute Field Ambulance with two prisoners who were employed to assist in digging shelter trenches at the dressing station at Bergerfurth. (Photo: Imperial War Museum)

201. Two wounded members of 6th Airlanding Brigade wait for treatment outside a dressing station. (Photo: Imperial War Museum)

202. One of the field ambulance dressing stations. (Photo: Imperial War Museum)

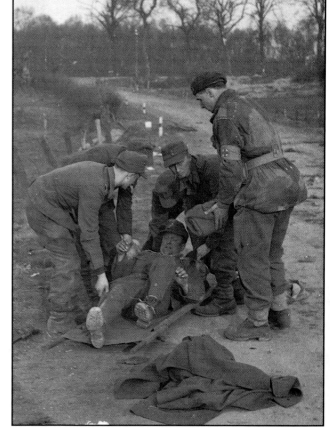

203. *Right:* A medical orderly of 224th Parachute Field Ambulance supervises movement of a German casualty near Bergerfurth. (Photo: Imperial War Museum)

204. The grave of Lieutenant Colonel Jeff Nicklin, Commanding Officer of 1st Canadian Parachute Battalion, who was killed by enemy machine gun fire after landing in trees on DZ 'A'. (Photo: 1st Canadian Parachute Battalion Association)

205. Corporal F. G. Topham of 1st Canadian Parachute Battalion who was awarded the Victoria Cross for outstanding bravery. (Photo: Airborne Forces Museum)

206. A sergeant of 6th Airborne Divisional Signals operating the divisional rear link radio. Behind him is the radio trailer which has been dug in and camouflaged. (Photo: Imperial War Museum)

207. A sniper of one of the parachute battalions. (Photo: Imperial War Museum)

208. Men of the 1st Battalion The Royal Ulster Rifles digging in on the banks of the River Issel. (Photo: Imperial War Museum)

209. Two glider pilots in conversation with men of an armoured car reconnaissance troop of 6th Guards Tank Brigade near Bergerfurth after they had linked up with 6th Airborne Division. (Photo: Imperial War Museum)

210. Vehicles of 6th Airborne Division's divisional troops, after crossing the Rhine, move up to rejoin the division.
(Photo: Imperial War Museum)

211. Headquarters 6th Airborne Division after the division had commenced its advance eastwards from the bridgehead on the 26th March.
Brigadier Chubby Faithfull, the CRA, is seen here standing in front of the jeep whilst Major General Eric Bols can be seen at the extreme
right of the picture. (Photo: Imperial War Museum)

The Advance To The Baltic

26th — 28th March

The morning of the 26th March found 6th Airborne Division on the move. Major General Bols's plan was for 6th Airlanding Brigade, which had been relieved during the night by 157th Infantry Brigade, to attack the high ground north-west of Brunen. Meanwhile, 5th Parachute Brigade would remain in its positions whilst 3rd Parachute Brigade moved south into 17th US Airborne Division's area and concentrated as XVIII US Airborne Corps' reserve.

6th Airlanding Brigade

By 0600 hours 6th Airlanding Brigade had been relieved and it commenced its advance eastwards at 0900 hours with a squadron of Churchill tanks of the 3rd Tank Battalion Scots Guards and a battery of self-propelled guns in support. The 12th Battalion The Devonshire Regiment, which had a troop of Shermans of the 44th Royal Tank Regiment and a troop of M10 self-propelled anti-tank guns under command, was in the lead. It was followed by the 1st Battalion The Royal Ulster Rifles which came up on the Devons' left after crossing the River Issel.

Approximately two miles after the start line had been crossed, the Devons encountered two companies of enemy infantry supported by some self-propelled guns and mortars. After supporting fire from a medium battery had been brought down on the enemy positions, an attack was put in by the battalion. Sixty prisoners were taken without loss and the Devons moved forward until they reached the area of their final objective, the high ground above Brunen. Here, however, they met stiff opposition.

B Company was given the task of taking the objective. The ground over which it had to assault was very open but the speed at which the attack was carried out proved to be a decisive factor and by 1500 hours the company had seized the objective. Unfortunately it had suffered losses, including its company commander, Major J. R. H. Fawkes-Underwood, who was wounded. The rest of the battalion then moved forward and consolidated its positions with B Company on the right overlooking the western end of Brunen, D Company in the centre astride the main road, C Company on the left and A Company in reserve with the battalion headquarters in the area of Haddermans.

The 1st Battalion The Royal Ulster Rifles experienced similar opposition, being assisted in the final stages of its assault on enemy positions on the high ground by Typhoons which attacked positions in the rear of the objective. The aircraft were guided on to their targets by orange smoke fired from a 25-pounder by gunners of the airlanding light regiment. The battalion suffered few casualties and captured several prisoners. During that

212. Men of 1st Canadian Parachute Battalion move into Greven on a tank of the 4th Tank Battalion Grenadier Guards on 4th April.
Left to right: Pte E. D. Aziz, Pte P. G. Mulroy, Sgt G. H. Jickels, Pte L. O. Fuson, Pte J. Humaniuk, Pte G. M. Brown, Pte R. H. Carlton.
(Photo: 1st Canadian Parachute Battalion Association)

night, patrols from 6th Airlanding Brigade entered Brunen and found that the enemy had withdrawn and that the town was deserted.

5th Parachute Brigade

On the 27th March 5th Parachute Brigade, which had concentrated just east of the Issel, was ordered to pass through 3rd Parachute Brigade and to secure the village of Erle. At 1100 hours, the brigade commenced its advance with 6th Airborne Armoured Reconnaissance Regiment reconnoitring in front. By 1200 hours the brigade had passed through Brunen where it met no resistance. There was no sign of the enemy until a report was received from the reconnaissance regiment that it had encountered some infantry and anti-tank guns and had lost two tanks. This enemy force turned out to be a company supported by a number of 20mm light anti-aircraft guns and some self-propelled guns.

7th Parachute Battalion was allotted the task of attacking and clearing the enemy positions which were astride the division's axis of advance. Once that had been achieved, 13th Parachute Battalion would pass through and establish itself on the high ground overlooking Erle. 12th Parachute Battalion would then move through and take Erle itself.

In the event, the clearing of the enemy positions astride the axis took longer than expected. Lieutenant Colonel Geoffrey Pine Coffin gave C Company the task of dealing with some self-propelled guns which were holding a crossroads ahead whilst the rest of the battalion carried out a flanking move. No.7 Platoon, commanded by Lieutenant Whitworth, was leading C Company when it came under very heavy fire from some enemy anti-tank guns and anti-aircraft guns being used in the ground target role. Major Bob Keene, the company commander, decided to use his other two platoons in a flanking attack under cover of smoke. However, he changed his mind after reconnoitring the ground from a position from which an attack could be mounted; the objective was about three hundred yards from the proposed start line and there were cattle fences across the line of advance. Moreover, the light was now failing as dusk approached.

C Company therefore took up positions on the edge of a wood. Meanwhile the enemy decided to illuminate the area by setting fire to some haystacks by firing tracer into them. This unfortunately had the effect of revealing C Company's positions which were on a forward slope. As a result, the company was quickly pinned down and was only rescued by a fighting patrol from B Company putting in an attack from the north and surprising the enemy. C Company immediately advanced and took the enemy positions at the crossroads, capturing some sixty prisoners in the process, after which it dug in.

It was not until midnight that 7th Parachute Battalion had completed the task. In the meantime, 13th Parachute Battalion had moved on through towards its own objective but unfortunately radio communications had broken down and thus there was no way of eventually knowing when and if the battalion had reached the high ground overlooking Erle.

By 0200 hours on the following morning, the 28th March, there was no news from 13th Parachute Battalion and it was decided that 12th Parachute Battalion would have to commence its advance on the town. The plan of attack was changed, however, and it was decided that the battalion would move across country and take up positions at the rear of Erle, cutting its line of

213. Elements of the division board transport in the area of Osnabruck. (Photo: Imperial War Museum)

communications to the east. The battalion carried out the initial five-mile leg of its advance via the high ground on which it discovered 13th Parachute Battalion was positioned and digging in. This took five hours and thus there was only another hour and a half of darkness in which to cover the remaining two miles to the battalion's objective.

Headquarter Company, under Major Douglas Freegard, was left with 13th Parachute Battalion together with the battalion's transport, the mortars and the Machine Gun Platoon. 12th Parachute Battalion then set off, with C Company in the lead followed by Battalion Headquarters, B and A Companies. It was raining heavily and thus visibility was reduced but this only served to improve the chances of surprise being achieved.

The battalion eventually hit upon the road leading from Erle and at first light started heading towards the town. A No.36 grenade lobbed into the back of the vehicle produced startling results when it detonated a cargo of stick grenades. This obviously alerted the enemy who responded by opening fire wildly. The battalion attacked immediately and within fifteen minutes each company had reached and taken its objective. Three self-propelled guns at the rear of the village withdrew rapidly, and without firing a shot, before they could be attacked. Within an hour, the village had been cleared and two hundred enemy had either been killed or taken prisoner.

The battalion immediately commenced digging in, whilst at the same time successfully ambushing a number of enemy vehicles and dispatch riders who approached the town in ignorance of the situation. Inevitably, however, enemy artillery fire was brought to bear and a very heavy concentration fell on A and B Companies and Battalion Headquarters. Fortunately, however, the battalion was by then well dug in and casualties

were consequently light. Whilst the shelling was still going on, Brigadier Nigel Poett arrived with some anti-tank guns and ambulance jeeps. From him Lieutenant Colonel Ken Darling learned that the rest of the brigade would be moving up to the village and that the battalion would be responsible for the defence of its northern exits.

3rd Parachute Brigade

Meanwhile, patrols from 3rd Parachute Brigade, which was released from corps reserve during the afternoon of the 26th March and had moved forward to the Issel, had found that the east bank of the river in its area had also been abandoned by the enemy. Accordingly, Brigadier James Hill decided to seize the bridgehead and was given permission to exploit forward towards his objective for the next day. 6th Airborne Division's objective was the town of Lembeck, and 3rd Parachute Brigade was tasked with securing the area of Klosterlutherheim and the high ground south-east of Lembeck. After crossing the river, the brigade continued its advance during the night with the 3rd Tank Battalion Scots Guards under command.

The early morning of 27th March found 1st Canadian Parachute Battalion moving after spending the night in farm buildings in the area of the Upper Issel. At 0530 hours, the battalion was advancing towards its objective which was the village of Burch. B Company was in the lead and took the village after encountering little opposition. The battalion then pushed on towards its second objective which was an area of wooded terrain overlooking another small village. The heavy rain stopped but visibility was bad due to thick fog.

At this point a Tiger tank suddenly appeared on the narrow

214. After the occupation of Minden, Canadians and 'friends' pose for the camera.
(Photo: 1st Canadian Parachute Battalion Association)

215. Lieutenant Colonel Fraser Eadie, Commanding Officer of 1st Canadian Parachute Battalion, in Ricklingen on the 8th April.
(Photo: 1st Canadian Parachute Battalion Association)

road along which No.4 Platoon of B Company, which was leading the battalion, was moving at the time. The tank opened fire but itself came under fire from a PIAT team and withdrew rapidly. The battalion followed up until it reached its objective where it immediately began to dig in. As it did so, it came under heavy shellfire from a number of self-propelled guns and tanks in a small wood about a quarter of a mile away. B Company was particularly badly hit, suffering a number of casualties.

The Commanding Officer, Lieutenant Colonel Fraser Eadie, decided that there was no alternative but to carry out an assault on the enemy guns in the wood, despite the fact that this would have to take the form of a frontal assault over open ground against concealed armour. To make matters worse, no artillery support was available.

As the battalion was preparing to mount its attack, two jeeps equipped with .50 calibre Browning heavy machine guns happened to appear. Their offer of assistance was accepted with alacrity and the two vehicles then proceeded to lay down a heavy volume of fire into the woods occupied by the enemy armour. The battalion assaulted across the open ground with B Company leading the way once more but when it reached the woods the enemy had departed in haste. When the battalion pushed through into the village beyond the woods, it found the enemy gone but several houses on fire. It took up positions in the village in which it spent the night.

Meanwhile 9th Parachute Battalion had attacked the small village of Klosterlutherheim in the early hours of the 27th March. With B Company in the lead, the battalion moved up to the village where there was a short sharp action which resulted in twelve enemy being killed and a hundred and eighty captured.

6th Airborne Division

At midnight on the 27th/28th March, 6th Airborne Division

had passed from under command of XVIII US Airborne Corps to that of 8th British Corps whose axis of advance towards the Baltic was intersected by two major rivers, the Weser and the Elbe. Thus the advance itself was divided into three phases: from the division's locations at that time to the Weser, from the Weser to the Elbe and from the Elbe to the Baltic.

On the morning of the 28th March, Major General Eric Bols received his orders from the commander of 8th Corps, Lieutenant General Sir Evelyn Barker. The division's initial objective was the town of Coesfeld which lay some thirty-five miles northeast of Erle. 6th Airborne Division, with the Inns of Court Regiment under command, would take the town whilst to its left 11th Armoured Division would advance on a parallel axis to the northeast, with the task of dominating the town from the north.

3rd Parachute Brigade

At 1200 hours, the advance began. 3rd Parachute Brigade, which had spent the night near Brunen and subsequently moved to an assembly area west of Erle, was in the lead, preceded by elements of 6th Airborne Armoured Reconnaissance Regiment. Next came 6th Airlanding Brigade.

Initial opposition was met about two thousand yards east of Erle but this was soon dealt with. Further heavier resistance was encountered between Rhade and Lembeck but 8th Parachute Battalion cleared this before continuing the advance towards Lembeck which by then was some six thousand yards away. At this point it became apparent that the enemy was not going to allow Lembeck to be taken without a fight, so 9th Parachute Battalion was dispatched to carry out a left flanking movement to approach the town from the rear and thus cut it off from the east.

8th Parachute Battalion continued its advance along the axis of advance towards Lembeck. Immediately west of the town,

216. Corporal Moody and other members of 9th Parachute Battalion pass through an enemy road-block near Brelingen on the 10th April.
(Photo: Imperial War Museum)

however, the leading company came under heavy fire from 20mm guns and was pinned down. 1st Canadian Parachute Battalion, which had been in brigade reserve, moved up to hold the main axis whilst 8th Parachute Battalion mounted a right flanking attack on the town, supported by 6th Airborne Armoured Reconnaissance Regiment.

The battle for Lembeck lasted for the rest of the day until dusk. At this point Brigadier James Hill decided to limit 8th Parachute Battalion's attack, ordering it to take and hold the high ground to the south of the town. The battalion's leading company at one point became separated whilst engaged in a fierce battle with two companies of a Panzer Grenadier training battalion. By midnight, however, the battalion had gained the upper hand and had either killed or captured all the enemy. The detached company had by then fought its way into the western suburbs of Lembeck where it was eventually joined by 1st Canadian Parachute Battalion.

Meanwhile, 9th Parachute Battalion had successfully carried out its flanking move to cut the enemy off from the rear. However, whilst crossing over some high ground north of Lembeck *en route* to its blocking position, the battalion had encountered a battery of four 20mm guns. These were engaged by A Company which pinned the gun crews down with a steady hail of fire from its Bren guns whilst a patrol, led by Lieutenant Harpley, carried out a flanking move to a position some three hundred yards from the guns. Accompanied by two other men, Harpley, without waiting for the rest of his patrol who were still moving up behind, went straight into the assault. Several of the German gunners were killed and over twenty prisoners were taken. The battalion then continued its march to positions where it effectively blocked any movement into or out of Lembeck to the east.

29th March — 2nd May

6th Airlanding Brigade

During the night of the 28th/29th March, 6th Airlanding Brigade had occupied Rhade. On the 29th March the brigade advanced and passed through 3rd Parachute Brigade, reaching Coesfeld in the late afternoon. The 2nd Battalion The Oxfordshire & Buckinghamshire Light Infantry was in the lead as the brigade approached the town. As the battalion emerged from a large wood into open fields, it came under fire from some 20mm guns. However, before an attack by A and B Companies could be put in with support from the battalion's mortars and Vickers machine guns, the enemy rapidly withdrew.

By now it was dark but Brigadier Hugh Bellamy decided nevertheless to continue the advance into Coesfeld via the main road approaching the town from the south. This was successfully carried out without incident except that when the leading company of the 2nd Battalion The Oxfordshire & Buckinghamshire Light Infantry arrived in the town, it was somewhat surprised to find vehicles of the battalion's mortar platoon already parked in the town square. It transpired that, on receiving orders to move forward in support of the leading company, the platoon had mistaken the head of the column for a gap in the battalion and had continued to drive on until it reached the square.

Shortly after arriving in the town, the battalion learned from local people that some SS troops had recently vacated the town and were located in a house on a hill near the town. This information was passed to the brigade headquarters and a short time later the 1st Battalion The Royal Ulster Rifles attacked and cleared the house.

The Royal Ulster Rifles, supported by No. 2 Squadron of 4th Tank Battalion Grenadier Guards, commanded by Major W. Pike, had encountered heavy opposition when capturing the high ground overlooking Coesfeld. The battalion had come under fire from five 88mm guns positioned in the area of the railway station and from 20mm light anti-aircraft guns being used in the ground target role. Major Huw Wheldon MC, commanding C Company, was wounded during the action. However, after darkness had fallen, the battalion moved into the town after

217. Sergeants 'Nobby' Horne and 'Stan' Hardy of F Troop 212th Airlanding Light Battery RA.
(Photo: Mr H. Hardy)

having earlier sent in some patrols to check the area.

3rd Parachute Brigade

On the following morning, the 30th March, 3rd Parachute Brigade moved through 6th Airlanding Brigade and continued the advance. Its objective was now the bridge across the River Ems at the town of Greven some thirty-five miles away.

1st Canadian Parachute Battalion was in the lead, mounted in trucks and supported by the Churchill tanks of Nos. 1 and 3 Squadrons of 4th Tank Battalion Grenadier Guards. After travelling some distance, the battalion halted and A Company was transferred to the backs of the tanks.

Not long afterwards, an enemy road-block was encountered and the column came under small arms fire. However, A Company dealt with this without any problem and the advance continued. There were other pockets of resistance encountered *en route*, mainly from small groups of enemy who would try and ambush the tanks with Panzerfausts and small arms. In each case, A Company would dismount and carry out a sweep on either side of the road whilst the tanks would open fire on likely enemy positions.

At 2130 hours, as dusk was falling, the battalion reached a point some three miles short of Greven where it dismounted. The battalion advanced on foot whilst the Grenadiers' tanks took up positions on a line along the river. The bridge was taken within a few minutes of the battalion's arrival at the town and shortly afterwards 9th Parachute Battalion joined the Canadians in Greven. Lieutenant Colonel Napier Crookenden, the Commanding Officer of 9th Parachute Battalion, and his reconnaissance group advanced down the main street of the town and spotted another bridge as they came to the river. As he and one of his company commanders went forward to reconnoitre it, the bridge was blown by the retreating enemy. To its dismay, 1st Canadian Parachute Battalion then discovered that its maps were inaccurate; they showed only one bridge whereas there were in fact two. The battalion had seized the wrong bridge which led to an island in the middle of the river. There was no alternative but to await the arrival of sappers and bridging equipment.

Meanwhile 9th Parachute Battalion withdrew and moved south-east along the river bank. At 0345 hours a footbridge across the river was found and just before dawn two patrols from A Company and one from C Company crossed over. As they did so, they came under fire and C Company's patrol commander, Lieutenant McGuffie, was killed. A fierce action ensued but an hour later the enemy positions had been overrun. By 0730 hours, the town had been captured.

1st Canadian Parachute Battalion, meanwhile, had been kept busy that night. An enemy troop train, carrying German soldiers on leave, arrived at the town's railway station. All of its passengers were immediately taken prisoner and marched away to a PoW cage. In the early hours of the 31st March the enemy destroyed an ammunition dump on the far side of the river and explosions and flames continued for some time. At the same time, the battalion's positions along the river bank were under fire throughout the night.

During the morning, 249th Field Company RE strengthened one bridge to the right of the town whilst a sapper company from 8th Corps built a Bailey bridge across the river in the main part of the town. 3rd Parachute Brigade continued its advance, with 8th Parachute Battalion in the lead, for a further ten miles until it arrived in the late afternoon on the west bank of the Dortmund-Ems Canal. On arrival, however, it was found that both the main canal bridge and a second, smaller one half a mile to the south had been destroyed.

No. 2 Troop of 591st Parachute Squadron RE, commanded by Captain Fergie Semple, subsequently arrived to tackle the task of repairing the canal bridge. A reconnaissance of both bridges was carried out by Captain Semple and the CRE 6th Airborne Division, Lieutenant Colonel J. R. C. Hamilton, and it was decided that the site of the smaller bridge was the most suitable. Early the following morning, the 1st April, the bridging of the canal

commenced, by which time two companies of 8th Parachute Battalion had managed to cross the canal at 1030 hours and had pushed forward about a mile. However, the bridging site and village near it on the west bank became the target for some very heavy shellfire, from some enemy self-propelled guns some distance away, which continued until midday and then stopped.

6th Airlanding Brigade

6th Airlanding Brigade had moved up to Greven on the 31st March and had passed through 3rd Parachute Brigade during the night. In the lead was the 1st Battalion The Royal Ulster Rifles headed by Major Tony Dyball's D Company. After passing through Greven the battalion encountered an enemy anti-aircraft battery which opened fire on it. A lucky hit by a D Company PIAT on the enemy's ammunition dump caused a massive explosion which added to the general din and pandemonium, whilst the battalion took up a defensive position and called down artillery and mortar fire on the enemy battery. This was rapidly forthcoming and it soon became apparent that the enemy were spiking their guns and rapidly withdrawing. At first light the following morning, the 1st April, this was confirmed by patrols and by A Company which was sent forward to search and occupy the enemy position.

During the night of the 1st April the brigade crossed the Dortmund-Ems Canal, men crossing via the remains of the destroyed bridge whilst vehicles crossed over at 0300 hours on the 2nd April via the bridge constructed by 591st Parachute Squadron RE.

The advance eastwards recommenced at 0400 hours with the 2nd Battalion The Oxfordshire & Buckinghamshire Light Infantry in the lead, its objective being the town of Lengerich which lay about eight miles to the north-east. Not long after passing through Ladbergen, which was held by 1st Canadian Parachute Battalion, D Company came under heavy small arms fire and shellfire from enemy positions on the edge of a large wood, suffering several casualties. Support was called for from the airlanding light regiment and a medium regiment, as well as from the battalion's mortars and medium machine guns, whilst Major John Tillett and

219. Guns of 3rd Airlanding Anti-Tank Battery RA at Wessenstedt on the 24th April. In the background are some of the battery's 6-pounders whilst on the right of the picture can be seen the barrels of the guns of the 17-pounder troop. (Photo: Major J. Slater)

218. *Left:* Lieutenant Joe Hunter *(left)* and Captain Johnny Maddox of 3rd Airlanding Anti-Tank Battery RA at Wessenstedt. (Photo: Major J. Slater)

his company put in an attack. This was successful and resulted in only a small number of Germans killed and taken prisoner but a large quantity of anti-aircraft guns being captured.

As the brigade approached Lengerich on the morning of the 2nd April, there were conflicting reports as to the strength of the enemy holding the town. It was therefore decided to shell the town prior to its being attacked. A ten-minute concentration of shellfire was brought to bear, augmented by the firepower of the mortars, anti-tank guns and medium machine guns of the 1st Battalion The Royal Ulster Rifles. Once this had been completed, the battalion's C Company, now commanded by Major R. Crockett, led the way into the town where a certain amount of opposition was encountered. C Company attacked the area of the railway station but was counter-attacked by men of the German NCOs' training school at Hanover and a fierce action ensued.

By midday, however, Lengerich was captured. At 1700 hours the 2nd Battalion The Oxfordshire & Buckinghamshire Light Infantry arrived with a squadron of Churchills of 4th Tank Battalion Grenadier Guards under command. The battalion was tasked with assisting in the mopping up of pockets of enemy in the area of the town. As C Company was moving out of the town to search a large wood to the north-east, it came under fire and suffered casualties. A troop of the Grenadiers' Churchills moved up and silenced the opposition with the help of the company.

Meanwhile, the 12th Battalion The Devonshire Regiment had been having a tough time dealing with troops of an officer cadet battalion. The battalion's task was to seal off Lengerich from the north and to seize the high ground dominating the town. Initially B Company had come under fire from enemy positions on the northern outskirts of the town. By 1030 hours this oppo-

sition had been overcome but A Company then encountered stiff opposition from the German officer cadets who were in the process of withdrawing to a ridge to the east. The company put in two unsuccessful attacks, during which Lieutenants Whalley and Drew became casualties. The battalion was also being troubled by a number of enemy who were behind it, trying to fight their way back to rejoin their units to the east. The Commanding Officer, Lieutenant Colonel Paul Gleadell, was twice ambushed whilst visiting B and C Companies. Major Pat Dobbin, who was commanding Support Company, was killed on the second occasion. The battalion's transport was also ambushed in some woods some miles to the rear and Regimental Sergeant Major Allen was killed whilst leading a small force in a counter-attack. By the end of the day, the battalion had taken fifty-one prisoners. Its own losses amounted to three officers and nine men killed, with one officer and three men wounded.

That night the brigade halted its advanced and took up defensive positions in the area of the town, the Devons holding the high ground beyond the town.

5th Parachute Brigade

On the 3rd April 5th Parachute Brigade, which had arrived at Greven on the 31st March, commenced its advance towards Osnabruck. 12th Parachute Battalion, supported by No. 3 Squadron of 4th Tank Battalion Grenadier Guards, commanded by Major Ivor Crosthwaite, was in the lead.

After crossing the Dortmund-Ems Canal, the brigade headed for Lengerich which was reached at 1400 hours that afternoon. C Company of 12th Parachute Battalion, acting as the brigade's

220. Members of 1st Canadian Parachute Battalion in Kolkhegen on the 29th April after several days of long marches. *Left to right:* Sgt F. T. Rudko, Pte E. N. Russenholt, Pte R. S. Foster and Pte W. E. Campbell. (Photo: 1st Candian Parachute Battalion Association)

221. Released Polish prisoners near the Elbe. (Photo: 1st Canadian Parachute Battalion Association)

vanguard, was riding on the backs of the Grenadiers' Churchills whilst the rest of the battalion had dismounted from its transport because of the threat from enemy shellfire. After passing through Lengerich, the battalion moved up to the forward positions of the 1st Battalion The Royal Ulster Rifles who had already had one of their supporting tanks knocked out by an 88mm gun about eight hundred yards away on the road which was the axis of advance. One of No. 3 Squadron's Churchills moved forward towards a position from which it could engage the enemy gun but was itself disabled by the 88mm which opened fire first.

A and C Companies carried out a left flanking move whilst the Grenadiers laid down a heavy volume of fire on the area of the enemy gun position, at the same time putting down smoke on the right flank in order to deceive the enemy as to the direction of attack. On reaching a position from which the gun position could be attacked, No. 8 Platoon, which was commanded by Sergeant Wilson, went straight into the assault and knocked out the gun and its crew. C Company then advanced up the road where it consolidated, whilst A Company closed up and occupied the enemy position as the rest of the battalion moved up.

Dusk was now falling and the Grenadiers, unable to operate at night with their tanks, moved to a harbour area to refuel and replenish with ammunition whilst 12th Parachute Battalion continued the advance on foot, led by A Company.

After covering about a mile, sounds of digging were detected by Lieutenant Phil Burkinshaw's No. 1 Platoon which was in the lead. Soon afterwards, two enemy sentries were encountered on the outskirts of a small village called Natrup. After silently dispatching these, No. 1 Platoon worked its way to within thirty yards of the enemy positions and opened fire. A Company, led by Major George Ritchie, immediately attacked the enemy positions with No. 1 Platoon taking the left, No. 2 Platoon going straight through the village and No. 3 Platoon swinging to the

right. Lieutenant Adams, Private Menzies and Sergeant Torrie, all of No. 3 Platoon, were wounded by a grenade although Sergeant Torrie squared the account by killing, with his knife, the German soldier responsible.

After a two-hour halt, the advance was continued at 0230 hours on the 4th April, B Company now leading 12th Parachute Battalion. About an hour later the company encountered an enemy road-block and Sergeant Gerrard-Smith, a section commander in No. 9 Platoon, was killed on the road. At this point, Lieutenant Colonel Ken Darling decided that rather than follow the main axis of advance along the road, a better alternative would be to carry out a left flanking move round to the rear of a village called Hasbergen. This lay beyond the high ground in front and at the far end of it was a road junction from where a road led direct to the battalion's objective, the town of Osnabruck. Darling's plan was to position a force, consisting of A and C Companies, together with himself and his advance battalion headquarters, on the road junction and thus cut off any enemy escape route to the east whilst at the same time securing a hold on the high ground which dominated the area. B and Headquarter Companies, under the battalion second in command, Major Frank Bucher, would remain in their positions and hold the main axis. The operation would be in two phases: the flanking move being the first; the second phase consisting of an attack on Hasbergen from the rear whilst B and Headquarter Companies advanced towards the village along the road.

At this point, Brigadier Nigel Poett arrived at the battalion headquarters and directed that the high ground must be taken by dawn which would be at 0630 hours. The time was by then 0430 hours so the battalion had exactly two hours to carry out the task.

A and C Companies, together with the advance element of Battalion Headquarters, moved off at 0520 hours. B Company

222. German troops after surrendering at Wittenburg. (Photo: 1st Canadian Parachute Battalion Association)

provided a diversion by laying down fire in order to cover any noise from the movement of the flanking companies who of necessity would have to pass within a hundred yards of enemy positions. At one point the leading element of A Company, which was in the lead, came under fire and it was feared that it had been spotted but the firing ceased and there was no further enemy activity. The flanking force continued its advance and by dawn had reached its objective undetected. A and C Companies blocked the exits from the village and each sent a platoon into Hasbergen to clear it. This was completed within an hour, with over a hundred enemy being taken prisoner.

Meanwhile B and Headquarter Companies had advanced, B Company with its three platoons astride the road. Between the company and the wooded ridge to their front was a small row of houses on the right of the road. On the left was two hundred yards of open ground, then a small wood which bordered on the road and finally another two hundred yards of open ground which led to the foot of the ridge.

No. 4 Platoon, under Sergeant Dobson, cleared the first three houses whilst a section of No. 6 Platoon, under Corporal Tighe, managed to reach the forwardmost house. Unfortunately Captain Kauffmann, the second in command of D Company, was killed during this action. He had previously served as Lieutenant Colonel Darling's adjutant when the latter had commanded the 11th Battalion The Royal Fusiliers before joining airborne forces.

At 0625 hours the battalion's Vickers guns, under command of Sergeant Dennison, opened fire to protect B Company's right flank. Under cover of this fire, No. 4 Platoon advanced and occupied some houses on the forward edge of the ridge. At the same time, the Machine-Gun Platoon was engaged by two enemy 75mm guns and snipers. Despite this, however, the platoon continued to provide support until it was ordered to withdraw at 0700 hours.

The Mortar Platoon had been able to give only limited sup-port of some three to four rounds before it had to cease fire because of the risk of causing casualties amongst B Company whose mortar fire controller could not contact the mortar baseline on his radio. First light came at 0700 hours at which time Nos. 4 and 6 Platoons, under Major Rip Croker, were in the houses at the foot of the ridge. Unfortunately radio contact with them had been lost so Major Bucher decided to join them with the rear element of Battalion Headquarters and No. 5 Platoon. As he attempted to do so, he and his men were pinned down and suffered two casualties.

A troop of the Grenadier Guards' Churchills responded to Major Bucher's call for support and moved up. Bucher clambered on to the leading tank but, as he did so, it was hit by a 75mm gun and he was blown off its turret. The second tank, on orders from him, attempted to carry out a flanking attack from the right but was immobilised when it shed a track.

At 0730 hours, Brigadier Nigel Poett had come forward to check on the progress of the battle. On seeing the situation, he ordered 13th Parachute Battalion to advance and mount a battalion attack. However, this proved unnecessary as B Company then pressed home an assault supported by the remaining third Churchill. At this point the enemy surrendered. Twenty-seven Germans had been killed and five 75mm guns knocked out.

At 1100 hours 13th Parachute Battalion, with the Grenadiers' tanks in support, passed through Hasbergen to take over as leading battalion in the brigade, relieving a very tired 12th Parachute Battalion. Lieutenant Colonel Darling and his men had been operating for thirty hours, had led the advance for a distance of about twenty-five miles, fought four major engagements and had killed or captured over three hundred enemy. During this time there had been little opportunity for food and none at all for rest. Nevertheless, as the Commanding Officer found when he visited his companies after the battle and before they continued the advance to Osnabruck, which was subsequently reached at midnight, the battalion's morale was extremely high and its fighting spirit as keen as ever.

3rd Parachute Brigade

On the 3rd April, 3rd Parachute Brigade advanced on Wissingen which was some six miles east of Osnabruck, the entire brigade travelling on the backs of tanks and in half-tracks and armoured troop carriers. 9th Parachute Battalion was in the lead, followed by 8th and 1st Canadian Parachute Battalions. Wissingen was reached in the late afternoon and was taken by 9th Parachute Battalion after some heavy fighting.

The advance continued on the following morning, this time with 1st Canadian Parachute Battalion leading. The brigade was heading for the town of Lubbecke, with Minden on the River Weser as its final objective for the day. The rate of advance was very swift, the brigade passing through a succession of small villages. On the way, large numbers of surrendering enemy troops were encountered but there was no time to interrogate them or take them prisoner. They were merely disarmed and sent back towards other formations following behind.

Lubbecke was reached without loss or incident and the brigade pressed on to the outskirts of Minden where the advance was halted. As darkness was falling, 8th Parachute Battalion, which had led from Lubbecke, was engaged by the enemy and was pinned down. After a reconnaissance patrol had reported that the enemy were not in strength, Brigadier James Hill decided to carry out a night attack.

At 2345 hours, the tanks of the Grenadier Guards led the assault, bursting through the enemy positions into the city. 1st Canadian Parachute Battalion followed them with B Company in the lead. There was fierce fighting which lasted throughout the night as the brigade's three battalions cleared the enemy from the streets but by 0230 hours on the 5th April all opposition had been overcome and Minden had fallen.

3rd Parachute Brigade had advanced thirty-six miles from Greven to Minden in seventy hours, a remarkable feat. The city had in fact been an objective of General Simpson's 9th US Army but 3rd Parachute Brigade had beaten the Americans to it and had saved the city from destruction by a planned mass bombing raid. On the afternoon of the 5th April, units of 9th US Army arrived to take over whilst 3rd Parachute Brigade moved to the village of Kutenhausen, about three miles to the north.

6th Airlanding Brigade

Whilst 3rd Parachute Brigade had been attacking Minden, 6th Airlanding Brigade had meanwhile been advancing on the River Weser over which it was to establish crossing points at Petershagen and in the area of Todtenhausen. The brigade was led by the 2nd Battalion The Oxfordshire & Buckinghamshire Light Infantry, with C Company acting as vanguard whilst travelling on the Churchill tanks of a squadron of 4th Tank Battalion Grenadier Guards. Behind came Headquarters 6th Airlanding Brigade, the 12th Battalion The Devonshire Regiment and the 1st Battalion The Royal Ulster Rifles

The approach to the river was over ten miles of flat, low-lying terrain which was intersected by dykes and small canals. Initially, little opposition was encountered and this was mainly dealt with by the Grenadiers' Churchills. On arriving in the area of Kutenhausen, however, stiff resistance was met by enemy troops well armed with anti-tank weapons. Two of the leading Churchills were knocked out and the vanguard force, commanded by Captain Hardy Nankivell, had to put in an attack to clear the village. However, the leading battalion now came under enemy artillery fire and thus had to dismount from its transport and advance on foot, supported by the guns of the airlanding light regiment and a battery of medium guns.

As the river itself was approached, the vanguard was engaged by enemy in positions in some woods north of Todtenhausen but these were neutralised by the tanks. However, the brigade was

223. No. 1 Detachment of the Mortar Platoon of the 2nd Battalion The Oxfordshire & Buckinghamshire Light Infantry at Schwarton, across the Elbe. This was the last occasion on which the battalion's mortars were dug in for action. *Left to right:* Pte Plumb, Capt G. P. M. Clift, Pte Goodwin and Pte Smith '39. (Photo: Major G. P. M. Clift)

still being shelled by enemy artillery which caused casualties amongst its leading elements. Nevertheless, by midday C Company of the 2nd Battalion The Oxfordshire & Buckinghamshire Light Infantry had established itself in positions on the west bank of the Weser.

At 1500 hours that afternoon, B Company of the 2nd Battalion The Oxfordshire & Buckinghamshire Light Infantry, commanded by Major Gilbert Rahr, crossed the river under cover of smoke and supported by a field regiment of 25-pounders, a battery of 5.5-inch medium guns and the battalion's mortars. The river was approximately two hundred yards wide and was fast flowing. However, the company succeeded in reaching the far bank without incident, despite the continued shelling by enemy artillery. As soon as it had landed, it formed up and put in an attack on the village of Wietersheim which it cleared and occupied without any problems.

A and D Companies followed soon after whilst sappers of 591st Parachute Squadron RE constructed a raft to ferry the battalion's mortars and anti-tank guns across the river. Both companies then advanced on the village of Frille which lay about two miles further to the east. Here they found enemy troops well dug in and putting up a stiff resistance. Fierce fighting ensued with the two companies having to clear the village house by house before the enemy were finally overcome at about 2000 hours.

During the night the process of rafting the battalion's support weapons and heavy equipment across the river continued under the supervision of the battalion second in command, Major J. S. R. 'Flaps' Edmunds, although it was made none the easier by the continual enemy shelling and mortar fire. In spite of this, and despite the casualties that they suffered in the process, the men of the Pioneer and Reconnaissance Platoons succeeded in ferrying across the mortars and two 6-pounder anti-tank guns.

At dawn on the 6th April A Company, under Major Harry Styles, attacked a German flak train, consisting of six heavy anti-aircraft guns on railway mountings, which had been located south-east of Frille and which had been largely responsible for the harassing fire during the river crossing. Supported by mortars, the attack was successful and a small number of prisoners were captured.

That afternoon saw the completion of the bridge at Petershagen and by 1600 hours the whole of the 2nd Battalion The Oxfordshire & Buckinghamshire Light Infantry was across the Weser. At dusk that evening A and D Companies detected enemy movement east of Frille and the battalion's mortars and supporting artillery fired defensive fire tasks. However, no enemy attack took place.

On the following day, the 7th April, C Company cleared the east bank of the Weser between Petershagen and Dohren which was eight miles to the north. This was to enable 11th Armoured Division to build a bridge south of Dohren. Supported by a squadron of the 11th Armoured Division Reconnaissance Regiment, the company successfully completed the task by 1600 hours.

That afternoon, the forward companies of the battalion spotted enemy infantry and tanks forming up further to the east. At the same time they were subjected to mortar fire but artillery support was called down and the enemy moved north. As darkness fell, noise of further movement was heard and it was later discovered that the enemy had withdrawn. Brigadier Hugh Bellamy therefore decided that the battalion should attack the hamlets of Frillerbank and Heinrichs Teich which were about two thousand yards east of Frille.

At dawn the following day, the 8th April, D Company advanced on the two hamlets. In support were A Company, the battalion's mortars, the Machine Gun Platoon, the Reconnaissance Platoon and the guns of 53rd (Worcestershire Yeomanry) Airlanding Light Regiment RA. In the event, no enemy were encountered and the hamlets were occupied.

Meanwhile the 12th Battalion The Devonshire Regiment had made its way to the western edge of the Heisterholz Forest where it dismounted from its transport and, supported by a troop of Churchills, moved through the forest to the area of a large brick factory situated on the west bank of the river. D Company made the initial crossing, supported by the Vickers guns of the MachineGun Platoon firing from the top floor of the factory. Unfortunately there had been a breakdown in radio communications and thus the supporting artillery fire was not forthcoming.

The Devons' B Company crossed the river at midnight without mishap and, at 0400 hours on the 6th April, took up positions in the village of Lahde. However, attempts to ferry the battalion's mortars and anti-tank guns had failed because of the strong current. This had repercussions later when, at 1500 hours, D Company was moving over open ground towards the village of Masloh when it encountered four Panther tanks. The company commander, Major Gerry Palmer, his company headquarters and one platoon managed to take cover in two houses where they were continually shelled by the tanks at close range. Private Meeks scored several direct hits with his PIAT but it was not until Major Palmer succeeded in bringing down artillery fire that the tanks withdrew. However, when they did so they took fifty-one of the company prisoner.

Shortly afterwards, the battalion's 6-pounder anti-tank guns were brought forward over a hastily constructed bridge and were moved up to support C Company which by then was established in the village of Bierde. They arrived just in time to engage five enemy tanks which attacked the company, knocking out three of them.

On the following day, the 7th April, an attack was launched by the Devons on the villages of Masloh and Quetzen in order to secure the bridgehead. Supported by artillery fire which succeeded in driving the enemy from their positions, A and B

224. Captain Alan Finlayson RCA *(third from right)* and his forward observer party of 2nd Forward Observation Unit (Airborne) RA near Wismar. (Photo: Col P. R. R. de Burgh)

Companies attacked the two villages and occupied them without encountering any opposition.

The 1st Battalion The Royal Ulster Rifles had been reserve battalion in the brigade and on the 5th April, whilst on the way towards the Weser, had been tasked with taking Petershagen. Before reaching the town, the battalion was met by a deputation of German civilians who indicated that they wished to surrender the town itself. Nevertheless, fire was brought to bear on it from the guns of 212th Airlanding Light Battery RA and from the battalion's mortars and machine guns. This measure proved highly effective and the battalion took Petershagen without difficulty.

By 1345 hours on the 6th April, the battalion had crossed the Weser in assault boats and established a bridgehead, although its anti-tank guns were still on the west bank due to the lack of a bridge. However, during the early part of the night the bridging of the river was completed and the battalion's guns and vehicles were able to move up. By this time, D Company was in action, supported by a section of mortars and the MachineGun Platoon. This action lasted all night until D Company finally got the better of the enemy.

On the 7th April, 11th Armoured Division moved through the area. By this time the enemy had been identified as a battle group consisting of three companies of infantry, three Tiger tanks, five Panthers, three 75mm guns, a number of 105mm guns and a section of 81mm mortars.

The following day, the battalion moved to Munchausen which it occupied without difficulty after capturing some forty prisoners.

5th Parachute Brigade

The 5th April found 5th Parachute Brigade concentrated at Fried Walde as Osnabruck had been rendered uninhabitable by Allied bombing. Initially it had been planned that 15th (Scottish) Division would move through 6th Airborne Division and take over the lead in the advance to the Baltic. However, it was unable to move up in the time required and so 6th Airborne Division remained as the spearhead of 8th Corps.

On the 7th April, the brigade received orders to continue its advance on the following day. Its tasks would be to seize two bridgeheads over the River Leine at the towns of Neustadt and Bordenau which were about thirty-five miles away. The brigade's advance would be via Petershagen, on the River Weser, where bridgeheads had already been secured by 6th Airlanding Brigade, and then along a route via Roisenhagen, Bergkirchen, Altenhagen and finally to some high ground a short distance north of the town of Wunstorf and two miles from the River Leine. From there 12th Parachute Battalion, which would again be leading the brigade, would take the bridge at Bordenau and establish a bridgehead whilst 7th Parachute Battalion did likewise at Neustadt, some three miles further north up the river.

To support it in this task, the brigade was given No. 3 Squadron 4th Tank Battalion Grenadier Guards, 15th (Scottish) Division Reconnaissance Regiment, one troop of 4th Airlanding Anti-Tank Battery RA, a field battery and a medium battery. These were allocated to 12th Parachute Battalion in its role as vanguard.

The advance started at 1000 hours on the 8th April, by which time 12th Parachute Battalion and its supporting arm units were on the move. The reconnaissance regiment was deployed forward, reconnoitring the axis to the front and to the flanks. Behind came the battalion's C Company mounted on the Grenadier squadron's Churchills. Next came the two artillery batteries which moved individually in bounds so that one was always in action, ready to provide supporting fire. Finally the rest of the battalion, under the second in command, Major Frank Bucher, brought up the rear in RASC troop carrying vehicles.

After the brigade had crossed the River Weser, the first enemy were encountered at Rosenhagen but these were dealt with and

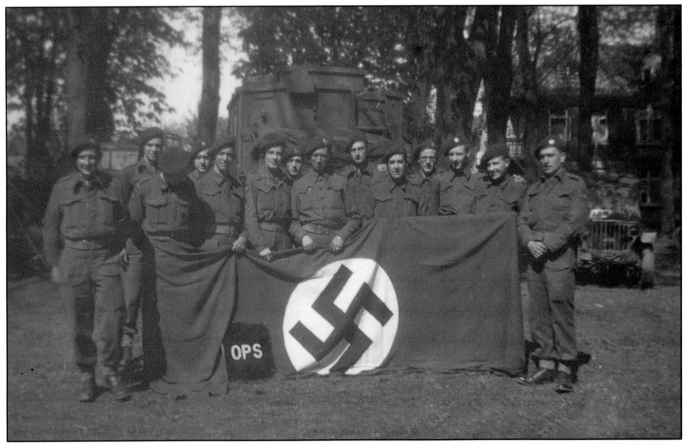

225. Men of 'G' Operations Branch of Headquarters 6th Airborne Division near Wismar. *Left to right:* S/Sgt Mitchell, L/Cpl Radford, Pte Pettitt, Pte Edwards, Cpl Porter, Pte Younger, Pte Owen, Pte Chapman, Pte Downing, Pte Hutchings, L/Cpl Flack, Pte Laycok, Cpl Horlock and SSM Walker. (Photo: Mr B. Downing)

226. The bridge at Bordenau which was captured by 12th Parachute Battalion. This photograph was found by Lt Col Ken Darling in a house by the bridge shortly after the action. (Photo: Gen Sir Kenneth Darling)

the advance continued. Lieutenant Colonel Ken Darling takes up the story:

"As we neared Wunstorf, C Company and the Grenadier squadron reached the village of Altenhagen. Shock tactics were again employed and after a few 17-pounder shells had been sent bouncing down the street by our troop from 4th Airlanding Anti-Tank Battery, the enemy fled.

The vanguard was now five miles short of the River Leine and the decision had to be taken as to which of two routes, which led to the objective, should be taken. The one to the north ran through a series of small villages and then on to some high ground north of an airfield at Wunstorf.

Major Ivor Crosthwaite, the Grenadier squadron leader, and I discussed the choice open to us. I had developed a very close liaison with him since the start of the advance after the break-out. I travelled behind his squadron, sitting on the scout car of his liaison officer, Major Bill Agar. Curiously enough, Bill Agar and I had known each other as boys in Sussex before I went to Sandhurst in 1938. Ivor Crosthwaite and I considered which route to take and how we should proceed. We both felt that there was a good chance of 'bouncing' the bridge if we went via the route to the south through open country.

At this point, Brigadier Nigel Poett, our brigade commander, and Major General Eric Bols arrived. I might say, they were frequently well up in the line of advance. This was a great help to me as the vanguard commander. They both confirmed the decision that Ivor Crosthwaite and I had taken.

We therefore instructed the vanguard to "bash on" (this subsequently became 12th Parachute Battalion's battle cry) towards the bridge on the southerly route. All went well for three miles but after C Company and the Grenadiers had passed through Wunstorf, resistance was met on the edge of the airfield. C Company dealt with the problem very quickly and without much trouble. The enemy were a motley collection of soldiers, some of them with wooden legs which amused our men enormously.

The fighting at the airfield was creating a delay and so I instructed the reconnaissance regiment to watch the enemy whilst the vanguard bypassed the airfield and moved to Bordenau by an alternative route. The bridge was now just two miles away and C Company and the Grenadiers "bashed on" towards it.

This now had the makings of an interesting race as by now the enemy must have realised that trouble was brewing and they

might have time to blow the bridge. The Grenadiers had very definite ideas on the subject and covered those two miles at record speed. As the leading tank rounded the last bend, the bridge could be seen intact but on it was a German lorry and a couple of men moving about and obviously up to no good.

As the column roared towards the bridge, parallel to the river for about a thousand yards, a hail of fire from every weapon — Besas, Stens, rifles and Brens — was quickly brought to bear on the lorry. This had the desired effect and the Hun decamped at speed. In a twinkling of an eye the Grenadiers' leading tanks were on and over the bridge."

As the tanks crossed the bridge, Lieutenant Colonel Darling and the men of C Company leapt off and immediately proceeded to disconnect the demolition firing circuits which they found, whilst taking up defensive positions to establish a bridgehead. Lieutenant Colonel Darling later recapped on his battalion's feats that day:

"This brought to a close a very successful day's work. The battalion had covered forty-nine miles between 0400 and 1700 hours and had captured a Class 40 bridge intact. Success was due to the fine co-operation between C Company and the Grenadiers. The latter's bold handling and the tactics of outflanking and getting behind enemy positions crushed all resistance with very few casualties to ourselves. These numbered precisely two: Lieutenant Jenkins wounded and Private Cunningham killed."

Subsequently the bridge at Bordenau was christened the "Yorkshire Grenadier Bridge" in honour of 12th Parachute Battalion and No. 3 Squadron 4th Tank Battalion Grenadier Guards.

Meanwhile 7th and 13th Parachute Battalions had cleared the airfield at Wunstorf. Once this task had been completed, 7th Parachute Battalion had continued its advance to Neustadt where it found the bridge intact. However, as B Company, under Major D. R. 'Tiger' Reid, started to cross the bridge, Corporal Taylor, who was one of the sappers of 591st Parachute Squadron RE attached to the company, noticed that the bridge had been prepared for demolition and shouted a warning. Unfortunately he was not heard. Seconds later, as the leading platoon of B Company was half-way across, the bridge was blown and twenty-two men were killed and several others wounded. Nevertheless, a bridgehead was established by Captain E. G. Woodman, Lieutenant G. B. Gush and two soldiers who had been the first to run across.

By the evening of the 7th April, 5th Parachute Brigade had advanced the furthest into Germany of any troops of 21st Army Group.

On the 11th April, 15th (Scottish) Division took over as leading division in 8th Corps whilst 6th Airborne Division was tasked with clearing up the axis of advance.

The advance to the Baltic continued, with the division moving north-east through the large town of Celle, on the Luneberg Heath, where the *Wehrmacht's* chemical warfare units had once been based.

On the 16th and 17th April, several villages east of the town of Uelzen were taken and held by the division to prevent any enemy withdrawal when Uelzen itself was attacked by 15th (Scottish) Division on the 18th April. Enemy resistance in the area of the town was the most determined that 6th Airborne Division had yet encountered east of the Rhine and the enemy artillery, mainly self-propelled guns, was particularly troublesome. It was not until units of 15th (Scottish) Division had fought their way into Uelzen, and 6th Airborne Division had bypassed it and advanced on the town of Rosche to the east, that the enemy was finally overcome. Rosche itself was attacked at night and captured by the 12th Battalion The Devonshire Regiment.

Once Uelzen had been taken, 6th Airborne Division was concentrated east of the town and was tasked with reconnoitring the roads which led from Uelzen to Luchow and Dannenberg.

By the morning of the 23rd April, the whole of 8th Corps had reached the River Elbe and was deployed along it on a thirty-eight mile wide front. The river itself was a major obstacle, being three hundred yards wide. On the west bank the terrain was flat marshland offering no cover and it was dominated by enemy positions on the far bank which consisted of a steep wooded escarpment.

The crossing of the Elbe was to be carried out in an operation consisting of five phases. In the first phase 15th (Scottish) Division, with 1st Commando Brigade under command, would carry out an assault river crossing and establish a bridgehead at Lauenburg. If possible, it was also to try and seize intact the bridges over the Elbe-Trave Canal east of Lauenburg. In the second and third phases, 15th (Scottish) Division was to extend the bridgehead initially to the town of Kruzen, two miles north of Lauenburg, and subsequently out to a ring including some villages seven miles north and north-west of Lauenburg. The fourth phase of the operation would see the division regrouping and handing over the eastern sector of the bridgehead to 6th Airborne Division which would subsequently extend it eastwards to include two villages five miles from Lauenburg. During the fifth and final phase, 6th Airborne Division was to secure the final limit of the bridgehead by deploying 15th Infantry Brigade of 5th Infantry Division to secure the area west of the Elbe-Trave Canal and to seize two bridges crossing the canal approximately eight miles north of Lauenburg. Once it had crossed the canal, 6th Airborne Division would once again come under command of XVIII US Airborne Corps.

Initially it was decided that 5th Parachute Brigade should drop on an airfield at Lauenburg on the far side of the river, ahead of 15th (Scottish) Division and 1st Commando Brigade. However, it was then discovered that the enemy was withdrawing and so the drop was cancelled.

D-Day for the crossing of the Elbe had originally been set for the 1st May but this was brought forward to the 29th April because of the potential problem of thousands of German refugees pouring westwards into Lubeck in their haste to escape the Russian forces advancing from the east.

By the evening of the 29th April the first two phases of the operation had been successfully completed, with the third being carried out during the following day. 3rd Parachute Brigade and 15th Infantry Brigade crossed the Elbe on the same day via one of the bridges just completed by 8th Corps sappers. 3rd Parachute Brigade then headed eastwards to an area beyond Boizenberg where it linked up with American forces. The rest of 6th Airborne Division followed and took over the eastern sector of the bridgehead as planned.

On the evening of the 30th April, Major General Matthew

227. A 'werewolf' lies dead in a street of Wismar. He was shot after firing on British troops. His body was left to lie in the street as a warning to others. (Photo: Imperial War Museum)

228. Debris is carried out of the building housing 317th Field Security Section (Airborne) after a grenade had been thrown through the front entrance by a 'werewolf' during the previous night despite a curfew being in force and the war being officially over. (Photo: Imperial War Museum)

229. German troops assist in the disarming of stick grenades. (Photo: Imperial War Museum)

Ridgway, the commander of XVIII US Airborne Corps, arrived at Headquarters 3rd Parachute Brigade. His orders were that the entire division, mounted in trucks with an armoured squadron of the Royal Scots Greys in support, was to advance with all haste to the town of Wismar on the Baltic coast. It was to arrive there before the Russians in order to prevent them from entering Denmark.

Brigadier Nigel Poett's 5th Parachute Brigade had been nominated to lead the advance but Brigadier James Hill had other ideas as he was determined that his brigade would reach Wismar first. The division set off the following morning, the 1st May, each of the two parachute brigades advancing along separate routes in a headlong dash to Gadebusch which was fifteen miles to the south of Wismar. From there it was a single route to Wismar and so whichever brigade reached Gadebusch first would be the first to arrive at the objective. At times the two brigades were held up by crowds of refugees on the roads. In the event, 3rd Parachute Brigade was successful and 1st Canadian Parachute Battalion was the first unit to enter the town on the morning of the 2nd May. On the way, the division had driven past formations of fully armed German troops lining the roads as the tanks of the Royal Scots Greys, with B Company of 1st Canadian Parachute Battalion aboard, had thundered past them. There were the occasional pockets of resistance but these were met with shellfire from the tanks as they advanced.

When 1st Canadian Parachute Battalion entered Wismar at 0900 hours on the 2nd May, it encountered some resistance in the form of a road-block and enemy troops dug in around it. However, these were cleared by B Company who dismounted and cleared the positions whilst the Royal Scots Greys proceeded to shoot their way through the road-block.

By midday the rest of 3rd Parachute Brigade had also arrived at Wismar. At 1600 hours that afternoon, the first Russians were met when C Company of 1st Canadian Parachute Battalion, which was covering the bridges on the eastern side of the town, encountered a Russian patrol.

At 1600 hours that afternoon, Lieutenant Colonel Napier Crookenden, the Commanding Officer of 9th Parachute Battalion, was sent by Brigadier James Hill to make contact with the Russians. Accompanied by two Russian-speaking sergeants from 1st Canadian Parachute Battalion, Lieutenant Colonel Crookenden set off in a jeep and shortly afterwards met a column of armour. Whilst he was in conversation with the senior Russian officer, another column of tanks sped past him towards Wismar. Crookenden, now accompanied by a Russian officer, went after them in hot pursuit and just managed to overtake the tanks as they reached the outskirts of the town and found themselves facing a troop of 17-pounder anti-tank guns.

Subsequently there was a meeting between Major General Bols and a senior Russian officer who stated that his mission was to capture Lubeck. General Bols made his position perfectly clear by stating, in as many words, that he had an airborne division and five regiments of artillery at his disposal and would use them if necessary. Needless to say, the Russian backed down.

During the ensuing period of the division's stay in Wismar, there was a series of meetings between British and Russian officers at brigade and divisional level, with Major General Bols meeting Marshal Rokossovsky. Ultimately it was agreed that Field Marshal Montgomery would meet the Marshal at Headquarters 3rd Parachute Brigade on the 7th May.

Meanwhile the division maintained its positions. Russian troops were allowed to enter the city in small numbers but their armour remained on the outskirts. On the 5th May the Russians erected a road-block one hundred yards from one of 1st Canadian Parachute Battalion's barriers and moved up a troop of tanks to a position nearby. By the 7th May relations between the two sides had deteriorated further. British troops were not permitted to enter the Russian zone but high level communication was maintained.

On the 7th May, Field Marshal Montgomery arrived in Wismar to meet Marshal Rokossovsky who was greeted by a nineteen-gun salute fired by 53rd (Worcestershire Yeomanry) Airlanding Light Regiment RA. On the 8th May, the war in Europe officially

230. Major General Bols and some of the senior officers in the division. (Photo: Imperial War Museum)

ended, the day being officially proclaimed "VE Day" and being celebrated in style by all units in the division.

For 6th Airborne Division the war was over. It had come a long way since the 3rd May 1943 when Major General Richard Gale had started building it from an embryo formation into a full airborne division. In the two years since then it had become one of the most formidable fighting formations in the British Army, frequently facing an enemy that outnumbered and outgunned it but more often than not emerging the victor because of the skill and fighting spirit of the men of its battalions and supporting arms.

The latter half of May saw 6th Airborne Division return home to its bases in Wiltshire. On the 31st May it said a sad farewell to the officers and men of 1st Canadian Parachute Battalion as they departed on the start of their long journey back to Canada. The gallant Canadians had been so much part of the division and had established a tremendous reputation as an airborne unit second to none.

For the rest of the division it was some well earned leave. However, the thoughts of all ranks were already turning to the future and what it might hold for them, together with some speculation over rumours of deployment to South East Asia.

231. Enemy troops surrender en masse. (Photo: Imperial War Museum)

232. Surrendered enemy troops in
the town square of Wismar.
(Photo: Imperial War Museum)

233. Col M. 'Old Technicolour' Mc Ewan, ADMS
6th Airborne Division, talking to an officer of one
of the parachute field ambulances whilst surrendered
enemy personnel stand around in the main square in
Wismar.
(Photo: Imperial War Museum)

234. Trooper Barry Boswell, of 6th Airborne
Armoured Reconnaissance Regiment, with Russian
troops after linking up with them near Wismar.
(Photo: Mr B. Boswell)

236. Members of No.2 Troop, B Squadron 6th Airborne Armoured Reconnaissance Regiment meet a unit of the Stalingrad Armoured Division on 1st May. (Photo: Mr N. Stocker)

235. *Left:* Gunner H. V. Mellenger of 2nd Forward Observation Unit (Airborne) RA at the barrier which divided British and Russian forces on the road near Wismar. (Photo: Col P. R. R. de Burgh)

237. The guns of 53rd (Worcestershire Yeomanry) Airlanding Light Regiment RA drawn up outside Wismar in preparation for firing a salute on the arrival of Marshal Rokossovsky. (Photo: Mr H. Hardy)

238. A pack howitzer and its crew awaiting the arrival of Marshal Rokossovsky. (Photo: Mr H. Hardy)

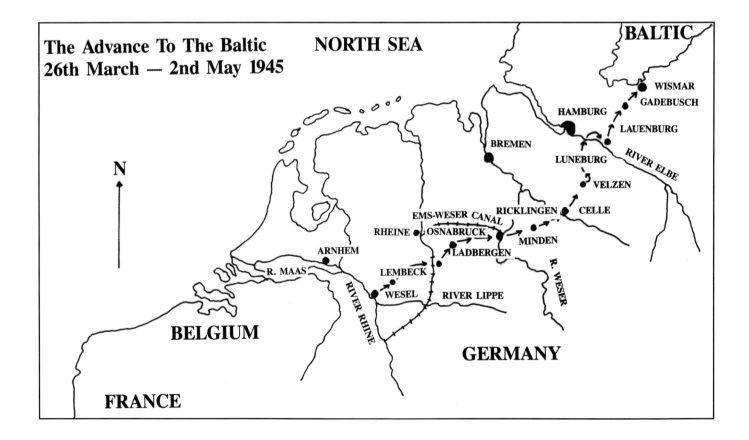

The Advance To The Baltic
26th March — 2nd May 1945

NORTH SEA

BALTIC

WISMAR
GADEBUSCH
HAMBURG
LAUENBURG
BREMEN
RIVER ELBE
LUNEBURG
VELZEN
RICKLINGEN
CELLE
EMS-WESER CANAL
RHEINE
OSNABRUCK
MINDEN
ARNHEM
LADBERGEN
R. MAAS
LEMBECK
R. WESER
RIVER RHINE
WESEL
RIVER LIPPE

N

BELGIUM

GERMANY

FRANCE

5th Parachute Brigade In South East Asia

Only a few weeks after its return from Germany, 6th Airborne Division was once again warned to prepare itself for possible action. Whilst the war in Europe had ended, the conflict against Japan in the Pacific was still being waged. The plans to defeat the Japanese, who by this stage were being forced back throughout South East Asia by the Allies, included an airborne operation which was to be carried out by 6th Airborne Division.

Brigadier Nigel Poett was salmon fishing on the River Tweed in the Scottish borders when he received an urgent message from Major General Eric Bols, summoning him back to divisional headquarters. On his arrival there, he discovered that 5th Parachute Brigade had been placed under orders for service in South East Asia and that he himself would be accompanying the divisional commander and two of his staff to the headquarters of the Supreme Allied Commander, Admiral Lord Louis Mountbatten, in Ceylon. At the same time, the division would be sending groups to India for attachment to units which were highly experienced in jungle warfare.

On their arrival, Major General Bols's party was met by Lieutenant General 'Boy' Browning who was by then Admiral Mountbatten's Chief of Staff. From him they learned that 5th Parachute Brigade's task would be to carry out an airborne operation to seize the causeway between Singapore and the mainland of Malaya. This would take place once an initial beachead had been established after seaborne landings had taken place and would form part of a major operation, codenamed 'Zipper', to recapture the Malay Peninsular. Within a few days, however, it became apparent that this would only be a brigade operation and that there would be no involvement for 6th Airborne Division. Major General Bols and his staff therefore returned to England whilst Brigadier Poett moved to Bombay to prepare for the arrival of his brigade.

5th Parachute Brigade Group, including 22nd Independent Parachute Company, 4th Airlanding Anti-Tank Battery RA, a detachment of 2nd Forward Observation Unit RA, 3rd Airborne Squadron RE, 225th Parachute Field Ambulance and other supporting arm units, arrived in July and immediately started to prepare for Operation 'Zipper'. In early August, however, two atomic bombs were dropped on Japan and the operation was cancelled. Nevertheless the brigade was dispatched to Malaya by sea, sailing from Bombay on the 9th September and arriving on the Morib beaches, on the west coast of Malaya, on the 17th September. Disembarking from landing craft, the troops were forced to wade ashore five hundred yards through chest-deep water and thick, knee-deep mud. Only 7th and 12th Parachute Battalions landed that day and moved a short distance inland, subsequently spending the night under rubber trees whilst sheltering from heavy rain.

Brigadier Poett was unsure as to what reception he and his men were going to receive from the local people. He was aware that the Communists had gained a strong foothold in Malaya and he therefore felt that he could take no chances during the brigade's advance towards Kuala Lumpur, which was its first objective, the following day. However, during the night, the brigade received a signal informing it that the city was in British hands and that it was to return to the beaches and re-embark for Singapore.

Once again aboard the P&O liner *Chitral* in which it had travelled from India, 5th Parachute Brigade Group sailed for Singapore. Here Brigadier Poett went to visit General Miles Dempsey who was the Commander-in-Chief Allied Land Forces South East Asia and who knew 6th Airborne Division well from his days in Normandy as the commander of 2nd Army.

The major problem in Singapore at that time was law and order. The situation was one bordering on chaos, the police having been virtually broken up by the Japanese. The brigade's primary task was therefore to assist in the restoration of order in the city. This it proceeded to do, whilst at the same time helping to rebuild the police force.

In early December 1945, 5th Parachute Brigade Group was sent to Indonesia where it was deployed in Batavia (now known as Djakarta), the capital city of Java. In August, a declaration of independence had been proclaimed by Dr Sukarno, an Indonesian politician who had proclaimed himself President at the same time. He was supported by several Indonesian politicians and a large number of armed extremists.

Java was in a state of chaos. A Dutch colony when overrun by the Japanese in 1942, its pre-war administration had not been popular with the Indonesians who had not been unhappy to see their former masters incarcerated. When the Japanese surrendered in August 1945, however, they had handed some of their arms over to the Indonesians and had withdrawn to some large camps inland to await their surrender to Allied forces. This was contrary to the orders which had been issued by Admiral Mountbatten who had instructed Japanese forces to remain in their respective positions and maintain law and order. As a result there was turmoil, with the Indonesians seizing the opportunity to settle old scores and long-harboured grudges whilst at the same time indulging in a wave of crime and terrorism throughout the country. Only one factor united them, a hatred of the Dutch and a determination that their country would not return to its previous status as a Dutch colony.

The problem facing the Allies was that there were still thousands of prisoners-of-war and civilian internees in Java who were threatened by the violence. There were no Dutch troops in the country and the restoration of law and order was becoming a matter of increasing urgency. It thus fell to the British to step in and take control.

When 5th Parachute Brigade Group arrived in Batavia the town was already in British hands. Elsewhere, there was serious fighting on the outskirts of the towns of Semarang and Surabaya. At that point the brigade had not been allotted a role and its arrival was not greeted with any enthusiasm by the British units already in Java because those who had fought in Europe were not popular with the Indian Army units and others which had fought with the 14th Army during the long and bloody campaigns in Burma. Nevertheless, undeterred by this, the brigade set to work in its usual highly professional way and, almost immediately after its arrival, was committed to Operation 'Pounce' — the clearing of Batavia. This involved carrying out internal security operations which ranged from patrolling sniper-infested streets at night to conducting searches and dispersing riots by day.

However, Brigadier Poett was not happy with the situation and felt that his brigade was not being used to its full potential. He therefore approached the commander of 23rd Indian Division, Major General D. C. Hawthorn, under whose command the brigade was operating, and requested that 5th Parachute Brigade Group should be given a role more in keeping with its capabilities. At that time a certain amount of regrouping and redeployment of units was in progress and it was thus decided that the brigade would be sent to the town of Semarang, located on the coast between Batavia and Sorabaya. It would be operating in an independent role and would have a number of additional supporting arm units under command, including A Squadron 11th Cavalry (Prince Albert Victor's Own) and 6th Indian Field Battery Royal Indian Artillery.

The most important town on the northern coast, Semarang was a port which handled much of the export traffic from Central Java. The main part of the town, which included the business area, lay nearest to the sea on flat low-lying terrain. About three miles inland the ground rose and it was here that the residential areas of the town were located. Two miles further inland was the dominating feature of Gombel Hill which not only overlooked the town but also the surrounding areas for many miles in all directions. An airstrip, capable of accommodating Dakota transport aircraft, lay about three miles to the west of the town.

Within Semarang itself there were different ethnic groups. These comprised Indonesians who numbered about 185,000 and thus were in the majority, some 40,000 Chinese and approximately 5,000 Dutch, many of the latter having held key positions prior to the Japanese occupation. The violence which had erupted after the surrender of the Japanese had served to cause a deterioration in the relations between the three groups. The Indonesians now no longer regarded their former masters with the same respect accorded them in pre-war days, whilst the Dutch in turn now regarded the Indonesians with distrust. The Chinese suffered the worst of all. Having been treated harshly by the Japanese, they were now treated with hostility by the Indonesians who accused them of co-operating with the British.

The town, which was well laid out and consisted mainly of modern buildings, was totally dependent upon the hinterland for supplies of food as there was little in the way of agriculture in the immediate areas surrounding it. Electricity and water were both supplied from Oengaran which was about fifteen miles inland.

Prior to the brigade's departure for Semarang, Brigadier Poett was approached by a group of former Dutch officials who wished to resume their administration of the Semarang District. However, Poett firmly but politely refused their request, stating that he and his brigade would be perfectly capable of undertaking any tasks with which they would be faced, including clearing up the aftermath of any fighting, setting up medical facilities, restoring the water supply and repairing roads and drainage. The brigadier was also approached by an Indonesian named Sjahrir who announced himself to be Prime Minister of Dr Sukarno's so-called government. He received a similar response from Poett.

The brigade arrived in Semarang on the 9th January 1946, just as troops of 49th Indian Infantry Brigade, under Brigadier de Burgh Morris, had completed the final phase of operations to secure the town and had successfully evacuated to Batavia a large number of Allied prisoners of war and civilian internees, the latter being mainly British and Dutch women and children. Whilst the evacuation was in progress, fighting between the troops and Indonesian guerillas broke out, with murder, arson and looting taking place. The town itself was virtually intact although some buildings in the Bodjong area had been damaged by RAF bombing two months earlier. Law and order had, however, been maintained as far as possible by Brigadier de Burgh Morris's troops, the local police being incapable of taking any action. Indonesian extremists had, however, cut off all power and water supplies and were refusing to allow any food to be brought into the town.

To assist it in its tasks of maintaining order, the brigade had attached to it a battalion of Japanese troops. This unit, commanded by a Major Kido, had been based in and around Semarang at the time the Japanese had surrendered. Initially the situation remained calm until Dr Sukarno took it upon himself to declare "independence". This roused the radicals amongst the Indonesian population and a certain amount of unrest began to develop. At the same time, RAPWI (Recovered Allied Prisoners of War & Internees), an organisation tasked with providing medical and humanitarian relief for prisoners of war and internees, opened its headquaters in Semarang. For some reason, this resulted in increased suspicion and unease amongst the Indonesian extremists. Major Kido and his troops thus assumed responsibility for maintaining order. However, the situation began to deteriorate further when Indonesians set up checkpoints in and around Semarang, stopping all traffic and interrogating locals and Europeans alike.

Major Kido intervened and ordered the Indonesians to remove their check points, at the same time explaining to them the nature of RAPWI's work. The Indonesians complied and there was an uneasy peace for a while. Nevertheless, Kido increased the guards at the internment camps, which held over twenty thousand European internees, and at the airstrip. The situation, however, soon started to deteriorate further and eventually the railway line was cut, leaving the airstrip as the only way in which supplies could be brought into the town.

The Indonesian extremists increased in numbers and entered Semarang once again, setting up checkpoints and harassing the local population. On the 12th October, they attacked the Japanese barracks, demanding that the battalion lay down its arms and surrender. In order to resolve this very threatening situation, Major Kido took an Indonesian delegation to meet his area commander, Major General Nakamura, at the headquarters at Magelang. During the ensuing conference the Indonesians repeated their demands for a Japanese surrender of all arms and ammunition. However, a signal from the Japanese senior commander in Java arrived whilst the conference was still in progress, instructing Japanese forces to retain their arms.

The resulting aftermath was one of increasing violence, with attacks being carried out by armed Indonesians and British, Dutch and Eurasian civilians being arrested and incarcerated. All telephone links had been cut. On the 14th October, the RAPWI and Red Cross offices in Semarang were attacked, whilst the detachment of Japanese troops at the airstrip was overpowered and imprisoned. Shortly afterwards, news arrived that Major General Nakamura and his staff at Magelan had also been attacked and imprisoned. On the same day, fighting broke out between three hundred Japanese civilians, who were workers in the Semarang Steel Company, and Indonesian police who were under orders to arrest all Japanese personnel in the town.

The situation was by then such that Major Kido had no alternative but to take matters into his own hands. In the early hours of the 15th October his battalion deployed from its barracks, clearing the area of Djomblang and clearing and recapturing the internment camps at Bangkong, Sompok and Halmaheira. Subsequently it recaptured key buildings and areas, such as the hospital and the railway station, which were occupied by extremists, whilst being constantly harassed by snipers and machine guns. Operations continued throughout the night, with the Japanese troops working their way towards the centre of Semarang and at one point coming under heavy fire from the Governor's residence which the extremists had fortified. This was only overcome after an anti-tank gun was used to shell the opposition into submission.

On the following day, the 16th October, Major Kido and his men stormed the Boeloe Jail which was captured after very heavy fighting. Here they found the bodies of eighty-five Japanese soldiers, airmen and some civilians slaughtered by the extremists, together with a further fifty Japanese and over three hundred Europeans due to be executed the next day.

Fighting continued on the 17th October but by then the extremists had begun to withdraw from Semarang, leaving behind snipers and some small groups to harass the Japanese troops. On the night of the 18th October, however, attacks were mounted on Japanese positions on Gombel Hill and some fierce fighting ensued but the extremists were repulsed after suffering heavy casualties.

On the 19th October, extremist elements were still in possession of the British American Tobacco factory on the eastern outskirts of the town. These, together with others who had infiltrated back into the town during the night from the areas of Demak, Koedoes and Pati, were cleared out by the Japanese.

At this point, elements of the 3rd Battalion 10th Princess Mary's Own Gurkha Rifles, under the command of Lieutenant Colonel Dick Edwards, arrived. They landed at Semarang docks, in landing craft from HMS *Glenroy*, but came under fire from a mobile patrol from the Japanese battalion. In the ensuing firefight, two Japanese soldiers were killed. Major Kido and his men were subsequently placed under Edwards' command.

The 10th Gurkha Rifles were followed by the rest of a composite brigade of 23rd Indian Division which was commanded by the division's Commander Royal Artillery (CRA), Brigadier Richard Bethell DSO. This force commenced the task of organising a massive evacuation of eleven thousand Allied prisoners of war and civilian internees. By mid-December these had been transported from camps at Magelang, Ambarawa and Banjobiroe to Semarang for subsequent evacuation by aircraft or ship to Batavia. The move from the hinterland was successfully carried out despite the fighting which continued in and around Semarang.

The CRA's Brigade had also restored law and order to the best of its ability whilst coping with the evacuation. Brigadier Bethell adopted a tough but humane line with looters, arresting them and sending them to the docks where they were put to work under the watchful eyes of Japanese soldiers. Any sniping from kampongs was met with an immediate and ruthless response, the respective kampong being evacuated and burnt to the ground.

Subsequently, the CRA's brigade was relieved on the 17th December by 49th Indian Infantry Brigade which remained in Semarang until the arrival of 5th Parachute Brigade Group on the 9th January.

Brigadier Nigel Poett's first move was to review the layout of the defensive positions, with particular emphasis on the security of key features such as Gombel Hill and the airstrip into which all resupply for the brigade would have to be flown. Gombel Hill was vital to the defence of Semarang but its inclusion resulted in a perimeter which was larger than was desirable. Brigadier Poett thus decided to establish a perimeter running along a canal on the eastern side of the town, this including Gombel Hill, and then along another canal on the western side. In all, this measured twelve miles. However, the limited forces available meant that it was impossible to man the perimeter throughout its entire length, and thus company and platoon bases were established at the main approaches to Semarang whilst patrols covered the areas between them. A company base was also established at the airfield whilst all keypoints, such as the docks, public buildings and railway station, were all guarded by detachments. Needless to say, the manpower requirement for all these locations taxed the brigade's resources heavily.

One problem which arose was the deployment of the Japanese battalion. When the brigade arrived, it found Major Kido and his men deployed on guard duties throughout Semarang. However, their presence was causing resentment amongst the local people, and in particular amongst those who had suffered at Japanese hands during the occupation. However, Kido and his men were needed to help in the onerous task of guarding the town. The problem was resolved by deploying the battalion to Gombel Hill and the south-eastern sector of the perimeter where it was out of the town and thus out of sight.

5th Parachute Brigade Group soon settled into Semarang, delighted at the opportunity to once again carry out a worthwhile role. 13th Parachute Battalion was responsible for the docks and the central area of the town whilst 12th Parachute Battalion looked after the western sector of the perimeter and the airfield. 7th Parachute Battalion meanwhile remained in brigade reserve in the main residential area of the town and at the same time provided guards for the RAPWI camps.

In order to prevent infiltration into the town by extremists, a patrol area was established outside the perimeter to a depth of some two thousand yards. Frequent patrols by all three battalions were carried out, including visits to local villages or 'kampongs' which were possible concentration points for extremist groups. The guerillas, against whom the brigade was operating, were concentrated mainly in the area around Semarang and consisted of groups of bandits who appeared to owe little allegiance to anyone except their individual leaders. They devoted their energies as much to the terrorising of the local population through robbery and murder as they did to carrying out attacks on troops. Their frequently-avowed aim was the expulsion of the British and the massacre of all the Dutch and Chinese. They were armed with an assortment of weapons which included small arms, a few 75mm and 105mm guns and some mortars. Initially, guerilla mortar and artillery fire was wildy inaccurate but it improved with practice in the area of Gombel Hill. To counter this, a number of observation posts were established from which sound bearings could be taken and reported. These proved successful as a counter-measure, with artillery counter-bombardment fire

being brought to bear within minutes of an enemy gun or mortar opening fire.

Within the area of Semarang itself there were a large number of small kampongs, each of which was a warren of huts positioned haphazardly amongst trees and undergrowth. Inevitably these provided good concealment for guerillas. Initially, a series of dawn cordon and search operations were carried out but these did not prove particularly successful, although some arms and equipment were discovered on occasions. They did, however, cause resentment amongst the local people, partly because of damage caused to property during the search phases, who were somewhat understandably alarmed by large numbers of troops descending on them without warning. This practice was subsequently abandoned and replaced by an effective intelligence system operated by the brigade's field security section. This resulted in information being obtained which in turn resulted in successful searches of pinpointed houses.

The brigade made its mark very quickly. Law and order was imposed swiftly, a major factor being the imposition of a curfew between 2230 hours and 0430 hours the following morning. The gunners of the detachment of 2nd Forward Observation Unit RA, 4th Airlanding Anti-Tank Battery RA and 6th Indian Field Battery RIA carried out the task of policing the town under the command of Major John Bamford.

Essential services, such as power and water, were soon restored by 3rd Airborne Squadron RE under Major Peter Moore DSO MC. Medical facilities were organised by 225th Parachute Field Ambulance, commanded by Lieutenant Colonel John Watts MC, and the roads, railways and docks, which had been badly damaged by Allied bombing, were once again put in working order. The brigade's signal section was tasked with maintaining and operating the town's telephone system and the two civilian exchanges, whilst the brigade's RASC detachment organised the distribution of food. All this impressed the local inhabitants who soon learned to like and trust the efficient and friendly paratroopers.

To assist the brigade in the civil administration of the town, the Allied Military Administration Civil Affairs Bureau (AMACAB) was formed on the 15th January 1946. This was headed by Dr Angenent, a Dutchman who had served in a number of administrative posts in Java for some considerable time. Attached to him as a staff officer and as the brigade commander's liaison officer was Major Kenneth Milne of the King's Royal Rifle Corps who was also the Commanding Officer of RAPWI Mid-Java.

AMACAB was divided into different branches covering health, engineering, food and law and order. The head of each branch worked alongside and officer of the brigade who was responsible for providing technical advice and for obtaining assistance from the appropriate resources within the brigade. Thus Lieutenant Colonel John Watts of 225th Parachute Field Ambulance was also the Medical Officer of Health whilst Major Peter Moore of 3rd Airborne Squadron RE was the Town Engineer. Likewise, Major John Bamford of 2nd Forward Observation Unit RA was the Commissioner of Police and Captain Harry Pollak MC of 13th Parachute Battalion was Head of the Food Committee.

Much of the burden of returning conditions within the town to normal fell on the sappers of 3rd Airborne Squadron RE who were supported by a number of civilians who had worked as engineers in the town before the war. New waterpoints were constructed whilst existing ones were repaired. Considerable repairs were carried out on the main power station whilst electricity substations were put in working order and new generators installed. The sappers also carried out extensive repairs in the docks, putting the two dry-docks back into commission, whilst also providing technical assistance which enabled the gasworks and a refrigeration plant to be restored to running order. In addition, the squadron constructed a railway culvert, redecked two bridges and overhauled four locomotives. It also constructed two sawmills, repaired roads, demolished unsafe buildings and converted warehouses within the docks area into accommodation for five thousand Japanese internees.

Another principal task was the formation of a new police force, and this was carried out by Major John Bamford and the officers and gunners of the brigade's artillery units. The force was organised as a headquarters and four divisions of which two were staffed by Indonesians and one each by Dutch and Chinese respectively. Each division was commanded by a British officer who was assisted by twenty gunners. Police posts were established throughout the various areas of Semarang and these were visited each night by troops who patrolled the streets in jeeps. The provision of uniforms, regular rations and pay contributed greatly to the morale of this new force and gradually a genuine *esprit de corps* began to manifest itself. Gradually the local population's confidence in the police was restored and this resulted in people bringing their problems and complaints to local posts for investigation. Indeed, such was the success of the brigade's law and order operations that one policeman, who had served in the town's pre-war force, stated that there was less crime in Semarang at that particular time than during any comparable period before the war.

In early February 1946, Brigadier Nigel Poett received a visit from General Dempsey who toured the brigade and was impressed by what he saw. He subsequently wrote, saying that he had never seen the brigade "looking in better form — in every way" and asking Brigadier Poett to pass on his congratulations to the commanding officers of all units.

During the general's visit, Brigadier Poett was told that he was shortly to be posted to the War Office as Director of Plans. This was sad news for him because he had formed 5th Parachute Brigade and had commanded it for three years. He would be leaving many old friends alongside whom he had fought during the Normandy campaign, at the Rhine Crossing and the advance through northern Germany to the Baltic. However, as General Dempsey reminded him, he had been fortunate in having had a wonderful command and was leaving it on a crest of a wave.

A few days later, on the 16th February, he handed over to Brigadier Ken Darling, the much respected former commanding officer of 12th Parachute Battalion who at that time had recently been appointed to command 1st Indian Infantry Brigade. Brigadier Poett received a splendid send-off which was attended not only by elements of 5th Parachute Brigade but also by Major Kido and some of his men, as well as by the Chinese business community.

At the end of February, Brigadier Darling was informed that 5th Parachute Brigade Group was to be relieved by 'T' Regiment Group of the Royal Netherlands Army. Initially there were severe reservations as to what the reactions of the local population would be to the return of the Dutch and it was clear to Darling and his staff that matters would have to be handled with the utmost delicacy.

The first step was to ensure that there would be no friction between the Dutch and British troops and all elements of the brigade received instructions to this effect. Following this, the heads of the different ethnic communities were informed of the impending arrival of the Dutch troops and were reassured that these would be under British command until such time as 5th Parachute Brigade Group withdrew. Brigadier Darling also went to great lengths to assure the local leaders that the Dutch would be fully capable of defending them against Indonesian extremist elements. Finally, he persuaded them that any form of disturbance would be futile and would only serve to destroy the peaceful conditions prevailing in Semarang.

Darling's words were heeded and the arrival of the Dutch forces, under the command of Colonel Van Langen, at the end of the first and second weeks of March, took place without any disturbance. A small number of locals did leave Semarang for a few days but they soon returned after having been robbed of most of their possessions by extremists outside the town.

239. Men of 12th Parachute Battalion wading ashore from landing craft on arrival in Malaya in September 1945. (Photo: Mr R. Dixon)

Each Dutch unit had a liaison party, of three officers and a small number of NCOs, attached to it from 5th Parachute Brigade Group for the initial three weeks after arrival. In addition, the brigade supplied teams, to provide assistance in training signallers, mortarmen and machine gunners of which there were few in the Dutch ranks. The men in the Dutch units were generally of good calibre, many of them having served during the war in either the Resistance in Holland or in the Dutch forces which operated as part of the Allied armies. However, 'T' Regiment Group was weak in its supporting arm elements. This was rectified to a certain extent when a Dutch field artillery battery arrived. 5th Parachute Brigade Group also gave as much assistance as possible in terms of logistical and maintenance support, the RASC and RAOC officers of the brigade were kept busy checking and handing over stores of all natures to the Dutch.

The arrival of Colonel Van Langen and his force meant that the Kido Battalion and all Japanese civilians could be evacuated from Java. Prior to his unit's departure, Major Kido presented Brigadier Ken Darling with his sword as a sign of respect. On the 23rd March, he and his men arrived at the evacuation staging camp at Galang Island from which the following signal was received by the brigade:

''Message:

Addressed to:- Maj Stenning

Addressed by:- Maj Kido
　　　　　　　Kido Unit, Galang Island.

Text:

Under very kind care and direction of local British forces, Kido Unit completed landing here on the 23rd inst., without anything unusual to the entire personnel.

Taking this opportunity, I wish to express my hearty thanks to you as well as all the British troops for your exceptional courtesy extended to us, and all the troubles taken for us during our residence in, and at the time of our departure from, Semarang.

Kindly convey our best wishes to His Excellency Brigadier of your Brigade.''

On the 24th March the first anniversary of the crossing of the Rhine was celebrated. The entire brigade, together with all of its attached supporting arms units, paraded through Semarang and the salute was taken by Lieutenant General Sir Montagu Stopford, the Allied Commander Netherlands East Indies.

On the 15th May, 5th Parachute Brigade handed over Semarang to Colonel Van Langen and his force and left Java. The peaceful state of the town and the harmonious state of co-existence amongst the different ethnic communities were a great tribute to the immense effort and dedication which had been shown by the brigade during its tour of duty in Semarang. The smart but friendly paratroopers had won the hearts of the local people, as is evidenced by the following tribute published in the brigade's own newspaper *Pegasus*:

''Dear Sir,

Will you kindly allow me the use of a few lines in your daily to express, also on behalf of my countrymen, my great gratitude and appreciation for the splendid work the 5th Para Brigade has done in the reconstruction of Semarang.

All of you have done great and have thus again enhanced the reputation which Great Britain enjoys throughout the world for fair play and hard work.

We shall all miss you, and your smiling smartness and tenacity to create order out of disorder will forever remain in our memory.

Fare thee well!

Dr P. H. Angenent''

After leaving Java, 5th Parachute Brigade Group returned to Malaya for a brief period before moving to Singapore. In July it moved to Palestine to rejoin 6th Airborne Division, arriving at Port Said on the 7th August. Here the brigade and its battalions were disbanded, its officers and soldiers being absorbed into other units of 6th Airborne Division.

240. The CIGS, Field Marshal Lord Alanbrooke, inspects men of 12th Parachute Battalion during his visit to 5th Parachute Brigade on 6th December 1945. (Photo: Imperial War Museum)

241. Privates G. McGreigh and G. Lewis of 12th Parachute Battalion search suspects before passing them on for interrogation. (Photo: Imperial War Museum)

242. *Above:* Men of 7th Parachute Battalion take cover after coming under fire from Indonesian snipers during operations in the Kramat quarter of Batavia. (Photo: Imperial War Museum)

243. *Left:* A 2-inch mortar team of A Company 13th Parachute Battalion during operations in Semarang. (Photo: Mr F. G. Murphy)

244. *Below left:* A Bren LMG group of A Company 13th Parachute Battalion during operations in Semarang. (Photo: Mr F. G. Murphy)

245. Below: A 6-pounder anti-tank gun of 4th Airlanding Anti-Tank Battery RA at Gombel Hill, Semarang, engages guerilla positions. (Photo: Major J. Slater)

246. 7th Parachute Battalion marches past the Commander-in-Chief during the Rhine Crossing anniversary parade by 5th Parachute Brigade at Semarang on the 24th March 1946.
(Photo: Mr F. G. Murphy)

247. 6th Indian Field Battery Royal Indian Artillery drives past the Commander-in-Chief during the Rhine Crossing anniversary parade.
(Photo: Mr F. G. Murphy)

248. Honey light tanks of A Squadron 11th Cavalry (Prince Albert Victor's Own) drive past the Commander-in-Chief during the Rhine Crossing anniversary parade.
(Photo: Mr F. G. Murphy)

Palestine

Whilst 6th Airborne Division had initially been assigned a role in South East Asia, 1st Airborne Division had been earmarked for deployment in the Middle East as part of the Imperial Strategic Reserve. However, the dropping of the atomic bombs on Japan in early August brought a cessation of hostilities in the Far East and thus all ideas of dispatching 6th Airborne Division to that part of the world were abandoned.

With the war now over, it was considered no longer necessary to have two airborne divisions in the British Army's order of battle. Whilst 6th Airborne Division was the junior of the two formations, it was nonetheless decided that it would be retained and that 1st Airborne Division should be disbanded.

Consequently 6th Airborne Division became part of the Imperial Strategic Reserve. Shortly afterwards, during the period 15th September to 6th November 1945, it moved to Palestine.

The division's order of battle underwent some changes at this time. 5th Parachute Brigade was replaced by 2nd Parachute Brigade, comprising 4th, 5th and 6th Parachute Battalions, which was commanded by Brigadier C. H. V. Pritchard DSO. 3rd Parachute Brigade, now commanded by Brigadier Gerald Lathbury DSO MBE, still formed part of the division, as did 6th Airlanding Brigade which was still commanded by Brigadier Hugh Bellamy DSO.

Amongst the battalions of the division, 3rd Parachute Battalion had replaced 1st Canadian Parachute Battalion whilst the 1st Battalion The Argyll & Sutherland Highlanders had replaced the 12th Battalion The Devonshire Regiment in 6th Airlanding Brigade. Within the supporting arms, 1st and 9th Airborne Squadrons RE had replaced 3rd and 591st Parachute Squadrons RE whilst the role of pathfinding was now carried out by the 21st Independent Parachute Company. 127th Parachute Field Ambulance had replaced 225th Parachute Field Ambulance which, together with 3rd Airborne Squadron RE, had accompanied 5th Parachute Brigade to South East Asia. The division was later joined by the 3rd The King's Own Hussars who had previously been stationed in Syria.

The main body of the division travelled to Palestine by sea, arriving at the port of Haifa after a voyage of ten days. From there it moved by rail to Nuseirat Hospital Camp, near the town of Gaza, where the divisional main headquarters was already established. It was joined there on the 27th September by the divisional tactical headquarters which had flown out via Egypt.

The different elements of the division were based in a number of camps which were grouped within easy reach of each other, about six miles from Gaza. Conditions were very spartan and the weather extremely hot whilst the terrain was barren and sandy.

6th Airborne Division's role in Palestine was to act as Britain's strategic reserve in the Middle East. Palestine had been chosen, as opposed to Egypt, Cyrenaica or other alternative locations, due to its superior training facilities and airfields. However, in the event, very little parachute or airlanding training was carried out, particularly after the RAF began to reduce its strength in the country.

The Political Situation

Palestine was a country sorely beset by internal trouble and strife between its Jewish and Arab inhabitants. These had existed since 1917 when the British Government had given an undertaking that it recognised the requirement for a home state for Jews but had taken no further action. At the end of the First World War, Britain had received a mandate from the League of Nations, which came into force in 1923, to administer Palestine which had previously formed part of the Turkish Empire. The mandate, amongst other things, provided for the formation of a Jewish body to advise the government of Palestine on issues affecting the Jewish national home and the interests of the Jewish community in Palestine. This role was carried out by the Zionist Organisation until 1929 when its terms of reference were increased, a number of non-Zionists were admitted and it was transformed into the Jewish Agency. This organisation had no governing function but inevitably exercised a great deal of influence over the Jewish community by virtue of its functions.

At that time the majority of the Palestinian population were Arabs. During the period from 1918 until 1939, however, there was a small but steady flow of Jewish immigrants. In 1939 the British placed a limit on Jewish immigration of 75,000 over a period of five years. After that there would be no further immigration without the consent of the Arab population.

At the end of the Second World War, however, there were large numbers of displaced Jews who were homeless as a result of the Nazi holocaust. Somewhat naturally, Palestine appeared very attractive to them. At the end of 1945 the Jewish Agency, which by then was responsible for handling Jewish affairs in Palestine, mounted a campaign to try and force the British government to remove the restrictions on Jewish immigration whilst at the same time trying to promote the cause of a national home state for Jews. The fact that Palestine already belonged to the Arabs did not seem to occur to the agency or to any of the Jews already living in the country.

When 6th Airborne Division arrived in Palestine, it was met by a hostile reception from the Jewish press which referred to its troops as "Gestapo". This was highly objectionable to the division, many of whose members had been Jewish and many of whom, during the advance to the Baltic, had seen the results of the Nazis' treatment of Jews. Moreover, many of its members had been killed, wounded or maimed whilst fighting the Nazis and thus the division as a whole resented the Jews' attitude towards it. Small wonder then that, in the main, many of its members sympathised with the Arabs.

The Jews possessed their own underground defence force in the form of the Hagana which was formed in Palestine in 1920 during anti-Jewish riots that had taken place at that time. It was organised on conventional military lines, many of its members having served in the Allied armies during the war, and was well-equipped with small arms and mortars. Within the Hagana was the Palmach which was a highly trained elite element which operated on a full-time basis and whose commanders were highly experienced.

In addition to the two underground military organisations, there were two Jewish guerilla forces. The first of these was the Irgun Zvai Leumi (National Military Organisation — IZL) which was formed from a splinter group of revisionists and extremists which broke away from the Hagana in 1937 over a disagreement concerning the subject of armed reprisals against Arab aggression. During the war the IZL had maintained a low profile until February 1944 when it had commenced a campaign of sabotage and violence against the Palestinian government. Thereafter it had continued to oppose British rule through violence and terrorism.

The second guerilla organisation was the Stern Gang. This organisation had been formed originally by an individual named Abraham Stern and consisted of some fifty members of the IZL who disagreed with the organisation's policy of quiescence which it adopted during the war years until February 1944. In their opposition to British rule, Stern and his men actively co-operated with the Italians and then the Germans whilst at the same time conducting operations against the British. In 1942, Stern himself was killed during an encounter with the British Palestine Police, and a Pole named Nathan Freedman Yellin assumed command of the gang. The following year the gang adopted the title of Lachamey Heruth Israel (Hebrew Fighters for the Freedom of Israel).

The majority of Palestinian Arabs were followers of the Mufti of Jerusalem, Haj Amin al Husseini. He had been exiled previously by the British but exercised control through several loyal lieutenants who carried out his commands and policies. However, despite the fact that they were united in their wish for independence, the Arabs were riven by dissension between their different factions. Tribal politics tended to take prime place in the order of political priorities.

In 1936 the Arab Higher Executive Committee was formed. With the Mufti as its president, this body consisted of the heads of the various Arab political parties and was intended to organise and control the Arab rebellion which took place in the same year. The committee was declared illegal by the Palestinian government but during the war no other body replaced it.

In November 1945 the Arab Higher Committee was formed. This body incorporated representatives of all political parties but it was shortlived, its downfall being brought about by dissension between the different factions within it. The Arab League, which had also been formed in 1945 and whose ruling council consisted of representatives of all Arab countries, then ordered that a new body was to be formed under the leadership of Jamal Husseini, a cousin of the Mufti. This was the Arab Higher Executive which was tasked with developing and sustaining some form of national unity amongst Palestinian Arabs. The Arab League itself also exerted influence, not only because of its interest in the affairs of all Arab states but also because of the lack of any really effective Arab political organisation in Palestine.

To the British troops arriving in Palestine, the political situation seemed to be almost unfathomable. The reception that they received on arrival also confused them initially. On the one hand were the Arabs with their politics in a continual state of instability; on the other were the Jews with their implacable hostility towards Britain as well as to the Arab population. It was thus an unpleasant situation in which the members of 6th Airborne Division found themselves.

The Military Situation

At the time of the division's arrival in Palestine, there was a considerable number of British troops already in the country. These included 1st Infantry Division and several additional units which were engaged in guard duties. Some of these were colonial troops and included the 23rd Battalion The King's African Rifles and the 5th Battalion The Northern Rhodesia Regiment as well as units of the Transjordan Frontier Force and the Arab Legion.

Palestine was divided into three military sectors: 15 Area in the north, with its headquarters at Haifa; 21 Area in the south, its headquarters based at Sarafand; and 156 Sub-Area with its headquarters in Jersalem. The area headquarters controlled all static units and installations whilst the field formations were responsible for internal security operations and thus were deployed so that maximum control could be maintained during civil unrest.

By the time 6th Airborne Division arrived, the worsening political situation was such that internal security was becoming a matter of growing priority. Even before the division had been fully assembled, warning orders were received for the regrouping and redeployment of all forces in Palestine in order to meet the growing threat of civil unrest. The Southern Sector, which consisted of the districts of Lydda, Gaza and Samaria (minus the sub-district of Jenin), was to be the division's area of responsibility in the event of trouble breaking out. As the three brigades and supporting arms arrived, they were allotted their respective tasks and immediately commenced carrying out reconnaissances of their areas.

Training

By the end of the war, all formations and units within 6th Airborne Division were highly trained in all the skills required of them for offensive operations. The very nature of airborne operations required parachute and airlanding troops to possess a high degree of aggression and *elan* to compensate for the lack of heavy weapons and equipment.

Internal security operations, on the other hand, placed different requirements on troops. Whilst such fundamentals as discipline, physical fitness, professionalism and military skills still remained important, the emphasis was on diplomacy and the use of minimum force when necessary. With two separate communities continually at loggerheads, troops were likely to have to act as mediators or to protect one from the other. Such a role called for a sound knowledge of the historical background and political situation, tact, diplomacy and firm action when required.

As well as learning the principles of internal security operations, troops were instructed in techniques such as cordon and search — the throwing of a cordon around a village or settlement and the methods of searching for well-concealed caches. Others included crowd dispersal and riot control, as well as the setting up of checkpoints and road-blocks. Troops also had to learn the regulations governing the powers available to them: imposition of curfews, rules for opening fire and powers of search and arrest.

Instruction was also given in the religions and customs of both the Jewish and Arab communities in order that no offence was caused during operations which involved the searching of property or individuals.

Due to the fact that they would be working closely with the police, all troops were also briefed on its organisation and role. The Palestine Police was a British colonial force of which the officers and some NCOs were British whilst the constables were recruited from the local communities. Under the command of a Commissioner, it was organised in districts and divisions and possessed specialist branches such as the Criminal Investigation Department.

Troops were also required to be fully familiar with the system of government and administration in Palestine, reminding them that their role was to support the civil authorities. The responsibilities of government lay with the High Commissioner. In turn, he was empowered to delegate powers to the military authorities in the person of the General Officer Commanding in Palestine. Embodied in the Defence Emergency Regulations of 1945, these were considerable and extensive. Palestine itself was divided into six districts, each administered by a District Commissioner who was responsible to the Chief Secretary.

Operational Deployment

No major regrouping of troops in Palestine had been considered likely until at least three weeks after the arrival of 6th Airborne Division. On the 7th October, the plan for the takeover of the Southern Sector was issued. This called for the division to assume operational responsibility as soon as it was required to do so, and after 3rd Parachute Brigade, which was only semi-mobile, was ready for deployment. Until that time, the brigade was to be available to Headquarters 21 Area if needed.

On the 14th October, a modified plan was issued. This provided more details which included the deployment dispositions for all formations and units. 3rd Parachute Brigade was required to provide two mobile columns which were to be on call to Headquarters 21 Area and at six hours notice to move.

On the 20th October, 6th Airborne Division received orders to deploy to its predetermined operational locations. On the same day, the divisional tactical headquarters moved to Sarafand where it was co-located with Headquarters 21 Area. The following day, 3rd Parachute Brigade moved north to the district of Lydda which incorporated the towns of Tel Aviv and Jaffa.

Meanwhile 6th Airlanding Brigade prepared for its deployment to the Samaria district. Brigade Headquarters moved to Lydda Airport on the 23rd October and two of its battalions, the 1st Battalion The Royal Ulster Rifles and the 2nd Battalion The Oxfordshire & Buckinghamshire Light Infantry, deployed to their operational stations. Under command of the brigade was the 6th Battalion The Gordon Highlanders which was based at Tulkarm.

2nd Parachute Brigade arrived on the 22nd October from England and was immediately moved to Gaza which was potentially the quietest of the six districts. It was initially planned that all three brigades would change districts every six months, Gaza affording the opportunity for refresher training in airborne and tactical skills.

During this period the situation was one of an uneasy lull during which there were a number of minor incidents. On the 31st October, however, a number of sabotage attacks were carried out on the railway network, including the rail junction at Lydda, and the oil refinery at Haifa. Main lines were cut by explosives in a total of two hundred and forty different locations by saboteurs of the Palmach who suffered only one casualty. At Lydda the security forces and railway staff suffered four killed and eight wounded. Two days later, however, all main railway lines were in operation once again.

In the middle of the following month, the British Government made its long-awaited statement on the problem of Palestine. In essence, this stated that Palestine itself could not solve the problem of Jewish homelessness and that an Anglo-American committee would be set up to examine political, economic and social conditions in Europe which had bearings on the problems of Jewish immigration and settlement, and to examine the status of Jews in Europe who had been the victims of Nazi and Fascist persecution. The statement also indicated that the British Government would meanwhile hold consultations with the Arab population in Palestine to ensure that there would be no interruption of the immigration of fifteen hundred Jews each month.

Whilst they were undoubtedly disappointed by this statement and voiced it accordingly, the Jewish Agency and the Jewish community in general were well aware that any resort to violent protest would be highly counter-productive. However, the younger and more foolhardy elements of the community ignored any such considerations and riots broke out in Jerusalem and Tel Aviv on the afternoon of 14th November.

As 3rd Parachute Brigade moved into Tel Aviv, the situation began to deteriorate rapidly after attacks were carried out on British property and troops were stoned. During the evening the District Offices were set on fire and the police became heavily committed in several areas of the city during attempts to break up rioting mobs. Before too long a company of 8th Parachute Battalion was called for and it moved into position at Colony Square. Almost immediately, the troops were subjected to stoning by a large mob and injuries were caused amongst policemen and soldiers. Despite massive provocation, great restraint was shown but, after several warnings, weapons eventually had to be used to restore order. A few rounds were fired and this achieved the desired effect of dispersing the mob which then proceeded to attack the Post Office and government offices which were ransacked and set ablaze.

Later that evening the rest of 8th Parachute Battalion arrived and an hour later order had been restored and a curfew imposed. Early the following morning, the 15th November, however, trouble broke out again when large crowds set buildings on fire and indulged in looting. Weapons were once again used to disperse them. Eventually the rest of 3rd Parachute Brigade was ordered into Tel Aviv, arriving at midday with A Squadron of the 3rd The King's Own Hussars under command. Order was soon restored but to ensure that control of the city was maintained, the brigade was reinforced by the 1st Battalion The Royal Ulster Rifles, the 6th Airborne Armoured Reconnaissance Regiment and the remainder of the 3rd The King's Own Hussars.

The operation, codenamed 'Bellicose', continued until the early morning of the 20th November when all troops were withdrawn from Tel Aviv. Casualties amongst the Jewish rioters amounted to six killed and sixty wounded, whilst those amongst the security forces totalled twelve wounded and thirty slightly injured. This was the division's first operation carried out in Palestine and reflected great credit on the steadiness and restraint shown by the troops in what had proved to be a series of very difficult situations.

Cordon & Search Operations

Late November 1945 also saw the first cordon and search operations carried out by the division.

On the night of the 24th November, two groups of armed Jews, later reported to be Palmach, carried out attacks on coastguard stations at Givat Olga and Sidna Ali. These were located north and south of a location at which a schooner had been boarded by the Royal Navy two nights previously whilst it was in the process of landing illegal Jewish immigrants. The crew and twenty Jews had been arrested and sent to the detention camp at Athlit.

The attacks on the coastguard station were a reprisal on the part of the Jews. Both buildings were blown up and fourteen casualties were suffered by the police.

Follow-up operations by the police indicated that the group which had attacked the station at Givat Olga had come from two settlements at Givat Haiyam and Hogla, whilst those who had attacked Sidna Ali were from Rishpon and Shefayim which were only a short distance away.

On the early morning of the 25th November, 8th Parachute Battalion moved to Sidna Ali to take part in an operation in support of the police searching the two settlements to the south. On making their entry, the police encountered violent resistance from the occupants who were soon joined by Jews from neighbouring settlements. The majority of Jewish reinforcements were halted by the cordons of troops around the settlements and confrontations took place as a result. The police, meanwhile, were making little headway and were eventually forced to withdraw. Cordons were reinforced and left in position during the night. 8th Parachute Battalion was replaced by 3rd Parachute Battalion and the 2nd Battalion The Oxfordshire & Buckinghamshire Light Infantry who were placed under command of 3rd Parachute Brigade. By this time 6th Airlanding Brigade, now commanded by Brigadier R. H. Bower CBE, and 3rd Parachute Brigade were deployed on the operation, each with a squadron of the 3rd The King's Own Hussars under command.

On the following day, the 26th November, the police again attempted to carry out a search of the two settlements in the north but without the support of troops. Once again, they were met by violent resistance and troops were called in during the morning to quell the rioting. Jews from neighbouring settlements once again attempted to break through the cordons but were stopped by troops who, after warnings had been given, opened fire and inflicted casualties.

In the south, where 3rd Parachute Brigade was covering Rishpon and Shefayim, 8th Parachute Battalion entered Shefayim at 0700 hours with the police. Baton charges and CS gas had to be used before order could be imposed. The occupants of the settlement adopted a policy of non-cooperation and nine hundred Jews were arrested and placed under guard. At Rishpon, meanwhile, the cordon came under attack from a crowd numbering approximately fifteen hundred and troops were forced to open fire, inflicting casualties. Later in the morning a crowd of some three thousand approached a platoon in the cordon, led by a man on horseback. After due warning, he was shot and the crowd dispersed without further ado. After a search of the settlement, explosives were discovered and eleven Jews, including the head of the settlement, were arrested.

By 1700 hours, cordon and search operations at all four settlements had been completed and all troops and police withdrew. Six Jews had been killed and approximately forty-two wounded, with one hundred and sixty being sent to the detention centre at Athlit for interrogation. The casualties amongst troops and the police consisted of a number with slight injuries.

During this operation it became apparent to the security forces that the Jews were highly organised, with reinforcements being deployed in answer to alarm signals from settlements. Troops also learned how quickly a small incident could escalate into a large and violent confrontation. Further lessons learned were that it was essential that Jewish reinforcements should be intercepted as far as possible from the scene of any cordon and search operation in order to prevent any interference, and that the maximum

249. A Jewish illegal immigrant ship at Nahariya after being run aground by a Royal Navy destroyer in April 1946.
(Photos: Mr B. Boswell)

number of troops available should by deployed for this type of operation, including an adequate reserve.

In this particular operation, a total of the equivalent of eleven infantry battalions from 1st Infantry and 6th Airborne Divisions was deployed. Those units which took part included: 1st Battalion the Loyal Regiment, 2nd Battalion The North Staffordshire Regiment (both 2nd Infantry Brigade), 1st Battalion The Argyll & Sutherland Highlanders, 1st Battalion The Royal Ulster Rifles, 2nd Battalion The Oxfordshire & Buckinghamshire Light Infantry (all 6th Airlanding Brigade), 3rd and 8th Parachute Battalions (both 3rd Parachute Brigade), 6th Battalion The Gordon Highlanders and a company of the 1st Battalion The Hertfordshire Regiment. In addition, 195th Airlanding Field Ambulance and 224th Parachute Field Ambulance supported their own individual brigades, whilst the 3rd The King's Own Hussars deployed squadrons under command to 6th Airlanding Brigade and 3rd Parachute Brigade.

After a temporary lull of about a month, the Jews renewed their operations. On the night of the 26th December the police headquarters in Jerusalem and Jaffa were attacked, as were railway installations at Lydda and a military armoury in Tel Aviv. In all instances, these attacks were attributed to the IZL.

The result of this was concentrated action by the security forces. 3rd Parachute Brigade was once again sent into Tel Aviv where a curfew was imposed. Intelligence indicated that those responsible for the attacks in Jaffa and Tel Aviv had gone to ground in Ramat Gan, a large settlement just outside Tel Aviv.

Operation 'Pintail', involving 3rd Parachute Brigade with 4th Parachute Battalion under command, was launched on the 29th December. Fifteen hundred Jews were interrogated, fifty-nine being arrested and detained. In the following month of January 1946, Operations 'Heron' and 'Pigeon' took place in which the settlement of Rishon-le-Zion and the Shapiro Quarter of Tel Aviv were searched respectively.

The end of February 1946 saw the IZL launch a series of attacks against RAF bases in Palestine. On the night of the 25th February, raids were carried out against airfields at Lydda, Petah Tiqva and Qastina. The immediate effect of these raids, which resulted in an estimated £750,000 of damage, was the withdrawal of aircraft to Egypt and the consequent loss of airborne training by 6th Airborne Division. Eventually the aircraft returned but responsibility for the security and protection of the airfields now fell on the division which was already heavily committed in providing guards.

The Raid At Sarafand

On the 6th March, the IZL attempted a raid on the ammunition store of the 3rd The King's Own Hussars who were based at Sarafand. Nine Jews, dressed in the uniform of British airborne troops, arrived at the Rishon Gate at lunchtime in a stolen military vehicle and a car. At the guardroom they overpowered the Jewish guards and, leaving a small group at the gate, drove to the hussars' ammunition tent. Here they held the sentries at gunpoint whilst

they commenced loading cases of ammunition aboard their truck. However, they were soon spotted and, as the alarm was raised, the Jews withdrew rapidly towards the gate under fire. As they did so, they placed an explosive charge in the ammunition store which exploded without causing any casualties.

Meanwhile, the hussars' Signals Officer, Captain Gerry Barrow, had run with a small group of other officers to the Rishon Gate to close it and cut off the Jews' retreat but had found it occupied by the rest of the IZL group. He succeeded in overpowering one of the Jews but came under fire at closer range and was forced to take cover. He was subsequently awarded the MBE for his part in this action.

The IZL gang was pursued by some of the hussars in armoured cars but they eventually evaded pursuit in the area of Rishon-le-Zion. Subsequently two of the gang, both of whom had been seriously wounded, were captured and the two vehicles were discovered together with nearly all of the small quantity of ammunition which had been taken from the ammunition store.

The only British casualty during the raid was Mrs Jean Marjoribanks, one of the YMCA team who ran a canteen service for the troops. She was seriously wounded by Jewish gunfire during the raid but fortunately made a complete recovery. A widow, she subsequently married Lieutenant Colonel Johnny Frost DSO MC, the Commanding Officer of 2nd Parachute Battalion.

A Farewell To Gliders

During the early part of 1946, 6th Airborne Division underwent several changes in both command appointments and order of battle.

Major General James Cassels CBE DSO, who had until then been commanding 51st Highland Division, arrived to take over command on the 5th March from Major General Bols who departed for the Imperial Defence College.

March also saw the disbandment of 6th Airborne Armoured Reconnaissance Regiment, commanded by Lieutenant Colonel C. P. D. Legard. The majority of its members transferred to the 3rd The King's Own Hussars which assumed the role of divisional reconnaissance regiment.

The main change, however, was the loss of 6th Airlanding Brigade which was replaced in the division by 1st Parachute Brigade. Commanded by Brigadier Hugh Bellamy DSO, the previous commander of the gliderborne formation, this comprised 1st, 2nd and 17th Parachute Battalions.

1st Parachute Brigade arrived at Port Said on the 1st April. Two days later the brigade headquarters reached Camp 21 near Nathanya, the rest of the brigade arriving by the 7th April. The following day it assumed operational control of the Samaria District less the sub-district of Jenin.

On the 15th April, 6th Airlanding Brigade was redesignated 31st Independent Infantry Brigade and on the 26th April took part in a farewell to the division parade at which it wore red berets for the last time. It remained in Palestine until November when it was disbanded.

On the 5th August, 5th Parachute Brigade returned to the divisional fold from its period of operations in South East Asia. Soon after its arrival, however, the brigade was disbanded. 7th Parachute Battalion was amalgamated with 17th Parachute Battalion but, as senior battalion, retained its numerical disignation. 12th Parachute Battalion was disbanded and its members dispersed to other battalions within the division. 13th Parachute Battalion had already been disbanded prior to the brigade's departure from Malaya.

On the 13th September, 21st Independent Parachute Company was also disbanded. The pathfinder role was handed over to the divisional reconnaissance regiment and thus many members of the company transferred to the 3rd The King's Own Hussars whilst others joined parachute battalions within the division.

Training

Due to the continuing operational situation in Palestine, airborne and tactical training were forced into second place. Opportunities for battalions or companies to conduct airborne exercises were thus few and far between.

6th Airborne Division was supported by No.283 Wing RAF which was commanded by Group Captain R. B. Wardman OBE AFC. This formation consisted of Nos.620 and 644 Squadrons which were equipped with Halifax bombers.

Parachute training was carried out at the Airborne Training School at Aqir, the number of descents during 1946 and 1947 being in excess of twenty thousand. The majority of those carried out were during refresher training for the trained parachutists within the division, although a number of basic courses were also conducted for those personnel who could not be sent back to No.1 Parachute Training School in England.

6th Airborne Division operated its own Divisional Battle School which was based at Ein Shemer before moving to St Jeans near Acre. It carried out all types of training, except airborne training, and catered for all the division's requirements at different levels.

Brigade exercises were impossible to organise, given the operational demands at that time. Battalion level training was rare, although one exercise did take place in Sudan in May 1946 when a battalion group, consisting of 3rd Parachute Battalion, a company of 8th Parachute Battalion and supporting arms detachments, was flown from Palestine to Khartoum. The exercise itself was deemed to have been successful, although there was a high casualty rate during the parachute drop of the 8th Parachute Battalion company. However, some valuable lessons in the deployment of parachutists in a hot climate were learned, including the necessity to wear smocks and long trousers despite the heat in order to avoid injury on landing. There was also a faster rate of descent due to thinner air and down-draughts.

Several company level airborne exercises took place outside the country in such places as Iraq, Transjordan and Cyprus. Other planned exercises, destined to take place in Libya, Aden and elsewhere in the Middle East, had to be abandoned due to the operational situation in Palestine at the time.

Internal Security Operations April 1946 — January 1947

On the 2nd April the IZL attacked the railway network at two locations, one north of Haifa and the other in the area of Isdud-Yibna between Lydda and Gaza.

The attack north of Haifa was carried out by some twenty armed Jews who overpowered the police detachment and caused damage to a bridge at Na' amin. The sabotage attack in the south was carried out by a larger group and resulted in five bridges being damaged, the railway line being cut in several places, an engine being destroyed and roads being mined. Initially, an attack was carried out on the railway station at Yibna and a police defensive position nearby. At that point, however, a patrol from 9th Parachute Battalion arrived in the Yibna area, encountering some of the IZL's mines in the process. The patrol followed up and the IZL withdrew but the pursuit was delayed due to an unfortunate and lengthy exchange of fire between the Arab railway policemen and the patrol in the dark, fortunately without any casualties on either side. At this point a patrol from 5th Parachute Battalion arrived, with a company of 6th Parachute Battalion arriving in the area further to the south at about midnight.

At dawn the following morning the pursuit was taken up again, with patrols following three trails. Reports indicated a group of about thirty Jews moving north across the Rishon ranges, whilst police tracker dogs followed trails to settlements at Kefar Marmorek and Ezra Bitsaron and another from Isdud. The group heading north was sighted by an observation aircraft which guided troops from 8th Parachute Battalion to its location. Eventually, an action took place which resulted in the capture of twenty-four Jews and a considerable number of weapons.

Towards the end of April, the Stern Gang carried out an attack which was notable only for the degree of brutality displayed by its perpetrators and which was remembered long afterwards by all members of 6th Airborne Division serving in Palestine

at the time.

At 2030 hours on the 25th April an attack was carried out by approximately thirty Jews on a detachment of troops of 5th Parachute Battalion guarding a vehicle park in Tel Aviv used by recreational transport. At very short range, fire was opened from a commandeered house opposite the entrance to the park whilst twenty or so Jews entered the park itself. Unarmed troops taking cover inside the tents in the park were gunned down without mercy, after which the terrorists withdrew into the Karton Quarter of the town.

The following morning, a search was carried out of the quarter and a total of seventy-nine suspects were detained. Major General Cassels summoned the Mayor of Tel Aviv and expressed his anger and revulsion at the outrage, as well as his belief of the complicity of certain elements of the Jewish community. However, little or no effort was made to punish the Jews other than the imposition of a road curfew and the closing of all bars, restaurants and places of public entertainment between 2000 and 0500 hours.

Needless to say, there was considerable bitterness and anger amongst all elements of 6th Airborne Division. The following night some troops took the law into their own hands and vented their anger on some of the inhabitants of the nearby settlement of Beer Tuvya, damaging property and beating up several Jews in the process. This breach of discipline, despite the massive provocation, could not be permitted and the ringleaders were caught and duly punished.

The following month of June featured the kidnapping of five British officers by the IZL from the British officers club in Tel Aviv. The Jews' objective was to take hostages which they intended to hold in exchange for commutation of the death sentences passed on the two Jews captured after the raid on the 3rd Hussars' ammunition store at Sarafand.

Two of the five officers were released in Tel Aviv four days later, possibly under pressure from the more moderate Hagana or the Jewish Agency who it was thought possibly feared drastic repercussions against key Jewish leaders. The release of two of the hostages was probably a compromise, the remaining three still providing an effective negotiating asset.

The other three hostages were released on the 4th July, by which time the death sentences on the two Jews had been commuted. Having been chloroformed, they were placed in wooden boxes and left on a street corner in Tel Aviv. On regaining consciousness, the three officers forced their way out of the boxes and found themselves in the middle of passers-by who ignored them completely.

Operation 'Agatha'

During the period from November 1945 to the end of June 1946, the Jews had continued to wage a campaign of terrorism and sabotage against the security forces despite every effort having been made to curtail them. It was suspected that the Jewish Agency and the leaders of the Jewish community condoned, if not actually assisted, the activities of the illegal armed organisations.

It was therefore decided to carry out an operation designed to obtain evidence from the headquarters of the Jewish Agency and to arrest those members of Jewish political organisations suspected of being implicated in terrorist activities or of indirectly assisting with them. In addition, buildings suspected of being the headquarters of illegal armed organisations would be occupied and as many of their members as possible would be arrested. The operation would take place across the whole country and would involve the major proportion of military units in Palestine. 6th Airborne Division was given all the tasks with the exception of the occupation of the headquarters of the Jewish Agency.

2nd Parachute Brigade, now commanded by Brigadier J. P. O'Brien Twohig CBE DSO, was stationed in the Lydda District and had operational responsibility for Tel Aviv. It was tasked with arresting suspect Jews within its own area. 1st Parachute Brigade was to search six settlements in the north whilst 3rd Parachute Brigade was given the task of searching Givat Brenner and No'ar Oved in the south.

250 & 251. 9th Airborne Squadron RE carry out rescue operations in the aftermath of the bombing of the King David Hotel in Jerusalem.. (Photos: Mr A. W. Sweetlove)

The main initial problem was that of security, and elaborate precautions were taken to ensure that this was maintained. Normal routine was maintained by all formations and units taking part, and knowledge of the operations was restricted to the minimum number of personnel. In addition, a certain amount of deception was carried out and briefing of troops was left until the last possible moment, after they had been confined to camp.

On the morning of the 29th June, the operation commenced. Between 0345 and 0515 hours small groups from 6th Airborne Divisional Signals, escorted by men of the Glider Pilot Regiment, took over civilian telephone exchanges without any warning. At the same time, telephone lines to those settlements about to be searched were cut.

In Tel Aviv, detachments of police and troops moved carefully into areas where listed suspects were living and made unobtrusive approaches to houses before carrying out arrests. In the areas of the settlements in the north and south, cordons were placed in position quickly and quietly. Troops had been furnished with exact details of those Jews to be arrested for subsequent screening by the police.

By the end of the operation on the 1st July, the total number arrested was two thousand, seven hundred and eighteen which included fifty-six women. Five hundred and seventy-one were released during the following week and the majority of the rest during the following months. Six hundred and thirty-six were sent to the detention centre at Latrun, of whom a hundred and thirty-five were suspected of being members of the Palmach.

Due to the careful planning and extremely tight security beforehand, the operation was successful. One of the effects of it was that the Palmach and Hagana became far more circumspect in their operations against British forces in Palestine.

The Bombing of the King David Hotel

During the early afternoon of the 22nd July, a group of about twenty Jews, disguised as Arabs, entered the King David Hotel in Jerusalem. The hotel at that time housed the Secretariat of the Government of Palestine and Headquarters British Troops in Palestine and Transjordan. It was also still in use as a hotel and thus no one looked twice at the group which, pretending to be a party of workmen, unloaded from a truck several milk churns filled with explosives and placed them in the basement of the part of the hotel housing the government secretariat. As they were doing so, a British officer became suspicious and was shot whilst investigating. The alarm was raised as the fuses were lit and the Jews made their escape. Unfortunately there was no time to evacuate the hotel and the charges exploded, demolishing the entire wing of the hotel. A large number of people were killed, with many more being trapped and injured.

9th Airborne Squadron RE, commanded by Major E. W. J. Cowtan MC, was tasked with carrying out rescue operations. Based at Qastina, some forty miles from Jerusalem, it moved with all haste to the city. As they arrived in Jerusalem, the sappers encountered Jewish road-blocks through which they had to force their way whilst being stoned. Nevertheless, by 1600 hours the squadron was already at work clearing the rubble from the wrecked building. For the next three days the sappers worked ceaselessly and tirelessly in three shifts, one sapper driving his bulldozer for thirty hours without a break.

Six survivors were rescued from the wreckage. By the time all the rubble and debris had been cleared, ninety-one bodies had been found. The squadron had performed magnificently and this was recognised by the award of the MBE to Major Cowtan.

On the 23rd July, 8th and 9th Parachute Battalions moved into Jerusalem as part of the operation to track down the Jews responsible for this horrendous outrage. Two of the perpetrators were discovered, one dead and one wounded, whilst thirty-seven Jews were arrested. However, it was difficult to prove their involvement in the crime and the authorities could only send them to a detention centre.

On the 24th July, the British Government published a White Paper which gave details of the connections between the Jewish Agency and the terrorist organisations in Palestine. Needless to say, this caused no little consternation and embarrassment amongst the Jewish community.

Operation 'Shark'

In the immediate aftermath of the bombing of the King David Hotel, it was decided to carry out a thorough search of Tel Aviv because of evidence that some of those responsible for the bombing were hiding in the city. The task of doing so was considerable, bearing in mind that the inhabitants numbered about one hundred and seventy thousand.

Four brigades were assigned to the operation, together with three independent battalions, three regiments of armour and the supporting arms of 6th Airborne Division. A cordon was to be placed around the entire city before dawn on the 30th July, after which a curfew would be imposed and inner cordons established. These would divide the city into four different areas, each of which would be cordoned and searched by one of the four brigades.

Before dawn on the 30th July 1st, 2nd and 3rd Parachute Brigades, together with 2nd Infantry Brigade from 1st Infantry Division, moved into their positions. Surprise was complete and the outer cordon was in position before the alarm could be raised. As dawn came, the inner cordons were established and the curfew imposed. All buildings were thoroughly searched and all inhabitants, with the exception of the elderly and children, were screened. All males between the ages of fifteen and sixty were sent for screening at brigade headquarters by police CID teams who were equipped with extensive details of wanted Jews. Suspects were then sent to the detention centre at Rafah where further screening took place.

During the four days of the operation, one hundred thousand people were screened by the battalions and ten thousand by the four brigade headquarters and police screening teams. Seven hundred and eighty-seven were detained and sent to Rafah. Five arms caches were discovered, including one in the basement of the Great Synagogue where, in addition to a large quantity of weapons, search teams discovered £50,000 worth of forged bearer bonds and forging equipment.

The operation, which finished in the early afternoon of the 2nd August, was deemed a great success and Major General Cassels sent a special message of thanks and congratulations to all units which had taken part:

"...It was clear from the beginning that it was going to be a long, difficult and laborious task involving great tolerance and cheerfulness on the part of everybody concerned. It was impossible to foresee every contingency and a great deal had to be left to the initiative and common sense of the individual. The fact that the search was completed far quicker than I had ever hoped, and with virtually no incidents of any kind, speaks volumes for the great work, good spirit and example of every one of you.

I consider that this was one of the most difficult operations that I have ever had to undertake and its scope was, I believe, more ambitious than any similar operation ever staged. It has now been completed expeditiously and well. There is absolutely no doubt that we have achieved very considerable success. This is entirely due to the great loyalty and support that you have given me throughout..."

Operations 'Bream' and 'Eel'

Throughout 1946, the subject of Jewish immigration continued to pose a problem to the government of Palestine. The Jews had every intention of flooding the country with immigrants, thus making life virtually impossible for the British who were still enforcing the limit of fifteen hundred a month. Thousands had been arriving in Palestine, only to find themselves interned in camps to await their turn for legal entry within the restricted monthly quota.

In the middle of August, the government announced that henceforth all Jews arriving in Palestine would be sent to Cyprus and interned there in camps until some decision could be reached concerning their future.

The Hagana at this time was not involved in a general offensive against the security forces but was confining itself to operations connected with illegal immigration. On the 21st August, a week after the government's announcement, three of its members attached a limpet mine to the hull of the *Empire Rival*, one of the vessels used in deportations, whilst she was anchored in Haifa Bay.

The reaction of the authorities was swift, with searches being carried out at S'dot Yam and other settlements. 6th Airborne Division was tasked with searching for arms at two settlements in

252. A 25-pounder gun of 53rd (Worcestershire Yeomanry) Airlanding Light Regiment RA during firing at Beer Sheeba.
(Photo: Mr W. L. Blunt)

the Negev, Dorot and Ruhama, which were situated close to each other some ten miles east of Gaza. Both were known to have elements of the Hagana amongst their inhabitants who numbered approximately two hundred and thirty-five and a hundred and seventy respectively. It was also known that the Hagana carried out training in both settlements and that large quantities of arms were concealed in them.

8th and 3rd Parachute Battalions, with 9th Airborne Squadron RE under command, carried out the two search operations of Dorot and Ruhama respectively. Cordons were positioned before dawn on the 28th August and these remained for the six-day duration of the operations.

The searches of all buildings produced little results for the first two days, although there was evidence of plenty of illegal military training; spent cartridge cases found on a rifle range at Ruhama was only one indication of the presence of weapons. Towards the end of the second day, however, ten metal-detecting dogs arrived with their Military Police handlers. On the following morning the dogs discovered caches in both settlements which contained large quantities of weapons, ammunition, explosives, mines and military equipment.

In September an incident occurred which was to have particularly serious repercussions. On the 13th, the IZL raided the branches of the Ottoman Bank in Tel Aviv and Jaffa. The terrorists achieved little success, their haul totalling little more then £4,000. During their attempted escape, however, they encountered the police and in the ensuing action thirteen of the terrorists were captured. One of these was a youth named Benjamin Kimchin who was subsequently tried and sentenced to eighteen years imprisonment and eighteen strokes of the cane.

The IZL responded immediately by warning that they would kidnap and flog a British soldier if the sentence on Kimchin was carried out. The youth was caned in accordance with his sentence and on the 29th December the IZL carried out their threat. The Brigade Major of 2nd Parachute Brigade was kidnapped whilst visiting units in Nathanya and was taken out into the country where he was stripped and flogged. In Tel Aviv and Rishon-le-Zion three NCOs were also kidnapped and treated likewise.

Needless to say, the reaction amongst all British troops was one of fury and all units were confined to their bases in order to prevent retaliation against the Jews. However, there was some compensation in that a road-block manned by men of 1st Parachute Brigade at Wilhelma, north of Lydda, stopped a car in which five IZL terrorists were travelling. After a short action in which one of them was fatally wounded, they were captured and were found to be in possession of two rawhide whips as well as weapons. All were subsequently tried and three of them were hanged.

During the closing stages of 1946, the division had conducted operations against rail saboteurs during Operation 'Earwig' in which the engineer squadrons played a principal role in dealing with mines and booby traps laid by terrorists. In November, Captains Newton and Adamson were killed and another officer and two other ranks were wounded whilst disarming mines.

In the early part of December a bomb attack was carried out by the Stern Gang on South Palestine District Headquarters, part of which was blown up by a large explosive charge hidden in a vehicle parked inside the headquarters compound. The explosion caused considerable damage and caused casualties totalling one officer and one other rank killed, as well as twenty-three officers and men and five civilians wounded.

There then followed a lull in terrorist activity during the middle part of the month. On the 13th December Major General James Cassels handed over command of the division to Major General Eric Bols who returned to Palestine on the 6th January. During the previous month Brigadier Gerald Lathbury had handed over command of 3rd Parachute Brigade to Brigadier F. D. Rome DSO.

On the 30th December 1st Parachute Brigade, with 8th Parachute Battalion and the 3rd The King's Own Hussars under command, carried out Operation 'Prawn' which was a search of the Yemenite quarter of Petah Tiqva for members of the IZL and the Stern Gang. Meanwhile 2nd Parachute Brigade, with a squadron of the 12th Royal Lancers under command, was engaged on Operation 'Noah' which involved a search of the south-east quarter of Nathanya. On the following day, 3rd Parachute Brigade, with a company of the 2nd Battalion The King's Royal Rifle Corps under command, carried out Operation 'Ark' in which a search of the Yemenite quarter of Rishon-le-Zion was carried out.

These three operations brought 1946 to a close for 6th Airborne

253. Parachute course instructors and trainees at Aqir Aerodrome. (Photo: Mr B. Boswell)

Division but there was no cessation in operations which continued into the New Year. The Areas of Tel Aviv, Rehovot, Sht Hat Tiqva and Montefiorre were searched, nine thousand people being screened and a hundred and thirty detained.

In early January a number of raids were carried out by small groups of police and troops on known areas of terrorist activity. Codenamed Operation 'Octopus' and based on sound intelligence, these proved very successful and led to a reduction in activity by terrorists in areas such as Rishon-le-Zion, Rehovot and Petah Tiqva. Ninety suspects were arrested, a large proportion of whom were subsequently detained.

The Move North

On the 18th January 6th Airborne Division left the Southern Sector of Palestine, which it handed over to 3rd Infantry Division newly arrived from Egypt, and commenced its move to the Northern Sector to assume responsibility from 1st Infantry Division.

A few days later, on the 24th January, 2nd Parachute Brigade sailed from Haifa for England where it was to reorganise before eventually moving to Germany. There it would concentrate on the airborne training which had been so lacking during its time in Palestine.

Operations in the Northern Sector January 1947 — May 1948

On arrival in the Northern Sector, 1st Parachute Brigade moved to Galilee whilst 3rd Parachute Brigade took up station in Haifa which was regarded as an area where trouble was most likely to occur. The 3rd The King's Own Hussars were assigned to Afula whilst the division's artillery units were deployed throughout the sector. Headquarters 6th Airborne Division was based in a Carmelite monastery at Stella Maris.

The environment and terrain were totally different to those of the Southern Sector. Whereas the south of Palestine was mostly flat, with orange groves and fertile areas interspersed with stretches of barren desert, the north was hilly with spectacular views over the Jordan Valley and the Sea of Galilee.

The relationship between British troops and local inhabitants in the north was a great deal better than that which the division had enjoyed in the south. 1st Infantry Division had not suffered the problems encountered by 6th Airborne Division and it was made plain to all that every effort had to be made to maintain any existing goodwill.

However, this was easier said than done because 3rd Parachute Brigade, almost immediately after its arrival in Haifa, was required to impose a curfew in Hadar hak Carmel which was the main Jewish quarter in the city. This was in response to the kidnapping by the IZL on the 27th January of Judge Windham, a district judge, and a British civilian named Collins. The IZL action was in reprisal for the sentencing to death of a Jew named Dov Gruner. Curfews and road-blocks were imposed throughout the sector during the search for the two men. Eventually the death sentence on Gruner was postponed and the two hostages were duly released. However, it was an unfortunate start to the division's tour of duty in the north.

Haifa was the main port in Palestine and located nearby were the oil installations of the Iraq Petroleum Company, Shell and other oil companies, as well as the refinery belonging to Consolidated Refineries Ltd. All these and the port installations were obvious targets for sabotage and thus the division had a heavy commitment in providing protection for all of them. Initially the 2nd Battalion The East Surrey Regiment and a squadron of the Arab Legion were placed under command to assist but the East Surreys were posted elsewhere a few months later and their responsibilities were shouldered by 3rd Parachute Brigade.

6th Airborne Division also had to cope with handling the transhipment of illegal immigrants who were still arriving at frequent intervals from Europe. Responsibility for this task was given to the division's artillery units which carried it out until it was assumed by the Royal Navy a year later.

1st Parachute Brigade had a very large area of responsibility in Galilee. With its headquarters based in Nazareth, it had the responsibility of covering the towns of Acre, Safad, Nazareth, Beisan and Tiberias. In addition to maintaining order, the brigade was also tasked with anti-smuggling operations and the prevention of illegal immigration along Palestine's northern and eastern borders with Lebanon, Syria and Transjordan. It also had the responsibility of providing protection for the Iraq Petroleum Company pipeline which stretched from the Haifa refinery to the River Jordan. For this particular task, the brigade had under command the 3rd Mechanised Regiment of the Arab Legion.

Two of 1st Parachute Brigade's battalions were based on the coast north of Acre and these were responsible for the prevention of illegal immigration from the sea. The third battalion was located at Rosh Pinna, north of Tiberias, and was responsible for taking any necessary action in Safad, a town which was liable to civil unrest. The brigade also had under command the 1st King's Dragoon Guards who left soon after and were replaced by the 17th/21st Lancers.

The first major task that involved 6th Airborne Division after its arrival in the Northern Sector was the evacuation of British civilians from Palestine. This was announced by the government on the 31st January and involved the movement of some fifteen hundred people, mostly women and children, to collection centres from where they were transported by rail to Egypt. There they embarked from Port Said for the sea voyage to Britain. Approximately one third of the evacuees came from the Northern Sector and the division was responsible for transporting them from their homes to the collection centre. This was located at Peninsula Barracks in Haifa which was the base of 9th Parachute Battalion which moved into other temporary accommodation.

The divisional RAOC, under Lieutenant Colonel R. J. Meech MBE, the RAMC and RASC units all played a major role in looking after and transporting the evacuees for whom this was a traumatic period. The evacuation from Palestine took place between the 5th and 8th February. The first stage was by rail from Haifa to Maadi in Egypt, the railway line being heavily patrolled by 8th Parachute Battalion. In the south, evacuees were concentrated at Sarafand and then moved by rail or by aircraft from Aqir.

Transhipment of Illegal Immigrants

Early February found 6th Airborne Division involved in the transhipment of illegal immigrants. This proved to the most unpleasant of all the tasks it was required to carry out during its time in Palestine.

Aspiring immigrants came from Europe in vessels of all types and sizes on which conditions were appalling. The ships themselves were old and in a barely seaworthy state. Facilities on board were non-existent, passengers being accommodated in tiers of bunks which were fitted into any available space and occupied on a communal basis. In several instances there was insufficient space for people to lie down, one vessel accommodating nine people in a space of six cubic feet. The conditions of hardship and filth belied description and Jews had to endure such conditions for anything up to a month during the voyage to Palestine.

The vessels, which were of varying sizes between 1,000 and 5,000 tons, were normally observed and shadowed by RAF aircraft which guided Royal Navy warships until contact was made. Once the three-mile territorial limit had been entered, the Royal Navy then moved in and intercepted the ships. Boarding parties were then sent aboard, more often than not encountering violent opposition. Once this had been overcome, the vessels were taken in tow to Haifa where troops waited to carry out transhipment of the immigrants.

The division's artillery units, under the control of HQRA 6th Airborne Division, were responsible for transhipment operations. When transhipment was in progress, the port was closed and 3rd Parachute Brigade deployed troops to quell any disorder that might have arisen in the town.

The initial phase of a transhipment operation involved an

254. The Shell oil refinery at Haifa after being blown up by the Irgun on the 30th March 1947. Twenty thousand tons of oil were destroyed. (Photo: Imperial War Museum)

Army boarding party taking over from the Royal Navy. Any sick immigrants were taken to a first aid post and then by ambulance to hospital. All others were sprayed with disinfectant as a precaution against disease, after which their baggage was searched for arms, explosives or any items of an illegal nature. Thereafter, immigrants were embarked on British ships whick took them under guard to Cyprus where they were detained in camps pending their eventual processing for immigration into Palestine. Meanwhile, the vessels in which they had travelled from Europe were searched for any explosive charges that might have been concealed aboard them, and timed to explode whilst the vessels were still in the port after unloading, before being towed to a location outside the harbour breakwater where they joined other hulks.

In July 1947, some four-and-a-half thousand Jews embarked from France in a 4,275 ton vessel called *Exodus*, a former American river steamer previously named the *President Warfield*. Departing from the small port of Setye, near Marseilles, on the night of the 11th July, the ship sailed for Palestine.

The ship itself had been specially prepared to resist boarding by the Royal Navy. Barricades, reinforced with barbed wire and netting, had been fitted around her decks. Round the outside of these ran a pipe to which were fitted steam jets, at twelve-inch intervals, which were powered by the ship's boilers.

The Royal Navy shadowed the *Exodus* from almost the start of her voyage. On her entry into Palestinian territorial waters, a boarding party of fifty men was successfully put aboard and eventually the crew and passengers surrendered. The vessel reached Haifa on the afternoon of the 18th July and on its arrival the normal transhipment operation took place, the passengers being transferred to three British ships. In the early hours of the following morning, the 19th July, the convoy sailed from Haifa under escort of the Royal Navy. It was not until they were at sea that the Jews were told that their destination was not Cyprus but the south of France from which they had departed at the beginning of their journey. Needless to say, this information caused no little consternation amongst them.

On each of the three transports was a detachment of one hundred guards supplied by 6th Airborne Division. On board the *Ocean Vigour* and *Runnymede Park* were men of 87th Airborne Field Regiment RA, which had joined the division earlier in the year, who were commanded by Major R. L. Ellis and Captain A. C. Barclay respectively. On board the *Empire Rival* were troops of 1st Parachute Battalion under the command of Lieutenant Colonel M. I. Gregson MBE, the Commanding Officer of 87th Airborne Field Regiment RA.

The voyage to France took nine days, during which all Jewish males were confined to their quarters, in order to reduce the risk of sabotage, whilst women and children were permitted to move around. The relationship between the British troops and the Jews became surprisingly good once the latter realised that the soldiers were somewhat different to the image of evil monsters broadcast by the Jewish propaganda machine. The soldiers soon struck up friendly relationships with the children on board and this undoubtedly helped in breaking down many barriers. Aboard each ship was a medical officer and orderlies who found themselves fully occupied during the voyage with coping with health problems that occurred *en route*. They were assisted by suitably qualified volunteers from amongst the immigrants.

On arrival at Port de Bouc, near Marseilles, on the 28th July, the convoy was met by a number of vessels organised by the Hagana. Propaganda was broadcast from these through loudspeakers, encouraging the Jews on board the three transports to resist any attempt to disembark them. Added to this was a certain amount of agitation carried out by the more die-hard elements amongst the immigrants. As a result, only a few sick Jews were disembarked in France.

Finally, after three weeks of fruitless negotiations between the British, the Jews and the French authorities, the convoy sailed for Germany where it arrived in Hamburg on the 8th September. The Jews were by this time determined to resist any attempt to evict them from the ships and when the time came for disembarkation, a violent battle took place. Eventually, with the help of some military police and detachments of other British troops, all the immigrants were disembarked and the operation was complete. After two weeks leave in England, Lieutenant Colonel Gregson and his men returned to Palestine.

During the *Exodus* operation, the violence in Palestine continued. The reaction of the Jewish population to the news of the transhipment to Europe was one of disbelief followed by anger. This manifested itself initially in attacks against the police by the Stern Gang. The response from the security forces was the imposition of a curfew in Hadar hak Carmel, the main Jewish area of Haifa, with patrols being deployed in force on the 20th July. On the afternoon of the same day the whole of 3rd Parachute Brigade, reinforced by the 3rd The King's Own Hussars and two troops of the 17th/21st Lancers, cordoned off the area.

On the 21st July, attacks were carried out by the Palmach on two radio stations. The second one of these took place in the area of Headquarters 6th Airborne Division at Mount Carmel when a group of six saboteurs were spotted by sentries. The Jews came under fire and withdrew, leaving behind some fifty-pound explosive charges and one of their number who was seriously wounded.

The IZL was also active, mining roads and railway lines as well as carrying out a series of attacks on oil pipelines and military establishments. The British transport vessel *Empire Lifeguard* was sunk by an explosive charge in Haifa harbour, the finger of suspicion subsequently being pointed at the Palmach.

Changes of Command & Reorganisation

The latter part of 1947 saw a number of changes in command appointments. On the 20th July, Brigadier J. P. O'Brien Twohig took over command of 1st Parachute Brigade from Brigadier Hugh Bellamy who returned to Britain to assume command of 2nd Parachute Brigade.

On the 19th August, Major General Hugh Stockwell CB CBE DSO arrived to take over command of the division from Major General Eric Bols. General Stockwell immediately distinguished himself in the division's eyes by attending a parachute course at Aqir which he passed without any problems.

In October, details of the proposals to reduce the division to two parachute brigades were sent to Major General Stockwell by the War Office. In essence, these laid down that 3rd Parachute Brigade would be disbanded and that amalgamations would take place between 2nd and 3rd Parachute Battalions, 4th and 6th Parachute Battalions and 8th and 9th Parachute Battalions. The 1st (Guards), 5th (Scottish) and 7th (Light Infantry) Parachute Battalions would each retain their separate identities because of their regimental affiliations.

1st Parachute Brigade would consist of 1st (Guards), 2nd/3rd and 8th/9th Parachute Battalions whilst 4th/6th, 5th (Scottish) and 7th (Light Infantry) Parachute Battalions would constitute 2nd Parachute Brigade.

When 2nd Parachute Brigade sailed for England at the end of January it took with it, in addition to 4th, 5th and 6th Parachute Battalions, 211th Airlanding Light Battery RA, 300th Battery of 2nd Airlanding Light Regiment RA, No.1 Section of 2nd Forward Observation Unit (Airborne) RA, 3rd Airborne Squadron RE, 'K' Troop of 6th Airborne Divisional Signals Regiment, a detachment of 249th Airborne Park Squadron RE, 63rd Composite Company (Airborne) RASC and 127th Parachute Field Ambulance RAMC. In addition, it also took sections of 6th Airborne Division Provost Company, 6th Airborne Division Ordnance Field Park RAOC, 6th Airborne Division Workshops REME and a REME airlanding light aid detachment.

During 1947 a number of changes had taken place within the divisional order of battle, particularly after the disbandment of 6th Airlanding Brigade and its gliderborne units. Several of these had occurred amongst the Royal Artillery units within the division. By the end of the year these consisted of the 33rd Airborne Light Regiment RA (which had earlier replaced 53rd (Worcestershire Yeomanry) Airlanding Light Regiment RA), 66th Airborne Anti-Tank Regiment RA, 87th Airborne Field Regiment RA and 334th Forward Observer Battery RA. Sapper units in the division by then comprised 1st, 3rd, and 9th Airborne Squadrons RE and 147th Airborne Park Squadron RE, this last

unit having been originally designated 286th and subsequently 249th.

Other changes within the division's supporting arms included the conversion of 195th Airlanding Field Ambulance to the parachute role and its redesignation to 195th Parachute Field Ambulance. By the end of the year, 127th Parachute Field Ambulance had been redesignated to become 23rd Parachute Field Ambulance whilst the REME elements in the division now consisted of three separate workshops designated 1st, 2nd and 3rd Airborne Workshops respectively.

The amalgamations and reductions in the number of battalions within the division inevitably resulted in a greater workload for the remaining units which subsequently had larger areas to protect. The loss of 3rd Parachute Brigade was to be slightly offset by the arrival of the 2nd Battalion the Middlesex Regiment which arrived in mid-December and moved into Camp 253 which was located near the prison at Acre which was a permanent source of trouble. Shortly afterwards, 7th Parachute Battalion left for England to join 2nd Parachute Brigade.

The closing months of 1947 saw, at the end of November, the announcement by the United Nations of its approval for the partition of Palestine between the Jews and the Arabs. Whereas the former were delighted by this decision, the Arabs declared themselves totally opposed to partition and vowed to oppose it by force if necessary. All four Jewish organisations switched their attention from the security forces to the Arabs and it was not long before violence between the two communities flared up anew with increased vigour. This started on the 2nd December in Jerusalem and Jaffa, rapidly spreading to Haifa. On the 30th December the first major incident took place when members of the IZL threw bombs at a group of Arab employees of Cosolidated Refineries Ltd outside the refinery at Haifa. Six Arabs were killed and more than forty were wounded in the attack.

The Arab reaction was swift and furious, several Jews in the refinery being beaten to death. The police arrived soon after the outbreak of rioting but quickly found themselves outnumbered. Troops from 2nd/3rd Parachute Battalion arrived shortly afterwards and rapidly restored order, all Jews and Arabs being cleared from the refinery and escorted back to their respective areas by the 3rd The King's Own Hussars. Forty-one Jews were killed and forty-eight were injured in this incident. On the following night the Hagana carried out a reprisal attack on the Arab village of Balad es Sheik, killing fourteen Arabs and wounding eleven. Of those killed, ten were women and children.

Trouble on the Frontier

On the 13th December, trouble flared up in the town of Safad, in the Frontier Sub-sector, when a Jew disappeared after entering the Arab market in the town. Firing broke out between Jews and Arabs and the violence escalated rapidly, the police soon being obliged to call for troops to reinforce them. A troop of armoured cars of the Transjordanian Frontier Force arrived, followed by a company of 8th Parachute Battalion, and a curfew was imposed.

Five days later, on the 18th December, trouble flared up again when a number of armed Jews attacked the Arab village of Khissas which was located near the frontier with Syria. They killed ten Arabs and wounded five others, most of them being women and children. Pamphlets were left behind by the attackers, stating that the raid was a reprisal for the Jewish casualties in Safad and at Khissas where a Jew had been killed by Arabs.

To cope with the increasing threat of trouble, the Transjordanian Frontier Force was reinforced by 1st Parachute Battalion, the 17th/21st Lancers and detachments of divisional troops. One major problem facing the security forces was the defence of Jewish settlements near the frontier. These were overlooked by high ground and thus were vulnerable to sniping by Arabs.

On the 9th January 1948, settlements at Dan and Kafr Szold were attacked by two strong forces of Arabs. A troop of the 17th/21st Lancers was dispatched to each settlement where their armoured cars came under fire. The lancers replied initially with

255. A Cromwell of the 3rd King's Own Hussars in Haifa after fighting had taken place in the town the night before.
(Photo: Imperial War Museum)

256. Patrolling the Wadi Rushmiya in Haifa.
(Photo: Imperial War Museum)

machine guns before eventually being forced to use their 2-pounder guns which proved highly effective. Subsequently the Royal Air Force provided air support in the form of some Spitfires which carried out mock attacks on the Arabs' positions. During the afternoon 1st Parachute Battalion entered the fray, using its 3-inch mortars with good effect. Eventually, with an increasing amount of firepower being arraigned against them, the Arabs withdrew.

The early months of 1948 were difficult for 6th Airborne Division which was required to cope with increasing unrest between Arabs and Jews whilst the number of units available to it was steadily decreasing. January also saw the withdrawal of the Transjordanian Frontier Force and its replacement by the 1st Battalion Irish Guards. With Headquarters 3rd Parachute Brigade having been disbanded on the 18th January, a replacement formation was assembled for operations in the frontier areas. This consisted of 1st Parachute Battalion, the 1st Battalion Irish Guards and the 17th/21st Lancers. Designated 'Craforce', this was commanded by Brigadier C H Colquhon OBE who was CRA 6th Airborne Division.

Operations in Haifa

The brunt of operations in Haifa was taken by 2nd/3rd and 8th/9th Parachute Battalions which were commanded by Lieutenant Colonel T. H. Birkbeck DSO and Lieutenant Colonel J. H. M. Hackett DSO respectively.

The situation between the Jews and Arabs in the town started to deteriorate once the announcement about partition had been made. The latter part of December proved to be a particularly difficult period and the 3rd The King's Own Hussars and some of the division's artillery units had to be called in as reinforcements to help restore order.

Whereas the fighting between the two communities had consisted of little more than sniping, this escalated gradually over a period of time to a level where battles involving the use of small arms were taking place. Eventually, both sides started to use mortars and heavy machine guns. Despite this escalation, however, the security forces never lost the initiative nor let the situation get out of hand. Troops were deployed in platoon strength in static posts located in commanding positions throughout the town. At the same time, patrols were deployed so as to be able to take rapid action in response to any threat whilst covered by the static posts.

In March, it became apparent that the Jews might not wait for British withdrawal for the opportunity to defeat the Arabs who had by then received considerable reinforcements in the form of several hundred Syrian and Iraqi irregular troops. These were reported to be hidden in the Suq and other areas nearby. Consequently, a mixed troop of tanks and self-propelled guns of the Chestnut Troop of 1st Regiment Royal Horse Artillery was moved into the town to reinforce the squadron of the 3rd The King's Own Hussars already supporting the two parachute battalions in Haifa. Columns of armour, artillery and infantry thereafter patrolled the town at different times by day and night and would engage any Arab or Jewish position opening fire on the other side. This tactic had a marked effect on both communities and reduced the levels of armed confrontation between them.

Withdrawal and Disbandment

It had originally been planned that 6th Airborne Division should leave Palestine during the period of March and April and would return to England before eventually moving to Germany to become part of the British Army of the Rhine. It was therefore a somewhat bitter blow for the division to be told on the 18th February that it was to be disbanded and that several of its units would remain in Palestine until the end of the Mandate on the 15th May.

The withdrawal itself was to be phased and would take place when the Mandate ended. Until then, however, the administration of the country had to be supported and law and order maintained.

At the end of January, 40 Commando Royal Marines arrived in Haifa from Malta and was placed under command of 6th Airborne Division. It was tasked with the protection of the port and with covering the evacuation by sea.

The first elements of the division to leave Palestine were the divisional advance parties, 87th Airborne Field Regiment RA and 9th Airborne Squadron RE which embarked on the *Franconia* and *Samaria* on the 6th and 9th May. On the 12th May the divisional HQRA, 33rd Airborne Light Regiment RA and 66th Airborne Anti-Tank Regiment RA embarked for England on the *Otranto*.

On the 3rd April, Headquarters 6th Airborne Division closed down and control of the Northern Sector was passed to the divisional commander's tactical headquarters, now designated Headquarters GOC North Sector, which co-located itself with Headquarters North Palestine District near Headquarters 1st Parachute Brigade.

On the 6th April, 1st Parachute Brigade handed over control of Haifa to 1st Guards Brigade. On the 16th and 23rd April, Headquarters 1st Parachute Brigade and 2nd/3rd Parachute Battalion embarked for England on the *Empress of Australia*. On the 23rd April, Rear Headquarters 6th Airborne Division and 8th/9th Parachute Battalion sailed on the *Empress of Scotland*. Behind them they left the divisional commander with his tactical headquarters, Headquarters 'Craforce', 1st Parachute Battalion, the 3rd The King's Own Hussars, 1st Airborne Squadron RE and 317th Airborne Field Security Section.

On the 15th May, Major General Hugh Stockwell handed over operational control of the Northern Sector to 1st Guards Brigade and on the same day boarded an aircraft for England. Three days later his tactical headquarters, Headquarters 'Craforce' and 1st Parachute Battalion embarked on the the *Empress of Australia*. On the 30th June 1st Airborne Squadron RE left Palestine together with the last British troops.

The withdrawal from Palestine saw the passing of one of the British Army's finest fighting formations and the end of a saga which had begun five years previously during the dark days of the Second World War. During its brief period of existence, 6th Airborne Division carved for itself a unique place in the annals of British military history. The invasion of Normandy and the advance to the Seine, the crossing of the Rhine and the advance to the Baltic — in each of these campaigns 6th Airborne Division led the way, frequently outgunned and against seemingly overwhelming odds, but always eventually winning the day.

During the difficult and trying days of post-war operations in South East Asia and Palestine, the officers and men of the division were required to perform tasks of a very different nature which demanded restraint and minimum force - the very antithesis of those qualities required of them as airborne troops in battle. Whatever was required of them, and however difficult the task, they continued to display the same high degree of professionalism and skill which had earned them the respect of friends and foes alike. At all times they lived up to the division's motto of "Go to it!"

257. *Left:* Major General Hugh Stockwell, GOC 6th Airborne Division, *Right:* General Sir Alan Cunningham, High Commissioner of Palestine.

258. *Below:* Sergeant Bill Williams of 3rd Parachute Battalion at a roadblock at Az Zib, north of Haifa.
(Photo: Airborne Force Museum)

Epilogue:

Post-War Reorganisation of Airborne Forces

In 1948, the War Office decided that one parachute brigade group would constitute the Regular Army's airborne forces element. In order to maintain links with the wartime airborne formations, 2nd Parachute Brigade was redesignated 16th Independent Parachute Brigade Group (the numerals 1 and 6 representing the 1st and 6th Airborne Divisions). 4th/6th, 5th (Scottish) and 7th (Light Infantry) Parachute Battalions were reformed as the 1st, 2nd and 3rd Battalions The Parachute Regiment respectively. 1st (Guards) Parachute Battalion was reduced to company strength and was redesignated No.1 (Guards) Independent Company The Parachute Regiment, becoming the pathfinder unit for 16th Independent Parachute Brigade Group.

The previous year, 1947, had seen the formation of a Territorial Army formation, the 16th Airborne Division (TA). Commanded by Major General Roy Urquhart CB DSO, who was commander of 1st Airborne Division at Arnhem, the division consisted of 4th, 5th and 6th Parachute Brigades (TA) which comprised a total of nine parachute battalions designated 10th to 18th respectively. In 1956, these three formations were redesignated 44th, 45th and 46th Parachute Brigades (TA). Later in the same year, however, 16th Airborne Division (TA) was reduced to one brigade group. This brigade, 44th Independent Parachute Brigade Group (TA), initially retained five battalions: 10th (City of London), 12th (Yorkshire), 13th (Lancashire), 15th (Scottish) and 17th (Durham Light Infantry) Battalions The Parachute Regiment (TA). However, the 12th and 13th Battalions amalgamated in the same year to become the 12th/13th Battalion, reducing the number in the brigade to four. In 1967 this battalion amalgamated with the 17th Battalion and was redesignated the 4th (Volunteer) Battalion. The other two battalions were redesignated the 10th (Volunteer) and 15th (Scottish Volunteer) Battalions The Parachute Regiment respectively.

In 1977 the Regular Army's 16th Parachute Brigade was disbanded, its role being partly assumed by 6th Field Force which included a single parachute battalion with a limited airborne role.

The other regular battalions of The Parachute Regiment were deployed in non-airborne roles, taking their turn in the airborne role with 6th Field Force every four years.

In 1978, 44th Parachute Brigade (TA) was disbanded. The three parachute battalions survived intact but the brigade's supporting arm elements were lost. 16th (Lincoln) Independent Company, the brigade's pathfinder unit, was initially absorbed by the 15th (Scottish Volunteer) Battalion as a fourth rifle company but was eventually transferred to the 4th (Volunteer) Battalion.

In 1982, 8th Field Force was redesignated 5th Infantry Brigade. It comprised two parachute battalions and other airborne supporting elements which included 7th Regiment Royal Horse Artillery (a former parachute unit which at that time still had two parachute batteries and a number of forward observation parties formed from qualified parachutists) and 9th Parachute Squadron Royal Engineers.

In November 1983, 5th Infantry Brigade was redesignated 5th Airborne Brigade and was allocated Out of Area operations as its primary role. The brigade comprises two parachute battalions and two airlanding battalions, one of the latter being a Gurkha unit. Supporting arm elements include 7th Parachute Regiment Royal Horse Artillery, 9th Parachute Squadron RE, 23rd Parachute Field Ambulance RAMC, 5th Airborne Brigade Headquarters & Signal Squadron, 5th Airborne Brigade Pathfinder Platoon, 5th Airborne Brigade Logistics Battalion and an armoured reconnaissance regiment, provided by either The Blues & Royals or The Life Guards, of which elements are parachute trained.

All volunteers for the British Army's parachute units undergo training at The Depot The Parachute Regiment & Airborne Forces which is located at Aldershot in Hampshire. All must pass the 'P' Company selection course before undergoing training at No 1 Parachute Training School at RAF Brize Norton in Wiltshire. After qualifying for the famous maroon beret and parachute wings, they take their places in their respective units in 5th Airborne Brigade.